# MEN AND WOMEN OF THE BIBLE

## A READER'S GUIDE

# MEN AND WOMEN OF THE BIBLE

## A READER'S GUIDE

## NANCY M. TISCHLER

GREENWOOD PRESS
Westport, Connecticut • London

**Library of Congress Cataloging-in-Publication Data**

Tischler, Nancy Marie Patterson
    Men and women of the Bible : a reader's guide / Nancy M. Tischler.
      p. cm.
    Includes bibliographical references and index.
    ISBN 0–313–31714–3 (alk. paper)
     1. Bible—Biography. I. Title.
    BS571 .T57 2002
    220.9'2—dc21       2002075347

British Library Cataloguing-in-Publication Data is available.

Library of Congress Catalog Card Number: 2002075347
ISBN: 0–313–31714–3

First published in 2002

Greenwood Press, 88 Post Road West, Westport, CT 06881
An imprint of Greenwood Publishing Group, Inc.
www.greenwood.com

Printed in the United States of America

The paper used in this book complies with the
Permanent Paper Standard issued by the National
Information Standards Organization (Z39.48–1984).

10 9 8 7 6 5 4 3 2 1

Every reasonable effort has been made to trace the owners of copyright materials in this book,
but in some instances this has proven impossible. The author and publisher will be glad to
receive information leading to more complete acknowledgments in subsequent printings of the
book and in the meantime extend their apologies for any omissions.

# CONTENTS

Contents

# Contents

# INTRODUCTION

The men and women who step out of the pages of the Bible are varied and vivid. God's chosen people, their families, friends, and enemies are the characters in this, the "greatest story ever told." They delight, appall, and startle us with the freshness and naturalness of their actions and reactions. A woman yearns for a child and laughs at the angel who promises one; a man meets with his long-lost brothers and gently chides them as he forgives their betrayal; a prophet worries about how his people can survive in an alien land; and a disciple chops the ear off an arresting officer in defense of his master—these are the lively and universal people whom we meet in the books of the Bible.

This volume is an introductory study of more than one hundred biblical characters most frequently cited through the ages. It is aimed at students and general readers who want to discover authoritative information about these people, their heritage, their adventures and pronouncements, the periods in which they lived, the later discoveries about them and their times, and the traditions that have developed around them. Each entry discusses the name and etymology, the synopsis of the Bible story, the historical context, the archaeological evidence, and the ideas and interpretations of the character in later works.

Every man and woman of the Bible is an actor in its amazing narrative, which is full of new beginnings and reversals, promises and betrayals, chronicling humankind from that moment when "God created Man, male and female created He them," forming Adam from the dust of the earth and breathing the breath of life into him. The narrative extends to that final apocalyptic vision of Armageddon, the Feast of the Lamb, and the hope of the Second Coming.

The Bible is a great epic, with a scope unparalleled in all of literature: a record cherished by many people for more than three millennia, moving from prehistory to the end of human time. Although *Men and Women of the Bible* deals with humans, not angels or other supernatural beings, the hero of the Bible is God. The lesser figures in this epic of human history are the men and women who fight with God, follow his guidance, laugh at his advice, thunder his message, cringe at his power, accept his authority, and delight in his world. Our focus here is on the people who form the archetypes that dominate Western thought.

The Bible encompasses poetry and prose, prophecy and wisdom literature, sermons and stories, tragedy and comedy. Genesis starts with a poetic credo and then moves into a narrative. Exodus begins with narrative and then shifts into a declaration of the law. Some books are chronicles of births and deaths, wars and victories. Some are laments for the pain of God's people. Job is classical in its tragic form. The Song of Solomon is an erotic tribute to human love and the joys of the flesh. The Proverbs are thoughtful, often cynical statements of wisdom derived from centuries of experience. The Psalms are songs to be sung when celebrating the king's arrival, marching up Mount Zion, proclaiming God's fierce judgment on the enemies of Israel, or meditating on God's mercy or his law. Many of the books are short stories—Ruth or Judith—with narratives that reveal men and women in moments of temptation and quiet heroism. The Gospels combine narrative with poetry, parables, and tragedy. Paul's letters are still different in form—the epistolary, which is much like the sermon—addressed to particular people with their particular problems, reflecting universal truths. The Revelation of St. John, like Daniel, is apocalyptic literature, replete with symbols that startle and thrill the imagination. In short, the Bible is a veritable library of books that form a majestic story encompassing the story of man's relationship with God. The different characters fit their times and shape their expression in a dizzying catalogue of genres. Their words and actions fit into this larger context.

The text of the Bible—this vast collection of works by many different hands—has been saved in many ways: as oral history, on scrolls, in temples, and in monasteries. It has been edited, tested, copied, discussed, annotated, and translated over the centuries. Some of the stories—those of the Macabees, of Susanna and the Elders, of Judith and Holifernes—have been rejected by large segments of Christendom. Others have been denigrated by religious leaders as less than elevating. Many ancient documents, once respected, were eventually judged unreliable and discarded. Because authors often refer to legends that extend beyond the Bible, I have included stories that have developed around characters in the Bible, largely among the people who revered them as local folk heroes and heroines. I have also included comments on the "lost books of Genesis" (which were rejected very early by the Jewish scholars) because of their literary significance. Even though they have not found their way into orthodox texts of Scripture, their images and stories, such as the Battle of the Angels or Lilith, the "first wife" of Adam, find occasional mention elsewhere. In commenting on people from the New Testament, I have included references to the Gnostic Gospels, some of them only recently discovered, which were rejected by the early Christian scholars. They are interesting for their own sakes and because they are very popular among modern writers and academics. My task is not to determine orthodoxy but rather to tell the readers about the people and let them determine their authenticity.

Some tough choices had to be made about the translations used for this study. Among the thousands of translations of the Bible written over the years, many are beautifully wrought and richly annotated. Although I have relied on commentaries in several—especially those in the *New International Version* and the *HarperCollins Study Bible*—I have quoted primarily from the *King James Version*. This seventeenth-century translation had unparalleled influence on English and American literature, determining the rhythms and the word choices of generations of English-speaking poets and novelists. Because I have limited my comments to the literary influence of English and American writers on the English-speaking peoples of the world, this seemed an appropriate choice. For most of the basic research, however, I have used the *New International Version*—which I rarely cite because its presence is so pervasive in the text. For many of the articles on archaeology, I have referred to the Web site for *Bible Review* and *Biblical Archaeology Review*—www.biblicalarchaeology.org

In collecting materials for this dictionary, I have drawn heavily from a number of sources, particularly on scholarly notes in study Bibles, and on writers I respect. For many of the notes, I cross-referenced several dictionaries of the Bible and several encyclopedias before choosing the most common information as authoritative.

Since names have symbolic significance in much of ancient history and literature, I have sought out the meanings of the names and their linguistic sources, using the spellings I found in popular translations of Scripture and used by various commentators.

In some cases, the entries were complicated by multiple possibilities: not *Herod* but *Herods*; who governed with different levels of bloodthirstiness in the days of the Caesars, not just Caesar Augustus. There were also various Jameses, Philips, and Johns. In most of these cases, I have clustered them together under one name and then endeavor in the discussion to differentiate them.

The stories themselves come directly from the Bible narratives. I tried to cite the sources in Scripture and indicate the man or woman's heritage, work, time, situation, and story. If the person was a prophet or was supposed to have written one or more of the books of the Bible, I indicated the major ideas or forms involved in this activity. Depending on what appears to explain the appearance of this person in the pages of a particular book, I pointed to her as a faithful wife, a temptress, a heroic savior of her people. Or I noted that he is the heir to the covenant tradition, a tribal leader, a digger of wells, a tyrant, or a faithful disciple.

Some stories are too complex to tell effectively in a few words, forcing an uneven distribution of attention to those with complicated stories, while giving short shrift to heroic figures with simple tales. Tobit comes to mind as a minor figure with a baroque narrative line, involving a dog, a treasure, a fish, and a fatal bride. Many of the stories are startling in their realistic detail, breathtaking in their revelations of universal humanity. The starkness of the narrative forces the reader to guess at the tone of voice, the motives, and the true relationships between the bare words. We sometimes have only simple statements to cover whole centuries of change, for example, "Now there arose up a new king over Egypt, which knew not Joseph." In these few words, taken from the first chapter of Exodus, we realize that the Jews had changed from welcome guests with powerful friends in high places to despised slaves whose children were targets for slaughter by Egyptians, who had forgotten the wisdom and service of Joseph. The reader must fill in these lacunae as best he or she can, realizing that scholars may discover some of the reasons for attitudes and actions, explaining what we can only guess at. It is well to acknowledge that we "see through a glass darkly" and that our understanding is both cloudy and partial.

Framing the larger context for these people in the Bible is also a process of discovery. Working hand-in-hand with archaeologists, historians in the past century have opened up a much fuller picture of the worlds in which Abraham traveled with his caravan and Solomon entertained guests from far and wide in his wondrous court. For the history segment of each entry, I combined many of these sources and texts, relying especially on Werner Keller's delightful book, *The Bible as History*. For the study of the prophets, I found Edith Hamilton a useful and insightful critic. The background of the individual stories, which follows the Scripture narrative, is a quick sketch of the situation in which each person lived.

Ancient history is as fresh as today's newspaper, and so is its landscape. The places where Jacob buried his beloved Rebekah, where Abraham planned to sacrifice his son, where Jesus helped Peter pull a net filled with fish out of the Sea of Galilee, or where Deborah advised her husband to let the rainy season trap the Philistines with their iron chariots are still the places that form the geography of Israel, which is also the geography of our spiritual lives, precious to us because of the people and events we associate with that area. We know about Jerusalem and Bethlehem and Sinai, not only from Scripture, but also from current events in Israel and the Occupied Territories. Golgotha and the Mount of Olives have taken on a symbolic meaning for many of us. They form a kind of symbolic landscape, frequently cited in literature.

At the same time, archaeologists are constantly discovering literal facts about literal people who lived in these places. Shards of long-discarded pottery, outlines of old walls, pieces of baked clay marked with symbols, and jars filled with scrolls are the bits and pieces of history that hardy scholars seek to fit together into designs that testify to the long human history in these lands. Although there are good books about the excavations, I also found it valuable to go and visit the actual places and to track recent discoveries chronicled in journals of Biblical archaeology. (Various websites makes this resource particularly helpful, allowing the reader to check the most recent discoveries and commentaries.) Each discovery helps us to visualize more precisely the actual lives that these folks lived and the conditions at that time.

In each entry I also included a discussion of the influence of the named individual and track the references later. Individuals are listed in loose chronological order, noting how their contemporaries viewed them, how later Scripture characterized them, how other thinkers—Jewish, Christian, or secular—have presented them, how they are characterized in art and literature and sometimes even in music. These listings are no more than samples. The interested reader will find a much fuller study of literary tradition in David L. Jeffrey's *Biblical Tradition in English Literature*.

Many of the men and women in the Bible have entire libraries devoted to them, written by scholars who have studied them for a lifetime. At the end of each entry, I have provided a brief bibliography to encourage deeper study. The zealous student will find a more comprehensive bibliography at the end of the book, giving a hint of the rich resources available to scholars.

By limiting the study to its influence on Western literature, primarily in the English language, I have deliberately omitted much of the Eastern, near-Eastern, and African tradition, some of which develops very different characterizations of such people as the Queen of Sheba, Ishmael, and others. In spite of these tempting bypaths, I have forced myself to remain on the well-trodden road, mentioning only the most commonly understood traditions in the West. I have, however, tried to signal other colorful trails available to the curious reader.

Over the years, I have studied, taught, and written about the relationship between Scripture and literature. The alert reader will notice the frequent references to my all-time favorite scholar, Dorothy L. Sayers, who thought deeply about and spoke eloquently of the lively matter of Scripture. In addition, I have discovered many insights from conversations with friends and careful attention to texts in Bible study groups.

I am particularly grateful to my friend Jean Sherman, who spent many hours contemplating the ideas and prose of this book, seeking to make it more readable. Most of all, I have been blessed by the profound insights in sermons by many dedicated ministers, particularly Gordon Keddie, who has provided advice and corrections based on a far deeper knowledge of the Scripture and of the original languages and who possesses a greater scholarship than I do.

My overall approach has been simple: I have sought to attend first to the "plain meaning" of the words. I then look at the larger context—the shape of the story, the relationship with other people, the later commentary on this person. Scripture frequently interprets itself: one speaker comments on another, turns an earlier person into a symbol, transforms a person's life into a foreshadowing of later events. The careful reader must be open to this complex tapestry of meanings. With the help of many study guides, I have discovered that even the most insignificant person in the Bible may become a symbol for many generations to follow. All in all, the study of Scripture is never complete. Each reading yields fresh insights. The Bible is a remarkable book, ancient and fresh at the same time.

My hope in bringing together these portraits is to inspire readers to dig deeper into the stories of these heroes and villains, to see how their stories are relevant to our own trials and temptations, to seek to understand their times, and to consider the significance of each of them to our own lives and time. The pilgrimage of the scholar is a great joy, the discoveries dazzling, and the enrichment of one's life immeasurable.

# A

## AARON

**Name and Etymology.** *Aaron* comes from the Hebrew word meaning "uncertain," but it may mean "woe to this pregnancy," a response to Pharaoh's edict to slaughter the male children of the Hebrews.

**Synopsis of Bible Story.** Aaron was the older brother of *Moses, the younger brother of *Miriam. (His story appears in Exodus 4:27–30, 6:20, 8:25, 17:12; Numbers 3:1–3, 20:28.) Born of the house of *Levi, he was son of Amram and Jochebed. During his miraculous experience of God's glory with the burning bush, Moses argued that he could not lead the Hebrews because of his "uncircumcised lips" (Ex. 6:12); he protested, "I am slow of speech, and of a slow tongue" (Ex. 4:10). God named Aaron as his voice: "See, I have made thee as God to Pharaoh; and Aaron thy brother shall be thy prophet" (Ex. 7:1).

At God's command, they approached the Pharaoh, demanding that he let the Israelites go. In their first confrontation with the Pharaoh, God used Aaron's rod to demonstrate his power, first turning the rod into a snake, and then—when the court magicians matched this by transforming their own sticks to snakes—Aaron's rod swallowed up the others. This wondrous rod demonstrated God's dominance over Egyptian magic and over Egypt's gods.

With each of the Pharaoh's refusals and his hardening of heart, God used Aaron's rod to pronounce the plagues upon Egypt—the water turning to blood, then the frogs, the gnats, the dust, the flies, the cattle, the locusts—and finally, the horrendous killing of the firstborn of the Egyptians.

In the Exodus, Aaron continued to be spokesman and helper, not prophet or leader. Moses had visions, the direct experience of the glory of God, whereas Aaron had a more distant, secondary experience, giving voice to the event. It was he who explained to the people about the manna (the miraculous food provided each day by God); it was he who placed the omer of the manna in a jar for eternal remembrance. When Moses grew weary holding his hands aloft for the battle between Joshua, an Israelite warrior, and the Amalekites, an attacking tribe, Aaron and his companion, Hur, held up his hands. When Moses was summoned to go up the mountain to see God in all his glory, God asked that Aaron come up the mountain as well. More often, however, Aaron was warned not to approach God.

Aaron lacked the single-minded strength that Moses exhibited. Left without his brother when Moses was on Mount Sinai, Aaron agreed with the people's demand for visible gods to follow. He encouraged the Hebrews to melt down their jewelry and make a golden calf, proclaiming, "These be thy Gods, O Israel, which brought thee up out of the land of Egypt" (Ex. 32:4).

When Moses returned, he was horrified at their naked dancing, and "waxed hot" and demanded that the people decide, "Who is on the Lord's side?" (Ex. 32:19). At that crucial moment, the sons of Levi, including Aaron, gathered around Moses, escaping the mass slaughter that ensued. The faithfulness of the Levites at this moment endeared them to the Lord, giving them a permanent role as the keepers of God's sanctuary. In spite of his role in the rebellion, Aaron and his descendants were rewarded by being named the chief priests, a role denied the other Levites.

Later, when Aaron and his sister Miriam complained about Moses' Cushite wife (an Ethiopian woman from another country, and perhaps from another race), he was again forgiven (Num. 12). When the Levites murmured against him, Moses sided with Aaron (Num. 16:10–11). He joined Miriam in her rebellion against God's favoritism toward Moses, saying, "Hath the Lord indeed spoken only by Moses? Hath he not spoken also by us?" (Num. 12:2). God then punished Miriam horribly, but Aaron suffered only by watching his beloved sister suffer. Noted Hebrew scholar Elie Wiesel has called Aaron "The Teflon Kid" for his ability to escape the punishment he was due (Wiesel).

Aaron became the first head of the Hebrew priesthood, with his garments elaborately detailed for glory and for beauty (Ex. 28:4–43). His behavior and appearance were strictly outlined (Lev. 10). He was to have no loose hair, drink no wine, and avoid rending his clothes. He and his sons were to avoid marrying "unclean" wives, defiled or divorced, and no "blemished" offspring were to function as priests (Num. 21). The rituals he was to perform were precisely outlined in the Law given to Moses by God. He and his descendants became the anointed of the Lord, the priesthood, without holdings of their own because their "portion" was in Jehovah. As a mark of their special role, the Hebrews shared with the priest the offerings, the throw offerings, the blood offerings, and the cereal offerings. On the Day of Atonement, the priest alone might enter the Holy of Holies, changing from his elegant attire to a simple white linen robe.

As the first keeper of the flame, Aaron performed the usual functions of the priesthood while also protecting his God-given authority. When Korah, another Levite, revolted against Moses and Aaron and sought to usurp the power of his sons, Aaron had the task of taking the "brazen censers" (Num. 16) to mark the followers of Korah who were to be destroyed. When this tragedy was followed by a plague, it was Aaron who burned incense to atone for the people, and stood between the dead and the living.

His most remarkable feat is chronicled in Numbers 17, when the children of Israel continued their quarrel for supremacy. Moses used Aaron's rod to determine God's will. Left overnight in the tabernacle, Aaron's rod bloomed and bore almonds, marking the house of Levi, the lineage of Aaron, for the priesthood, to "bear the iniquity" and to "do the service of the tabernacle of the congregation" (Num. 18:23).

Although two of Aaron's sons died in the wilderness, after using unholy fire (Lev. 10), two others survived to continue the priesthood. When Aaron realized that his time was drawing near, he went up on Mount Hur, where Moses stripped his garments and put them on Eleazar, Aaron's son. Aaron died—like Moses—in the wilderness, forbidden to enter the promised land. The people mourned his passing for thirty days.

**Historical Context.** Historians assert that the Exodus occurred early in the reign of Ramses II, c. 1290 B.C. This was a turning point in Jewish history, leading to the establishment of the covenant at Sinai and the sense of identity as a special nation. Aaron is particularly important as the founder of the priesthood, serving as high priest for 40 years and setting the tradition firmly in place.

**Archaeological Evidence.** Tomb paintings from the Eighteenth Dynasty in Egypt show brickmaking, such as that performed by the Hebrews during their captivity. The skin color of the slaves is much lighter than that of the taskmasters, indicating that they were of a different race. Historical discoveries regarding Ramses II, his ambitions and building programs, reinforce the Biblical stories.

The scene of the golden calf fits into pagan practice. Golden bulls' heads and other images of objects of veneration, primarily fertility symbols, have been discovered all over the Middle East. The Hebrews probably knew the Apis bull at Memphis. Winged bulls were common in Babylonian art and a standard part of Canaanite bull cults. Baal worshipers—members of cults who celebrated fertility—also engaged in licentious dancing, perhaps a tradition the Jews were mimicking when Moses discovered them nude in front of the golden calf.

Much of the jewelry melted down for the creation of the calf, as well as the lavish embellishment of the garments listed in Exodus, chapter 28, matches discoveries among archaeologists in Ur and elsewhere—the precious stones, the engraving, the gold work. Scripture acknowledges that the earrings and other items were taken from Egypt, where tombs have preserved remarkable treasures. The Israelites were less inclined to have lavish personal embellishments, probably because the carvings on the jewelry were usually cult images.

**Character in Later Works.** Hebrew scholars have focused on every action and on every detail of Aaron's life. Their Midrash, the rabbinical commentary on Scripture, tends to explain away his flaws and focus intensely on the symbolism of his priestly garments.

As an ancestor of John the Baptist, Aaron provided a line between the Old and New Testaments. In Paul's epistles, Aaron became the type of priest (mentioned in Hebrews along with Melchizedek [the king-priest of Salem who blessed Abram in Gen. 14:18–20]) chosen by God and set aside from ordinary men in his work and his appearance. Paul indicates that the role of high priest is assumed by Christ, rendering this role no longer necessary on earth. Rather than following the "law of carnal commandment," the new priest, according to Paul, has the power of endless life. The Roman Catholic Church, however, saw in Aaron's sons the principle of apostolic succession, which the Reformation leaders (especially John Calvin) rejected, asserting rather the "priesthood of all believers." Calvinism also rejected elaborate and symbolic regalia, choosing plain black and white garb instead of gorgeous vestments.

Aaron's selection by God for a special role is often seen as the precursor of vocation, and his perseverance in spite of his errors points to the doctrine of election. As a character, Aaron is the symbol of the spokesman or the prophet—not the leader or the king, but the spiritual power and the interpreter of the Word.

The imagery of his clothing resonates all through the rest of Scripture. *Paul's clothing of the Christian warrior echoes Aaron's breastplate with its elaborate symbolism. The imagery of Revelation—with the gold and gems—has the flavor of these earlier descriptions. It also has become a rich source for iconography in medieval art. The symbolic meaning of each of the gems, the colors, the placement of each item, inspired artists in their precise choices. Later, in the Puritan tradition, we find this as a source for John Bunyan's imagery in *Pilgrim's Progress*.

The staff—Aaron's rod—became an image of power. The flowering rod was transformed into the root of *Jesse, an image of the Virgin birth of *Christ. It then became the bishop's staff in the Roman Catholic Church, and in modern literature D. H. Lawrence used it in the novel *Aaron's Rod* as a symbol of sexual and spiritual power. The music that springs from the piccolo, Lawrence's "Aaron's rod," blossoms into a symbol of the Holy Ghost, "putting forth new buds," and pushes past old limits. More recently, Aaron has shared honors in the opera *Moses and Aaron* by Arnold Schoenberg.

### SOURCES

Anderson, Bernard, *Understanding the Old Testament*, Englewood Cliffs, NJ: Prentice-Hall, Inc., 1966; Jeffrey, David L., ed., *A Dictionary of the Biblical Tradition in English Literature*, Grand Rapids, MI: William B. Eerdmans Publishing Company, 1992; Lawrence, D. H., *Aaron's Rod*, New York: Thomas Selzer, 1922; Propp, William Henry, *Exodus I-XVIII*, (Anchor Bible Series, vol. 2), New York: Doubleday, 1999; Wiesel, Elie, "Aaron: The Teflon Kid," in *Biblical Archaeology*, August 1998.

### ABRAHAM (ABRAM)

**Name and Etymology.** Abraham, for the first ninety-nine years of his life, was known as *Abram*, derived from the Hebrew for "exalted father." God later renamed him *Abraham*, meaning "father of many nations" (Gen. 17:5). By giving him a new name, God marked him as his special servant.

**Synopsis of Bible Story.** Abram's story appears in Genesis 11:25–26, beginning when he was already an old man, moving with his father, Terah, his nephew, *Lot, and his wife, *Sarai, from Ur of the Chaldees to Haran in the land of Canaan. After the death of his father, Abram had a call from God to set out on a grand adventure with the promise of blessings and protections and the hope of becoming a "great nation" (Gen. 12:2). Gathering his family and dependents, he journeyed through Canaan to Sichem, where he received from God the promise of the land. Because of famine, Abram took his tribe to Egypt, warning his wife to hide their relationship. When the Egyptian Pharaoh took Sarai into his house, plagues followed, leading the Egyptian to accuse Abram of causing him to incur God's wrath. From Egypt, the sojourners traveled to Bethel, where, earlier, Abram had set up an altar.

Lot, Abram's nephew, had by now accumulated many dependents and animals, causing some contention between his and Abram's men. He therefore sought a division of the land to maintain peace, a request that Abram honored, allowing his nephew to select the fertile Jordan plain.

Abraham and the three angels. The Art Archive/Museo Tridentino Arte Sacra, Trento/Dagli Orti (A).

Abram, assured by God of the blessings of the land and progeny, dwelt in the plain of Mamre, "which is Hebron" (Gen. 13:18). Later, notified that Lot was taken by warring tribes, he demonstrated his courage and generosity by pursuing Lot's captors as far as Dan, and bringing back his nephew, the other captives, and their goods. On his return, he received a blessing from *Melchizedek, King of Salem (Jerusalem) (Gen. 14:18).

Abram's concern then shifted from the land and battles to his need for an heir. He carefully followed the Lord's demands for a sacrifice, was blessed with a dream vision of his future and that of his progeny. The day ended with a covenant, the Lord promising the land around him as an inheritance for his seed. Sarai, also realizing the need for an heir and her own advanced age, gave her Egyptian handmaiden, *Hagar, to Abram, resulting in the subsequent birth of *Ishmael. This plan was to lead to conflict between the women and eventual casting out of Hagar.

In the meantime, the Lord fleshed out his covenant with Abram, including the mark of circumcision for all of the men in his tribe as a sign of that covenant. He also changed the names of Abram and Sarai to include an aspirate—thus *Abraham* and *Sarah*. In addition, Sarah was promised a son, a promise reinforced by visiting angels, who provoked Sarah's laughter at their announcement. She pointed to her being past the time of childbearing, but their response to her cynicism was, "Is any thing too hard for the Lord?" (Gen. 18:14).

While this promise was reaching fulfillment, Abraham once again found himself called upon to come to Lot's aid: recognizing that the evil city of Sodom was targeted for destruction, he pleaded with the Lord to be lenient, winning concessions. In spite of these efforts, the cities met disaster, while Abraham watched the smoke rise from the ruins. Lot, who escaped, did not rejoin him, but went another way.

Abraham then traveled south, once again hiding his real relationship with Sarah, telling a half-truth to the leader, Abimelech, that Sarah was his sister, but not mentioning that she was also his wife. Again God protected Sarah, and Abimelech demanded to know why Abraham was encouraging him to sin by keeping the full truth from him. It was after the restoration of peace with Abimelech and the blessing of a child on his family that the Lord allowed Sarah to conceive and bear *Isaac. It was at this point that the antagonism with Hagar intensified and Sarah demanded that she and Ishmael be expelled.

A final act in the drama came with God's demand that Abraham sacrifice his cherished son Isaac on an altar. At the last minute, a subsitutionary sacrifice of a ram was provided by divine intervention. Abraham's willingness to kill his "only son" in obedience to the Lord was rewarded with another blessing from God: ". . . for because thou hast done this thing, and hast not withheld thy son, thine only son: That in blessing will I bless thee, and in multiplying I will multiply thy seed as the stars of the heaven, and as the sand which is upon the sea shore; and thy seed shall possess the gate of his enemies; And in thy seed shall all the nations of the earth be blessed; because thou hast obeyed my voice" (Gen. 22:16–18).

The story ends with the death of Sarah and with Abraham's mourning for her. He bought the burial field from Ephron, the same field in the land of Canaan where he had first settled. He then arranged to obtain a wife for Isaac from his old country. Although Abraham took other wives in his final years, he gave all that he had to Isaac before he died "in a good old age, an old man, and full of years" and was buried in the cave with Sarah (Gen. 25:8–10).

**Historical Context.** Abraham's is the first of the specifically Hebrew narratives in Scripture, breaking from the larger explanations of human origins to focus on the history of the Jews.

Abraham left Ur, where the people worshipped the goddess of the moon, to live a nomadic life, probably following the traditional caravan route from the Fertile Crescent into Egypt (this route was used in ancient times to bring spices and other goods from the Middle East to Egypt and back). Abraham may have been a wealthy trader, which would account for his large entourage and his easy access to rulers of lands where he visited. As the first of the Patriarchs, Abraham became the basis of much of Hebrew thought: his covenant with God established the Israelites' claim to the land, the promise that they would become a great nation, and that they could rest on their faith in God.

The Muslims revere Abraham as their ancestor, claiming (according to the Koran) that Ishmael, not Isaac, was the designated sacrifice on the altar they believe to be on the Temple Mount in Jerusalem. Known as the Dome of the Rock or Mosque of the Dome, this site is also thought to be the original site of the Holy of Holies in Solomon's Temple. They also hold other sites sacred: the Cave of Machpelah in Hebron, where Abraham was buried, and the Oak of Mamre, where he is believed to have met the angels. The Jaffa Gate in Jerusalem is also known as "Abraham's Gate" because it leads to the road to Hebron.

**Archaeological Evidence.** He was a son of his age—the Middle Bronze. This was a time of transition from the last kings of Sumer, Isin, and Larsa, to the First Dynasty of

Babylon, whose greatest king was Hammurabi, the codifier of laws that resemble the Hebrew laws. The migration of the family of Terah, Abraham's father, from Ur to Haran (Gen. 11), has been dated in the twentieth or nineteenth centuries B.C.

There have been a host of discoveries in our century that shed light on the background of Abraham. Tablets unearthed at Mari on the Euphrates River; the finds of Sir Leonard Woolley at Ur, probably the early home of Abraham (Gen. 11:28, 31); and the research of L. Borchard all help set the approximate dates in Mesopotamian history during the second millennium B.C. The rich collection of clay tablets found at Ur reveal the life of the period. The Beni-hasan painting (discovered in this Egyptian village in 1890) suggests the physical appearance of Abraham and his clan (see Keller, 68). Recent excavations at Mari reveal that the towns cited in Gen. 24:10 correspond to actual locations of the Nuzi civilization.

Historians have discovered the caravan routes from ancient time in the Fertile Crescent, along which traders brought spices and other goods from the Middle East to Egypt and returned. Abraham may have been such a trader, in which case he would have been a very wealthy man.

Recent scholars, working with sophisticated tools for genetic tracking, have asserted that Jewish and Middle Eastern non-Jewish populations share a common genetic pool. This suggests that the people of the Middle East are descended from a common ancestral population (as suggested in the story of Abraham, Hagar, Sarah, Ishmael, and Isaac). (See M. F. Hammer's article in *Proceedings of the National Academy of Science*, 2000.)

**Character in Later Works.** Abraham's impressive history was quickly elaborated by tales of his birth, youth, perils, escapes, angelic protection, heroic adventures, vast learning, multiple marriages, extensive progeny, and his death. This great hero of monotheism was frequently mentioned in the New Testament as an image of the progenitor of Israel and a man of faith. Jesus defined his authority and deity in relation to Abraham (John 8:58): "Before Abraham was, I am." And *Paul identified Jesus as "the seed of Abraham" (Galatians 3:16), thereby connecting the Abrahamic covenant with fulfillment in Jesus as the promised Messiah. Paul identified the Christians' faith in Christ as "the faith of Abraham" (Rom. 4:12–16) and explained the doctrine of justification by faith—the great Protestant watchwords—*sola gratia, sola fides*—in terms of Abraham's being a believer before the law of Moses was given. (Also see Heb. 7:2, 11:8–17; James 2:23.)

St. Augustine followed Paul's lead, noting that all Christians are children (or "seed") of Abraham by their faith. Martin Luther, philosopher and theologian Søren Kierkegaard, among others, pictured him as the paradigm of the man of faith. The angelic visitors were seen as an early witness of the Trinity, the meeting with Melchizedek an anticipation of the Eucharist, and the offering of Isaac as an Old Testament type of atonement, prefiguring the sacrifice of Christ.

In English literature, Abraham appeared in Caedmon's *Genesis* and was frequently referred to in poetry (often as an image of paradise in comments on "Abraham's Bosom"). In the novel *Joseph Andrews*, Henry Fielding named his parson Abraham Adams. *Father Abraham* was the name that novelist William Faulkner planned at one time for the novel that became *The Hamlet*, in ironic reference to its impotent hero. Canadian novelist Margaret Laurence also uses him in *The Stone Angel*. One of the more interesting dramatic uses of him is Paul Green's *In Abraham's Bosom*, a play echoing the faith of African-American Christians. Even more stories focus on those characters who surrounded him—Hagar, Sarah, Isaac, Ishmael, and Lot. When Abraham appears, it is most often as the father, the wanderer, and the man of faith.

God's promises to Abraham and his seed has proven important to Jews, Christians, and Muslims through the centuries.

## SOURCES

Graves, Robert, and Raphael Patai, *Hebrew Myths: The Book of Genesis*, New York: McGraw-Hill Book Company, 1963; Hammer, M. F. et al., *Proceedings of the National Academy of Science*, U.S.A., 9 May 2000; Keller, Werner, *The Bible As History*, New York: Bantam Books, 1982; Kollek, Teddy, and Moshe Pearlman, *Jerusalem, Sacred City of Mankind: A History of Forty Centuries*, Jerusalem: Steimatzky's Agency, Ltd., 1968; Miller, Madeline, and J. Lane Miller, *Harper's Bible Dictionary*, New York: Harper and Row, 1961; Rogers, Phillip, "Abraham," in *A Dictionary of the Biblical Tradition in English Literature*, edited by David L. Jeffrey, Grand Rapids, MI: William B. Eerdmans Publishing Company, 1992.

## ABSALOM

**Name and Etymology.** *Absalom* comes from the Hebrew "father is/of peace."

**Synopsis of Bible Story.** Absalom, the third son of *David, appeared to be the heir to the throne. Handsome and clever, he was as headstrong as his father, but not so dedicated to God. His mother was Maacah, the daughter of Talmai, the king of Geshur (2 Sam. 3:3). She also bore to David a beautiful girl, Tamar, who became the sexual target of her half-brother, Amnon. This lustful brother lured the young woman to his bedside, pretending he was ill, and then raped her. Afterwards, he viciously rejected her, causing great shame and distress. Absalom, horrified at his half-brother's actions, which brought heartbreak and dishonor to his sister, plotted for two years to turn the tables on Amnon. He invited him to a sheep-shearing festival, and—while he was "merry with wine" (2 Sam. 13:28)—ordered his men to strike him down (2 Sam. 13:1–39).

Absalom fled to his mother's homeland of Geshur, where he remained for three years. David, though distressed at the fratricide, longed to see his beloved son and allowed himself to be convinced to permit Absalom's return to Jerusalem, but not to the court. Finally relenting, David welcomed him back into his presence, only to discover that this handsome son was now plotting to wrench the kingdom from him. Perhaps recognizing that palace politics would result in *Solomon's ascent to the throne, Absalom began currying favor with the people, sympathizing with their problems and claiming that, were he the judge, their lives would be vastly improved. Through his political promises and displays of glory (showing up daily with a chariot and horses and fifty men to run ahead of him at the city gates), Absalom "stole the hearts of the men of Israel" (2 Sam. 15:6).

Subsequently, Absalom went to Hebron. From there he sent secret messengers to incite civil war, joining with David's scheming counselor, Ahithophel, and other conspirators to take the throne from David (2 Sam. 15:12). The old king, recognizing the danger, fled from Jerusalem, taking some of his officials with him, but leaving behind a few spies and ten concubines. Pausing on their journey after crossing the Kidron Valley, David sent the Ark of the Covenant back to the city, while he continued up the Mount of Olives, weeping and praying (2 Sam. 15:31). Along the way, he was pelted with stones by a man who blamed him for *Saul's death, reminding him that he too was a "man of blood" (2 Sam. 16:9).

Absalom and his forces returned to Jerusalem to delighted crowds. In an act of arrogance, the young man lay with his father's concubines to signify his alienation from his father. His warriors then set out to attack the weary and weakened king, but David's spies informed him, allowing him to flee across the Jordan and escape the ambush and gather the loyal forces to defend his crown.

The story concludes tragically: Preparing for the final confrontation with the rebellious forces of Absalom, David's warriors asked him to stay behind, fearing that he would present the insurgents with a prize target. David's men defeated the revolutionary army and then chased Absalom, who was riding on a mule, under the branches of a large oak, where his long hair caught on the tree, leaving him dangling. Although his men were reluctant to kill the young man, Joab plunged three javelins into his heart, and ten of his armor-bearers finished him off. They threw him into a pit and piled up stones over his body, a place where David later erected a pillar, Absalom's Monument. They then reported back to David, anticipating a violent response to bearers of bad news. The old king/father was heartbroken. Going up over the gateway, he wept: "O my son Absalom, my son, my son Absalom! Would God I had died instead for thee—O Absalom, my son, my son!" (2 Sam. 18:33).

**Historical Context.** David's personal response to the death of a traitor was typical of his lovable frailty. He often showed himself to be more of a father than a king, thus weakening the kingdom and dividing his people. This period of civil conflict presages further divisions of the kingdom after Solomon's death when the unrest of the people became even more obvious. If he had strictly followed the law (Deut. 21:18–21), David would have stoned his utterly incorrigible son to death.

Geshur, the region that was home both to Absalom's mother and to him, in time of trouble, ceased to exist by the ninth century B.C. There are possible references to Geshur in the El Amarna letters. (These are clay tablets that describe fifteenth- and sixteenth-century life in Canaan. They were discovered in 1887 about 160 miles from the Nile Delta. (See Negev, 126–127.)

**Archaeological Evidence.** The monument David raised to memorialize his handsome son, two pillars in the "King's Valley" (2 Sam. 18:9–17), has traditionally been identified as Absalom's Monument in the Kidron Valley (*New International Version*, 446). Recent scholars indicate that this handsome relic is probably more recent than the events of this narrative—probably from Herod's reign instead of David's. (See Mare, 195 ff.)

**Character in Later Works.** A wealth of Jewish lore—including the story of Rabbi Joshua ben Levi's visit to the underworld—suggests that his act of treachery against his father is an unforgivable sin. St. Augustine used Absalom's perverse actions and his downfall as evidence of free will in confrontation with prevailing Providence. Most critics focused on David's grief and the complicated workings of divine justice. Many theologians have seen this tragic narrative as a vindication of Nathan's prophetic words to David at the time of his infidelity in his affair with Bathsheba and the plot to murder her husband to cover that shame (2 Sam. 12:10, 12:11).

This story of the handsome Absalom has been used throughout history as an admonitory tale of pride and over-reaching. Chaucer used the name for his amorous young parish clerk with the golden curls in "The Miller's Tale." The symbol of the beautiful hair that is Absalom's source of vanity and the means of his death reappears frequently in art and literature. The poet/painter William Blake has a moving picture of him with his ever-forgiving father, "The Forgiveness of Absalom." Renaissance writers were also interested in Absalom's reputation for false eloquence (2 Sam. 15:1–6), the proverbial attribute of the political schemer.

His clever schemes to undermine and overtake his father's authority intrigued the more political writers of the seventeenth century, serving as the subject of John Dryden's *Absalom and Achitophel*. More than sixty plays about David use the character of this famous son, often as the focal point in the drama. Among the recent writers who have used his tragedy in colorful ways are William Faulkner (in *Absalom, Absalom!*) and Alan Paton (in *Cry, the Beloved Country*). (For a lengthy listing, see Frans De Bruyn in Jeffrey, 13–14.)

## SOURCES

De Bruyn, Frans, "Absalom," in *A Dictionary of the Biblical Tradition in English Literature*, edited by David L. Jeffrey, Grand Rapids, MI: William B. Eerdmans Publishing Company, 1992; Mare, W. Harold, *The Archaeology of the Jerusalem Area*, Grand Rapids, MI: Baker Book House, 1987; Negev, Avraham, ed., *The Archaeological Encyclopedia of the Holy Land*, New York: Thomas Nelson Publishers, 1986.

## ADAM

**Name and Etymology.** *Adam* appears as a proper name for the first time in Genesis 4:25. The word appears to mean "that man" or "human being." The Hebrew root means "to be red" or "ruddy," a term tied to blood, or soil. Genesis 2:7 involves a Hebrew wordplay connecting the "man" (Adam) with the "ground" (adamah).

**Synopsis of Bible Story.** Genesis tells the epic story of the creation of man and woman, the Garden of Eden, the Temptation and Fall, life "east of Eden," the births of Adam's children, and, after 930 years, his death. Adam was married to *Eve, father to *Cain, Abel, and Seth, as well as other sons and daughters.

On the sixth day, God created man (male and female) in his own image, as the crowning glory of the creative acts. Man was set apart from the other animals by his dominion over them, and his capacity for fellowship with the Creator. At the time of creation, man was ordered to be fruitful and multiply. God looked on the creation of mankind and—as with the rest of his creation—found it "good" (Gen. 1:31).

In the expanded narrative, beginning with Genesis 2, Adam was created out of "dust" into which God breathed the breath of life. God placed man in the garden of Eden "to dress it and to keep it" (Gen. 2:15). He also explained that he could eat freely of every tree of the garden except for the tree of the knowledge of good and evil, "for in the day that thou eatest thereof thou shalt surely die" (Gen. 2:17). This first man named the animals in the garden, but found none suitable for his mate. Noting that is not good that man should be alone, God formed a "helpmeet" for Adam out of his rib—creating woman. They lived together in the garden as husband and wife, naked and unashamed in that golden age.

Both of these new creations were free to obey or disobey God. It was the wife who chose to converse with the subtle serpent, to risk temptation, and to eat of the fruit of the forbidden tree; and it was her transgression that ensnared Adam, who subsequently—at her invitation—ate of the fruit, knowing that he was disobeying God in this action.

They immediately understood that they were naked and hid from God, cowering and disobedient. In the confrontation that followed, Adam blamed Eve, who in turn

God creating Adam, illuminated letter A, folio 76R of Bible of Etienne Harding, c. 1109 Latin manuscript, from Abbey of Citeaux, France. The Art Archive/Bibliothèque Municipale, Dijon/Dagli Orti.

blamed the snake. God blamed them all, noting that Adam has become "as one of us, to know good and evil" (Gen. 3:22).

Adam would henceforth find the ground cursed: ". . . in sorrow thou shalt eat of it all the days of thy life; Thorns also and thistles shall it bring forth to thee; and thou shalt eat of the herb of the field; In the sweat of thy face shalt thou eat bread, till thou return unto the ground; for out of it wast thou taken; for dust thou art, and unto dust shalt thou return" (Gen. 3:18–19.)

God expelled them from the Garden of Eden, prohibiting their eating of the Tree of Life, and posting Cherubim with flaming swords to block their return. It was in their life "east of Eden" that they "knew" one another and Eve conceived and bore their first two sons, Cain and Abel. In Cain's murder of his brother, the curse took on meaning. A third son, Seth, was born to them later, as were other nameless children (Gen. 4:25).

**Historical Context.** The story of the Creation, which derives from a time long before written history, has parallels in many Eastern myths, including the Babylonian. Some version of the first man and woman is common in them, but only in the Hebrew story is man created in the image of God, which has been defined in various ways in various creeds of various faiths, usually involving knowledge, wisdom, righteousness, and true holiness. Nor is the bond between God and man so basic, and the relationship

Adam and Eve. The Art Archive/Rubens House, Antwerp, Belgium/Album/Joseph Martin.

between man and nature so clearly delineated in these other narratives. And, only in the Genesis telling is marriage so clearly defined as a heterosexual union, involving a separate unit of the family, reinforced by the directive to "be fruitful and multiply."

Unlike the rebellious and vindictive Prometheus, the Greek mythological figure who was thought to have created man by using a combination of water and clay, the

God of Genesis created man in his own image, making him the guardian and sovereign of nature. This is the crowning act of the great story of Creation.

Life in Eden bears some resemblance to the Greeks' Golden Age. In the Greek myths, man descended over time from the idyllic Golden Age to the more debased Silver, then to the Bronze Age. Each of these generations became more cruel, libidinous, and treacherous until the modern Iron Age. In Genesis, the life before and after the Fall is more stark and abrupt. Life in Eden is innocent and ideal; life "east of Eden" is filled with sin, guilt, and death.

**Archaeological Evidence.** As early as 3000 B.C. a seal impression of a bearded Adam standing by Eve was found in Tepe Gawra, near Nineveh in Assyria. It is now on exhibit in Philadelphia at the University of Pennsylvania Museum of Archaeology and Anthropology. Myths of Eden are numerous in Hebrew history. The story of Adam is so important in human history that men frequently proclaim the discovery of the earliest "man." The designation of the rivers in Genesis would seem to establish the region of Eden to be in the Fertile Crescent, but modern anthropologists have cited locations for discoveries as far away as Africa and China. Some in Jerusalem believe that Adam's grave is located near the Church of the Holy Sepulcher, the traditional site of the Crucifixion. This neat symbolism allows the idea of the Second Adam, crucified on a cross made from the wood of the tree in the Garden of Eden, to blend into the ancient image of the First Adam eating his guilty meal of forbidden fruit.

**Character in Later Works.** References to Adam occur regularly in Scripture (Job 31:33; 1 Cor. 15:22, 45; 1 Tm. 2:14). In some cases, they describe the creation story, in some the first occasion of sin, in some the image of the first man in contrast to Christ, the Second Adam. While Scripture presented Adam as an individual and a type, a theological explanation of man's nature and his depravity, theologians and others have argued over various facets of his historicity and meaning. From the beginning, Hebrew myth elaborated the stories of Adam, Lilith (thought by some to have been the first woman created), and Eve. Many of these stories are now available in collections such as *Hebrew Myths: The Book of Genesis.*

During the middle ages, the whole background of Satan, the battle of the angels, and the fall of man became an increasingly elaborate story of epic proportions, emerging as context for such poetic classics as Dante's *Divine Comedy* and John Milton's *Paradise Lost*—the fullest retelling of the narrative. Michelangelo's celebrated fresco on the ceiling of the Sistine Chapel portrays God touching Adam's finger—a dramatic image of the instant of life's beginning.

No story of Western culture is more significant to the literary imagination than the story of the Creation and the Fall. From the medieval mystery plays, which often begin with the story of Adam and Eve, to modern novels, the images and ideas of this story dominate our culture: not only John Milton's great epic, but also George Eliot's novel *Adam Bede*, Mark Twain's *Extracts from Adam's Diary*, and C. S. Lewis's *Perelandra*. William Blake bases his *Songs of Innocence* on the Eden narrative. The hero of Robert Penn Warren's novel *All the King's Men* derives both his name and innocence from this first hero.

In most cases, the image of the innocent man facing sin (usually involving woman) and falling into temptation (often in a garden setting) results in richer understanding and greater pain. Nathaniel Hawthorne placed his illicit lovers in a false Eden, a New

England forest, for his evocative scene of seduction in *The Scarlet Letter*. Milton explored the concept of the "fortunate fall," the idea that Adam's sin opened for mankind the greater knowledge of good through the understanding and experience of evil, and further provided the occasion for God's redemptive work through his son, Jesus Christ, who paid the price for that original sin.

The idea of the new creation, as a monster in Mary Shelley's *Frankenstein*, or a robotic test tube creature, as in Aldous Huxley's *Brave New World*, provides the alternate possibility of man reversing the roles, becoming the creator of the new Adam, making himself into God. It is impossible to overstate the centrality of this character in Western literature.

## SOURCES

Graves, Robert, *The Greek Myths*, vol. 1, Baltimore, MD: Penguin Books, 1955; Graves, Robert, and Raphael Patai, *Hebrew Myths: The Book of Genesis*, Garden City, NY: Doubleday, 1964; Platt, Rutherford Hayes, and J. Alden Brett, *The Lost Books of the Bible and the Forgotten Books of Eden*, New York: The New American Library, 1974; Reik, Theodore, *The Temptation*, New York: Braziller, 1961; Sayers, Dorothy L., *The Mind of the Maker*, Westport, CT: Greenwood Press, 1941.

## AMOS

**Name and Etymology.** *Amos* is apparently a shortened form of a name such as "Amasiah," meaning "the Lord carries" or "the Lord upholds."

**Synopsis of Bible Story.** A shepherd, or sheep-raiser from Tekoa, near Bethlehem, Amos was called by God to prophesy to Israel. He spoke directly to the sins of Damascus, Gaza, Tyre, Edom, Ammon, and finally Judah. In the first instances, he pronounced "three sins" of each, describing in detail the iniquities of the people. In the case of Judah, he pointed out that, led astray by false gods, the people had rejected the law of the Lord and had not kept his decrees. As a result, the Lord threatened that he would send fire that would consume the fortresses of Jerusalem (Amos 2:5). The injustices of Israel dominate the brief prophetic utterances of this poetic and forthright prophet; they are specific and blunt. He notes that Israel has evidence in history of God dealing with injustice and disobedience.

A poetic interlude, making a more richly philosophic statement and including a plea for transformation, rebukes and begs that Israel "Hear this word" (Amos 3:1, 4:1, 5:1). Ending this exhortation with a strong admonition against those who are "at ease in Zion" (Amos 6:1), he reveals a series of visions: the locusts, the fire, and the plumb line (Amos 7). In keeping with his stated background, not as a professional prophet nor as the son of a prophet, but as a shepherd and a "gatherer of sycamore fruit" (Amos 7:14), he describes a final vision—a basket of ripe fruit. God explains that Israel is ripe for the Day of the Lord. Following this picture of destruction and distress comes a restoration, a time of repair and revival when "the mountains shall drop sweet wine, and all the hills shall melt," (Amos 9:13) and the Lord will bring back his exiled people, Israel, to rebuild the ruined cities, plant gardens, and eat their fruit. God's final promise—through Amos—is that he will plant Israel "upon their land, and they shall no more be pulled up out of their land" which he has given them (Amos 9:15).

**Historical Context.** Amos was a minor prophet of the eighth century B.C. His beautiful words were apparently collected and transcribed quite early—shortly after the time of his sojourn in Israel. Though a native of the Southern Kingdom (Judah), he was called to prophesy to the Northern Kingdom (Israel), warning clearly of the threat of the Assyrian Empire, which was soon to overtake and decimate these peoples.

In Amos, for the first time, the Lord referred to Israel as "my people" (Amos 7:8, See notes in *New International Version*, 1348.) The general outline of Israel's history, from the time of Moses to the time of the "Return" (the eventual homecoming of the Jews after the Babylonian captivity), is beautifully described in this brief prophetic book.

**Archaeological Evidence.** Much of Amos's prophecy refers to specific places, activities, and people abundantly reflected in recent excavations in Dan and in Gath. Since the early 1990s, records in the *Biblical Archaeological Review* have made constant reference to Amos's prophecies borne out in earthquakes, battered walls, ruined cities, and shattered cult objects.

The affluence of the world to which he refers is evidenced by the recent discoveries of the opulent lifestyle in cities of the Northern Kingdom. The description of "winter house" and "summer house" or the "great house" and the "little house," (6:11), the carvings and inlays of ivory he describes (6:4) match discoveries in the ruined palaces in Samaria and other cities. In addition, Assyrian reliefs picture the prisoners of war being led away with a rope fastened to a hook that pierced the nose or lower lip, as described in Amos 4:2.

**Character in Later Works.** *Ezekiel and *Hosea both refer to Amos, but direct reference is rare in Scripture. St. Jerome pictured him "upon his crag blowing his shepherd's horn," a characterization reflected in literature. This rustic poet may be the inspiration for the medieval masterpiece *Piers Plowman* (Jeffrey, 35).

In medieval statuary, he is pictured as a rustic prophet of doom. In our century, there have been a number of minor plays based on his life and a novel by Dorothy Clarke Wilson. Generally, however, literary interest in him has been sparse.

The actual inspiration of Amos may be more subtle—the concept of the simple man, a plainspoken prophet of justice, who can see through the elegant trappings of the contemporary culture to the corruption beneath. Classics scholar Edith Hamilton sees him as the enemy of ritual, the prophet of righteousness— "a wild-looking figure . . . sunscorched and weather-worn, a rough herdsman's cloak wrapped around him"—sternly confronting the chief priest with those powerful words: "Take thou away from me the noise of thy songs, for I will not hear the melody of thy viols. But let justice well up as waters and righteousness as a mighty stream" (Hamilton, 75).

## SOURCES

Biran, Avraham, "Sacred Spaces of Standing Stones, High Places and Cult Objects at Tel Dan," *Biblical Archaeology Review*, September/October, 1998; Demsky, Aaron, "Discovering a Goddess," *Biblical Archaeology Review*, September/October, 1998; Hamilton, Edith, *Spokesmen for God*, New York: W. W. Norton & Co., 1949; Isaacs, Ronald H., *Messengers of God: A Jewish Prophets Who's Who*, Jerusalem: Jason Aronson, Inc., 1998; Jeffrey, David L., *A Dictionary of the Biblical Tradition in English Literature*, Grand Rapids, MI: William B. Eerdmans Publishing Company, 1992; Laughlin, John C. H., "The Remarkable Discoveries at Dan," *Biblical Archaeology Review*, September/October, 1981; Maeir, Aren M., and Carl S. Ehrich, "Excavating Philistine Gath: Have We Found Goliath's Hometown?" *Biblical Archaeology Review*, November/December, 2001.

# B

## BALAAM

**Name and Etymology.** *Balaam* is a Greek form of the Hebrew word for "a thing swallowed," or "ruin."

**Synopsis of Bible Story.** Balaam's story (in Num. 22:7–24:25, 31:16) is both colorful and confusing. The son of Beor, this pagan diviner found himself in the midst of a quarrel between Balak, the king of Moab, and the Israelites. Balak mistakenly thought that the crowd of Israelites flooding into his region posed a threat to the Moabites and the Midianites. Realizing that they were too numerous for his armies to battle, he called upon supernatural forces to help his side. He sent messengers to Balaam, who was a seer sensitive to spiritual forces, not limited to the worship of Baal. At first, Balaam listened to God, who refused to provide him with curses for the Israelites, dictating blessings instead. Balaam demonstrated an integrity in his response to Balak, refusing to pretend that he could curse that which God chose to bless. When offered bribes, he insisted that even a palace filled with silver and gold could not change his response.

On the night Balaam had refused the king a second time, God came to the diviner and told him to go with the messengers to Balak, and to follow God's orders. The following day, Balaam started on the journey, apparently planning to curse the Israelites rather than obey God, only to find his donkey was more sensitive to spiritual apparitions than he: she balked at the sight of the angel of the Lord, responded to repeated beatings by lying down under him, and finally cried out in response to his continuing abuse, asking him why he was beating her. With no sign of surprise that he was faced with a talking donkey, Balaam berated her for her disobedience. At that moment, the Lord opened Balaam's eyes, allowing him finally to see the angel that the donkey had already recognized. The Lord then commanded Balaam to follow his orders when he entered into the courts of Balak.

Once in the presence of Balak—who was disturbed that his prophet took so long in coming—Balaam began performing a series of sacrifices and oracles. In four long and three short poetic prophecies, he told of the blessings that Jehovah was planning to pour out on the Israelites. With each blessing, Balak suggested they change location and begin again, but Balaam continued to follow the command and the voice of God. The last of these oracles has the mark of messianic prophecy.

To this point, it would appear that this pagan was a valid conduit for God's message. There is, however, an abrupt change in the story. We next learn of a time of sexual immorality among the men of Israel, as they succumbed to the Moabite women in celebration of their fertility gods. At first this narrative does not appear relevant to Balaam. Somewhat later, when Balaam's death is noted, we discover that he was the instigator of Israel's apostasy, thereby bringing God's judgment down on the wayward men. These Israelites yoked themselves to Baal Peor and were consequently punished. Balaam was killed in Israel's war against Midian (Num. 31:8).

**Historical Context.** Balaam was a thirteenth-century B.C. soothsayer used to demonstrate Jehovah's power to the King of Moab and his followers. In actuality, *Moses had no plans to conquer the cities of Moab, and Balak's efforts against them were unnecessary.

Fertility rites among the worshippers of Baal become clear at the conclusion of Balaam's story and were to continue as a threat and temptation to the Israelites.

The tribes, which were the subject of the oracles, appear in later history, fulfilling the prophetic utterances here and echoing those in Jacob's final blessings of Joseph's sons and his own. Although these oracles about settlement of the land proved valid, the real interest was in the coming of a great leader—a "star" and a "scepter" in the distant future. This prophecy was picked up in the New Testament in references to the *Magi, the wise men from the East, who came in search of the "star." They are thought to have derived their interest in this star and in the coming of the Messiah—the king—from the Jews who had been in captivity in Babylon (Matt. 2:1–2).

Another link to New Testament thought is the interest in magic, these Magi being practitioners of the occult in some region to the "east." The magic powers we see in Balaam, which appear again in the story of Simon Magnus (Acts 8:9–24), indicate that supernatural explorations were not limited to the people of the Covenant. Ancient literature is full of references to oracles, prophecies, magic, and dreams.

**Archaeological Evidence.** One of Balaam's prophecies has been unearthed in an Aramaic text from Tell Deir Alla in the Jordan Valley, apparently from circa 700 B.C. (*New International Version*, 220). Ink inscriptions on a plastered wall of a large building, apparently destroyed by fire, survive, telling the story about Balaam the Seer. It may actually be a draft notation from a professional scribes' school located at that place. Given this late date, however, this is no verification of the historicity of the biblical passage.

Numerous statues of Baal are in the Archaeological Museum (in the Israel Museum in Jerusalem), showing him to be a human figure, most like the Greeks' vision of Zeus.

**Character in Later Works.** The talking donkey that sees the angel before the man became a favorite for artists. Balaam was an ambiguous figure (like *Lot or *Esau) whose portrayal troubled ancient interpreters. On the one hand, he was a true prophet of God, a man who "heard the words of God, and knew the knowledge of the Most High" (Num. 24:16) and who was effective at both blessing and cursing (Num. 22:6).

Such powers could hardly have come without God's help. In addition, his words were favorable to Israel, as was his prediction of the coming of their Messiah.

On the other hand, his balking donkey and his trip to Moab both argue against his virtue. He appears to have been an enemy of Israel, despite his lavish oracles. Ancients tend to believe he was "Balaam the Wicked," a prophet for hire, interested in his own material gain and self-aggrandizement In Deut. 23:3–5, Moses criticized Balaam for his curses, bought by the king of Moab, but serving no purpose. Later scripture references note that Balaam tried to curse Israel, but God would not listen (Mic. 6:5). We also see negative assessments in Joshua 13:22, 24:9–10, and in Nehemiah 13:2. Jews were interested in the idea that the "scepter" would not depart from Judah (Gen. 49:10). At Qumran, Balaam's words were understood as a prediction of a coming war and subsequent domination by Israel.

In the New Testament, Balaam was seen as a prototype of heretics and an example of permissive morality in 2 Peter 2:16, Jude 11, and Revelation 2:14. *Jude saw him as a prophet-for-hire (Jude 11). Later, Philo—one of the early Christian commentators— called him a "sophist." Christians were nonetheless interested in Balaam's foreseeing the Messiah (Num. 24:17–19) and interpreted his oracles as fulfilled in Christ (Matt. 2:1–2).

Naturally, the episode of the donkey was a favorite in medieval miracle plays, especially the Chester cycle. Apparently, though Balaam's story is often cited in literature, the only developed story is Charles Davy's "Balaam: An Attempt Towards an Oratorio" written in 1789.

This narrative of a non-Jewish prophet points to God's work beyond the scope of Israel and has proven particularly appealing to non-Jewish believers seeking evidence of the universality of God's rule. In addition, the charm of the wise donkey, more sensitive to spiritual truth than the "wise" man, becomes a favorite among those who admire Scripture for its aesthetic delight.

## SOURCES

Albright, W. F., "The Oracles of Balaam," *The Journal of Biblical Literature*, 63, 1994; Alter, Robert, *The Art of Biblical Narrative*, New York: Basic Books, 1981; Emmerson, Richard K., "Balaam," in *A Dictionary of the Biblical Tradition in English Literature*, edited by David L. Jeffrey, Grand Rapids, MI: William B. Eerdmans Publishing Company, 1992; Kugel, James L., *Traditions of the Bible: A Guide to the Bible As It Was at the Start of the Common Era*, Cambridge, MA: Harvard University Press, 1998; Mazar, Amihai, *Archaeology of the Land of the Bible: 100,000–586 B.C.E.*, New York: Doubleday, 1992; Young, Karl, *The Drama of the Medieval Church*, vol. 2, Oxford: Clarendon Press, 1967.

## BARABBAS

**Name and Etymology.** *Barabbas* is Aramaic for "son of the father"—perhaps an ironic reference to the status given exclusively to *Jesus, or perhaps a suggestion that he was the son of a rabbi. The ancient authorities, including the Sinaitic Syriac version, give his full name as Jesus Bar-Abbas (Mart. 27:16–26).

**Synopsis of Bible Story.** Nothing is known of Barabbas outside of the Gospels, which place him in prison for robbery (John 18:40). *Mark and *Luke say he was there for insurrection and murder (Mark 15:7; Luke 23:19), and *Matthew says that he was "notorious" as a rebel (27:16). This implies that he had taken part in a rebellion, presumably against the Romans, and may therefore have been a folk hero among the Jews (*New International Version*, 1484). Placing this in contemporary terms, we might view

Barabbas as not a common robber or a murderer, but as a terrorist, committed to some national cause (Sayers, 258). Mark's reference to "insurrectionists who committed murder in the uprising" implies that Barabbas was a member of Zealots, a revolutionary group of Jewish nationalists dedicated to the expulsion of the despised Roman occupation (Brownrigg, 38). He had probably killed some people in the course of one of the many rebellions against the Roman legions.

At the time of his arrest, Jesus argued with the chief priests and the officers of the Temple guard, asking, "Be ye come out, as against a thief, with swords and staves?" or as it is expressed in more modern terms in the *New International Version*: "Am I leading a rebellion, that you have come with swords and clubs?" (Luke 22:52) He may have been making a reference to the Zealots and their violent mode of insurrection as opposed to his own non-violent strategy. In contrast to Barabbas, Jesus consistently refused to become a political revolutionary, insisting that his kingdom was not of this world.

*Pontius Pilate, the Roman procurator who presided over Jesus' trial, noting that a Passover custom allowed him to free one prisoner, recommended that it be Jesus, but the multitude demanded the release of Barabbas instead. In this ironic reversal, Pilate freed the violent revolutionary and crucified the son of God.

**Historical Context.** The Zealots, who derived their spirit of rebellion from the tradition of the Jewish nationalistic Maccabees, were increasingly active in these days, especially under the clumsy administration of Pontius Pilate. Even before this, the Jews had risen up against the Roman procurators. There were no less than fourteen procurators in Judea during the period from 6 to 66, during which time the tensions between Rome and the Jews steadily increased. They found the Jews' stubborn resistance to Hellenistic religion, their zeal for their own faith and customs, and their refusal to compromise puzzling and troublesome. While the Romans considered the Jewish religion barbaric and superstitious, the Jews considered the Romans sacrilegious and brutal.

Over time, the Jews were drawn into groups of Zealots who favored armed rebellion. This eventually flared into open hostility under the heavy handed Felix (procurator of Judea A.D. 53–60), and led eventually to the fall of Jerusalem and the scattering of the Jews.

**Archaeological Evidence.** Josephus, the contemporary historian, described the Zealots as a party of patriots, founded by Judas the Galilean, who led a revolt against Rome in A.D. 6. They opposed paying tribute to a pagan emperor, insisting that God was Israel's true king. One of Jesus's disciples was called Simon the Zealot (Luke 6:15; Acts 1:13); and in addition, some believe that *Judas Iscariot was connected with this group of patriots. They remained active throughout the period of Jesus's life and for sometime afterwards. Their final stronghold, Masada, fell in May A.D. 74. Caves—especially in certain areas of the Galilee—were commonly the hiding places for the Zealots (Bruce, 1675).

Masada itself, the famous fortress of the brutal king *Herod, has become a favorite tourist attraction in recent years and a site for a great deal of archaeological excavation and study.

**Character in Later Works.** There is little patristic commentary on Barabbas himself; the focus is instead on the irony of the crowd's preferring a convicted murderer over the spotless Son of God. This led one early commentator, St. John Chrysostom, to note the viciousness of the crowd, increasing the inclination toward anti-Semitism among Christian thinkers.

Barabbas does appear frequently in the medieval mystery plays. In the York cycle (plays produced by the guilds in York), he makes a brief, gracious speech in response to Pilate's gesture. Christopher Marlowe names his protagonist after him in the play *The Jew of Malta*. Most references to him are incidental. In recent years, the writer Pär Lagerkvist developed a psychological study of him (*Barabbas*; Jeffrey, 76).

## SOURCES

Brownrigg, Ronald, *Who's Who in the Bible*, New York: Bonanza Books, 1980; Bruce, F. F. "Zealot," in *The Illustrated Bible Dictionary*, vol. 3, Sidney, Australia: Tyndale House Publishers, 1980; Jeffrey, David L., ed., *A Dictionary of the Biblical Tradition in English Literature*, Grand Rapids, MI: William B. Eerdmans Publishing Company, 1992; Kee, Howard Clark, Franklin W. Young, and Karlfried Froehlich, *Understanding the New Testament*, Englewood Cliffs, NJ: Prentice-Hall, Inc., 1965; Miller, Madeline S., and J. Lane Miller, *Harper's Bible Dictionary*, New York: Harper and Row, 1961; Sayers, Dorothy L., *The Man Born to Be King*, Grand Rapids, MI: William B. Eerdmans Publishing Company, 1943; Shaw, Gregory, "Barabbas," in *The Oxford Companion to the Bible*, edited by Bruce M. Metzger and Michael D. Coogan, New York: Oxford University Press, 1993.

## BARNABAS

**Name and Etymology.** *Barnabas* means "son of exhortation" or "of prophecy." He is also known as "Joses" or "Joseph."

**Synopsis of Bible Story.** Barnabas first appears in Acts 4:36–37, where he generously donates the money from the sale of his land to the church, contrasting starkly with two other members of the community of believers, Ananias and Sapphira, whose hypocritical pretense at generosity ended with their condemnation and death. Barnabas is identified as a Levite (Jew) from Cyprus. Later, when *Paul came to the church at Jerusalem, the Apostles were suspicious of his motives. Barnabas reached out to the new convert, vouching for his genuine faith and testifying to his bold preaching in Damascus in the name of Jesus (Acts 9:27). Later, Barnabas asked Paul to come from Tarsus to Antioch (Acts 11:22, 25), where the church needed additional helpers. They then carried a contribution from the church at Antioch to Jerusalem for the poor of Judea (Acts 11:22–30).

These men worked well together and teamed up as partners for the first missionary journey, an evangelistic tour that began with Barnabas's home region of Cyprus. They were joined by Barnabas's young cousin *Mark, who quickly abandoned the enterprise and returned to Jerusalem (Acts 12:13). Although Barnabas was Paul's elder in the faith, Paul began to assume the leadership role during this journey. In a comic scene in Lystra, the two were taken to be Greek deities. Apparently because he was large and handsome, Barnabas was thought to be Jupiter. The smaller, more articulate Paul was identified as Mercury, the messenger of the gods (Acts 14:12). Their ministry to the Gentiles led eventually to the Council of Jerusalem, where the matter of circumcision of converts was determined (Acts 15).

When Paul was planning his second missionary journey, he turned again to Barnabas. When his friend insisted on bringing along Mark, Paul chose to go with Silas instead. Although Barnabas then disappeared from the narrative, we do see references to him in Paul's epistles: the apostle mentions his old friend (1 Cor. 9:6; and in Gal. 2:1–13). Barnabas gave Mark another chance and took him to Cyprus as a companion. Paul eventually forgave him (Col. 4:10; Phil. 24) and finally admitted that Mark had indeed changed and was a great help to him (2 Tim. 4:11), "profitable" in his ministry.

**Historical Context.** The ease with which Barnabas accepted Paul and joined with him in his activities may be attributed to their common background. Both were educated in the Jewish law, and both came from commercial and cultural centers. Some critics speculate that they were of about the same age and interest in reaching out to the people of Asia Minor and beyond (M. Miller, 61). It is curious, however, that a Levite would own property. This suggests a change in the law, allowing Levites to accumulate wealth. It may, in fact, mark a breakdown (or a failure to recover) the pre-exilic tribal distribution to provide for the Levites.

**Archaeological Evidence.** Statues of Zeus/Jupiter, which are abundant in archaeological sites all over the Mediterranean region, where Hellenistic culture spread, help the reader to understand something of the appearance of Barnabas. The art works suggest a well-proportioned man of mature years.

**Character in Later Works.** An apocryphal epistle attributed to Barnabas, written after 100 A.D. was designed to deal with the historical link between Judaism and the Gospel. The writer of this letter indicates that the rites and ceremonies of the Jewish law were meant by God to be mystical pointers to Christ. The Jewish people were seduced by an evil angel into a literal understanding of them, leading them to believe these ordinances were sufficient unto themselves. Because of this failure among most of the Jews, the Covenant (established between God and the Israelites at Mount Sinai) had been taken away from them and reserved instead for the Christians. This epistle may have reinforced and elaborated the argument for Christians' selection of Sunday as the Sabbath, a custom adopted by the first generation of believers. (See Letter of Barnabas 15:3–5, in R. Miller.)

Barnabas did not play a significant role in Church tradition, usually being discussed only in connection with Paul's missionary journeys. John Milton does refer to him in *Considerations Touching the Likeliest Means to Remove Hirelings out of the Church*, and the term "Barnabas" is often used as a name for a loyal supporter, but this early leader of the Christian community has not proved consequential in art or literature.

### SOURCES

McCready, Wayne O. "Barnabas," in *A Dictionary of the Biblical Tradition in English Literature*, edited by David L. Jeffrey, Grand Rapids, MI: William B. Eerdmans Publishing Company, 1992; Miller, Madeline S., and J. Lane Miller, *Harper's Bible Dictionary*, New York: Harper and Row, 1961; Miller, Robert J., *The Complete Gospels*, San Francisco: HarperCollins, 1994.

## BARUCH

**Name and Etymology.** *Baruch* comes from the Hebrew word for "blessed" or "blessed of Jehovah." The name is a shortened form of other names like "Berechiah" and "Barachel"—more common names in Scripture.

**Synopsis of Bible Story.** Baruch was a friend and scribe to *Jeremiah who is mentioned in several places (Jeremiah 32:12–15, 36:4–5, 45). He served Jeremiah as a scribe or an amanuensis. Baruch, however, seems to have gone well beyond the normal scribal duties, serving as a confident and friend. At the time Jeremiah was in prison and receiving a series of oracles, Baruch brought ink and rolls of parchment to him and transcribed God's words as Jeremiah dictated them. Probably because Jeremiah was banned from the Temple area, it was Baruch who then read the prophecies to the people, that all Judah might hear. When the prophetic scroll was destroyed by the angry king, Baruch once again wrote them out on a scroll, adding still more prophecies. These words form the nucleus of the Book of Jeremiah, chapters 1–9, 10:17–25, 46–49:33, and possibly portions of chapters 11–20. Baruch is thought to have gone with Jeremiah into Egypt when Jerusalem fell, and perhaps then to Babylon.

According to Roman Catholic and Eastern Orthodox churches, he was also the author of *The Book of Baruch*, which is not accepted as canonical by either Jewish or Protestant scholars, though the Jews considered it especially significant. Regarding the story that Baruch left Egypt and traveled to Babylon, Carol A. Newsom notes the inconsistencies between Jeremiah 43:1–7 and the opening of the *Book of Baruch*, explaining: "It was a relatively common practice during the Second Temple period to compose edifying works that expanded the biblical tradition. . . ." (1617). It is only in the opening verses of *The Book of Baruch* that Baruch is mentioned as the author.

*The Book of Baruch*, which opens as it is being read aloud to the captive Jews in Babylon, includes an extended prayer of confession and petition modeled in part on Daniel 9:3–19. This is followed by a prayer praising Wisdom in the mode of Proverbs and other wisdom literature. Then the beautiful psalm of assurance that the people will eventually be redeemed and returned to Jerusalem concludes the brief book with a note of hope—which echoes the hope we also see in Jeremiah.

**Historical Context.** The historical Baruch, the son of Neriah, was a contemporary of Jeremiah during the reigns of the vassal kings Jehoiakim (609–598 B.C.) and Zedekiah (598–587 B.C.). He was present at the time of the destruction of the Temple in Jerusalem, and a partner with Jeremiah in exile. It is also assumed that he later went to Babylon, where he tried to comfort the people with words of praise for *Nebuchadnezzer and hope for the remnant.

**Archaeological Evidence.** An inscription occurs on a clay seal impression from the late seventh century B.C., reading "[belonging] to Berechiah, son of Neriah, the scribe." This is apparently a relatively rare example of the occurrence of the name of a biblical person in a nonbiblical source from the individual's own time (Coogan, 75).

**Character in Later Works.** In addition to *The Book of Baruch*, this famous scribe is also credited with *The Apocalypse of Baruch* and *The Rest of the Works of Baruch*. Perhaps because Baruch's actual authorship of such works remains in doubt, he is rarely mentioned in either Jewish or Christian literature. One scholar notes that "The one passage that had special significance for the church is Baruch 3:37, where the subject of the words 'appeared on earth' was mistakenly taken to be God rather than Wisdom . . . and the verse was therefore understood as a prophecy of the incarnation" (Dentan, 76).

SOURCES

Coogan, Michael D., "Baruch," and Dentan, Robert C., "Baruch, The Book of" in *The Oxford Companion to the Bible*, edited by Bruce M. Metzger and Michael D. Coogan, New York: Oxford University Press, 1993; Newsom, Carol A., "Baruch: Introduction," in *The HarperCollins Study Bible*, edited by Wayne A. Meeks, San Francisco, CA: HarperCollins, 1993; Wiseman, D. J., "Baruch," in *The Illustrated Bible Dictionary*, vol. 1, edited by J. D. Douglas, Sidney, Australia: Tyndale House Publishers, 1980.

## BATHSHEBA

**Name and Etymology.** *Bathsheba* means "daughter of the oath," or "daughter of the seventh day, or Sabbath."

**Synopsis of Bible Story.** Bathsheba, a well-born woman, the daughter of Eliam, the granddaughter of Ahithophel, David's counselor, and the wife of Uriah the Hittite, David's warrior, was apparently a great beauty. She was first mentioned in 2 Samuel 11:1–5, when David noticed her bathing on her rooftop and immediately sent for her.

When she informed him somewhat later that she was with child, he arranged for her husband's return, probably to trick him into believing the child was his own. But Uriah, a Hittite who showed more honor than the Hebrew David, refused to return to his wife while men were at war, staying with the troops while he was in town. David, increasingly aware of his guilt and the peril of discovery, arranged with his loyal commander Joab that Uriah be placed in danger's way.

When notified that Uriah had been killed, David waited only briefly to marry the pregnant widow, displaying an arrogance of power that captured the attention of *Nathan the prophet. Nathan invited David, by means of a parable, to convict himself. When David repented his adultery, Nathan signaled God's forgiveness, but also his punishment of the evildoers. The child was doomed to die (2 Sam. 12). In spite of David's deep remorse and constant prayer, Nathan's prophecy proved true.

Other children were born to David and Bathsheba thereafter. David promised his wife that Solomon, their second child, would be his heir to the throne. In the old king's final days, Bathsheba reminded David of this, while following carefully the trickery involving Adonijah. Bathsheba clearly helped procure the throne for Solomon (1 Kings 1:15–31).

Later, when Bathsheba made a plea to King Solomon on Adonijah's behalf for the maidservant Abishag (1 Kings 2:19–21), she apparently did not understand that the possession of the king's mistress would be a signal that he also deserved the throne. Solomon, more politically shrewd and more ruthless than his mother, saw Adonijah as a continuing threat to his power and had him killed. This forceful action on Solomon's part apparently brought a halt to the plotting by the old queen. Bathsheba lived out her final days as a queen mother, influential but not dominating her illustrious son.

**Historical Context.** The many battles that David fought, the habit of undertaking them in the springtime, and his own advancing years finally shifted his status from young hero to middle-aged monarch. Rather than fighting with his men, he now elected to remain at home, bored and lascivious.

The ritual bath of purification in which Bathsheba was first discovered is clearly directed in Hebrew law, which sets aside certain times in a woman's life—her menstrual periods and immediately after giving birth—during which she is "unclean" and may not be touched until after she is cleansed by a ritual bath and sacrifice (See Lev. 15:19–22). The frequent baths may have derived from the Hebrews' sojourn in Egypt, where priests were required to bathe four times a day (according to Herodotus 2:27).

**Archaeological Evidence.** Archaeologists have recently discovered references to the Davidic dynasty, but of course not to Bathsheba. Even her famous son's name—if it sur-

David and Bathsheba, illuminated letter E, folio 197R of late 12th–early 13th century Latin Bible. The Art Archive/University Library, Coimbra/Dagli Orti.

vives in stone artifacts—is buried amid the layers of construction on the Temple Mount in Jerusalem.

Bathsheba's famous bath, however, did suggest some interpretation of archaeological discoveries: Designs that have survived from the older civilizations do testify to flat roofs, often used as private gardens. Modern archaeologists have also uncovered ritual bath sites in numerous places, including the Temple Mount in Jerusalem, Sepphoris, and Qumran. These "mikvehs" appear to be pools used for ritual cleansing by religious communities rather than private baths like the one Bathsheba used.

**Character in Later Works.** From the beginning, this famous beauty, who incited King David to adultery and murder, and who bore King Solomon and helped him in his climb to power, has been interpreted as the agent of man's sinful ways and his hope of redemption. David wrote the beautiful, penitential Psalm 51, lamenting his wicked ways, in which he begged for mercy and forgiveness. Bathsheba's listing in Matthew 1:6 as an ancestor of Jesus symbolizes the good use God makes of human sin.

Early medieval commentators such as St. Augustine were reluctant to dwell on the negative side of the David and Bathsheba story, preferring to treat it allegorically. Gregory the Great, however, thought her to be a representative of the perils of carnal appetite.

In Christian art, Bathsheba has often served as a justification for painting the female body nude, as seen in the masterpiece by Rembrandt. She, like *Susanna, also contributed to the iconography of the bathing temptation scene in medieval and Renaissance art. In philosophy and literature, writers have interpreted the bare, objective narrative of the Scripture in various ways.

Bathsheba's compliance with David's lustful demands appeared to the fourteenth century writer of the Cornish (from Cornwall in England) biblical drama the *Ordinalia* to make her complicit in the sin. The author even shows Bathsheba urging David to kill her husband, and then hypocritically weeping at the consequences of her deed. Other writers, such as William Faulkner, have seen her as a type of *Eve, a seductress, luring a bored and willing David into lascivious indulgence (Belle tempting Horace Benbow in *Sartoris*). Thomas Hardy, always sympathetic to beautiful women, had earlier used her as Bathsheba Everdene in the novel *Far from the Madding Crowd*, and refers to her in *Tess of the d'Urbervilles*. She is particularly important in *The Scarlet Letter*, Nathaniel Hawthorne's meditation on adultery and faith. (Bathsheba's noble and ill-fated husband, Uriah, has been seldom used, but is the famous villain Uriah Heep in Charles Dickens' novel *David Copperfield*.)

Feminists use her as an example of woman's helplessness in most of human history: the classic victim, she was desired, taken, impregnated, and widowed. The Scripture does not say that she had any role in making decisions in these significant activities that changed her entire life. On the other hand, her later career, as the favorite wife of King David, the mother of the heir-presumptive, and an important queen mother, advising her son and seeking favors from him, suggests that she became a strong and impressive woman in her later years, using her feminine wiles to influence the prominent men around her.

## SOURCES

Douglas, J. D., "Bath, Bathing," in *The Illustrated Bible Dictionary*, vol. 1, Sidney, Australia: Tyndale House Publishers, 1980; LaBossière, Camille R., "Bathsheba," in *A Dictionary of the Biblical Tradition in English Literature*, edited David L. Jeffrey, Grand Rapids, MI: William B. Eerdmans Publishing Company, 1992.

# C

## CAESAR

**Name and Etymology.** The title *Caesar* was used by all the Roman emperors from the time of Julius Caesar until the third century A.D. It was also originally the name of a Roman family, prominent from the third century B.C. (Brownrigg, 50) which was used by the individual members from the triumph of Augustus (31 B.C.) until Nero's death (A.D. 68), and then used in a more general manner thereafter for the leader.

**Synopsis of Bible Story.** The first of the Caesars to impinge on the New Testament was Augustus, who mandated the census that brought *Mary and *Joseph to Bethlehem, their family's traditional home, where they were to be counted (Luke 2:1). Augustus died in A.D. 14, leaving Tiberius (A.D. 14–37) on the throne during most of *Jesus' ministry. He was still emperor when Jesus was crucified, died, rose, and ascended into heaven. He was the Caesar of the early Christian Church, when the Spirit filled the followers of Christ at Pentecost, when *Stephen was martyred, and when *Paul was converted.

It was Caligula (Gaius) (A.D. 37–41) who was emperor in the early days of the Church, and Claudius (A.D. 41–54) who reigned during Paul's first two journeys. It was the notorious Nero (A.D. 54–68) who was the Caesar of the early Christian persecution, and who presided over Paul's trial and *Peter's arrest and martyrdom. Galba (A.D. 68–9), Otho (A.D. 69), and Vitellius (A.D. 69) followed in a tumultuous time, but it was Vespasian (A.D. 69–79) who ordered the destruction of Jerusalem. Whereas *Matthew was written during Vespasian's reign, *Luke was written during the reign of Titus (A.D. 79–81). Most of the Gospels were written during reigns of the later Caesars. It was at the time of Domitian (A.D. 81–96) that the fourth Gospel was written and *John was exiled to Patmos (Brownrigg, 50).

The rule established by the Caesars was an unsystematic blend of legal and social powers, not technically a monarchy. With the elimination of the Cesarean family, this position of leadership was institutionalized, with the title assumed by its incumbents. A Caesar's power usually rested in part on the provincial command of frontier forces, including Judaea. This is the reason that the Jews customarily referred to Caesar as "king" (John 19:12, 15).

The Hellenistic tradition of royal leadership led to the universal oath of personal allegiance to the Caesarean house. Later, when the monarchs proclaimed themselves not only emperors, but gods, demanding worship of the imperial cult, both Christians and Jews found themselves faced with an agonizing problem. This became the basis for much of the persecution that was the background for the Book of Revelation.

**Historical Context.** In 63 B.C., Palestine had been eager to see Rome become an ally. This was early in the Wars of the Maccabees, and seemed to the Jews to be a welcome change from the lawless Hellenizers among Alexander the Great's successors, the Ptolemies and Seleucids. It was a troubling time, with merchants facing uncertainties in their business dealings, and villagers frightened by pillaging armies. It also saw the disruption of worship as different forces demanded the veneration of universal deities. By contrast, the Jews found Roman rule remarkably tolerant of regional religions and practices, allowing local control on many issues. Roman gods tended to be local and numerous. The Roman conquerors were willing to accept into their pantheon influences from Greece and the Orient, thereby increasing skepticism about traditional gods.

This tolerance by the state applied to Judaism and to early Christianity, which was considered a branch of Judaism. Later, after the determination that the emperors were gods, however, the conflict became increasingly obvious. Jews could not worship any god but Jehovah, and Christians found themselves frequently persecuted for their obstinacy in the face of official mandates.

Jesus was born in the latter days of Caesar Augustus, when this great lawmaker and warrior had destroyed his enemies and established a reign noted for peace and tolerance. While the family of Jesus had bowed to the requirements of the census, they fled from the tyranny of Caesar's local authority, *Herod. During his years of ministry, Jesus often dealt with agents of Rome—the Centurion, *Matthew the tax collector, and of course *Pontius Pilate, the procurator.

Later, Paul, a citizen of Rome, used the Roman legal system to appeal to Rome when he was accused by Jewish officials. Over time, however, the adversarial relationship intensified. Christianity was increasingly seen—like Judaism—as an affront to Roman sovereignty. The destruction of Jerusalem in A.D. 70 ended the historic tradition of worship at the Temple. And the increasing persecution of the Christians produced a host of martyrs.

**Archaeological Evidence.** Few elements in Scripture are so richly documented in archaeology as the reigns of the Caesars. It was as a tribute to Augustus Caesar that King Herod the Great built the lavish Roman metropolis Caesarea on the Mediterranean Sea. This was, in fact, a period of great public works. Monumental remains, sculpture, documents, coins, roads, viaducts, paintings, and many manuscripts testify to the impressive sweep of Roman power.

Because this was a time rich with arts, individualized portraits are available of each of the different monarchs who ruled over tiny Palestine. The Roman historians, notably Tacitus and Pliny, detail many of the activities of the Caesars. Eusebius, the early Christian chronicler, discusses the relationship between the Caesars and the early Christians.

**Character in Later Works.** Jesus used the term *Caesar* in a generic sense, standing for government. When he said, "Render therefore unto Caesar the things which are Caesar's," he was using the name for the secular powers. So long as Caesar was restricted to governing the political life of Palestine, it was not in conflict with Christianity, but when the emperor also demanded adoration, he was demanding "the things that are God's" (Matt. 22:21).

Later, John (in Revelation) saw Caesar—and Rome—as the Whore of Babylon, one more persecutor of God's people (Rev. 17:1–6). On the other hand, it was another emperor, Constantine, who eventually proclaimed Christianity the established faith of the Empire and became a Christian hero, celebrated in medieval tales for his wisdom.

When Rome fell to the barbarians, the reign of the Caesars took on a fresh luster, representing in retrospect a period of order and opulence. The establishment of the See of the Roman Catholic Church in Rome tended to merge the grandeur that was Rome with the Church itself, especially during the period when the dream of the Holy Roman Empire was central to much of the Christian imagination. Dante used the images of priest and king, which he took from Scripture, and the image of the ideal empire in the climax of the *Purgatorio*, when the hero reached the pinnacle of the holy mountain and is finally prepared for paradise. This dream of the Holy Roman Empire inspired Christians for many years, living in their imaginations as an ideal City of God on earth.

## SOURCES

Brownrigg, Ronald, *Who's Who in the Bible*, vol. 2, New York: Bonanza Books, 1980; Judge, E. A., "Caesar," in *The Illustrated Bible Dictionary*, vol. 1, edited by J. D. Douglas, Sidney, Australia: Tyndale House Publishers, 1980; Kee, Howard Clark, Franklin Young, and Karlfried Froehlich, *Understanding the New Testament*, Englewood Cliffs, NJ: Prentice-Hall, Inc., 1965.

## CAIAPHAS

**Name and Etymology.** *Caiaphas*, or Joseph ben Caiaphas, is an Aramaic name. *Joseph* was a traditional Hebrew name, dating from the Patriarchs, meaning "may God add children" (Comay, 225).

**Synopsis of Bible Story.** When *Jesus had proven to be more popular with the people than the jealous members of the ruling council of priests could endure, Caiaphas posed the famous speculation that led to the Crucifixion: ". . . it is expedient for us, that one man should die for the people, and that the whole nation perish not" (John 11:50). At this point, Caiaphas was the titular head of the Sanhedrin, but his father-in-law, Annas, appears to have been the real power. Later, during the trial, Jesus was brought, bound, from the house of Annas to the palace of Caiaphas (John 18:24), where some believe he was tortured, and then led to the judgment hall of *Pontius Pilate.

**Historical Context.** Joseph ben Caiaphas was part of a virtual dynasty of high priests. His father-in-law, Annas, the previous high priest, was appointed to that position by the Roman procurator Valerius Gratus. Caiaphas served from A.D. 18 to 37, remaining in office under Gratus's successor, Pontius Pilate, placing Caiaphas at the scene for the Passion of Christ. He was part of the infamous family that was influential in the powerful Sadducee faction of the Sanhedrin, the High Council, which at the time was the highest Jewish authority and combined within itself all spiritual and temporal power.

It functioned as the highest judicial court of the Jews. He was the high priest at the time of *John the Baptist's ministry (Luke 3:2) and he was eventually removed from office by Vitellius Caesar.

This corrupt family, nine of whom served as high priests, apparently derived much of their considerable wealth from the sale of sacrificial animals and offerings in booths on the Mount of Olives. The Jewish historian Josephus notes, "Such was the shamelessness and effrontery, which possessed the high priests, that they were actually so brazen as to send their servants to the threshing-floors to receive the tithes due to the priests" (Josephus, *Antiquities*, quoted in Brownrigg, 53). Jesus may have been referring to their activities when he condemned those who made God's house a "den of robbers" (Mark 11:15–19).

Some believe that Caiaphas was central in plotting to label Jesus as a traitor and a danger to imperial security before handing him over to Pilate, thus encouraging the Romans to kill him rather than punish the whole nation. In this action, the Sanhedrin might destroy Jesus, blame the Romans, and pretend at the same time that they were loyal to Rome (Brownrigg, 52–53).

Later, after taking a central role in the Crucifixion of Jesus, Caiaphas also tormented the early Christians. Along with other priests, he demanded of *Peter and *John by whose authority they had healed the man at the Temple gate (Acts 4:7). By this time, however, he and the other priests were aware of the increasing power of the Apostles and did not dare punish them (Acts 4:21). On the advice of Gamaliel, he had them beaten, warned, and discharged. He also presided at the trial of *Stephen, and later contributed to the Diaspora, providing Saul (later *Paul) with letters of authority to persecute Christians as far as Damascus.

**Archaeological Evidence.** The houses of Caiaphas the high priest and his father-in-law, Annas, were thought to be on the Western Hill of Jerusalem. The remains of a villa believed to be the house of Caiaphas have been discovered near the spot where Peter was said to have heard the cock crow three times (the Church of St. Peter in Gallicantu). In 530, Theodosius went from the Cenacle to the House of Caiaphas, "which is now St. Peter's Church," suggesting that this was a very old tradition in this location. There is some debate as to which of the villas may have actually belonged to the powerful priestly family. Some archaeologists believe this location to be the Herodian Mansion. Josephus said that Ananias, a later high priest, (A.D. 47–55) lived on the Western Hill, near the Hasmonean Palace, indicating that the general location of this family of high priests would be correct. The site currently identified as the House of Caiaphas is full of storage chambers for offerings, a cell for prisoners with a place for chains, and a rock-hewn channel for blood. The artifacts testify powerfully to the cruelty of the punishment of prisoners in this place.

This location in St. Peter's Church is within sight of the area where the family tomb of Caiaphas was discovered in November 1990 (Coogan, 97). This tomb held ossuaries, or bone boxes, inscribed with the priestly name of *Caiaphas*. One of the skeletons was of a man about 60 years old, now identified as the Caiaphas of the New Testament (Fine, 42–43).

**Character in Later Works.** Although the Fathers of the Church rarely mentioned Caiaphas and Annas, these men became significant actors in the Passion plays of the Middle Ages, often representing the old law. They were overdrawn stereotypes of villains who ranted and raved in the face of the gentle Christ. The role that Caiaphas and the Sadducees played in the trial and crucifixion of Christ is now considered one major source of anti-Semitism among Christians, who for centuries called Jews "Christ-killers." Although he was a corrupt member of a select group, Caiaphas was often seen as a representative figure. In actuality, the Disciples noted that all Israel mourned the crucifixion of Christ. The "daughters,"—a term used in Scripture to designate the common folk, often neglected by the powerful—were particularly pained.

## SOURCES

Brownrigg, Ronald, and Joan Comay, *Who's Who in the Bible*, vols. 1 and 2, New York: Bonanza Books, 1980; Coogan, Michael D., "Caiaphas," in *The Oxford Companion to the Bible*, 2 vols. New York: Oxford University Press, 1993; Fine, Stephen, "Why Bone Boxes?" *Biblical Archaeology Review*, edited by Bruce M. Metzger and Michael D. Coogan, 27(4) 39 ff. (2001); Jeffrey, David L., ed., *A Dictionary of the Biblical Tradition in English Literature*, Grand Rapids, MI: William B. Eerdmans Publishing Company, 1992; Keller, Werner, *The Bible as History*, New York: Bantam Books, 1982; Whiston, William, trans. *The Works of Josephus*, Peabody, MA: Hendrickson Publishers, Inc., 2001.

## CAIN

**Name and Etymology.** Cain's name means "smith" or "artificer" or "spear," perhaps because he is the ancestor of blacksmiths, or perhaps because Eve saw herself as a partner of God in "man-making" (Alter, 6; Genesis 4:1). In Hebrew folk etymology, the name means "acquisition," or "production" (Meeks, 10).

**Synopsis of Bible Story.** Genesis 4 traces the story of Cain, from his birth as firstborn of *Adam and *Eve and brother of Abel. Cain is designated as a "tiller of the ground," while Abel is a "keeper of sheep." Each brought an offering to the Lord, but with a difference: While Abel brought "fat" offerings of the "firstlings," Cain simply brought "of the fruit." This is assumed by many to be a careless and thoughtless offering rather than a careful selection of the first fruits. Thus, while the Lord respected Abel and his offering, he had no respect for Cain and his offering.

Cain's response was to be "very wroth, and his countenance fell." God admonished him that the error lay with him: "If thou doest well, shalt thou not be accepted? and if thou doest not well, sin lieth at the door." Then follows a curious scrambling of the words God spoke to the fallen Eve in Genesis 3:16, "And unto thee shall be his desire, and thou shalt rule over him" (Gen. 4:7). Rather than respond humbly to God's warning and accept his obligation to control his errant will, Cain went to his brother, talked with him, and "rose up against Abel his brother, and slew him" (Gen. 4:8).

When God again spoke to him, inquiring of him where his brother was, Cain responded: "I know not: Am I my brother's keeper?" (This again echoes the questions and answers of the fallen parents.)

The Lord demanded an honest confession of his crime: "What hast thou done? the voice of thy brother's blood crieth unto me from the ground" (Gen. 4:10). Like the response to Adam's lies in the earlier story (Gen. 3:17–19), the Lord announced the consequences of the sin and of the subsequent prevarications, "And now art thou cursed from the earth, which hath opened her mouth to receive thy brother's blood from thy hand; When thou tillest the ground, it shall not henceforth yield unto thee her strength; a fugitive and a vagabond shalt thou be in the earth" (Gen. 4:12).

Cain and Abel, bronze relief panel from main door, by Bonanno Pisano. The Art Archive/Cathedral of Monreale, Sicily/Dagli Orti (A).

Cain still refused to confess or seek forgiveness. Instead, he lamented that the punishment was "greater than I can bear. . . I shall be a fugitive and a vagabond in the earth; and it shall come to pass, that every one that findeth me shall slay me" (Gen. 3:16).

In a final act of grace, the Lord set a mark on Cain to protect him, proclaiming that ". . . whosoever slayeth Cain, vengeance shall be taken on him sevenfold."

Then Cain went out of the Lord's presence, dwelling in the land of Nod, where he married two women and became the progenitor of whole classes of people: the city dwellers, the tent-dwellers, musicians, and artificers in "brass and iron." One of his descendants, Lamech, proved even more bloody than Cain, proclaiming that he had slain a man "for my wounding, and a young man to my hurt. If Cain shall be avenged sevenfold, truly Lamech seventy and sevenfold" (Gen. 4:23–24).

His death is not recorded, nor is there any record of Cain ever acknowledging his guilt and shame.

**Historical Context.** From the earliest analyses, the clear parallels with the Eden story of temptation, sin, evasion, confrontation, curse, and expulsion were noted. Cain's self-pity, his loss of closeness with God, and his increased difficulty with the soil are parallel to Adam's. Later commentators used Cain to explain fratricide, the origin of polygamy, cycles of violence, tools of warfare, the growth of cities, and the beginnings of the arts.

The story may have explained the origin of nomadic, camel-herding Bedouins, who entered Palestine later than the goat-and-sheep-owning semi-nomads, and who still use tribal tattoos (Graves and Patai, 95). There is a likely connection between the fratricidal Cain and the tribe of Cainites (Queni), a desert people living to the south of Israel, who are referred to collectively as "Cain" (Num. 24:22; Judg. 4:11). They were known to the Israelites as both nomads and city dwellers and were considered to be hostile.

**Archaeological Evidence.** No archaeologists have located the land of Nod, though they do suggest that the genealogy in the story is a "historical concatenation" to explain the various divisions of labor and lifestyles. (See Alter, 19.) The emphasis on blood in the soil may have some relevance to the ancient practice of human sacrifice, thought to bring fertility to the land. Numerous civilizations in the Fertile Crescent had fertility rites, even as late as the Jewish settlement of Israel, when neighboring tribes continued to sacrifice their firstborn sons.

**Character in Later Works.** Cain's actions became the popular explanation for violence in human nature—a reordering of human existence. When Cain lost connection to the ground, the source of his livelihood, he was transformed into the eternal wanderer, no longer a son, a brother, a farmer (McEntire, 27).

By the time of the birth of Christ, the ancient Hebrew collection of traditions that were represented in the Talmud, the Mishnah, also included numerous stories regarding Cain: Cain was not really Adam's son, but Satan's; his hatred for Abel was the result of a longstanding rivalry over a twin sister; Cain murdered Abel in the field by striking him with a stone; his lineage was destroyed in the Flood, etc. (See Kugel, 146–169.)

In the New Testament, Cain is identified with Satan (the "wicked one") in 1 John 3:12 and is called "evil" in Jude 10–11. A continuing consideration has been the meaning of Abel's innocent blood, tied to his role as shepherd, relating him to the image of Christ, while Cain is pictured most often as the personification of human sinfulness.

Gnostics considered Cain the source of forbidden ideas, perhaps the offspring of the snake in the Garden of Eden; St. Augustine saw him as the basis for the evil city, in contrast with the City of God. Others were interested in his punishment, and that of his descendants. One frequent concern has been the "mark" which condemned and protected him.

In early English literature, Cain was the source of villainy, the sworn enemy of mankind. Thus *Beowulf* presents Grendel as the lineage of Cain, and Dante names the lowest part of hell after this original fratricide (*Inferno*, Canto 32).

Romantic writers, more inclined to be half in love with twisted heroes, were fascinated with the lonely and heroic nature of Cain. They pictured him as a rebel and often wrote works explicitly tied to Cain: for example, Samuel Coleridge's *The Wanderings of Cain* (1798) or Lord Byron's drama *Cain: A Mystery* (1821). This was, in fact, a type often referred to as the "Byronic hero." William Blake responded to the earlier Romantics by writing *The Ghost of Abel* (1822). James M. Dean notes that Cain has typically been romanticized in the modern period: becoming a visionary wanderer, estranged from ordinary society, both cursed and privileged with a terrible burden of guilt. As a kind of "Wandering Jew," he is implicit in Coleridge's Ancient Mariner, Melville's Ishmael, Mark Twain's Huck Finn, Conrad's Lord Jim, and so on. John Masefield's novel *The Everlasting Mercy* used a conflation of King Saul, Saul of Tarsus, and Cain as Saul Kane, the hero.

John Steinbeck's *East of Eden* is one of numerous modern American stories related to the character. William Faulkner was especially fascinated with the idea of spilled blood cursing the land, the cycles of violence, brother pitted against brother—all images of the history of the American South. These themes track though many of his stories and novels, such as *Absalom, Absalom!*

Cain continues to be the image of fraternal hatred. The recent revival of gnosticism among scholars and their concept of the role of the snake as an image of forbidden knowledge have renewed the ancient interest in Cain's origins.

## SOURCES

Alter, Robert, *Genesis: Translation and Commentary*, New York: W. W. Norton and Company, 1996; Dean, James M., "Cain," in *A Dictionary of Biblical Tradition in English Literature*, edited by David L. Jeffrey, Grand Rapids: William B. Eerdmans Publishing Company, 1992; Graves, Robert, and Raphael Patai, *Hebrew Myths: The Book of Genesis*, New York: McGraw-Hill Book Company, 1963; *The HarperCollins Study Bible*, Meeks, Wayne A., ed., San Francisco: HarperCollins Publishers, Inc., 1993; Kugel, James L., *Traditions of the Bible: A Guide to the Bible As It Was at the Start of the Common Era*, Cambridge, MA: Harvard University Press, 1998; McEntire, Mark, *The Blood of Abel: The Violent Plot in the Hebrew Bible*, Macon, GA: Mercer University Press, 1999; Pagels, Elaine, *The Origin of Satan*, New York: Random House, 1995.

## CORNELIUS

**Name and Etymology.** *Cornelius* is Greek, meaning "of a horn."

**Synopsis of Bible Story.** Cornelius, a centurion of the Italian contingent, was stationed in Caesarea Maritima, in the early days of the Church. Apparently a devout man, Cornelius was already noted for his almsgiving and his godly behavior when he had a vision of an angel who instructed him to send for *Peter. A man of action, Cornelius immediately sent messengers to Joppa.

At the same time, Peter himself had an angelic vision of an even more extended nature. He had gone up to the rooftop to pray before dinner when he fell into a trance. He saw heaven opened and a vessel descending to him, let down in a sheet. In it were "all manner of fourfooted beasts of the earth, and wild beasts, and creeping things, and fowls of the air" (Acts 10:12). Then Peter heard a voice instructing him to kill and eat, but Peter refused. Having never eaten anything unclean or unlawful, he could not accept this bounty (Acts 10:13). A voice spoke to him saying, "What God hath cleansed, *that* call not thou common" (Acts 10:15). This was repeated three times before the vessel was taken back up to heaven, leaving Peter puzzled. It was at this moment that the men came from Cornelius, requesting his presence in Caesarea. The Holy Spirit spoke clearly to Peter, telling him that these men were sent by God, and he was to go with them.

When Peter met with Cornelius, the centurion fell down before the disciple, but Peter raised him up, saying, "Stand up; I myself also am a man" (Acts 10:26). As they told one another of their recent experiences, Peter recognized that ". . . God is no respecter of persons: But in every nation he that feareth him, and worketh righteousness, is accepted with him" (10:34–35). From this time forward, Peter preached to any who would believe, both the circumcised and the uncircumcised, freely baptizing any who had received the Holy Ghost.

**Historical Context.** In this story we have the classic confrontation between the Jew and the Gentile, the Hebrew and the Roman, the old covenant of the Jewish law and the new covenant of believer's baptism. Cornelius appears to have been a pious man prior to the moment of the vision, one given to fasting and prayer. This ideal Gentile made a strong case for a greater openness in the Christian community, eventually leading to the Council of Jerusalem, where Peter joined *Paul in arguing that new converts need not be circumcised as Jews before being baptized as Christians.

Centurions were commanders of "centuries" (100 men) in the Roman army. Five centurions are mentioned in the New Testament, and three became followers of Christ (Miller, 96) Apparently, they were professional soldiers, well-disciplined and law-abiding, who brought their families with them and became a part of the local community. *Jesus expressed admiration for the unnamed centurion whose servant was healed at Capernaum (Matt. 8:5, 8:13; Luke 7:2, 6).

**Archaeological Evidence.** The vast area being excavated around Caesarea Maritima covers 235 acres on the Mediterranean coast between Tel Aviv and Haifa (also known as Joppa). It was occupied from the third or fourth century B.C. through the period of the Crusades. Under Roman rule from early times, it was the site of Paul's imprisonment as well as the place where Cornelius was posted. *Herod had built the city between 22 and 10 B.C., and named it in honor of his patron, Augustus *Caesar. Excavators have discovered a large artificial port, a well preserved aqueduct system, a theater, a circus, a waterfront warehouse complex, several baths, shops, and dwellings. There are also the remains of an early synagogue, as well as a Christian church built over the ruins of Herod's temple to Roma and Augustus. It was in this city's ruins that the inscription bearing the name of *Pontius Pilate was discovered.

**Character in Later Works.** Cornelius never became a significant image in Western art or thought. This decent, orderly, faithful man provided the opening wedge for the evangelism of the Roman Empire, but is not mentioned again in Scripture, and never figures prominently in poetry or prose.

## SOURCES

Brownrigg, Ronald, *Who's Who in the Bible*, vol. 2, New York: Bonanza Books, 1980; Miller, Madeline S., and J. Lane Miller, *Harper's Bible Dictionary*, New York: Harper and Row, 1961; Negev, Avraham, ed., *The Archaeological Encyclopedia of the Holy Land*, New York: Thomas Nelson Publishers, 1986.

## CYRUS (II) THE GREAT

**Name and Etymology.** *Cyrus* may have been a dynastic rather than a personal name, derived from Hebrew *Kores*, Old Persian *Kurus*, Babylonian *Kura*.

**Synopsis of Bible Story.** Cyrus II, grandson of Cyrus I, came to the throne of Persia c. 559 B.C. He conquered the King of the Medes (his mother's father), and founded the Persian Empire, taking the title "King of the Medes" and "King of Elam." By 539 B.C., he entered Babylon, acclaimed by jubilant crowds.

A sympathetic ruler, he issued a decree to return the exiles to their homes and he restored their temples. The Jews were thereby allowed to restore their Temple and its fittings (Ezra 6:3). *Daniel prospered during the first three years of Cyrus' rule in Babylonia (Dan. 1:21, 6:28, 10:1) but then, according to Josephus, he was removed to Media or perhaps to Susa. Daniel, *Ezra, and *Isaiah all presented Cyrus as a divinely designated shepherd and the Lord's anointed, the agent of a divine plan for Israel. Isaiah 44:28 and 45:1 speak of a "shepherd" and the Anointed.

Cyrus died on an expedition to the east in 530 B.C. and was buried in Pasargadae near Persepolis. Unfortunately, the chamber now stands empty and the inscription said to be over its doorway is missing. Cyrus was succeeded by his son Cambyses II.

**Historical Context.** After taking the throne, Cyrus took over the territories of the Medes and united them into a strong alliance, clashed with Croesus of Lydia, captured Sardis, and began the prolonged war with the Greek states. Eventually his empire extended over much of Asia as well as the Near East, encroaching on Europe. Apparently a shrewd and tolerant monarch, he governed through the use of local district satraps and allowed a high degree of religious freedom. (See 2 Chron. 36:22–23; Ezra 1:1–8); Isa. 44:28, 45:1.) Cyrus established the great Persian empire, which was destined to last for two hundred years, until the rise of Alexander the Great.

**Archaeological Evidence.** Josephus tells of Cyrus's career, as do most historians of the ancient world, including Herodotus, who includes a detailed history of Cyrus's mythic childhood.

The Cyrus Cylinder describes the capture of Babylon without a battle. It also tells of the edict restoring the temples and returning the gods to captive peoples. This baked clay cylinder is currently at the British Museum. The final words on this cylinder, "I am Cyrus, king of all, the great king, the mighty king, king of Babylon, king of Sumer and Akkad, king of the four corners of the earth. . . ." (Keller, 327) are echoed in 2 Chronicles 36:23, "Thus saith Cyrus king of Persia, All the kingdoms of the earth hath the Lord God of heaven given me. . . ."

The other impressive relic of Cyrus is his reputed tomb, built of limestone blocks tied together with iron cramps, which is at Pasargadae. The meager ruins of this terraced city have been found, along with a few buildings on which inscriptions claim the structures as the work of "Cyrus the king of Achaemenids."

**Character in Later Works.** The early life history of Cyrus is recorded by the Greek historians Herodotus and Xenophon in dramatic fashion, much like the tale of Oedipus, with prophecies, a father who tried to thwart fate, and the eventual triumph over his own father and grandfather. The Greek dramatists thought Cyrus's efforts to dominate the Greek city states helped to forge the short-lived Greek unity and encourage the Athenian rise to power. The wars the Greeks waged against the Persians were dramatized by the playwright Aeschylus in his play *The Persians*.

For the Jews, Cyrus took on the image of a pagan used as a divine instrument, chosen by God to deliver Israel. Christian writers have interpreted him as evidence of providential history. Milton pictured him as the liberator of the people of God in *Paradise Regained*, as did William Cowper in his poem "Expostulation."

## SOURCES

Anderson, Bernard W., *Understanding the Old Testamente*, Englewood Cliffs, NJ: Prentice-Hall, Inc., 1966; Jeffrey, David L., ed., *A Dictionary of the Biblical Tradition in English Literature*, Grand Rapids, MI: William B. Eerdmans Publishing Company, 1992; Keller, Werner, *The Bible as History*. New York: Bantam Books, 1982; Miller, Madeline S., and J. Lane Miller, *Harper's Bible Dictionary*, New York: Harper and Row, 1961; Wiseman, D. J., "Cyrus," in *The Illustrated Bible Dictionary*, vol. 1, edited by J. D. Douglas, Sidney, Australia: Tyndale House Publishers, 1980; Wiseman, Donald J., "Cyrus," in *The Oxford Companion to the Bible*, edited by Bruce M. Metzger and Michael D. Coogan, New York: Oxford University Press, 1993; Young, Edward J., *Daniel*, Carlisle, PA: William B. Eerdmans Publishing Company, 1949.

# D

## DANIEL (BELTESHAZZAR)

**Name and Etymology.** *Daniel* means "God is [my] judge"; Daniel also was assigned the name "Belteshazzar" by the Babylonians.

**Synopsis of Bible Story.** Sometime after *Nebuchadnezzar, King of Babylon, besieged Jerusalem, looted the Temple, and took the people hostage, he selected the brightest and best of the young Israelites for his service. Among these were four young men from Judah: Daniel, Hananiah, Mishael, and Azariah, whom the chief official gave new names: Belteshazzar, Shadrach, Meshach, and Abednego (Dan. 1:6–7). When confronted with the opulence of the court diet, Daniel sought permission to refrain from wine and royal food rations, probably because of his adherence to the law of Moses. A test proposed by Daniel and his companions proved that they were even healthier with their simple diet than the others who enjoyed the king's riches.

Next came the testing of Daniel's abilities at interpreting dreams. With God's help, he was able to explain the meaning of the picturesque statue in Nebuchadnezzar's dream—a giant man with a head of gold, chest and arms of silver, belly and thighs of bronze, legs of iron, and its feet partly iron and partly baked clay (Dan. 2:31–35). In another dream, figuring a great tree that was cut down, Daniel prophesied the tragic fall of Nebuchadnezzar (Dan. 4:25), which came to pass over time, teaching the folly of human pride and the power and glory of God.

The king's enthusiastic response to Daniel's insights, which he demonstrated by showering the young man and his companions with gifts, stirred jealousy among other of his courtiers. As a result, some Babylonian astrologers set a trap to force the king to punish the Jews for their worship of Jehovah by throwing Shadrach, Meshach, and Abednego into a fiery furnace (Dan. 3:13–23). The three companions were preserved by a mysterious fourth man who walked with them around the fire, all unbound and unharmed, and the fourth looked "like the Son of God" (Dan. 3:25).

When a new king, Belshazzar, came to the throne, he also tested Daniel's ability to interpret signs and dreams. Writing mysteriously appeared on the wall during a great banquet, written by the fingers of a human hand; the king grew pale and promised riches to the person who could explain the words. Rejecting the rewards, Daniel explained the words: "*Mene*: God hath numbered thy kingdom, and finished it. *Tekel*: Thou art weighed in the balances, and art found wanting. *Peres*: Thy kingdom is divided, and given to the Medes and Persians" (Dan. 5:26–28).

Again the prophecy came to pass, leading to the reign of Darius, who appointed 120 satraps to rule. These administrators, again sensing the threat posed by these resident aliens, focused on Daniel and his companions, trying to find a way to destroy them, finally trapping them by issuing an edict forbidding public prayer. Darius allowed them to put Daniel in a lions' den, where an angel protected him from harm (Dan. 6:16–22). After this, Daniel prospered through the reigns of Darius and *Cyrus, apparently spending much of his time in prophecy.

Daniel himself is presented primarily in the first chapters of the book that bears his name. Chapters 1–6 are largely historical narrative. The final six contain his visions, which have had as much influence on literature as the character himself. Among these visions are such images as the eternal kingdom, the four beasts coming up out of the sea, the judgment by the Ancient of Days, the ram and the goat, the new Jerusalem with the Messiah Prince, the great battle among the kings of the earth, the Son of Man, and the resurrection of both the good and the wicked, with the deliverance of those whose name is found "written in the book" (Dan. 21:1).

**Historical Context.** Because Daniel was portrayed as a Jewish exile in Babylon, the actual literary setting is the sixth century B.C. The Book of Daniel was probably completed c. 530 B.C., shortly after the capture of Babylon by Cyrus in 529. The prophet points to the coming of four kingdoms—apparently Babylon, Media, Persia, and Greece. Several of the prophecies in Daniel were fulfilled in the coming of the Roman Empire, the Anointed One or Messiah, and the restoration and rebuilding of Jerusalem (*New International Version* notes, 1289).

The book spans—at least prophetically—the rise and fall of the myriad empires which were to dominate God's chosen people. (Edward Young's commentary on Daniel contains a detailed listing of the historical figures and references.) Most critics note specific citation of empires and events.

**Archaeological Evidence.** Some scholars contend that the language of the book of Daniel argues for a date earlier than the second century. Linguistic evidence demonstrates that the Hebrew and Aramaic chapters of Daniel must have been composed at different times, making the book difficult to date with any accuracy.

One particular problem is the apparent reference in chapter 11 to Antiochus IV Epiphanes, the Seleucid ruler from Syria. He persecuted the Jews and desecrated the Temple, causing the *Maccabees to resist militarily. The more skeptical commentators contend that the inaccurate descriptions of the end of Antiochus's reign and of his death suggest that the book was written prior to the desecration of the Temple in 167 B.C. More conservative commentators note that Daniel, whom Jesus identified as the author (Matt. 25:15) predicted in broad strokes the end of the Seleucids and the end of the New Testament age. They insist there is no reason to doubt Daniel's authorship or his prophetic powers.

Daniel in the lions' den, detail. The Art Archive/Galleria di Storia ed Arte, Udine/Dagli Orti (A).

Daniel's portrayal of "great Babylon" is no exaggeration. Nebuchadnezzar was an assiduous builder. Hundreds of thousands of bricks bear his name, as do the plans of many buildings—suggesting constant building activity. "Babylon in fact surpassed all the cities of the ancient orient: it was greater than Thebes, Memphis, and Ur, greater even than Nineveh" (Keller, 316).

Fragments of the book of Daniel were discovered among the Dead Sea Scrolls.

**Character in Later Works.** As one of the best examples in Scripture of apocalyptic form, the book of Daniel had considerable influence on later Biblical and secular literature. The visions and their complex interpretations were to reappear frequently in other writings, particularly the Revelation of St. John, 1 Enoch and 2 *Baruch. The concept of the Antichrist, the great tribulation, and the various events leading to the restoration of the millennial kingdom in the final chapters have had enormous impact on eschatological literature, especially in recent times. Among the most important influences on later thought are its concepts of angelology, the resurrection, and the reign of the Son of Man. The numerology in the book has particularly fascinated later writers.

One of the more colorful sequels to the Biblical story is the apocryphal Bel and the Dragon. In this fast-moving narrative, Daniel continues his adventures by demonstrating for the king that his god is more powerful than the pagan god, using a trick to show that the priests of Bel are in fact eating the feasts left for the god. In a second episode, with the help of the prophet *Habakkuk, who is carried by an angel by his hair, Daniel is saved from death once again.

A set of prayers in poetic form make up the apocryphal Prayer of Azariah and Song of Three Jews. In addition, the story of *Susanna is sometimes identified as chapter 13 of Daniel, picturing this hero saving her from execution, confronting the malicious elders with the facts of the case.

The New Testament echoes Daniel with some frequency in Jesus' references to himself as the "Son of Man," in the Incarnation, the Resurrection, and the coming of the millennial kingdom. In his prophecies and his story of the glorious triumph of the martyr, Daniel is often seen as a type of Christ.

Most Christian tradition, including St. Augustine, emphasizes Daniel's chastity as a sign of his celibate state, reinforced by his purity in diet and apparent renunciation of fleshly pleasures. Chaucer's "Monk's Tale" draws on the ancient tradition that Daniel was a eunuch of royal descent.

Jewish tradition has emphasized the wisdom of Daniel, echoed in works such as Hawthorne's *The Scarlet Letter*, where he is cited for his ability to solve riddles. Others, such as Charlotte Brontë's *Shirley* and E. L. Doctorow's *The Book of Daniel*, emphasize his ability to interpret dreams. Dante drew on his image of the man with feet of clay, a symbol of the different ages of mankind. His name became useful for other authors such as George Eliot, who needed a Jewish hero for *Daniel Deronda*.

Belshezzar's Feast was the inspiration for a dramatic painting by the apocalyptic artist John Martin (1789–1854) (now in a private collection in Canada) and a dramatic oratorio by William Walton, the twentieth-century English composer.

## SOURCES

Keller, Werner, *The Bible as History*, New York: Bantam Books, 1982; Martin, Lawrence T., "Daniel," in *A Dictionary of the Biblical Tradition in English Literature*, edited by David L. Jeffrey, Grand Rapids, MI: William B. Eerdmans Publishing Company, 1992; Miller, Madeline S., and J. Lane Miller, *Harper's Bible Dictionary*, New York: Harper and Row, 1961; Milne, Pamela J., "Daniel," in *The HarperCollins Study Bible*, edited by Wayne A. Meeks, San Francisco, CA: HarperCollins, 1993; Whitcomb, J. C., "Daniel, The Book of," in *The Illustrated Bible Dictionary*, vol. 1, edited by J. D. Douglas, Sidney, Australia: Tyndale House Publishers, 1980; Young, Edward J., *Daniel*, Carlisle, PA: William B. Eerdmans Publishing Company, 1949.

# DAVID

**Name and Etymology.** *David* means "beloved of God."

**Synopsis of Bible Story.** David, the second king of Israel, proved to be the best loved hero of the nation. The first thirty years of his life are chronicled in remarkable detail in 1 Samuel 16 through 2 Samuel 2. His history is retold in 1 Chronicles. Descended from *Ruth and Boaz, father to *Solomon and the line of kings that followed him, he was Jesus' ancestor.

His story is a romantic one, beginning with his discovery by *Samuel at a time when King *Saul had failed in his covenant with God, and Israel was in need of a new king after God's heart (1 Sam. 13:14). The young shepherd, a talented musician from Bethlehem, was anointed privately by the old prophet, and then was called to the court of Saul to play and sing for the tormented old king. At first an armor-bearer to Saul, David became an unlikely hero when he responded to the challenge of the Philistine warrior *Goliath. With his slingshot in hand, David volunteered to confront the formidable and well-armed opponent. Using the peasant's weapon, he killed the giant and used Goliath's own sword to cut off his head.

David's story from this point on shows a rising vigor and power as he led men into battle after battle, causing the people to proclaim that he had killed his "tens of thousands" (1 Sam. 18:7, 22:11). He sought and won Saul's daughter, Michal, as a wife, and also won the friendship of Saul's son Jonathan. But his rising popularity alienated and frightened the fiercely jealous king, who tried one strategy after another to destroy him. With the help of his allies within the family, David "dodged the spear" and escaped time and again, finally settling in Hebron, safely out of Saul's reach (1 Sam. 19:10, 23:25–26).

Respecting the sanctity of the royal office, David refused to kill Saul. When the old king died by his own hand, David mourned both him and Jonathan. The forty years of King David's reign are chronicled in 2 Samuel and the first two chapters of 1 Kings, revealing a complex man, a lover of numerous women, a friend to many men, a "serial murderer" (Shanks), a powerful leader in war, a too-loving father who stirred revolts among his own sons, and finally an old man dying with a young maiden at his feet and his beloved Bathsheba by his side, giving advice to Solomon, their son and his heir.

**Historical Context.** The people of Israel saw David as the ideal king, the hero who enlarged the landmass of Israel, established Jerusalem as the capitol, and united the people as a fighting force with a national identity. He carved out an empire unequaled in ancient Israel's history. Recent scholars note that he was a charismatic leader with a genius for mediation, able to command diverse tribal, economic, and cultic allegiances, consolidating them into the centralized power needed to form a nation-state.

**Archaeological Evidence.** The whole landscape of Israel is full of places where David herded sheep, fought various enemies, hid from Saul, wept for friends, and worshipped God.

For example, the Elah Valley, about fifteen miles from Bethlehem, would have been a likely place for the confrontation with Goliath. Nearby stream beds are full of small stones to use in a slingshot. In addition there were at least two periods in which David went to the wilderness to hide from the pursuing Saul. The unattractive nature of the Judean wilderness made it an excellent place for refuge. Some of the places identified with

David in this region include "Masada," and perhaps the place later used by Herod for his fortress and En Gedi, the oasis, where David cut off Saul's shirt to prove his loyalty.

The excavation (between 1956 and 1962) of Gibeon, a town eight miles northwest of Jerusalem, revealed the pool mentioned in the combat scene between David's and Ishbosheth's twelve chosen men. (Ishboseth was Saul's son and his heir-apparent. He assumed the throne briefly before being defeated by David.) The pool is a large pit, 35 feet deep. At the bottom of the pit is a stairway down into a tunnel which leads to a subterranean pool with a stairway going around the inside that was apparently constructed to bring the water from the spring into the walled area of the city.

David's selection of the "threshing floor" that became the site for the City of David was crucial for later building and established the tradition of the entire Temple Mount. (See Harold Mare, especially the chapter on the City of David.) This natural fortress was at first David's home and later the site of the first temple, built by his son Solomon. David's capture of the city is described in 2 Samuel 5:6–7, ending with the capture of the fortress of Zion. He took the city by entering through the "conduit," which was probably the water tunnel. He then brought the Ark of the Covenant to Jerusalem with great fanfare, establishing it as the center of worship.

The City of David is a small tongue-shaped piece of land south of the Temple Mount, limited by the Kidron and Tyropoeon Valleys. Its history goes back to Abraham and Melchizedek, the King of Salem and priest of God Most High (Gen. 14:18–20). It now lies outside of the city wall and is a residential area with homes built over the rubble of thousands of years of habitation. An extensive area on the eastern slope of the city has been evacuated, revealing ancient city walls dating back to the time of King David and earlier.

It was from the roof of David's palace, probably on high ground toward the north, that David spied Bathsheba bathing. The court intrigue of David's family, with his sons vying for power, all took place within the confines of the small, fortified City of David. It was within the City of David that he was buried, as were most of the royal family thereafter.

Until recently, many skeptics had assumed David to be a mythic hero. A reference to the "house of David" uncovered in 1976 the ancient city of Dan made headlines in the *New York Times* (Sheler, 60). The twelve lines were the first reference to David found outside of the Bible. One commentator had noted that archaeologists are now discovering new material so swiftly that any archaeological treatment of David's life is likely to be outdated by the time it is published in book form (Shanks).

**Character in Later Works.** In both his person and in his works, David made an indelible mark on future generations. His psalms, which are beautiful examples of Hebrew poetry, are still used in worship all over the world. Even those psalms not written by him are often attributed to him or focused on him. David was always a man after God's own heart (1 Sam. 13:14), from the time old Samuel discovered this handsome young shepherd boy tending his father's flocks. His exploits and character have become the stuff of fable: his service as an armor-bearer and singer in the court of Saul, his heroic adventures against *Goliath and the Philistines, his time of flight and adventure during the later days of the old king, his numerous loves and deep friendships, his times of joy and agony, his brutal treatment of his adversaries, his loving errors in handling his rebellious sons, and his final deathbed scene.

Among the most famous portrayals of him as a young hero is Michaelangelo's handsome statue. Donatello has a parallel statue. One of the latest objects of mutilation by terrorists was the Gaza Synagogue mosaic of David playing the lyre, a portrayal thought to date from the sixth century A.D. We can most often identify him in medieval art by the crown and the harp or the psaltery, his images.

He became a fascinating subject of literature because he was not a perfect hero, but a realistically presented man of God, whose story was full of violence, deceit, greed and lust; a man who was both brutal and gentle, who confused his private hungers with public actions. Plays, novels, and poetry about him abound. (See the long list in Huttar and Frontain's entry, "David," 184.)

Among the more recent examples are D. H. Lawrence's *David* and Christopher Fry's *A Sleep of Prisoners*, but earlier authors had focused on his sinfulness, the chaos created by his sons, and his troublesome relationship with his many wives, especially Michal and Bathsheba. William Faulkner used him as a symbol of the failed father of a rebellious son in *Absalom, Absalom!*, and Joseph Heller even turned his death into comedy in *God Knows*.

In the past two centuries, artists have portrayed his love of Jonathan as homosexual, and feminists have pictured his use and abuse of Michal and Bathsheba as brutal, but generally, he remains the hero. A remarkable king, whether heroic, lyric, comic, or tragic, David has inspired artists over the centuries.

## SOURCES

Exum, J. Cheryl, *Plotted, Shot, and Painted: Cultural Representations of Biblical Women*, Sheffield, England: Sheffield Academic Press, 1996; Gunn, David M., "David," in *The Oxford Companion to the Bible*, edited by Bruce M. Metzger and Michael D. Coogan, New York: Oxford University Press, 1993; Hendel, Ronald S., "King David Loves Bathsheba," *Bible Review Archives*, February 2001; Huttar, Charles and Raymond-Jean Frontain, "David," in *A Dictionary of the Biblical Tradition in English Literature*, edited by David L. Jeffrey, Grand Rapids, MI: William B. Eerdmans Publishing Company, 1992; Mare, W. Harold, *The Archaeology of the Jerusalem Area*, Grand Rapids, MI: Baker Book House, 1987; McKenzie, Steven L., *King David: A Biography*, New York: Oxford University Press, 2000; Shanks, Hershel, "King David, Serial Murderer," *Bible Review Archives*, December 2000; Sheler, Jeffrey L., *Is the Bible True?* San Francisco, CA: Harpers, 1999.

## DEBORAH

**Name and Etymology.** *Deborah* means "bee." Scholars speculate there is some tie between her name and the beehive mentioned later in Judges in conjunction with *Samson's activities.

**Synopsis of Bible Story.** Judges 4 and 5 describe the remarkable female judge, Deborah, who was a unique example of a prophetess, warrior, wife, and judge. She dwelt under a palm tree between Ramah and Bethel, and was apparently so wise that people came from all over Israel for her advice. In a strong gesture, she sent for a military leader, Barak, and told him to unite the forces of the country to battle Sisera, the captain of Jabin's army. For whatever reason, Barak did not believe that he could manage without her help, and insisted he would not go unless she went also. Some speculate that he may have been her husband, and that his name and the name given for her husband *Lappidoth*, both mean "lightning" (Boling, 95). Deborah answered, "I will surely go with thee," while warning that the journey would not result to his honor, "for the Lord shall sell Sisera into the hand of a woman" (Judges 4:9).

Barak then gathered together 10,000 men, going up Mount Tabor with Deborah to wait for the chariots of iron that Sisera and his armies brought into the valley of Megiddo, to the river of Kishon. Then, on God's advice, they waited until the river flooded the "wadi," leaving the 900 chariots unable to maneuver in the mud and water. Sisera and his men all fell to the "edge of the sword," fleeing northward, abandoning the useless chariots in their haste. Barak pursued after them, killing the remainder, "and there was not a man left" (Judges 4:16).

In a colorful codicil—the famous Song of Deborah—we learn that Sisera fled to the tent of Jael, the wife of Heber the Kenite, a supposed ally. There, Jael went out to meet him, graciously invited him in, fed him with curdled milk, covered him, and when he fell asleep, placed a tent nail against his temple (or neck) and killed him with a hammer. Then, in fulfillment of the earlier prophecy, she came out to greet Barak, offering to show him the body of his enemy in her tent. The song concludes with praises to the Lord for avenging Israel.

**Historical Context.** In the time of the Judges (1229–1209 B.C.), the Israelites were gradually settling the land, often facing the various Canaanite factions as they did so. As this story illustrates, they were a weak, unequipped army, formed by volunteers from different tribes, not always willing to join the battle against the well-equipped modern armies of the Sea Peoples, with their iron chariots. This particular scene, with the army coming from the west, indicates that Sisera may have been one of the Philistines.

The clever strategy of taking the high ground and waiting for rains to flood the Esdraelon Plain, turning the ground to mud, inspired later warriors in this same region—at least one in 1799, and another in World War I. Travelers have noted that spring rains traditionally made the plain too muddy for wagons to travel easily, even causing horses to drown in the swollen Kishon River in 1903.

Megiddo, the region where this and many other battles took place, is the spot designated for the final great battle of Revelation—Armageddon. The control of Esdraelon and other territories belonging to the promised land was essential for the survival and growing power of the Israelites. Their prosperity depended on cutting off the caravan routes through this valley. Deborah's important role was the unifying of several of these scattered tribes, thus giving her the honored status of "mother."

Deborah herself is unique in Israelite history. She was not only a judge in the sense of a military leader, but also a judge in the law or court sense of the title. She is also the only judge to be called a "prophet," in fact, the first prophet since the days of Moses (Keddie, 49), and the only judge who was a woman. Female prophets, however, do appear elsewhere in the Old and New Testaments, e.g., Miriam (Exod. 15:20), Huldah (2 Kings 22:14), Noadiah (Neh. 6:14), and Anna (Luke 2:36).

Deborah's victory hymn is a familiar form of ancient poetry, with examples surviving from the fifteenth to twelfth centuries B.C. in Egypt and Assyria and paralleling the triumphant songs on crossing the Red Sea sung by Miriam and Moses.

**Archaeological Evidence.** The most interesting and widely studied of the sites mentioned in Deborah is Megiddo. Archaelogists have discovered a gap in occupation levels at Megiddo, suggesting that the site was either abandoned or lightly occupied from 1125 to 1100 B.C., thereby associating the destruction of the twelfth-century city with the events celebrated in the Song of Deborah (Boling, 116).

Although most of the other places mentioned in Judges do not have specific reference to Deborah, the city of Hazor also interests scholars: it was prominent in the field of metallurgy and importing raw materials, the economic and political leader of its region. Destructive levels of Hazor suggest that Israel may have destroyed the city twice, under both Joshua and Deborah. The ideal location of this city makes the repeated settlements there understandable.

If, as some critics assume, Sisera was one of the Sea Peoples, then the reliefs depicting "feather-helmeted" Sea Peoples in battle chariots with six-spoked wheels (Mazar, 304–305; *The Anchor Bible*, vol. VI-A, 146) would be relevant to Deborah's story. Mazar suggests that they were apparently migrants, not merely military invaders, who may have come from Crete. The Bible identifies the homeland of these people, whom they call "Philistines," as "Caphtor" (Amos 9:7; Jer. 47:4).

**Character in Later Works.** Deborah is a puzzle of sorts for later critics, serving in a particularly unfeminine role. Since women were traditionally wives and mothers, Hebrew critics were inclined to view her as the "mother" of Israel, using her womanly ways to unite a divided people in time of war. It is not she, after all, who brutally kills Sisera; it is Jael who violates the rules of hospitality and destroys her guest. Some rabbis discovered references to the Messiah and to the world to come in the last verse of her song, but she herself remains an ambiguous figure.

The character has not been popular among the Church Fathers or the poets until recent time, when she has delighted the feminists as a kind of "warrior woman." (See the parallels with Maxine Hong Kingston's *The Warrior Woman*.) She first reappeared in the nineteenth century, at a time when women's rights became a political issue of some importance and women were considering going to the battle front as nurses. More recently, her name appears as a kind of Joan of Arc figure, and she is sometimes seen as an early version of the woman leader like Golda Meir, Indira Ghandi, and Margaret Thatcher. (Gordon Keddie argues that these are inappropriate parallels, considering Deborah's clear call from God to exercise a redemptive purpose in his plan for his people's salvation. [Keddie, 49].)

Most recently, Deborah has dominated many studies of women in Scripture, representing the role of women in leadership positions in Judaism and Christianity, a significant concern which has torn many congregations apart. Also valuable in the Song of Deborah is the indication of the traditional roles of women in warfare, either enslaved by the enemy or mourning their dead sons.

## SOURCES

Boling, Robert G., *Judges*, Anchor Bible Series, vol. VI-A, New York: Doubleday and Co., Inc., 1969; Bruce, F. F., "Deborah," in *The Illustrated Bible Dictionary*, vol. 1, edited by J. D. Douglas, Sidney, Australia: Tyndale House Publishers, 1980; Cline, Eric H., *The Battles of Armageddon: Megiddo and the Jezreel Valley from the Bronze Age to the Nuclear Age*, Ann Arbor, MI: University of Michigan Press, 2000; Globe, Alexander, "Deborah," in *A Dictionary of the Biblical Tradition in English Literature*, edited by David L. Jeffrey, Grand Rapids, MI: William B. Eerdmans Publishing Company, 1992; Keddie, Gordon J., *Even in Darkness*, Darlington, England: Evangelical Press, 1985; Keller, Werner, *The Bible as History*, New York: Bantam Books, 1982; Mazar, Amihai, *Archaeology of the Land of the Bible: 10,000–586* B.C.E., New York: Doubleday, 1992; Meyers, Carol L., "Deborah," in *The Oxford Companion to the Bible*, edited by Bruce M. Metzger and Michael D. Coogan, New York: Oxford University Press, 1993.

## DELILAH

**Name and Etymology.** *Delilah*, a Hebrew name, has had various interpretations, including "weakness," "impoverish," and "flirtatious."

**Synopsis of Bible Story.** Delilah appeared late in *Samson's life, after his first marriage and his brutal confrontations with the family of his Philistine wife. After he had served his long term as judge of Israel, he again found himself attracted to Philistine women who lived among his old enemies (Judg. 16). First, a prostitute in Gaza almost cost him his life. Some time later, still unable to learn from experience or to control his lust, Samson turned to Delilah, the only one of his women who was named in Scripture.

The text does not designate her as a prostitute or a wife, but the Philistines quickly identified Delilah as a useful tool for bringing Samson, their old adversary, to destruction. They offered her a small fortune in silver to discover the source of Samson's great strength. Delilah relied on Samson's love for her. Repeating the devices employed by Samson's now-deceased bride, she nagged him and tested his response on successive occasions. The first time she asked, he replied that he could be tied with new ropes; the second time, he said he could be trapped by having his braids woven into fabric; only on the third challenge, when she insisted that his disclosure was truly a test of his love for her, did he admit that he could lose his strength if he cut his hair. His long, uncut hair was the sign of his covenant with God as a Nazirite (Judg. 16:17). She relayed this secret to her countrymen and invited men to cut Samson's hair as he slept in her lap. He awoke to find himself a powerless captive.

There is no record of Delilah having any further role in his imprisonment, blinding, or enslavement. Nor does Scripture tell whether she was a worshipper at the temple of Dagon when he pulled down the pillars and killed the multitude. Later commentators enjoyed the image of this final scene being Delilah's wedding feast, but there is no such evidence in Scripture.

**Historical Context.** As a Philistine woman, Delilah was a forbidden mate for a leader of the Israelites. From the days of Abraham, Isaac, and Jacob, the tribe had been warned to marry within their faith community. Samson's own family had warned him against his misguided pursuit of foreign women with their foreign gods. Later, Proverbs 6 vividly portrayed the lures of the lustful woman; and Paul even later warned Christians about being "unequally yoked" (2 Cor. 6:14). Throughout Scripture, the woman of another faith and another nation was seen as a threat to the family and the covenant community.

It is not unusual that the Philistines would have used Samson's weakness against him, nor that this woman would have used her opportunity to become wealthy while serving her own people. The fact that she is named suggests that she was of a higher social status than the prostitute who attracted Samson earlier. Using the traditional weapons of the weak—her beauty and her feminine wiles—she was able to defeat his superior strength. She did not, however, understand that ultimately this strength derived not from Samson's hair, but from his relationship with God. From her point of view, her actions would have been justified as patriotic and pragmatic.

**Archaeological Evidence.** Archaeological evidence about the Philistines is plentiful. Philistine women (if the statues and frescoes of Crete and the Palace of Knossos tell the truth) were wasp-waisted, big-busted worshippers of the "Great Goddess." Love of splendor, quite alien to the Hebrew tradition, is also evident in the remains of Aegean cultures.

**Character in Later Works.** Delilah, like Omphale, who humiliated Hercules, became the very image of the temptress. The Bible does not refer to her again by name, and the scribes and Church Fathers cited her as playing a small part in Samson's sordid career. The Jewish historian Josephus viewed her as a harlot, and in the writings of the early commentator Pseudo-Philo, she became Samson's wife. St. Ambrose and St. Cyril of Alexandria, like most of the early writers, saw her as a treacherous, avaricious woman. She was commonplace in homiletic literature—an example used from the pulpit. If Samson was seen as a type of Christ, Delilah became the synagogue, causing the crucifixion. She was often portrayed as the female threat to male power, flesh seducing the spirit.

Writers such as Chaucer often referred to her in this role, but it was Milton who fleshed out this portrayal in *Samson Agonistes*—the only extensive literary portrayal of her. Milton viewed her as a tantalizing woman, who represented the lures of the flesh, leading the man of God away from his sacred vows. In music (Saint-Saëns) and in film (de Mille), artists have continued to portray Delilah in this manner.

Among nineteenth century mythic critics, she was associated, like Omphale, with the solar or sun god myth, as was Samson. Modern critics see her actions—binding, weaving, and cutting—as traditional means of entrapment and emasculation by the female. Modern feminists see her as a wronged woman, forced to use duplicity and sexuality to overcome superior power. The point of view of Scripture toward Delilah and the Philistines is clearly negative, portraying her as an enemy of God and his people

### SOURCES

Boling, Robert, *Judges*, Anchor Bible Series, vol. VI-A, Garden City, NY: Doubleday and Co., Inc., 1969; Richardson, Brenda E., and Norman Vance, "Delilah," in *A Dictionary of the Biblical Tradition in English Literature*, edited by David L. Jeffrey, Grand Rapids, MI: William B. Eerdmans Publishing Company, 1992.

E

## ELIJAH

**Name and Etymology.** *Elijah* means "My God is the Lord" or "Yahweh is God."

**Synopsis of Bible Story.** Elijah, Israel's most famous prophet of the Northern Kingdom stood as the staunch adversary to Baal's prophets and the regal tyranny of Ahab and *Jezebel. The story of this ninth century B.C. prophet appears in six episodes that constitute his story (1 Kings 17–19:21; 2 Kings 1–2).

A Tisbite from Gilead, Elijah was unconventional in appearance and dress: he dwelled in caves, traveled long distances on foot, and spoke with authority. He predicted the famine in the land—an ironic commentary on the "fertility" worship of the new monarch. During this time, he lived through the miraculous intercession of God, with bread supplied by ravens. He also performed the miracle of bringing a child back to life—another indication that Jehovah, his God, was the source of life and fertility. He then challenged Baal's prophets to a contest of power on Mount Carmel, demonstrating the superiority of Jehovah and ending the famine. To avoid Jezebel's wrath, he fled to Mount Horeb, the sacred mountain, to remind Israel of her covenant with her God.

He confronted Ahab when he confiscated Naboth's land, foretelling the tyrant's violent death. He prophesied a judgment of fire on the disobedient people of God, and was himself translated into a whirlwind—becoming one of only two Old Testament people to escape death. Before his passing from the earth, he appointed *Elisha as his successor.

**Historical Context.** When Ahab chose Jezebel, the princess of Tyre, for his wife, he brought not only an overweening queen, but also her country's gods, Baal and Astarte. Apparently committed to these deities, the queen feted their prophets and priests in her palace, while disdaining the prophets of Jehovah, the native god of Israel. Baal-melquart was the official protector of Tyre.

Elijah himself was part of the Old Testament tradition of so-called "ecstatic prophecy," which had been characteristic from *Samuel's day, and was the forerunner of the eighth-century rhapsodists that moderns call "writing prophets." He was a man of action, firmly spiritual, recalling his people to the religion of *Moses by going back to Horeb, the traditional site of Moses' witness of Jehovah's theophany in the burning bush (Ex. 3:1).

The location of his homeland, Tishbeh, is uncertain. It may have been in the Kingdom of Jordan, southeast of the Sea of Galilee. Elijah left no written records; his story was apparently transcribed by someone who had intimate connection about the court life in Samaria.

**Archaeological Evidence.** Mount Carmel has a church commemorating the contest between Elijah and the prophets of Baal (1 Kings 18). It is an ideal site for such a contest, with visibility from the summit for miles around and located on the border between the plain of Ahser of the Phoenician cities of Tyre and Sidon.

Baal was the god of thunder, storms, fertility—the source of rain. Thus the contest is appropriately in terms of rain and lightning. There are numerous statues and carvings that illustrate this popular diety's physical appearance; for example, the stela in Ugarit of Baal where he holds a symbol of lightning in his left hand. He appears to be parallel to the Greek deity Zeus.

Astarte or Ashtar also appears with great frequency in the Old Testament. She also is a fertility god, often worshipped in groves of trees in high or mountainous places.

The ritual "limping" dance performed by the prophets of Baal, which was accompanied by the gashing with knives, has parallels among Tyrian seafarers who performed such a dance, and modern Arabs have a similar custom. It was also a funeral rite for Baal—involving laceration and the shedding of blood—a common practice in fertility cults (Gaster, 507).

**Character in Later Works.** Elijah was one of the most colorful of the prophets and was seen as the forerunner of *Amos. He, like Amos, was a stern and vociferous critic of paganism and social injustice who possessed considerable political influence and made a deep impression on the Hebrews. Because Malachi (4:5) had prophesied that a new Elijah would announce the coming of the Messiah, Elijah was also important to the New Testament. *John the Baptist seemed to many to be a new Elijah—living in the desert, proclaiming the dreadful "Day of the Lord." The priests and the Levites of Jerusalem were particulary anxious to learn whether Elizah had been reincarnated as John (John 1:21). And it was Elijah, along with Moses, who appeared at the Mount of Transfiguration (Mark 9:4). Apparently some of those who witnessed *Christ's miracles assumed that Jesus was Elijah returned to earth.

It is this influence that appears in Mendelssohn's oratorio "Elijah," which presents a thoroughly Christ-centered interpretation of the prophet's significance. Elijah is not usually a central character in British or American literature: Chaucer alludes to him in the "Summoner's Tale," as does Milton in *Paradise Regained;* William Blake, also a mystic, delighted in this charismatic prophet; Hardy referred to him in *Tess of the D'Urbervilles;* and he appears opposite Ahab as a mad old prophet in Melville's *Moby Dick.* Alan Jacobs notes that certain frequently used terms derive from Elijah, even though they are rarely attributed to him: "the still small voice" and "inheriting another's mantle" (Jacobs, 234).

The sojourn in the desert also became a type and pattern for others, including Christ. The whirlwind, a parallel to the theophany in *Job, also recurs in literature as a form in which man comes closer to God. The story of the helpful birds who feed the hero in distress, which delighted Renaissance painters, has its parallels in popular literature and Christian saints legends, including those of St. Catherine, St. Vitus, and St. Cuthbert. The raven is a particularly interesting choice, since it is usually considered a bird of ill omen (see Poe's "The Raven," for example).

In the African American community, where slaves used the River Jordan as a symbol for freedom, the fiery chariot that appeared at his death (2 Kings 2:11) was a particularly compelling image. Thus, the spiritual "Swing Low, Sweet Chariot" combined the slaves' dreams of escape with Elijah's wondrous translation from earthly existence. This imagery draws from an ancient and glorious tradition dating from early times and continuing through the Roman emperors, who were thought to ride to the Sun-god after death.

In Palestine, the "Place of the Burning" on Mount Carmel is invariably pointed out to pilgrims, and there is a monastery named for Elijah in Wadi el Quelt—a monument to his memory. This is thought to be the location of the brook "Cherith," to which the prophet retired when the drought he prophesied came to the land.

For many of the orthodox, Elijah has not died and continues to be a presence still wandering the earth. Some orthodox Jews continue to set a chair for him at the rite of

Elijah's Chariot of Fire, folio 200 of 1526-29 manuscript Latin Bible from Abbey of St. Amand, France. The Art Archive/Bibliothèque Municipale, Valenciennes/Dagli Orti.

circumcision. At the Jewish Passover, the door is opened in expectation of his return, and a cup of wine is poured for him. He is expected to reappear to usher in the Messiah and the final redemption of mankind: "Elijah the Prophet . . . may he come quickly to us with the Messiah" (Comay, 115).

## SOURCES

Comay, Joan, *Who's Who in the Bible*, vol. 1, New York: Bonanza Books, 1980; Gaster, Theodor H., *Myth, Legend, and Custom in the Old Testament*, vol. 2, New York: Harper and Row, Publishers, 1918; Jacobs, Alan, "Elijah," in *A Dictionary of the Biblical Tradition in English Literature*, edited by David L. Jeffrey, Grand Rapids, MI: William B. Eerdmans Publishing Company, 1992; Miller, Madeline S., and J. Lane Miller, *Harper's Bible Dictionary*, New York: Harper and Row, 1961; Smith, B. L., "Elijah," in *The Illustrated Bible Dictionary*, vol. 2, edited by J. D. Douglas. Sidney, Australia: Tyndale House Publishers, 1980.

## ELISHA

**Name and Etymology.** *Elisha* means "God has granted salvation."

**Synopsis of Bible Story.** This ninth-century prophet was the successor to *Elijah. Elisha was the son of Shaphat, a native of Abel-Meholah in the northern kingdom of Israel (1 Kings 19:16). His series of miraculous stories appears in 2 Kings 2–9 and 13:14–21.

We first meet him as the disciple of Elijah. Although apparently from a wealthy family, Elisha responded to the call by abandoning his wealth, sacrificing his twelve yoke of oxen, and meekly following his solitary master (1 Kings 19:19–21). Elisha was anointed by the aging Elijah and inherited his mantle, the symbol of his prophetic office. He served faithfully as a disciple, became a witness to Elijah's transcendence in the whirlwind, and his successor as God's prophet to Israel.

When Elijah asked his younger disciple what he desired, Elisha requested a double measure of Elijah's powers, which he apparently received. Scripture chronicles twice as many miracles for Elisha than it does for Elijah. Elisha was less the solitary antagonist of the house of Omri, more a leader of prophetic guilds, occasionally in friendly contact with the Israelite kings.

In Scripture, Elisha is the subject of two types of stories: one in which he or his servant Gehazi was involved with great figures of the day. These include the kings of Judah and Israel, who were at war with Moab (2 Kings 3:11–27) and with Naaman the Syrian (2 Kings 5); and Jehu (2 Kings 9). His upper-class background and courtly manner apparently allowed him easy access to people in positions of power.

The other kind of Elisha story involves miracles he performed. These include the healing of injurious waters (2 Kings 2:19–22), the cursing of the mocking boys (2 Kings 2:23–24), the feeding of the Shunammite woman and healing of her son (2 Kings 4:1–37), the detoxification of a cooking pot and multiplication of loaves of bread (2 Kings 4:38–44), and the floating of an ax head (2 Kings 6:1–7). Some of the miracles he performed echo those of *Moses, some Elijah, and some prefigure those of *Christ.

His prestige is suggested by King Joash's visit to his bedside when he was dying. Even after his death, many incredible tales circulated regarding events around his burial place.

**Historical Context.** Like earlier prophets *Samuel, *Nathan, and Elijah, Elisha confronted his people's kings regarding their moral or religious misdeeds, but was apparently also sought out for his gifts of foresight to advise them on military and political as well as personal and social concerns. He served as an advisor of sorts to kings of Israel, Judah, and Edom in their war with Moab; he played a part in wars between Syria and Israel; and he fomented the rebellion of Jehu. The historical events alluded to in his time of prophecy, and those in which he was involved, are extensive and complex, some of them overlapping Elijah's. His ministry covered a long period, spanning four reigns, from Joram (c. 849–842 B.C.) to Joash (c. 801–786 B.C.)—more than fifty years.

Elisha was also a prominent leader among the prophets. It seems to have been common among the prophets of ancient Israel to live in communities or guilds. The "sons of prophets" and the "company of prophets" are terms that suggest groups of seers or prophets, first apparent in Samuel's time, who lived simply, studied the law, and prophesied. He lived at times among such a group of professional holy men or mystics in the Gilgal area, on the plain of Jericho. As we know from the testimony of Qumran, such communities were often located in desert areas, where the men lived monastic lives, in conditions of extreme poverty assuaged only by religious ecstasy. One commentary notes that, although Elisha belonged to the prophetic tradition that produced the eighth-century rhapsodists, he had more affinities with the ecstatic prophets of the eleventh century (Smith, 442).

**Archaeological Evidence.** As the successor to Elijah in the crusade against the moral laxity of the time and the toleration and even veneration of foreign gods, Elisha touched on many of the elements verified by archaeologists. The Phoenician culture, the cities he visited, the pagan deities he confronted are all richly documented. The Arab village of Solem in the Jezreel Valley, for example, has been identified with Shunem, where a wealthy woman prepared a room for Elisha.

One of the few archaeological finds specifically related to Elisha is the reference to the "third" man with the king, apparently a rider who would hang onto the chariot. The defeat of the Israelites by King Mesha of Moab was documented by a stela discovered in 1868 by F. A. Klein. This statement regarding the victory of Moab is thought to be the oldest surviving Palestinian document, from 840 B.C. Others have noted that the "bloody water," which saved the allies from dying of thirst, may be the reddish color of the waters that seep into trenches beside the Dead Sea. (See the full description of this remarkable discovery in Keller, 248 ff)

**Character in Later Works.** Tradition holds that a dead man tossed into Elisha's tomb was restored to life on coming into contact with the prophet's bones (Jacobs, 235). Some believe that there was once an extensive cycle of Elisha miracle stories, most of which have been lost. Certainly, many of his miracles, activities, and attributes, including the waters purified by salt, the "baldpate" reference and the significance of hair, and the image of the chariot of the sun, do find parallels in other ancient literature. Gaster notes, for example, that the "inexhaustible cruse" (2 Kings: 1–7) is "simply a Hebrew version of a familiar folktale regarding the miraculous increase of food as a reward for hospitality to itinerant gods or saints. The leprosy that is cured by bathing (2 Kings 5:10) is related to "illution"—the washing "in of the properties of primordial waters," akin to baptism, and to a medieval magic charm involving the cure of the leper by dipping him seven times in a river (Gaster, 519). Many of the magic procedures we find in Elisha's miracles also find parallels in western thought. Thomas Hardy, in his *Wessex*

*Tales,* tells the story of "The Withered Arm" in which a cure is effected by touching the neck of a man who has been hanged. (See full listing in Gaster, 516 ff.)

Elisha's miracles find echoes in the New Testament, especially in the narratives of Jesus' miracles. The Church Fathers did not make extensive reference to him, and he does appear regularly in church architecture, carved or painted as with other prophets.

He was often included in the parade of prophets who appeared in the Corpus Christi plays, processions that established Jesus' genealogy in the Scriptures. Allusions to Elisha in Milton, James Joyce, and Charles Lamb are slight. These authors make use of his miracle-making ability and his bald head rather than his full career as a prophet of God. Because much of his advice was oral and specific and most of his miracles, though spectacular, were of limited spiritual meaning, he has not retained the grandeur of Elijah in religious thought.

## SOURCES

Clifford, Richard J., "Elisha," in *The Oxford Companion to the Bible,* edited by Bruce M. Metzger and Michael D. Coogan, New York: Oxford University Press, 1993; Comay, Joan, *Who's Who in the Bible,* vol. 1, New York: Bonanza Books, 1980; Gaster, Theodor H., *Myth, Legend, and Custom in the Old Testament,* vol. 2, New York: Harper and Row, 1975; Jacobs, Alan, "Elisha," in *A Dictionary of the Biblical Tradition in English Literature,* Grand Rapids, MI: William B. Eerdmans Publishing Company, 1992; Keller, Werner, *The Bible as History,* New York: Bantam Books, 1982; Merrill, Eugene H., *An Historical Survey of the Old Testament,* Nutley, NJ: The Craig Press, 1972; Smith, B. L., "Elisha," in *Illustrated Bible Dictionary,* vol. 1, edited by J. D. Douglas, Sidney, Australia: Tyndale House Publishers, 1980.

## ESAU

**Name and Etymology.** *Esau,* or "hairy," is probably a reference to Esau's appearance as well as to Seir, a city in Edom. "Ruddy" or "adom" is an additional reference, both to his coloring and his descendants, the Edomites.

**Synopsis of Bible Story.** Esau was the son of *Isaac and *Rebekah, a fraternal twin of *Jacob, born before Jacob, but in battle with him from the womb (Gen. 25:22). Another example (like Ishmael) of the firstborn who is set aside in favor of the second son, Esau was a "cunning hunter, a man of the field" (Gen. 25:27), and a favorite of his father, who apparently loved the venison Esau brought and cooked for him. A vigorous and overly hasty man, Esau was an easy prey for the quick-witted and more devious Jacob, who tricked him into selling his birthright for a mess of pottage (Gen. 25:29–34).

When Isaac was old and blind, on the verge of death, Esau again became the victim of a shrewd plot: this time he was stripped of his father's blessing. Making use of Isaac's love of venison, and disguising his smooth skin by the use of goatskins, Jacob won the irrevocable blessing before Esau came home from the hunt. Not realizing he was too late, Esau "also made savoury meat, and brought it unto his father, and said unto his father, Let my father arise, and eat of his son's venison, that thy soul may bless me" (Gen. 27:31). When he begged for some blessing, Esau won a painful response from his anguished father: "Behold, I have made him thy lord, and all his brethren have I given to him for servants; and with corn and wine have I sustained him: and what shall I do now unto thee, my son?" Then, responding to Esau's impassioned plea, Isaac pronounced these tragic words of "blessing": "Behold, thy dwelling shall be the fatness of the earth, and of the dew of heaven from above; And by thy sword shalt thou live, and shalt serve thy brother; and it shall come to pass when thou shalt have the dominion, that thou shalt break his yoke from off thy neck" (Gen. 27:37–40).

His guilty brother, Jacob, escaped to Haran to seek a bride from among his mother's people. By this time, Esau had married Hittite women, who irked his mother and whose presence worried his father. In an effort to please Isaac, he married Mahalath, the daughter of *Ishmael, thus allying himself with another displaced firstborn of the family of *Abraham.

By the time Jacob returned to claim the land he had inherited, Esau had apparently mellowed, welcoming his brother and forgiving him in a touching reconciliation scene (Gen. 33:9–15). Even though Jacob appears to have distrusted him, Esau proved a generous man, asking no tribute from his brother, returning peacefully to Seir.

**Historical Context.** The story of Esau is the story of a people, the Edomites, who were in constant struggles against the family of Jacob, the Israelites. The land of Edom was rugged and difficult, a region reaching from the Dead Sea to the Gulf of Aqaba, where the grazing and agriculture were unprofitable, driving the inhabitants to a life of hunting and extortion. The hatred between Esau and Jacob helped the Israelites to explain the subsequent actions of the Edomite peoples, who attacked Israel at various times in history (2 Chron. 21:8–10). Modern scholars are inclined to see the story as a justification for the treatment of these "cousins" as enemies of God's chosen people, the Israelites.

**Archaeological Evidence.** The peoples of Edom, their lifestyle, and the city of Seir are all part of documented history. Negev notes that the Edomites were of Semitic stock. They seem to have flourished from the thirteenth to the eighth centuries B.C., declined, and were finally destroyed in the sixth century B.C. Remains of fortified towns and numerous villages have been found, revealing that agriculture was highly developed as was local pottery. The inscriptions indicate it was richer than the other countries in the vicinity, in part because of the exploitation of copper. The Israelites were not allowed to use the roads passing through Edom on their way to Canaan (Negev, 122; Num. 20:17–21).

The law of primogeniture provided that the firstborn should inherit at least a double share of the father's property when the father died. Parallel practices have been discovered in Nuzi, in Larsa in the Old Babylonian period, and in Assyria in the Middle Assyrian period (*New International Version*, 42). Although Isaac and Esau tried to separate the birthright from the blessing, scholars note that the first led inevitably to the latter, both being the inheritance of the firstborn (*New International Version*, 47).

**Character in Later Works.** The descendants of Esau were seen by the Old Testament prophets as foes of Jacob's descendants (Mal. 1:2–3; Isa. 63:1–3). Paul saw the story of Esau as an example God's sovereign choice, which is justified by the subsequent evil done by the Edomite peoples (Rom. 9:10–13). Later Christians saw the prophecy of Isaiah as referring to Rome, which like Edom, would be the object of God's wrath in the last days (Alter, 358).

St. Augustine, among others, was convinced that Esau was a type of proud and carnal man who thoughtlessly bartered away his birthright. He saw him as a parallel to the Jews, who lost their birthright to their younger brothers—the Christians. Martin Luther saw the fall from glory and honor as a typical member of the wicked and hypocritical church, who, despising his primogeniture, lost his treasure, the Church of

Rome. John Calvin, noting the preference for the meal over the birthright, saw Esau as an example of the profane man whom God would not elect, and Jacob as the man of God's predestined choosing. John Wesley was more interested in the aftermath of the story, focusing on Esau's repentance and possible salvation.

Creative authors have made some references to Esau over the years, but generally have preferred Jacob. The term "a mess of pottage" has become commonplace in language, but the character of Esau became popular only among the Romantics and moderns. William Blake used Emanuel Swedenborg's mystical interpretation of the prophecy to reverse the roles of the damned and the chosen in *The Marriage of Heaven and Hell*. Esau served the romantics as a wanderer who married beneath himself. Later, writers such as John Galsworthy (*Flowering Wilderness*) and Samuel Butler (*The Way of All Flesh*) continued this interpretation. As a kind of wild man, he might well be seen as the model for the Brontë sisters' heroes, Heathcliff and Mr. Rochester. The dark, fierce outcast (like Cain) is a favorite romantic figure—the Byronic hero. The actual event of the stolen birthright was more interesting to William Faulkner, who used it as the key to the novel *Go Down, Moses*. The double path of the brothers does work effectively as the story of the South's tormented history of two races from shared parentage.

## SOURCES

Alter, Robert, *Genesis: Translation and Commentary*, New York: W. W. Norton and Company, 1996; Jeffrey, David L., ed., *A Dictionary of the Biblical Tradition in English Literature*, Grand Rapids, MI: William B. Eerdmans Publishing Company, 1992; Negev, Avraham, ed., *The Archaeological Encyclopedia of the Holy Land*, New York: Thomas Nelson Publishers, 1986.

## ESTHER (HADASSAH)

**Name and Etymology.** Esther's Hebrew name was *Hadassah*, meaning "myrtle." The name *Esther* is probably derived from the Persian word for "star" or perhaps from the Babylonian goddess Ishtar (*New International Version*, 712).

**Synopsis of Bible Story.** Esther, a Jewish orphan living in Susa, was raised by a kinsman, Mordecai, at the time that Xerxes (or Ahaseurus) was the ruler of the Medes and the Persians. An argument at court, when Queen Vashti refused the king's orders to appear before a group of drunken revelers to display her beauty, resulted in her banishment and the search for a new queen. The virgins of the empire were rounded up, brought to the harem, given extended beauty treatments, and then paraded before Xerxes. Swept up in this action was Esther, whose guardian wisely advised her to keep her nationality a secret. She was selected by the king as his queen and was celebrated in the court for a time.

One day, Esther's cousin Mordecai overheard rumors of a plot against the king among court officials. He told Esther, who warned the king, crediting the discovery of this treason to Mordecai. The king punished the villains, but failed to reward the informer. He lavished favors instead on the wily Haman, a member of the court who may have been part of the eunuchs' plot, giving him unusual authority. Puffed up by this power, Haman demanded and received respect and obsequious behavior from everyone in the kingdom. Only the Jews refused to honor him by bowing down. Angered by this proud group in general and Mordecai in particular for their unwillingness to abase themselves before him, Haman used his position to incite Xerxes against this people who—he insisted—were not loyal to their king or his laws. In this description, he neglected to mention that he was describing the Jews. Using the powers granted him, Haman issued a proclamation to the kingdom, setting a time for the genocide of the Jews.

Esther and Mordecai met secretly and determined that she was ideally situated to help her people, and that it was her obligation, regardless of the perils involved. Planning to use her womanly wiles, she bathed and dressed in her most elegant costume, went uninvited to the king's presence, and asked that he and Haman come to a special banquet she had prepared. A second opportunity for making a request appeared, but again she asked only that they come to the banquet she arranged.

Buoyed by his role as the queen's favorite courtier, Haman celebrated his new importance as he arranged for the construction of gallows to hang Mordecai. Before this final banquet, however, Xerxes recalled that he had not properly rewarded Mordecai. He asked Haman how he might honor such a loyal follower and unintentionally tricked him into suggesting great rewards for his sworn enemy.

In a parallel scene the following day, Esther told Xerxes that someone in his court had arranged for the slaughter of her people. When he discovered that the villain was Haman, Xerxes ordered that Haman rather than Mordecai be hanged from the gallows Haman had erected, and that the order for the slaughter of the Jews be rescinded.

In memory of Esther's heroic act, which saved her countrymen, the festival of Purim is celebrated annually by the Jews, beginning with Ezra (Esther 9:28–29).

**Historical Context.** This lively story about the Persian empire and the life of the Jews who did not return to Israel is unusual for its failure to mention God. The expanded Greek version included in the Apocryphal writings begins with Mordecai's prophetic dream and ends with a godly interpretation of the dream. It also shows Haman to be a darker villain, suggesting that he was in league with the eunuchs, who were executed for their murder plot against the king.

The story as transcribed in Protestant Bibles is more about the salvation of the Jews of the Diaspora than about a triumph of faith. Xerxes (486–465 B.C.) is well documented in history, largely because of his campaigns against Greek city-states. The Jewish historian Josephus, for example, speaks of "Artaxerxes II" as does the Greek historian Herodotus. On the other hand, critics note that details of the narrative appear not to be supported by other discoveries: Persia never had 127 provinces, and no records mention either Vashti or Esther (Williams, 401). So little does survive of court records, outside of Scripture, that these seem minor issues.

Yet the details of harem life, of palace intrigues, and the laws of the era do have marks of authenticity. The Greek version of the story includes more detail about the furnishings, the food, and the habits of the time, including a suggestion that Vashti had a drinking party for the women at the same time the king was having one for the men. Women's lives at the time were quite circumscribed, even marginal in public arenas—as they are in many orthodox or Muslim communities today. The Book of Esther is a rare glimpse of this world.

The letters are documented in greater detail in the Greek version, which otherwise follows the plot and wording of the Hebrew text.

**Archaeological Evidence.** Susa was one of several cities where archaeologists have discovered ruins of Persian palaces. The festivals in that city were legendary, including a form of New Year's festivities. Apparently the Diaspora Jewish communities were caught up in the celebrations, even joining in the casting of lots to determine the destinies of peoples and nations for the coming year. W. Lee Humphreys suggests this may be the base for the popular celebration called "Mordecai's Day" in 2 Maccabees 15:36 (Humphreys, 736–37).

Evidence suggests that the gallows mentioned in Esther was to be used for the display of executed prisoners, who were actually killed by impaling them. Herodotus discusses the income of the Persians and the slaughter of peoples for their wealth, suggesting that Haman's plot had a historical basis.

The book of Esther was not found among the Dead Sea Scrolls, and has been a continuing source of debate over the centuries—largely because of the omission of any mention of God. Jerome, in preparing his Latin Vulgate, recognized errors in the manuscript of the book of Esther and removed some verses, placing them at the end as a mark of their dubious authenticity. Later, during the Reformation, these verses were isolated as a separate book of the Apocrypha. Some of the Reformers objected to considering the book Scripture.

**Character in Later Works.** Although Esther has long been celebrated for her beauty and courage, and has been a heroine for the Jewish people, her book has been troubling for many theologians. From the earliest times, the rabbis considered it dubious, especially in its emphasis on vengeance, and Martin Luther thought it not sufficiently moral or religious to be included in the canon (Madoff, 241–43). Esther herself appears only as a casual reference in much of English literature, serving authors from Chaucer to Dickens as a type of a woman who makes shrewd use of her beauty.

The book has remained part of Scripture primarily because it serves as the basis for the celebration of Purim, and because of Esther's legendary power as a figure of female virtue, piety, resolve, and national resistance. The Book of Esther is one of the Five Scrolls read on festivals or commemorative days in the Jewish year. Purim is especially important as an indication of God's power to protect his chosen people in times of persecution. For modern Jews, the story is a bleak reminder of the Holocaust and the constant threat of annihilation by jealous powers in governments. It is also a comfort as a portrayal of the triumph of good over evil.

SOURCES

Humphreys, W. Lee, "Esther: Introduction," in *The HarperCollins Study Bible*, edited by Wayne A. Meeks, San Francisco, CA: HarperCollins, 1993; Madoff, Mark S. "Esther," *A Dictionary of the Biblical Tradition in English Literature*, edited by David L. Jeffrey, Grand Rapids, MI: William B. Eerdmans Publishing Company, 1992; Merrill, Eugene H., *An Historical Survey of the Old Testament*, Nutley, NJ: The Craig Press, 1972; Williams, J. C., in *Perspectives in Old Testament Literature*, edited by Woodrow Ohlsen, San Diego, CA: Harcourt Brace Jovanovich, 1978; Tucker, Gene M., "Esther," in *The Oxford Companion to the Bible*, edited by Bruce M. Metzger and Michael D. Coogan, New York: Oxford University Press, 1993; Trawick, Buckner B., *The Bible as Literature*, New York: Barnes and Noble, 1970.

EVE

**Name and Etymology.** Eve's name comes from the Hebrew "life," and is also connected with the Arab word for "serpent." It is the name given to his wife by *Adam, who also called her the "mother of all living" (Gen. 3:20).

**Synopsis of Bible Story.** The human female enters the Biblical narrative in the first chapter of Genesis, with the creation of man in the image of God, "male and female created he them" (Gen. 1:27). God then blessed both man and woman, admonished them to be fruitful and multiply, "replenish the earth, and subdue it; and have dominion over the fish of the sea, and over the fowl of the air, and over every living thing that moveth upon the earth" (Gen. 1:28). The subsequent narrative of the Garden of Eden fleshes out the story of woman's creation and her role, indicating that she was created as a companion and helpmeet for man (Gen. 2:18); born from man's rib, "bone of my bones, and flesh of my flesh," called "Woman because she was taken out of Man" (Gen. 2:23). This expanded explanation introduces the idea of marriage as a union of man and woman, becoming once again "one flesh" (Gen. 2:24).

The story of the "Fall" begins with the serpent, which tempts Eve to eat of the forbidden fruit. It first challenges God's law, insisting that she will not die when she eats of it, and then throws doubt on God's motives: "For God doth know that in the day ye eat thereof, then your eyes shall be opened, and ye shall be as gods, knowing good and evil" (Gen. 3:5). This temptation to power through understanding proves too much: "And when the woman saw that the tree was good for food, and that it was pleasant to the eyes, and a tree to be desired to make one wise, she took of the fruit thereof, and did eat. . . ." Following this act of disobedience, the woman gave the fruit also to her husband, who also did eat, "And the eyes of them both were opened, and they knew that they were naked. . ." (Gen. 3:7).

The subsequent effort to cover their shame and nakedness and to escape God's judgment quickly turned into a game of blame, in which *Adam blamed Eve, who, in turn, accused the serpent. God's firm declaration follows, first noting that the offspring of the woman and the serpent would have eternal enmity, and then that the woman would see her sorrow multiplied: ". . . in sorrow thou shalt bring forth children; and thy desire shall be to thy husband, and he shall rule over thee" (Gen. 3:16).

After the expulsion from the garden, the prophetic words were quickly realized: Eve did find herself pregnant, and she knew not only the pain of childbirth but also the sorrow of watching her first son, *Cain, grow jealous of his younger brother, Abel. In his anger, Cain killed Abel, leaving her bereft—one son dead, the other a murderer, now an eternal wanderer. More children followed, but the rest of Eve's life is undocumented. Her death is unnoted and her daughters are unnamed in Scripture.

**Historical Context.** From the earliest Rabbinical tradition, Eve's story explained the subordinate position of women. *Paul quoted Genesis 3 in 2 Corinthians 11:3 to suggest that sin entered from the serpent's beguiling of Eve, and her beguiling of Adam. In 1 Timothy 2:13–15, Paul cited Eve's sin as the basis for the subordination of women. This has remained fairly standard orthodoxy through the ages, being questioned most extensively in modern times. The subordinate role continues to be part of the rationale for forbidding women in the clergy in many denominations over many centuries.

**Archaeological Evidence.** The story of Eden lies too far back in prehistory to be recovered, but there have been periodic efforts to locate Eden. In recent times, numerous discoveries of ancient fossil remains have been proclaimed to be "African Eve" or "Australian Eve." The clear testimony of Genesis is that the garden of Eden was located in the Fertile Crescent, but the actual place is deliberately shrouded in mystery.

Nonetheless, the concept of the "mother of all living" continues to reappear, as recently as the discovery of a "shared" DNA among Jews and Arabs.

This aspect of Eve finds parallel expression in the many fertility goddesses worshipped throughout the ancient world (Astarte, Ashtoreth, Ceres, Diana, Venus, the Snake Goddess of Crete, and so on). The ancient clay and stone figures discovered in the Cycladic Islands (in the Mediterranean), Palestine, and all through the Fertile Crescent testify to the female as the lifegiver.

Her role as temptress, the source of man's many torments, parallels the Greek story of Pandora and her box of troubles, opened because of her curiosity.

**Character in Later Works.** Both Judaic and Christian tradition have seen Eve as the conduit for sin's entrance into the human race. In rabbinical tradition, her name is linked with the serpent, identifying the first sin with sexual knowledge, and making female sexuality the key to man's temptation and fall. In some Jewish allegory, Adam is the mind and Eve the senses.

Yet Eve's bond with her husband, as one flesh, is also the source of the "Bride" imagery for the Jews and later for the Christian Church. Among the Fathers of the Church, for instance, she represented the Church in relation to Christ and the soul in relation to God. (See references to St. Augustine, St. Thomas Aquinas, and St. Bonaventure in Danielson's article, 252). Many Christian writers have balanced her willful sin with the *Virgin Mary's modest acceptance of God's will for her life. One brought sin into the world, the other redemption.

In the Middle Ages, she was a staple character in the mystery cycles, many of which began with the story of the Creation and the Fall. Writers such as Chaucer make regular reference to her as the errant wife with the weak mind who leads her husband astray.

Although in the medieval world, Eve's sinful nature was emphasized, her physical beauty became a snare for sculptors, who carved her image as an object of delight. (See, for example, the twelfth-century Ghilberti carvings in the Autun Cathedral.) By the Renaissance, her image was a frequent justification for painting female nudes by such artists as Jan van Eyck, Michelangelo, Masaccio, and so on.

The finest of the literary portrayals of Eve was, of course, John Milton's in *Paradise Lost*. In his vision of her in the halcyon days before the expulsion from Eden, Milton pictured Eve as the ideal female, gentle and lovely. Others have used her either as a central or secondary character in the poems, plays, and novels: William Blake, in *The Ghost of Abel*; Lord Byron in *Cain*; Elizabeth Barrett Browning, in *A Drama of Exile*; Christina Rossetti in "Eve"; James Stephens in "Eve"; G. B. Shaw, in *Back to Methuselah*, Robert Frost in "Never Again Would Birds' Songs Be the Same"; and Archibald MacLeish, in *Songs for Eve*, among others (Danielson, 254). A recent update of Genesis appeared on Broadway, called *Songs of Paradise*, inspired by the "Purimspiel," a type of eastern European folk play based on biblical tales and performed by itinerant Yiddish actors at the Purim holiday.

Especially since the rise of romanticism and the development of the Cult of Domesticity, the female has become an object of adulation, at first in the tradition of Maryolatry (veneration of the Virgin Mary) and gradually as blatantly sexual, deliberately opposing the images of traditional Judeo-Christian theology. With the emancipation of women in Western culture, Eve has undergone a major transformation and reevaluation.

In the last two centuries, the feminists have devoted much of their attention to Eve. Seeing her as the patriarchal justification for woman's low estate, they have focused primarily on the "androgynous" creation they perceive in Genesis 1, where she was created in the image of God—male and female. Some of the more radical feminist theologians have studied the "lost" books of Genesis to discover the myth of Lilith, the first wife of Adam, and celebrate her independent spirit. News stories regularly note Lilith celebrations by feminist groups, including musicals, art shows, and other events.

As our first woman, Eve remains our most central and compelling female image.

## SOURCES

Danielson, Dennis, "Eve," in *A Dictionary of the Biblical Tradition in English Literature*, edited by David L. Jeffrey, Grand Rapids: William B. Eerdmans Publishing Company, 1992; Van Gelder, Lawrence, "An Update of Genesis, Leaning Toward Yiddish," *The New York Times*, Theatre Review Section, 14 November 2001.

## EZEKIEL

**Name and Etymology.** *Ezekiel* means "God strengthens."

**Synopsis of Bible Story.** The son of Buzi, Ezekiel was a man of priestly lineage who was deported along with his countrymen to Babylon after the surrender of Jehoiachin in 598–597 B.C. In Babylon, he felt called to be a prophet, receiving divine revelations from approximately 593 to 571 B.C. We know little about him as a person other than that he was married and that his wife died. Ezekiel was a remarkably self-controlled man, even refraining from mourning his wife's death (24:15–18). He was obviously distressed that he was called to prophesy Judah's doom, comforted that he could provide guidance for his countrymen in exile, and jubilant that he could also prophesy the affirmation of the eternal covenant and the new Temple.

The many images and details of the long prophetic book, covering many countries and problems, reveal a man of wide learning. Edith Hamilton notes that he was also a man who transformed the Jews, making them into a recognizable and separate people able to withstand the temptations of captivity in Babylon (Hamilton, 171ff). She notes his lavish detail, chronicling the rich clothing and splendid decorations of golden Babylon, treasures that poured in from all parts of the great empire. Ezekiel, realizing that their old way of life was lost to his countrymen and that they could no longer be herdsmen and farmers, encouraged them to engage in mercantile activities. Although he clearly yearned for the brooks and trees he remembered—and probably exaggerated—in his native landscape, he followed *Jeremiah's advice and settled into the new "dry and thirsty" (Ezekiel 19:13) land for some 13 years.

During this time of exile, Ezekiel turned his fellow countrymen back to their love of ceremony, tradition, and features of the law—such as the rite of circumcision, the importance of keeping the Sabbath, and always remembering their special status as God's chosen people. This zeal for Deuteronomic codes served to set the Jews apart from their neighbors. This separation, in turn, has allowed them to maintain their identity throughout history. Hamilton sees it as a divinely inspired stroke of genius—a pattern of organization to preserve the people and the faith through the centuries of Diaspora, the great dispersion of the Jews, that were to follow.

**Historical Context.** The book of Ezekiel is filled with 15 dates in their correct chronological order. They separate into three segments: the coming doom of Judah and

Jerusalem, the judgments against the foreign nations, and the eventual restoration of Jerusalem and the Temple (Begg, 218).

Historians note that, unlike *Jeremiah, Ezekiel accompanied the Jews into captivity, saw first hand the great Babylon and the rule of *Nebuchadnezzar, delighted in the splendors of the lavish city with its giant buildings and wide streets, and worked feverishly among the exiles to keep them separate from the pagans who surrounded them.

His prophecy traces the history from 593 to 539 B.C., when *Cyrus the Persian crushed the Babylonian empire. Ezekiel prophesied during the first 22 years of this dramatic history, and his prophecies predict events beyond his own lifetime. Some believe they extend even to the final days of earth at the great "Battle of Armageddon."

**Archaeological Evidence.** Because the Book of Ezekiel has more dates than any other prophetic book of the Old Testament, it is possible to provide precise calendar equivalents for the prophecies and events, using the discoveries of modern archaeology—Babylonian annals on cuneiform tablets, and astronomy—eclipses referred to in ancient archives.

Excavations of Babylon have provided extensive evidence of the city described in *Daniel and Ezekiel. Apparently Nebuchadnezzar was an assiduous builder, leaving indications that Babylon surpassed all the cities of the orient: "it was greater than Thebes, Memphis and Ur, greater even than Nineveh" (Keller, 316).

**Character in Later Works.** Although the Scripture does not describe his death, later traditions hold that Ezekiel was murdered by one of the leaders of the exiles whose idolatry he had denounced, and that he was buried near Babylon.

The apocalyptic tone of Ezekiel's prophecy was echoed in John's Revelation, particularly his reference to "Gog and Magog" (Ezek. 38:18; Rev. 20:8), which is placed in the promised millennium, the thousand-year period of the reign of the Messiah (Barnes, 256–57). The description of the restored Temple is also echoed in Revelation, becoming more specifically God's dwelling place—his Holy City.

Other imagery has also proven influential throughout the ages: the wheels-within-wheels, the scroll that the Lord commands his prophet to eat, and the valley of the dry bones. Ezekiel himself brought together many earlier streams of imagery; he in turn served as a source for much of the literary development of early Christian writing (Begg, 219).

Ezekiel is often criticized for his emphasis on ritualism and is regarded as having laid the foundation for all the narrow pedantries of the Scribes and Pharisees (Hamilton, 192), but he was much more than a rigid Puritan. This return to strict adherence to the law and the codes of conduct developed in Hebrew tradition allowed his people a sense of continuity and cohesion.

His concern with sin, his refusal to weep for either Jerusalem or his wife make him seem cold and unyielding, but his emphasis on God's grace and his redemption of his people, the restoration of the "dry bones" reveals him to be a joyful visionary. It is he who insisted that God no longer be judged by the old proverb, "The fathers have eaten sour grapes, and the children's teeth are set on edge" (Ezek. 18:2).

Due to his extensive catalogue of the Old Testament's apocalyptic traditions, he has a distinctive place within the literary genre, as the writer who has visions and is accompanied by a guide or interpreter. This image of being lifted up and carried away appears again in Chaucer, and is an interesting portrayal of transcendent visions. In Christian literature, authors have used his image of the New Jerusalem, the Holy City (Dante, Bunyan), of Armageddon (Styron, Faulkner), of the Valley of the Dry Bones (Eliot), of the eating of the scroll (Flannery O'Connor), and of the watchman (Emily Brontë). His massive prophecies have proven rich resource for poets.

## SOURCES

Barnes, William H., "Messiah," in *The Oxford Companion to the Bible*, New York: Oxford University Press, 1993; Begg, Christopher T., "Ezekiel," in *The Oxford Companion to the Bible*, edited by Bruce M. Metzger and Michael D. Coogan, New York: Oxford University Press, 1993; Bullock, C. Hassell, *An Introduction to the Old Testament Prophetic Books*, Chicago: Moody Press, 1986; Jeffrey, David L., ed., "Ezekiel," in *A Dictionary of the Biblical Tradition in English Literature*, Grand Rapids, MI: William B. Eerdmans Publishing Company, 1992; Hamilton, Edith, *Spokesmen for God*, New York: W. W. Norton & Company, Inc., 1949; Keller, Werner, *The Bible as History*, New York: Bantam Books, 1982; Paterson, John, *The Goodly Fellowship of the Prophets*, New York: Charles Scribner's Sons, 1948.

## EZRA (ESDRAS)

**Name and Etymology.** *Ezra* means "help," and is *Esdras* in Greek and Latin.

**Synopsis of Bible Story.** Ezra was a priest who returned to Jerusalem during the reign of Artaxerxes (465–424 B.C.). He belonged to a Jewish family of high priests, was a descendent of Aaron, and was described as "a ready scribe" (Ezra 7:6).

Unlike many other Babylonian Jews, Ezra was concerned with the rebuilding of the Temple and the faith in Jerusalem. He sought and won an imperial edict permitting him to lead a pilgrimage of 1,496 men and their families to Jerusalem, taking with them the sacred vessels that had been removed earlier.

Once settled in Jerusalem, under the leadership of *Nehemiah, he led these families in the renewal of their faith, reading the law of *Moses to them, reinstituting the rituals and festivals, and exhorting them to dissolve the mixed marriages with "strange wives" (Ezra 10:11). He apparently left the families in Jerusalem, returning to Babylon, but returned to visit them in 433 B.C. He is generally believed to be the "chronicler," who brought together much contemporary history of the Jews, including the work of *Nehemiah.

**Historical Context.** The Book of Ezra, like Chronicles and Nehemiah, provides a good supply of catalogs of emigrants, official letters and documents, and details of the ritual and activity of the time. It is also an invaluable first-person account of some of the events during the time of the return of the Jews to Palestine.

Scholars believe that Ezra 1:5–6 describes the return of the Jews to Jerusalem in 539 B.C., when he led a caravan of pious Jews back to reestablish their faith and rebuild their Temple. He brought with him a large number of priests and ecclesiastics, and immediately set to purify their lives and practices. Of major concern was their temptation to marry women outside their faith, which he condemned and forbade. He issued a proclamation for a gathering, at which time he ordered the removal of all foreign wives. This action and subsequent faithfulness marked a great revival of adherence to the covenant in his day.

As both a scribe and a spiritual leader and interpreter of the law, Ezra revived in his people a zeal for the law and ceremony. He is also credited with the rise of the synagogue movement, including careful study of the Torah. He and his spiritual heirs are also thought to have influenced the final shaping of the Old Testament canon.

Their initial attempts to rebuild the Temple were apparently frustrated by their enemies. Sometime around 446–445 B.C., the Jews were forced to stop their work on the walls and buildings. Hostile neighbors not only destroyed their constructions, but also sent a message to Artaxerxes I telling him that the Jews were reestablishing a cult and fortifying their city, accusing the Jews of being a notoriously seditious people. This led the king to call for the work to stop until he should choose to allow them to resume. Later, Zerubbabel resumed the building of the Temple under the Persian king, Darius, completing it in 515 B.C.

The historical setting of the book (and of the additional materials found in the Apocrypha under Esdras 1 and 2,) is confusing, in part because ancient historians were often more interested in the presentation of a viewpoint than in chronologically ordered facts. Some scholars suspect that the events listed are not in chronological order. The book quotes from other sources, including documents of Persian origin, some written in Imperial Aramaic—the official government or chancellery language of the Persian empire.

Ezra's narrative follows the story told in 2 Chronicles, which the same author may have written. The same person apparently composed both Ezra and Nehemiah, though there is no record of these two men actually meeting. Between them, they dominate the period of the "Return" and rebuilding of the second Temple in Jerusalem.

**Archaeological Evidence.** The text of Ezra was regarded by scholars prior to Origen (third century B.C.) as a portion of the book of Nehemiah, including the materials now isolated as Esdras 1 and Esdras 2. Nehemiah probably arrived in Jerusalem c. 457 B.C., some years after Ezra departed. (*New International Version*, 667)

Recently, extrabiblical texts have been discovered that show the special interest of Persian authorities in their subjects' religious activities. The official documents and letters in Ezra's book, all in Aramaic or Hebrew, include the decree of Cyrus, the accusation of Rehum and others against the Jews, the reply of Artaxerxes, the memorandum of Cyrus's decrees, Darius's reply to Tattenai, and the authorization given by Artaxerxes I to Ezra. (See listing in *New International Version*, 662.) The combination of these documents and the autobiographical form of the book make it an invaluable though confusing source for understanding the political history of the Jews during the Persian period.

**Character in Later Works.** Ezra has become a symbol of the most orthodox form of Judaism. He is described as a purist, a priest who was faithful to his calling, and a leader who insisted on strict observance of the law, including marriage within his faith. He also represents an emotional attachment to tradition, leading the public reading of the law and preaching to the Jews regarding their guilt, bringing them both celebration of God's goodness and weeping at their own unworthiness.

As an author who presented his ideas in diary form, not intending his words to be published, he became the first writer of autobiography whose work still survives. This has become a favorite form for the cataloging of historical events—as in Samuel Pepys diary of eighteenth-century England. In recent years, diaries have become an increasingly popular form of documenting history and the lives of ordinary people in various periods.

SOURCES

Fensham, F. Charles, "Ezra," in *The Oxford Companion to the Bible*, edited by Bruce M. Metzger and Michael D. Coogan, New York: Oxford University Press, 1993; Merrill, Eugene H., *An Historical Survey of the Old Testament*, Nutley, NJ: The Craig Press, 1972; Miller, Madeline S., and J. Lane Miller, *Harper's Bible Dictionary*, New York: Harper and Row, 1961.

# G

## GIDEON (JERUBBAAL)

**Name and Etymology.** *Gideon* means "hewer"; he was also called *Jerubbaal*—"contender against Baal."

**Synopsis of Bible Story.** Judges 6–8 tells of Gideon, the son of Joash of the Manasseh clan of Abiezer, who was a modest man and a loyal leader of his people. When his region in the central highlands was invaded by marauding Midianites, Gideon was called by God to drive the nomads back to their homeland. At the time of his first experience with God, his theophany, Gideon was secretly threshing his grain in a wine press (Judg. 6:11). Confronted by an angel of the Lord, who hailed him as "mighty man of valour" and assured him that "the Lord is with thee," Gideon complained that if God was indeed with him it was not clear why bad things were happening to his people (Judg. 6:13). In a refreshingly frank exchange with the angel, Gideon learned that he was the designated savior of his people, chosen to lead them to victory over the Midianites with God's help. He responded in a hospitable gesture of preparing and offering food to his visitor, only to have this "offering" flame up when touched by the Lord's staff. This miracle convinced Gideon of the reality of the supernatural experience and of his calling.

His first assigned task was to cleanse his own people of their worship of Baal and Ashteroth. By night, Gideon tore down their pagan altars and used the materials for an altar to Jehovah; he then performed a sacrifice on the new site. The men of the town were outraged and threatened to kill him, but his father, Joash, confronted the hostile crowd, insisting that Baal could defend himself, if he was indeed a powerful god. He also challenged the crowd with death before morning if they took up arms against Gideon. In this courageous confrontation with pagan deities, Gideon won the new name *Jerubbaal*.

Ever the reluctant hero, Gideon tested God yet again, requiring two miracles involving fleece and dew, one the reversal of the other. Only after this did this judge of Israel agree to be her deliverer from Midian. Following in the footsteps of *Joshua, another God-led warrior, Gideon summoned his followers and planned his strategy with God's help, using a reduced force of men so that God might be glorified in the victory. In a series of tests, he winnowed 32,000 men down to 300 sturdy warriors. Then, carefully following the guidance of the Lord, he prepared his men, spied on the enemy camp, and organized a surprise attack using trumpets and empty jars with torches inside and shouting out of the dark at the astonished Midianites, "The sword of the Lord, and of Gideon" (Judg. 7:20). Gideon and his men then chased the army across the Jordan, over the landscape, and back to their own country.

Along the way, when two cities refused to help the hungry and weary fighters. Gideon threatened them with punishment, but continued in his headlong pursuit until the enemy was driven back along the path of the nomads. In the end, he captured the kings, and routed the entire Midianite army. He then plotted his return home, following through on his earlier threats, pulling down the tower of Peniel, killing the men of the town, thrashing the men of Succoth with desert thorns and briers, and avenging himself on those who had killed his brothers.

In a concluding act of his saga, he refused the Israelites' wish that he rule over them as king, insisting that they should look to God as their king. He asked only that each give him a gold ring for his share of the plunder. These he melted down and made into an ephod.

The final years of Gideon's life were apparently placid: he returned home and had seventy sons (including the wicked Abimelech) by his many wives and concubines. He died at a ripe old age and was buried in the tomb of his father in Ophrah.

**Historical Context.** "Midian" is the name of a desert confederation that the Bible traces back at least as far as Moses' day. Midianites, Amalekites, and other easterners from the Arabian peninsula would occasionally overrun central Palestine as far west as Gaza in search of water, food, and plunder. The revival of Midian in the days of Gideon was probably due to new waves of immigration from eastern Anatolia and northern Syria, bringing with them the domesticated camel and thus presenting a whole new military configuration (Boling, 122). Many of the Israelite homesteaders hid for safety in mountain caves and dens. Since enemies would know that harvest time was the ideal time for plundering the countryside, the opening scene, with Gideon secretly threshing his grain, would fit neatly into this context.

The judges—of whom Gideon was the fifth to be specifically named—sometimes functioned as military leaders as well as wise adjudicators of disagreements. Like the final judge, *Samuel, Gideon believed that Israel should remain a theocracy that relied on God's rule, not a kingdom that relied on God's emissary. The final elements in the story, with Gideon acting like an Oriental potentate surrounded by wives and concubines, suggest that his heroism may have led him into disobedience with Hebrew law, which implied (if not required) monogamy.

By the twelfth century B.C., the Israelites had settled in Canaan, where they tended to adopt the local fertility worship of both male and female deities. Sacred groves or sanctuaries were constant components of Canaanite religion, variously accommodated at Israelite festival centers (Boling, 134).

Ephods were originally designed for Aaron and his priestly tribe; a golden ephod would be extremely valuable and heavy, less valuable for use in worship than as a vain relic of human glory. The Hebrews, to whom any "graven image" was forbidden, found the golden "ephod" that Gideon placed to honor Jehovah to be a snare. Apparently, it became the center of a pagan worship before which the people would "prostitute themselves" (Judg. 8:27).

**Archaeological Evidence.** The region in which Gideon lived and fought is well documented by archaeologists. It is the favorite path of the caravans, a route that nomads often took. Most of the cities and physical landscapes parallel those we see in the other judges, the caves used for others who hid in the mountains, the crossing places of the Jordan paralleling references for *Joshua, the region around Shechem (modern-day Nablus) having been the traditional burial place for *Joseph, Abraham, Isaac, and Jacob. Much of this is still disputed territory between the modern Palestinians and Israelis.

**Character in Later Works.** Isaiah referred to Gideon (Isa. 9:4) as an example of God's power to act in history, protecting his people against enemies. Paul saw him as one of his great "cloud of witnesses" (Heb. 11:32; 12:1); Church fathers thought each detail of his life signified some element of the Christian experience; John Calvin used him as evidence that in every saint there is something reprehensible.

Because of Gideon's detailed confrontations with the Lord, his colorful exploits, and his interesting personality, he has often been used in literature. In religious tradition, he was seen as the ideal warrior, an antetype of Christ. Seventeenth century poets frequently referred to him or used some symbol extracted from his narrative. Both John Milton and John Bunyan made reference to him in their great works. In the eighteenth century, William Cowper found him particularly interesting as a mixture of saint and sinner. Nineteenth century authors found parallels to military events of the time. Thomas Carlyle and John Ruskin both referred to him, and Thomas Hardy speaks of the "sword of Gideon." In the twentieth century, he was the subject of a play by Paddy Chayefsky, who saw him as a conflicted modern hero.

## SOURCES

Boling, Robert G., *Judges*, The Anchor Bible Series, vol. VI-A, New York: Doubleday and Co., Inc., 1969; Comay, Joan, *Who's Who in the Bible*, vol. 2, New York: Bonanza Books, 1980; Jeffrey, David L., ed., *A Dictionary of the Biblical Tradition in English Literature*, Grand Rapids, MI: William B. Eerdmans Publishing Company, 1992.

## GOLIATH

**Name and Etymology.** "The name *Goliath* is at home in Anatolia, one of the places from which the other Sea Peoples (1 Sam. 4–53) came; it occurs only here in the older version of David's fight with the Philistine champion. . . ." (Meeks, 443).

**Synopsis of Bible Story.** Shortly after the old prophet *Samuel searched out and anointed *David, the young shepherd had his first test of valor. The Philistines had gathered their armies for battle at Socoh, in the valley of Elah, confronting the Israelites, who stood on the opposing mountain. They sent out their champion, Goliath of Gath, an enormous man almost ten feet tall, wearing elaborate mail, carrying a bronze javelin, who shouted a challenge to his adversaries. "Why are ye come out to set your battle in array? am not I a Philistine and ye servants of Saul? choose you a man for you, and let him come down to me . . ." (1 Sam. 17:8).

This hand-to-hand contest (more common among Greek heroes than Hebrews) would determine which of the two forces would serve the other. Frightened, the Israelites could not answer this braggart until young David stepped forward. He had been tending his father's sheep when his father sent him to inquire after his brothers and take them supplies. Upon hearing of Goliath's challenge and the rewards offered by King *Saul—riches and his daughter in marriage—David responded, "Who is this uncircumcised Philistine, that he should defy the armies of the living God?" (1 Sam. 17:26).

His brother Eliab sought to keep David from displaying his pride and the "naughtiness" of his heart, but the brash young hero told King Saul that he stood ready to fight the giant Philistine. Although he was still young, he had experience as a shepherd in fighting wild animals, and thought—with God's help—that he could triumph.

Saul dressed him in his own armor, but David soon discovered that another man's clothing and weapons did not suit him, choosing instead to go in his own simple garb, carrying a slingshot and five smooth stones out of the brook. Goliath was furious at the insult implied by the choice of an unarmed youth, saying to David, "Am I a dog, that thou comest to me with staves?" (1 Sam. 17:43).

But David took out a stone, "slang it," and "smote the Philistine in his forehead," felling him instantly. He then took Goliath's sword and "slew him, and cut off his head therewith." Horrified, the Philistines fled with the men of Judah in hot pursuit (1 Sam. 17:49–52).

**Historical Context.** This eleventh century B.C. tale provides early evidence of David's power and God's support. The story is important in David's narrative: the events led the jealous Saul into plots of murder, because he assumed that David would challenge him for the throne. It has even greater importance in establishing David as the hero/king who would unite the tribes of Israel into a significant power.

David's placing of Goliath's sword in the sanctuary at Nob (1 Sam. 21:9) endowed this event with religious significance—as did the God-inspired nature of his victory. His carrying of Goliath's severed head to Jerusalem (1 Sam. 17:54), though also symbolic, is surprising, since the city was not a home to the Israelites until David became king (2 Sam. 5:7). The victory over the Philistines was an essential first step toward establishing authority over the "promised land" and uniting the descendants of *Jacob into a coherent force.

**Archaeological Evidence.** The Philistines, or the "Sea Peoples," who had the culture and appearance of Aegeans, were taller than the men of Judah. They were also more sophisticated in their use of metallurgy, and probably had superior armor and weapons. Recovered skeletons and bas-reliefs prove that men as tall as Goliath lived in Palestine. The Dead Sea Scrolls and the Septuagint give Goliath's height as somewhat smaller than it is in Scripture—approximately 6'9". Carvings that depict Philistines in contrast with the Israelites do display them as looking much taller and often wearing headdresses that make them appear even larger. The weapons and armor described have interested historians, who note that there may be some symbolic meaning to the wearing and adornment of armor, symbolizing status in the ancient world.

It was in the seventh century B.C., under the Babylonian monarch *Nebuchadnezzar, that the Philistines, this once-powerful fighting force, seem to have been carried into exile with the Israelites to Babylon. At this point, they appear to have lost their ethnic identity and then simply disappeared from historical records.

David attacks Goliath, from the manuscript Hours of Engelbert of Nassau, c.1470, Flemish. The Art Archive/Bodleian Library, Oxford/The Bodleian Library, Douce 220 folio 186v.

**Character in Later Works.** The old Hebrew scholars thought Goliath was descended from *Samson; his armor had the insignia of the Canaanite deity Dagon, whose temple in Gaza Samson had demolished in his final violent act of rebellion against the

Philistines. Later, patristic commentary allegorized him as a type of Satan, contending against Christ (the descendant of David).

This classic tale of David's simple faith and cunning against superior force has long been a subject of artistic and symbolic reference. The term "David and Goliath" has entered the language as a trope for battle against apparently impossible odds. Literary artists make reference to him, but do not as a rule make him the focus of attention in their poetry. Jeffrey cites A. M. Klein's "Sling for Goliath" and Margaret Avison's *Winter Sun* poems as modern uses of this figure (315). Among the artists who have portrayed the young David facing Goliath are Donatello and Michelangelo. The giant himself usually appears as only a head, severed from the body.

## SOURCES

Avalos, Hector Ignacio, "Goliath," in *The Oxford Companion to the Bible*, edited by Bruce M. Metzger and Michael D. Coogan, New York: Oxford University Press, 1993; Jacobson, David, "When Palestine Meant Israel," in *Biblical Archaeology Review*, May/June 2001; Jeffrey, David L., ed., *A Dictionary of the Biblical Tradition in English Literature*, Grand Rapids, MI: William B. Eerdmans Publishing Company, 1992; Meeks, Wayne A., ed. *The HarperCollins Study Bible*, New Revised Standard Version. San Francisco, CA: HarperCollins, 1993; Miller, Madeline S., and J. Lane Miller. *Harper's Bible Dictionary*, New York: Harper and Row, 1961.

# HABAKKUK

**Name and Etymology.** The prophet's name is probably Babylonian and refers to a kind of garden plant. (See notes in *New International Version*, 1381). It may come from the Akkadian *hambaquau*, a fragrant herb. Luther called him *Herzer* (the embracer) as if the name were derived from the Hebrew *habaq* (to embrace; Paterson, 126).

**Synopsis of Bible Story.** Nothing is known of the prophet Habakkuk himself. According to legend, he was the son of the Shunammite woman. Some believe that he may have been a Levitical Temple musician. He may also have belonged to the professional guild of prophets attached to the Temple, thereby accounting for the final address to the "director of music" and his last words, "On my stringed instruments" (Hab. 3:19). He was clearly a philosophical prophet who, from his watchtower, surveyed the historical events of his own day and asked God piercing questions about justice and goodness. He was also a powerful poet, recording great rhetorical questions in splendid phrases, picturing God as a mighty warrior who strode in anger through the earth, threshing the nations and delivering his people to save his anointed one.

Habakkuk's prophecy is a dialogue between God and the prophet, beginning with a general complaint. The Lord responds with a promise that Judah will see punishment "in your days" (Hab. 1:5–8). In specific terms, he promises to raise up the Babylonians (or Chaldeans), "that bitter and hasty nation, which shall march through the breadth of the land to possess the dwelling-places that are not theirs. . . . Their horses also are swifter than leopards, and are more fierce than the evening wolves. . . ." This vivid portrayal of the cleansing force coming forth provokes Habakkuk to complain that God, who is the most Holy Judge, is planning to use a treacherous and wicked people and yet remain silent as they destroy a folk more righteous than they (Hab. 1:12–13).

Again, God responds to the prophet, this time portraying, in a series of "woes," a time of judgment for those who break his commandments. God commands the prophet to write down his words "that he may run that readeth it" (Hab. 2:2), and then wait for the day of judgment. Comforted, in chapter 3 the prophet ends his short book with a prayer announcing his awe of the Lord. The magnificent theophany that concludes the prophecy proclaims his trust in God's providence. As he confronts the Lord and hears his voice, he says: "When I heard, my belly trembled; my lips quivered at the voice: rottenness entered into my bones. . . ." He then goes on to proclaim, "The Lord God is my strength, and he will make my feet like hinds' feet, and he will make me to walk upon mine high places" (Hab. 3:16, 3:19).

**Historical Context.** Habakkuk, who predicted the coming Babylonian invasion, apparently lived in Judah and wrote at the end of *Josiah's reign (640–609 B.C.) The prophecy is generally dated near the time of the battle of Carchemish (605 B.C.), when Egyptian forces were routed by the Babylonians under Nabopolassar and Nebuchadnezzar and pursued as far as the Egyptian border. Habakkuk may have lived long enough to see the initial fulfillment of his prophecy when Jerusalem was attached in 597 B.C. by the Babylonians.

**Archaeological Evidence.** The popularity of the Book of Habakkuk in ancient times is proven by the presence of a commentary on its two chapters among the Dead Sea Scrolls. The scroll, two strips of leather joined with linen thread, with writing on the smoothly dressed hair side ruled with lines, is badly mutilated.

Numerous details of battle and of everyday life in the book have been verified by historians. For example, the use of the term "catch them in their net" in 1:15 refers to the custom of the Babylonians, who captured the enemy in fishnets. Other elements of the fighting techniques, such as the mounding of earth to breach walls, also match historical investigations.

The "violence in Lebanon" (2:17) may refer to the same activity that appears in Assyrian inscriptions, of hunting expeditions in the Lebanon range and of the Babylonians who apparently ravaged the cedar forests of Lebanon to adorn their temples and palaces.

**Character in Later Works.** The Apocryphal book Bel and the Dragon tells of Habakkuk's ministering to Daniel in the lions' den—obviously legendary rather than historical. In this story he is represented as Daniel's rescuer when Daniel is cast for a second time into the den.

The final words of Habakkuk, a benediction and a musical direction, suggest that the last chapter may have formed a part of temple prayers that were chanted to the accompaniment of instruments (1 Chron. 18:4–7).

Paul quotes the book in both Romans (1:17) and Galatians (3:11) in his discussions of justification by faith. Hebrews 10:37–38 identifies the vision of Habakkuk (2:2–3) with Christ and relates it to the persecuted Church. According to Rabbi Simlai, a second-century scholar, Habakkuk based all of the 613 Mosaic commandments on a single principle, "the righteous shall live by his faith" (Isaac, 177). This, in turn, was a seminal thought of the reformers, who developed the doctrine of "Justification by Faith." Martin Luther exalted it to be the watchword of the Protestant Reformation.

For such a brief book, Habakkuk is amazingly diverse in form, containing the first-person account in the dialogue between God and the prophet, liturgical and musical elements, and the concluding ode to the Lord. The image of the watchtower from which the prophet saw the vision, the hope of a messiah and a saving remnant of the people, the powerful images of justice and injustice, confidence and doubt, salvation and judgment, God and humankind—and the central question of how a pure God can bear to behold evil—these all have helped to make this tiny book a jewel invaluable to many of the faithful.

## SOURCES

Achtemeier, Elizabeth, "Habakkuk," in *The Oxford Companion to the Bible*, edited by Bruce Metzger and Michael D. Coogan, New York: Oxford University Press, 1993; Isaacs, Ronald H., *Messengers of God: A Jewish Prophets Who's Who*, Jerusalem: Jason Aronson, Inc., 1998; Miller, Madeline S., and J. Lane, *Harper's Bible Dictionary*, New York: Harper and Row, 1961; Paterson, John, *The Goodly Fellowship of the Prophets*, New York: Charles Scribner's Sons, 1948; Richards, Kent Harold, "Habakkuk: Introduction," in *The HarperCollins Study Bible*, edited by Wayne A. Meeks, San Francisco, CA: HarperCollins, 1993.

## HAGAR

**Name and Etymology.** *Hagar*, or *Agar* in the *American Version of the New Testament*, means "One who fled" or "to flee"; this name seems to be related to the Hegira or flight of the Arabian Mohammed. Although she was Egyptian, her name is Semitic.

**Synopsis of Bible Story.** Hagar, whose story appears in Genesis 16:1–4 and 21:8–21, was the Egyptian or North Arabian maidservant, apparently given to *Abram by the Pharaoh. Abram in turn gave the woman to *Sarai as a bondswoman. When Sarai found herself still barren after many years of waiting, although God had promised that Abram would be the father of multitudes, she gave Hagar to her husband as a surrogate wife. Apparently younger and more fecund than Sarai, Hagar soon became pregnant and held her mistress in scorn. Offended, Sarai demanded that Abram choose between them. Her husband gave Sarai permission to do as she pleased with her maid, and Sarai apparently abused her to the point that Hagar fled into the wilderness of Shur.

In this time of trouble, an angel of the Lord came to Hagar and announced that she would bear a son, whom she would call "*Ishmael," "a wild man; his hand will be against every man, and every man's hand against him; and he shall dwell in the presence of all his brethren" (Gen. 16:11–12). Comforted by this mixed prophecy, she named the place of her meeting with God "Beerlahairoi" ("the well of him that liveth and seeth me").

God commanded her to return to her mistress and "submit." Scripture does not chronicle that, but she did bear the son and raise him with Abram's family; when he was thirteen, he was circumcised with the rest of the men (17:23) and was present at the time of Sarah's son, *Isaac's, birth.

As a member of the clan, Ishmael was also one of the guests when Isaac was weaned. It is at this point that the contention between the two women once again flared, this time because Ishmael "mocked" *Isaac (21:9). In a repetition of the earlier argument, Sarah once again demanded that this bondswoman be cast out, adding that "the son of this bondswoman shall not be heir with my son." Once again, Abraham acquiesced to his wife's demands, this time with the comfort from God that this "son of a bondswoman will . . . make a nation" because he was Abraham's seed (Gen. 21:13).

Sent into the wilderness of Beersheba with modest supplies, Hagar soon ran out of water and found that Ishmael was unable to continue. She put the young man in the shade and settled down at a distance, weeping, to await his death. Again she was rewarded with a theophany. The Lord responded to Hagar's cries, commanded her to lift up her son, and she opened her eyes to a well of water. She quickly brought water to Ishmael and revived him.

The story ends with Ishmael's career in the wilderness as an archer and Hagar's later journey to Egypt—her home—to find him a wife from among her people. Her death is not chronicled.

**Historical Context.** The Midrash, the ancient Hebrew commentary on Genesis, makes Hagar "Pharaoh's daughter." Bondage was a standard part of Hebrew life throughout much of the Old Testament and continued in Roman times. A female slave of child-bearing age was considered particularly valuable. In later Hebrew law, following the patriarchal precedent, foreign slaves could be enslaved permanently. Ordinarily, a person could be enslaved by capture, by purchase, or by birth. While Hagar may have been a captive prior to being a gift to Abram and then to Sarai, her son would be a slave by birth. Apparently, the abandonment by Sarai would have served as an act of liberation for both Hagar and her son.

The contest between the two women is a preparation for the historical conflict between their sons' descendants—the Israelites and the Ishmaelites—or the modern Jews and Arabs.

**Archaeological Evidence.** The Code of Hammurabi contains a close parallel to the strange relationship among Abram, Sarai, and Hagar, allowing for a man to substitute a bondswoman for his wife in order to produce a legal heir. Tablets from Ur and Nuzi testify to this custom among the people of the Near East.

In recent days, one of the most remarkable discoveries has been that Arabs and Jews do indeed share a common genetic marker, suggesting that they do come from a single forebear.

**Character in Later Works.** The relationship between these two strong women, each of whom became the mother of a dynasty, has fascinated scholars over the years. Jewish scholars elaborated on the Biblical account, adding adventures in Egypt and Gerar. Amplified stories of Hagar appear in both the Talmud and Islamic writings. The only other Old Testament references to Hagar and her descendants are in 1 Chronicles 5:10, and Psalm 83:6, where they are referred to as "Hagrites" and "Ishmaelites," enemies of the Israelites. Ezra 10:3 refers to a custom, probably derived from Hagar's example, that allows mothers who have been divorced to retain custody of their children.

Paul saw Sarah and Hagar as allegories of two different covenants, the old covenant of the law and the new covenant of the promise. In Galatians 4:21–31 and 1 Peter 3:6, we see Sarah as a symbol of faith and obedience, foreshadowing Mary because of the miraculous nature of her child's conception. In his writings, St. Augustine described Hagar as an image of the earthly city, continuing Paul's allegorical treatment.

For nineteenth- and twentieth-century writers, Hagar has become a rich example of the slave woman. Harriet Beecher Stowe in *Uncle Tom's Cabin* gave this name to the devoted old slave mother whom Tom meets on his journey south. Having seen all her children sold off into slavery, she begs for her final son, who is mercilessly wrenched from her hands. The painful relationship between the legal wife and the slave has proven a prophetic commentary on the life among white and black women in the American South under slavery. A number of southern writers have used Hagar's role as concubine/slave to describe the experience of African American slave women. The complicity of Sarah in this abuse of another woman parallels the Southern slave-owner's deliberate blindness to the obvious miscegenation on plantations. In the nineteenth and twentieth centuries, Hagar became the heroine of a "spate of quasi-historical fictions" (Jeffrey, 326). She clearly has the qualities that elicit sympathy and admiration, ideal for romantic novels.

More recently, the curious relationship between the two women is explored in a modern feminist novel, *The Handmaid's Tale* by Margaret Atwood. Atwood approached this as a patriarchal narrative that focuses on the woman as the nurturer of the seed, in which the barren woman is required to produce an heir through a surrogate's womb. In this case, the Hagar figure is an independent woman who is taken captive and forced into a slave relationship—a modern equivalent of the Egyptian captive, though considerably exaggerated. Another Canadian writer, Margaret Laurence, in her novel *The Stone Angel*, named her heroine Hagar, and Hagar's husband Bram, again suggesting Biblical parallels.

## SOURCES

Graves, Robert and Raphael Patai, *Hebrew Myths: The Book of Genesis*, New York: McGraw-Hill Book Company, 1963; Jeffrey, David L., ed., *A Dictionary of the Biblical Tradition in English Literature*, Grand Rapids, MI: William B. Eerdmans Publishing Company, 1992; Kitchen, K. A., "Hagar," and Judge E. A., "Slave," in *The Illustrated Bible Dictionary*, vols. 2 and 3, edited by J. D. Douglas, Sidney, Australia: Tyndale House Publishers, 1980; Miller, Madeline S., and J. Lane Miller, *Harper's Bible Dictionary*, New York: Harper and Row, 1964.

## HAGGAI

**Name and Etymology.** *Haggai* derives from the Hebrew "festal," perhaps "born on a feast day."

**Synopsis of Bible Story.** Haggai prophesied in the second year of Darius the Persian (c. 520 B.C.) for three months. His audience comprised the pioneers who were seeking to rebuild Jerusalem, and who had discovered that the promises of *Ezekiel and *Isaiah, which had spurred them to return from exile, were not being fulfilled. Harvests were poor and there was a drought in the land. He linked the struggles of the community in Jerusalem to the fact that the Lord's house remained a ruin: "Is it a time for you, O ye, to dwell in your cieled [paneled] houses, and this house lie waste?" (Hag. 1:4). Haggai insisted that, if they wanted prosperity and fertility, they must, "Go up to the mountain and bring wood, and build the house" (Hag. 1:8).

A short narrative section in this book tells of the energized community that responded to Haggai's preaching, and did begin work on the Temple under the leadership of Zerubbabel, the governor, and Joshua, the high priest (Hag. 1:12). Haggai continued to encourage them with assurances that Yahweh was present in the task and was measuring their work and insisting that they give careful thought to this construction (Hag. 2:15–19). God also promised to bless the remnant doing his work.

Haggai also predicted the coming of God's reign as universal king, a time of divine judgment, when God would overthrow the kingdoms of the world and the Jews would again be an independent nation. Then the new Temple would shine with a splendor greater than that of Solomon's Temple, filled with the glory of God—"for I have chosen thee," declared the Lord Almighty (Hag. 2:23).

**Historical Context.** We know nothing about Haggai the man except what is revealed in his book of prophecy. Hebrew tradition declares, on the one hand, that he had priestly connections, was a member of the Great Synagogue, and was born in Babylon during the Exile, and, on the other hand, that he was an old man who remembered the splendor of the Temple and the city before its destruction (Miller, 241).

This sixth century B.C. postexilic Hebrew prophet played a part in the life of Jerusalem after the return of the Jews from Babylonian captivity in the time of *Cyrus, king of Persia. In the summer of 520 B.C., Haggai, along with *Zechariah, brought moral pressure to bear on the Jews, forcing the resumption of work on the destroyed Temple. The Temple was completed in 515 B.C., but we learn no more about it from Haggai after his three short months of preaching.

**Archaeological Evidence.** This book vividly presents the social and economic conditions of Jerusalem sixteen years after the first return of the Jews from the Babylonian captivity. Although the crops were suffering, the pilgrims had found time and energy to rebuild their ruined residences. From the reference to the "paneled" homes, we assume that there were luxurious private homes. By contrast, these Jews had done little work on the rebuilding of the Temple. The message from God in the second chapter suggests that they had been shortchanging the reconstruction, refusing to live up to their promises.

A Persian silver coin minted in Jerusalem, probably in the sixth century B.C., shows the combination of the imperial eagle and the Aramaic name for Judah (Comay, 145). This provides some evidence of the combined governance of Judah in postexilic times. The history of the rebuilding of the Temple is, of course, well documented in Scripture.

**Character in Later Works.** The concept of the Temple as God's house, a place of his eventual enthronement, was to resonate throughout history. The image of God as a glorious king above all kings inspired Handel's *Messiah* which proclaims him, "King of Kings." The image of the Day of the Lord, when the glory of the Temple would shine forth in splendor was part of the inspiration for the gorgeous medieval cathedrals, flooded with light and sparking with gold (Hag. 2:77–9). The contrasting curse on the land as a result of human iniquity is a recurrent image in Western literature echoing *Ezekiel's Valley of the Dry Bones. From the earliest New Testament documents, through the Book of Revelation, to the image of the wasteland in modern literature, we can see the powerful influence of Haggai's vision (Hag. 1:11).

SOURCES

Comay, Joan, *Who's Who in the Bible*, vol. 1, New York: Bonanza Books, 1980; Mason, Rex, "Haggai," in *The Oxford, Companion to the Bible*, edited by Bruce Metzger and Michael D. Coogan, New York: Oxford University Press, 1993; Miller, Madeline S., and J. Lane Miller, *Harper's Bible Dictionary*, New York: Harper and Row, 1961.

# HANNAH

**Name and Etymology.** *Hannah* comes from the Hebrew word for "grace."

**Synopsis of Bible Story.** In the first two chapters of 1 Samuel, we learn of an Ephraimite woman named Hannah who mourned because of her barrenness. Her husband, Elkanah, had two wives. The other one, Peninnah, had children and taunted

Hannah. This was a family who went regularly to pray at Shiloh. Because he loved her and joined in her sorrow at her failure to bear children, her husband favored Hannah by giving her double portions of the meat.

Finally, after many years of listening to her rival's taunts and witnessing her husband's distress, she refused to eat. In "bitterness of soul" she finally made a vow before Eli the priest, who was sitting in their midst, saying: "O Lord of hosts, if thou wilt indeed look on the affliction of thine handmaid and remember me, and not forget thine handmaid, but wilt give unto thine handmaid a man child, then I will give him unto the Lord all the days of his life, and there shall no razor come upon his head" (1 Sam. 1:11). Her prayer continued with her lips moving, but no sound came forth and the priest believed her to be drunk. She explained that she was deeply troubled, pouring out her soul to the Lord: "Count not thine handmaid for a daughter of Belial: for out of the abundance of my complaint and grief have I spoken hitherto" (1 Sam. 1:16).

Eli blessed her and prayed God's blessing on her. Comforted, she ate, slept, and worshipped at the shrine before returning home. Subsequently, she became pregnant and gave birth to a son, whom she named *Samuel, "Because I have asked him of the Lord" (1 Sam. 1:20). Honoring her obligation, she waited the traditional three years until he was weaned and then took the boy with her to Shiloh, along with a three-year-old bull, an ephah (3/5 bushel) of flour, and a skin of wine. After a sacrificial ceremony, she brought the boy to Eli, dedicating him to the Lord for his whole life. The prayer of rejoicing and triumph over her enemies that follows is properly famous: "My heart rejoiceth in the Lord, mine horn is exalted in the Lord. . . ." (1 Sam. 2:1).

The child remained at Shiloh with Eli, serving God and ministering to the priest. Hannah came each year, bringing a little robe she had made, and offering animal sacrifice. Eli blessed her, praying that she would have other children to replace the one she had dedicated to the Lord. "And the Lord visited Hannah, so that she conceived, and bare three sons and two daughters," while the boy Samuel grew up in the presence of the Lord (1 Sam. 2:21).

**Historical Context.** Three times a year every Israelite male was required to appear before the Lord at a central sanctuary (Exod. 23:14–19, 34:23; Deut. 16:16–17). The Festival of Tabernacles, which is probably the one this family attended, commemorated God's care for his people during the desert journey to Canaan as well as gratitude for the year's crops. At a "fertility" celebration, it would have made Hannah particularly aware of her own barrenness.

The vow Hannah made dedicated her son as a Nazirite for a lifetime rather than a limited period, which was more common. Nazirites, who did not cut their hair and refrained from strong drink, were seen consecrated men and women.

**Archaeological Evidence.** The town of Ramathaim-zophim, in the hill country of Ephraim on the western slopes of the Judean hills, was also near the place where *Saul died and where *Joseph of Arimathea had his home.

Shiloh was a religious center for the tribes, the place where Joshua set up the tabernacle of the congregation (Josh. 18:10). It was still well known in the Middle Ages, and in the nineteenth century, it was correctly identified with Khirbet Seilun, about 20 miles north of Jerusalem. Negev notes that the mound is about 12 acres in area and contains the remains of biblical Shiloh. Trial digs were made there by various archaeologists over the years and have been renewed as late as the eighties by Bar-Ilan

University. A variety of remains have been discovered, but not the shrine itself (Negev, 346).

**Character in Later Works.** Hannah is regarded in Jewish tradition as a prophetess. Later writers noted the relationship between the way Eli judged her prayers the result of strong drink and the events of the Pentecost, when once again religious inspiration was thought by spectators to be drunken behavior.

Her exultant song has been widely translated and adapted, and is thought to have been the model for the Magnificat of the Virgin *Mary (Luke 1:46–55). Augustine, noting that her name means "grace," saw her as an example of the "pious mother" or a type of the true Church. In Latin, her name was translated as "Anna."

She rarely appears in English or American literature or art, although her name has become a common choice for baby girls.

### SOURCES

Jeffrey, David L., ed., *A Dictionary of the Biblical Tradition in English Literature*, Grand Rapids, MI: William B. Eerdmans Publishing Company, 1992; Negev, Avraham, ed., *The Archaeological Encyclopedia of the Holy Land*, revised edition, New York: Thomas Nelson Publishers, 1986.

## HEROD

**Name and Etymology.** *Herod* is the name of a dynasty of princes who ruled from c. 55 B.C. to c. A.D. 93; they may have come from Ashkelon. They were not Jews, but Idumaeans from Edom (the land associated with Esau; Miller, 254).

**Synopsis of Bible Story.** Several of the Herods impacted New Testament stories. It is thought to have been Herod the Great (in power from 37 B.C. to 4 B.C.) who ruled at the time of *Jesus' birth. A bloodthirsty man, he was clearly capable of ordering the Slaughter of the Innocents (Matt. 2:1). Archelaus (Herod the Ethnarch) replaced him on the throne from 4 B.C. to A.D. 6, but was not given the title "king" (Matt. 2:22).

It was Herod the Tetrarch (Antipas) (Luke 3:19) who was responsible for the imprisonment and execution of *John the Baptist (Mark 6:14–28). He was also the Herod to whom Jesus was sent by *Pilate in an effort to force Jewish authorities to sentence him (Luke 23:7–10). *Luke also mentions that Jesus referred to Herod Antipas as "that fox" (Luke 13:31). And finally, it was "Herod the king," otherwise known as Agrippa, who attacked the apostles (Acts 12:1–6). His death (". . . he was eaten of worms") is recorded by Luke (Acts 12:20–23).

His son Agrippa, born in A.D. 27 was given the title of "king" by Claudius and was the Herod before whom *Paul was brought. In this encounter (Acts 25:13–26–32), he listened to Paul's defense of his faith and laughingly noted that the apostle was trying to make a Christian of him (Acts 26:28).

**Historical Context.** The Herods were brought to power by the Romans, who used them as a replacement for the powerful Hasmonaean house, which was in decline at the time. They were generally resented in Judea as foreigners and as tools of Roman power. They apparently understood how to keep the Jews in order, protect their own positions, and build massive monuments to themselves and to Rome.

Herod the Great was the most flamboyant of them all, building great fortresses such as Massada and Jericho, as well as in Jerusalem. In Jerusalem he also built himself a grand palace and rebuilt the Temple. He proved his ruthlessness by killing many of his

Herod's banquet (detail). The Art Archive/Klosterneuburg Monastery, Austria/Dagli Orti.

own family, including sons, a wife, and other relatives whom he thought to be threats to his own authority.

His son Herod Antipas demonstrated some of the same traits, building the great city of Tiberius to honor the emperor, and involving himself with a complicated pattern of marriage, divorce, and incest that John the Baptist criticized—at his own peril. The famous scene of Salome's Dance of the Seven Veils and the beheading of John the Baptist has made this tyrant the most famous of the Herod family in art and in literature.

Herod Agrippa apparently worked to avoid the Jewish uprising against Rome in A.D. 66, choosing to remain loyal to Rome rather than Judea, thus increasing his own power. He died childless in A.D. 100, thus ending the long and bloody dynasty (Bruce, 644–5).

**Archaeological Evidence.** Israel has many relics of the century of Herodian rule, bits of their vast building programs scattered over the entire country, most of them in ruin. Excavations have revealed much of the lifestyle of the era, including the lavish entertainment and rich decoration. Records, coins, historical accounts, and statues make this a fully documented period in history. Among the most interesting subjects for archaeologists are the designs for the Temple and the Temple Mount.

Historical accounts date from the first century, when Josephus celebrated Herod for his creation of the magnificent seaport of Caesarea. Augustus Caesar is thought to have noted, when discussing Herod's vicious behavior with his family, "I had rather be Herod's pig than Herod's son" (Tamburr and Murphy, 351).

**Character in Later Works.** A villain in all of Christian history, Herod the Great is often portrayed in literature as a ranting maniac. His encounter with the *Magi and his Slaughter of the Innocents are frequent themes in paintings. Salome's dance and the beheading of John the Baptist by Herod Antipas have also served subjects as melodramatic for generations of artists. Karl Tamburr and Michael Murphy trace the evolving character of Herod through the medieval mystery plays into the culture that Chaucer describes, demonstrating how the various Herods are conflated over time into a single vicious figure capable of any action. Herods are often given an Italian accent and have a tendency to shout at subordinates. The hideous death, "a fearful combination of palsy, itch, leprosy, dropsy, and other ailments," (Tamburr and Murphy, 351) which was apparently suffered by Herod Agrippa I is attributed to Herod the Great and used as a symbol of God's judgment on him for the Slaughter of the Innocents (Tamburr and Murphy, 351).

### SOURCES

Bruce, F. F., "Herod," in *The Illustrated Bible Dictionary*, vol. 2, edited by J. D. Douglas, Sidney, Australia: Tyndale House Publishers, 1980; Miller, Madeline S., and J. Lane Miller, *Harper's Bible Dictionary*, New York: Harper and Row, 1961; Tamburr, Karl, and Michael Murphy, "Herod," in *A Dictionary of the Biblical Tradition in English Literature*, edited by David L. Jeffrey, Grand Rapids, MI: William B. Eerdmans Publishing Company, 1992.

## HOSEA

**Name and Etymology.** *Hosea* means "salvation" or "savior."

**Synopsis of Bible Story.** Hosea, son of Beeri, was a contemporary of *Amos, one of the earliest of the so-called "writing prophets." He apparently prophesied for thirty-eight years, primarily in the Northern Kingdom, Israel—a land he knew and loved. His speech, which is full of images of the soil, suggests that he may have been a peasant farmer. He knew about flax and wool, grapes, figs and olives, weeds, and harvests.

Commanded by God to wed a prostitute, Hosea married Gomer, daughter of Diblaim, who conceived and bore him a son named Jezreel. The next child, a daughter, was named Lo-Ruhamah, and the third, a son, was named Lo-Ammi. Each of the names symbolized a dire prophecy for the people of Israel. Gomer's infidelity led to a separation, followed by a reconciliation, when Hosea was instructed to "Go, show your love to your wife again, though she is loved by another and is an adulteress" (Hos. 3:1). This act of grace became a symbol of God's redemptive love for Israel, a people who "whored" after other gods, yet were continually loved and redeemed by Jehovah.

The final part of the story is the judgment and prophecy that Hosea carried to Israel over his long ministry, warning of the impending judgment on this errant people unless they should repent. "For they have sown the wind, and they shall reap the whirlwind," Hosea told them, in his most famous poetic proclamation (Hos. 8:7). He recalled for them the long history of Jehovah's love for Israel and his continuing disappointment, leading finally to their destruction unless they should turn from their evil ways. Even after cataloguing Israel's many sins, Hosea nonetheless felt a deep sorrow over their exile from their hereditary land.

**Historical Context.** Hosea's descriptions of the sins of Israel and her rulers match the events of the eighth century B.C. In his lifetime, four kings were assassinated in twenty years. His warnings to Judah suggest that part of the prophecy was written after Assyrian attacks, in hopes that the fate of the Northern Kingdom would serve to bring Judah to repentance before it was too late. Hosea's repeated use of "Ephraim" for Israel in the latter part of the book suggests that the Israel was by then narrowed to the central highlands.

The home of the prophet seems to have been in the hill country between Bethel and Jerusalem; his original habitation may have been east of the Jordan, a place of religious conservatism, "for the religion of Jehovah kept its pristine purity on the borders of the wilderness and in the desert" (Paterson, 38–39).

It is not entirely clear what is meant by "prostitute" in Hosea. Gomer may have been a cult prostitute, typical of Canaanite religion, connected with the fertility worship of these people. This is an unusual term for these cultic officers, according to some critics. The term "sacred prostitute" simply means "consecrated person." Sections of the prophecy, however, seem to refer quite specifically to cult prostitutes (Hos. 4:14).

Under Hebrew law, prostitution was a crime punishable by death (Gen. 38:24; Deut. 22:20–21). Apparently, there was also a tolerated class of people set apart for this sexual service, but priests were forbidden to marry prostitutes or to force their daughters into prostitution (Lev. 19:29, 21:7). On the other hand, the term may have had a broader interpretation, as we know from Rahab, who was seen as heroic and may have been nothing more sinister than an innkeeper.

**Archaeological Evidence.** Quotations from the book of Hosea (2:8–9, 10–14) are among the treasures discovered among the Dead Sea Scrolls in Qumran, Cave 4 (photograph in *The Illustrated Bible Dictionary*, vol. 2, 664).

There is ample evidence of the invasion by the Assyrians in 734 B.C., ending in the crushing of Israel in 711 B.C. The metaphors of sickness and sores referred to in Hosea 5:13 finds archaeological backing in Assyrian records, which tell of the tribute paid to Tiglath-Pileser III by the Israelite kings Menahem and Hoshea (2 Kings 15:19–20). (See *New International Version* notes, 1320.)

Regarding the fertility cults of the Caananites (referred to in Hosea 4:13–14), a number of images of Baal have been uncovered that indicate that silver and gold were used to craft images of him, in hopes of controlling the weather and leading to the fecundity of the crops and the people. Ancient Ugarit texts and later writings of Eusebius, the early Christian historian, testify to the religious practices of the Caananites that Hosea was protesting.

**Character in Later Works.** Hosea had a profound influence on *Jeremiah, perhaps because of his connection with Benjamin. They shared a vision of God's judgment, his anger, and his forgiveness.

The nature and reality of Hosea's marriage has been a continuing puzzle to critics, who love the poetry and power of the book. *Paul and other early commentators on the story (Rom. 9:25–26) see Hosea's life as partially symbolic, pointing to the New Testament fulfillments, whereas moderns believe that the actual torments of Hosea's life made him more sensitive to the anguish of God in his troubled relationship with his chosen people, focusing more on the psychological interpretation. A famous classical scholar, for example, says, "Hosea's greatness is that he rejected the idea of power as divine and the idea of anything else as divine except the perfect goodness of perfect love" (Hamilton, 120).

Numerous scholars have tried to determine whether Gomer was a prostitute before she married Hosea or a weak woman who became unfaithful immediately after their wedding. The suggestion is that she may have borne him the first child, but the others were products of her forbidden lovers. Whatever the case, the New Testament takes a fresh look at prostitutes, who are grouped with tax collectors as representing the lowest class in moral terms (Matt. 21:31–32). Yet *Jesus invited them to follow him and seek forgiveness.

The use of this imagery of whoredom is richly developed in the book of Revelation, with the whore of Babylon (Rev. 17:1, 18:3). Thus, Hosea's love for his weak and wicked wife becomes a great symbol of God's love for his people.

Hosea's love of the land, the flowers and fruits, the animals and the geography suggest that he was a country man, concerned with details of wind and weather. His parallel concern with the political life of the times led him into an extended parable, transforming his domestic anguish into a powerful allegory of God's redeeming love. His influence is clear in the echoes of his book in Jeremiah and in the extensive quotations from his book in the New Testament. (There are more than 30 direct and indirect quotations in the Gospels and Epistles.)

Generally, Hosea reappears in literary tradition as a name and a parable with a few quotations, rather than as a character who serves as a central figure in stories or plays. In modern times, he has appealed to Thomas Hardy (in *Tess of the d'Urbervilles*), Robert Louis Stevenson (in *Kidnapped*), and Isaac Bashevis Singer (in "Gimpel the Fool"). (See longer listing in Laurence Eldredge's entry on "Hosea," in *A Dictionary of the Biblical Tradion in English Literature*, 364–65).

In recent feminist criticism, his imagery is considered "prophetic pornography." J. Cheryl Exum considers the masculine image of God and the wife/prostitute image of Israel, with the critique of the fallen woman to be symptomatic of the whole culture and its abhorrence of women. She even suggests that the prophet—and his culture— encourage sexual aggression and violence against the "transgressive" women, who show signs of lust and fail to act in a sufficiently submissive manner. (See Exum, 100ff.) This critique includes the use of parallel imagery in *Ezekiel. It would also appear to miss the tormented tone of Hosea, a husband who was deeply in love with the woman who repeatedly betrayed him.

## SOURCES

Baldwin, J. G., "Hosea," in *The Illustrated Bible Dictionary*, vol. 2, Sidney, Australia: Tyndale House Publishers, 1980; Bullock, C. Hassell, *An Introduction to the Old Testament Prophetic Books*, Chicago: Moody Press, 1986; Eldredge, Laurence, "Hosea," in *A Dictionary of the Biblical Tradition in English Literature*, edited by David L. Jeffrey, Grand Rapids, MI: William B. Eerdmans Publishing Company, 1992; Exum, J. Cheryl, *Plotted, Shot, and Painted: Cultural Representations of Biblical Women*, Sheffield, England: Sheffield Academic Press, 1996; Hamilton, Edith, *Spokesmen for God*, New York: W. W. Norton and Company, Inc., 1949; Isaacs, Ronald H., *Messengers of God: A Jewish Prophets Who's Who*, Jerusalem: Jason Aronson, Inc., 1998; Miller, Madeline S., and J. Lane Miller, *Harper's Bible Dictionary*, New York: Harper and Row, 1961; Paterson, John, *The Goodly Fellowship of Prophets*, New York: Charles Scribner's Sons, 1948.

# I

## ISAAC

**Name and Etymology.** *Isaac* derives from the Hebrew word for "he laughs." This may be based on Sarah's laughter when she heard she would bear a son at her advanced age or it may signal the joy she and Abraham felt at this promised birth.

**Synopsis of Bible Story.** Isaac was a major figure in the line of the Patriarchs, the long anticipated heir, the beloved son, "emphatically the child of promise" (Fairbairn, 155) and later the prosperous and pious old man. Although successful and decent, he seems to have been more a caretaker than a hero; he was a stable, loving, forgiving, faithful man. One of his few critics, Alexander Whyte, notes that he was but a "pale appearance" between such powerful figures as his father and his son Jacob, a man more honored for the pious gesture of his youth than in his old age, when he became the gluttonous old man, who lay blind, sulky, and peevish except when his favorite son brought him a dish of savory venison (93–99).

The son of *Abraham and *Sarah late in their long marriage, Isaac was promised by angelic visitors (Gen. 17:19). Sarah, delighted at his birth and at her ability to provide milk for him, celebrated his weaning—probably when he was about two or three years of age—with an event that precipitated an argument with *Ishmael and his mother, *Hagar (Gen. 21). She demanded that Abraham designate Isaac, rather than his first born—Ishmael—to be his heir. When Abraham was later instructed to sacrifice his "only son" on Mount Moriah (Gen. 22:2), he assumed that this would be Isaac. The young man accompanied his father, ignorant of his own role as the intended sacrificial lamb, asking innocently about the animal that they would need (Gen. 22:8). After carrying the wood for the fire, Isaac was tied on the altar and watched his father raise the knife to slay him. Then followed the miraculous interruption, the substitution of the ram, and the release from the impending horror.

In the story of marriage, he proved, once again, to be a passive figure. Abraham, apparently concerned that Isaac remain in the land the Lord had promised Abraham and his seed, sent a servant back to their home to find a suitable wife for Isaac. When *Rebekah, Abraham's grandniece, offered water not only for the parched servant, but also for his camels, she demonstrated a graciousness and hospitality that impressed the servant, who rewarded her with jewelry. The servant subsequently went to her home and offered more gifts, requesting that she return with him to Canaan and marry his master. Isaac was forty years old when he saw the young Rebekah for the first time, took her to his mother's tent, and married her (Gen. 25:20).

The following years repeat the pattern of his father's marriage—the barren wife, the prayer for an heir, and—after 20 years—God's gracious response. At the time when Isaac's twin sons, *Esau and *Jacob, were born, God told the proud parents of their sons' futures, including that the older would serve the younger. This reversal of the standard order of

Sacrifice of Isaac—Abraham restrained by angel, c.1630. The Art Archive/Museo del Prado, Madrid/Album/Joseph Martin.

the sons' inheritance repeated the earlier pattern in the lives of Isaac and his older brother Ishmael. In another echo from an earlier story, when there was a famine in the land, Isaac went with Rebekah to Gerar and—like his father—pretended to Abimelech that the woman he was with was not his wife, repeating Abraham's lie and rationale—that a beautiful woman was a treasure for which a ruler would kill. When Abimelech saw the couple embracing, he castigated Isaac for trying to fool him and taking a chance of leading his people into sinful activity.

Like Abraham, Isaac was prosperous; like him, he dug wells and avoided quarrels whenever possible. He also made treaties, worshipped God, and built altars to honor the Lord. He also was close to God, experiencing theophanies—direct meetings with God (Gen. 26:23–25). Like Abraham, he also had a son, Esau, who married foreign women (Hittites). And he also arranged for the marriage of his second son, Jacob, to a woman from Paddan Aram.

His sons also struggled for his favor, but in Isaac's case, the triumph of Jacob was due largely to the plotting of Rebekah. She tricked the old, blind patriarch into giving his blessing to Jacob by eavesdropping on Isaac's private conversation with Esau, disguising Jacob, and coaching her favorite in his deceit. The old man was suspicious, checking the feel and smell of the visitor, but finally fell into the trap and gave the blessing to the wrong son. Isaac, saddened that his beloved Esau would not be his heir, nonetheless was faithful to his word.

When he died, at 180, his sons came together for his burial (Gen. 35:29).

**Historical Context.** This hard-working and gentle man, who seemed totally lacking in heroics or glamour, was the right man for the period, conforming perfectly when he was required to settle the land God had given his father. Rather than leaving to marry—as was the usual practice at the time, when marriages were matrilocal (husbands lived with their wives' families)—he married the woman chosen for him, and had her brought to his own country. When famine struck, he remained in the land, holding firmly to the promise. In a time when there was little law, when might made right, land ownership depended on populating and defending the property. Isaac was not a pioneer, but was rather a man who redug his father's wells, preserved the family, and made peace with his neighbors (Gen. 26:18).

The portrait of the pitiful old Isaac in his tent anticipating his death is made more poignant by his blindness and the manner in which his wife and younger son dishonored him by finding a devious means to circumvent his will. Among many ancient peoples, blindness was a common problem in old age (*New International Version* notes, Gen. 27:1). Old people were usually honored for their wisdom among the Hebrews and retained the authority in the family.

**Archaeological Evidence.** The sacrifice of the firstborn son was common among the Canaanites (See 2 Kings 3:26–27). Some believe that circumcision of the male child replaced this brutal offering of the sons of the Ammonites to Molech (Lev. 18:21, 20:2). Archaeologists note the relation of the statues of rams found in Sumerian art to the ram that God provides for substitutionary sacrifice for the firstborn son. They also cite parallels to the Cadmean story of Athamas and Phrixus in Greek myth (Athamas was ordered by Apollo's priestess to sacrifice his son Phrixus in order to restore fertility to the land, but Heracles interrupted the ritual, substituting a golden fleeced ram sent by Zeus.) (Graves and Patai, 174–76).

The Nuzi, from Larsa in the Old Babylonian period and from Assyria in the Middle Assyrian period, had texts testifying to the importance of primogeniture. The firstborn son was provided at least a double share of the inheritance.

Apparently, among the ancient Israelites, oral statements, including deathbed bequests, had legal standing, perhaps even magical power (*New International Version* notes, Gen. 27:4). This would explain Isaac's refusal to reverse his pronouncement of the blessing.

**Character in Later Works.** As one in the line of Patriarchs, Isaac was usually included in lists throughout both the Old and New Testaments. Jehovah is often referred to as the God of "Abraham, Isaac, and Jacob," the God of your fathers. Isaac's selection by his father and Jacob's selection, in turn, both violating the rule of primogeniture, were interpreted by *Paul as proof of God's sovereign right to choose by grace alone (Rom. 9:6–13).

There were extrabiblical tales that supplemented the story of Abraham's sacrifice of his beloved son, Isaac. One was that the boy was taken away to paradise, where he dwelled for three years studying God's law (Graves and Patai, 174). The experience of the binding of Isaac—known as the *Aqedah*—was associated with the site of the Temple, and Isaac emerged as the paradigm of the martyr and the perfect sacrifice, bringing merit and redemptive value to his descendants. The New Testament refers to the Aqedah as an example of redemptive faith as well as action (Hebrews 11:17–19; James 2:21). It is also thought that Isaac's sacrifice bore relationship to the death and resurrection of *Jesus. The early Church Fathers Clement and Tertullian understood it in this manner (Nathanson, 43).

While Christians interpreted Isaac as the sacrificial lamb, foreshadowing Christ, the "Lamb of God" (John 1:29, 36), early Muslim exegetes disagreed. By the tenth century, it was the consensus among Islamic scholars that Ishmael, the ancestor of the northern Arabs, was the voluntary sacrificial offering. That argument continues as the great religions battle over the site of the sacrifice, the Temple Mount in Jerusalem. Even today, the Jewish New Year ritual commemorates the binding of Isaac with the blowing of the ram's horn.

Wall paintings, statues, and paintings by such artists as Ghiberti, Donatello, Titian, Caravaggio, and Rembrandt have portrayed the Aqedah in dramatic forms.

In literature, the story of the binding of Isaac and the tricks of Jacob became standard fare in medieval plays, which tended to focus on the son rather than the father. One English mystery, the Townley play, and several other lesser-known plays from later periods dealt with the powerful sacrificial story. In the seventeenth century, Isaac was frequently mentioned in poetry, but was not a central figure. Novelists and philosophers have also used the image of the sacrifice effectively. Sir Walter Scott used Isaac of York as a key figure in his novel *Ivanhoe*. Probably the most thoughtful consideration of the feelings and meanings involved in the sacrificial event is Søren Kierkegaard's philosophical meditation, *Fear and Trembling*. In the sacrifice of Isaac, demanded of Abraham, Kierkegaard saw a transgression of deeply held ethical values as proof of faith.

## SOURCES

Fairbairn, Patrick, *Imperial Standard Bible Encyclopedia*, vol. 3, Grand Rapids, MI: Zondervan, 1957; Graves, Robert, and Raphael Patai, *Hebrew Myths: The Book of Genesis*, New York: McGraw-Hill Book Company, 1963; Nathanson, Barbara Geller, "Aqedah," in *The Oxford Companion to the Bible*, edited by Bruce M. Metzger and Michael D. Coogan, New York: Oxford

University Press, 1993; Whyte, Alexander, *Bible Characters From the Old and New Testaments*, Grand Rapids, MI: Kregel Publications, 1990.

# ISAIAH

**Name and Etymology.** *Isaiah* means "Jehovah is salvation."

**Synopsis of Bible Story.** Isaiah, the son of Amoz, is still considered the greatest of the Hebrew prophets. The story of his life and work may be partially reconstructed from fragments scattered through his prophecy and in 2 Kings 19–20. He was born c. 770 B.C., apparently of a prominent family, and lived in Jerusalem; he married a woman he called "the prophetess" (Isa. 8:3) and had two sons (Isa. 7:3, 8:3). Some scholars believe that his wife died and he remarried and had another son. His famous call to be a prophet came in the year that King Uzziah died (c. 742 B.C.). He had a vision of "the Lord sitting on a throne," along with a host of angels. Isaiah was horrified at his own unworthiness in the face of God's holiness. He then heard the voice of the Lord asking, "Whom shall I send?" To this, Isaiah responded, "Here am I; send me" (Isa. 6:1–8).

His understanding of the people and events of his day leads us to believe that Isaiah was a friend and counselor of kings, a statesman and formulator of national politics. On the other hand, he was not blind to the needs of the poor and the afflicted, openly attacking the social ills of his day. He became a teacher and prophet who proclaimed God's messages to his people in the longest set of prophecies in the Old Testament.

Tradition has suggested that he met his death at the hands of King Manasseh for making unflattering speeches. According to the Mishnah (Hebrew traditions collected c. 200 B.C.), he was sawn in half. Whatever the details, he died a martyr.

It is not his life but his remarkable scope of understanding and expression that has made an impression on subsequent people of his own and other faiths. His prophetic writings range from flat historical narrative, to impassioned judgmental warnings, to richly imaginative descriptions of the land and its people, to the apocalyptic visions of a messianic age.

**Historical Context.** "Even before the collapse and captivity of Samaria there had arisen in Judah a man whose prophetic ministry was to make him one of the most illustrious figures in history" (Merrill, 282). Isaiah lived at a time when there was a confusion of petty wars, city feuds, and palace assassinations, when the Assyrian and later the Babylonian powers threatened Judah from one side and Egypt from the other. He was a counselor to the court during the reigns of Uzziah, Jotham, Ahaz, and Hezekiah.

While *Amos and *Hosea were prophesying in the Northern Kingdom, the young Isaiah undoubtedly heard their strong condemnations of their country's failures and their warnings of Assyrian aggression. About the middle of the eighth century B.C., Assyria, under Tiglath-Pileser III, threatened the security of her small western neighbors with plans to attack Egypt. The strategic location of Israel and Judah made them prime targets in the larger plan. While Israel fell early to this aggressor, Judah was able to negotiate and bribe her way to survival for 135 years after the fall of Samaria. Isaiah saw the efforts of this tiny kingdom struggling in the face of overwhelming odds.

With Isaiah's warnings and God's miraculous intervention, Jerusalem did not fall, even in the face of the eastern powers like *Sennacherib. When this leader invaded in 689 B.C., Isaiah recommended that Hezekiah stand fast and watch the Lord work his miracles, allowing Hezekiah to witness the amazing death of 185,000 troops.

Isaiah foresaw the Babylonian captivity and the subsequent return of the remnant of God's people with the advent of Cyrus. He also prophesied the coming of the Messiah and the coming of the Day of Judgment.

**Archaeological Evidence.** One of the most prized finds at Qumran was the Isaiah Dead Sea Scroll, discovered by Bedouins of the Ta'amira tribe, in a cache of documents and fragments secreted in a remote cave above the north end of the Dead Sea.

Recent historians, in studying the language and history of the book of Isaiah, have speculated that the book deals with three separate periods: "First Isaiah" deals with Assyria and the folly of relying on Egypt in the face of this formidable foe. "Second Isaiah," chapters 40–66, appears to focus on the fall of Jerusalem in 587 B.C., when the better part of the population was deported to Babylon. This section includes the famous "servant songs" thought to be a prophesy of the Messiah. "Third Isaiah," chapters 56–66, seems to reflect the period just before or during Nehemiah's return to Jerusalem after the exile (444 B.C.) It has a number of close parallels to the life of Christ. (See Miller, 284–287 for fuller detail.) (The division of Isaiah was conceived in Perthsire, Scotland, by George Adams Smith, a nineteenth-century critic.)

For the past two centuries, linguists and historians have puzzled over the jumble of names and confusion of periods that appear in the book of Isaiah. One modern scholar, Edith Hamilton, notes that, "He was one of the great minds of the world, and the way his book has been edited wrongs him" (133). While earlier modern scholars have sought to divide the authorship among three separate prophets, some recent scholars have developed a technique for textual analysis that suggests the whole of the book may well have been written by the same author, as attested by patterns of word usage. On the one hand, the three different segments have sometimes been attributed to disciples of Isaiah, while on the other, more traditional readers have noted that a faith in God's foreknowledge of human history could easily explain the prescience of the entire prophecy, not requiring the strained reading of these critics. We need not date prophecy by the actual events.

**Character in Later Works.** For most of modern history, the earliest known version of Isaiah was one completed in the ninth century A.D. The discovery of the Dead Sea Scrolls revealed a complete manuscript on leather parchment from a Jewish sect living about the first century B.C. in a monastery at Qumran. These scrolls are now on display in The Shrine of the Book in Jerusalem.

The book of Isaiah is full of richly suggestive imagery on which generations of poets and worshippers have drawn. The hot coals placed on his lips when he was called by God, the suffering servant going like a lamb to slaughter, the highway of the Lord, the mother in birth pangs, her child held to her comforting breast, the great Whore of Babylon, God trampling out the "Grapes of Wrath," the fiery sword of God's vengeance, the gentle protection of the remnant of his people, the images of the "Holy Mountain," the "Heavenly City," and of the "New Heavens" and the "New Earth"—these and a host of other images stir the imagination. Many of these vivid images echo other prophets such as *Hosea, *Amos, *Elijah, and *Joel. It would seem that these centuries of turmoil were a time of rich creative expression, vivid expressions of God's message to his people.

Isaiah has been celebrated for the brilliance of his style and metaphorical language. Stories of his life and death also became part of the Jewish commentary on his prophecy.

Christians love Isaiah for his messianic expectations. Such passages as "Behold, a virgin shall conceive, and bear a son, and shall call his name Immanuel" (7:14), or "For unto us a child is born, unto us a son is given. . . ." (9:6) have become traditional in Christmas pageants and sacred music. Handel's *Messiah* draws heavily on Isaiah.

The seventeenth-century writer, John Milton, like many medieval theologians, speculated on Isaiah's portrayal of the disobedient angel, Lucifer, the morning star, which has fallen from on high (14:12); Blake used Isaiah's images of Lucifer in *The Marriage of Heaven and Hell*. The famous painting of the *Peaceable Kingdom* derives from the image of the lion and the lamb lying down together, found prominently in Quaker tradition. When the United Nations was born, the stone wall facing the building in New York was inscribed: ". . . and they shall beat their swords into ploughshares, and their spears into pruninghooks: nation shall not lift up sword against nation, neither shall they learn war any more" (Isa. 2:4).

David Jeffrey notes that Isaiah is frequently cited in English literature but seldom appears as an individual character except in the medieval "Prophets" plays (381). From early times, the book of Isaiah has played a central role in Christian liturgy, theology, and art; it is sometimes called the "Fifth Gospel." In the words of St. Jerome, Isaiah tells the life of the Messiah so as to make one believe he is "telling the story of what has already happened rather than what is to come" (Sawyer, 328–9). The work also remains prominent in synagogue lectionaries, having left its lasting imprint on Jewish literary and religious tradition, particularly the Zion-centered visions of justice and peace. His great dedication to Jerusalem reverberates in contemporary life as it did in St. Augustine's *City of God*.

In modern literature, Isaiah's imagery and his description of desert lands and ruined cities with the heaps of broken lives continue to echo through such pieces as T. S. Eliot's *The Waste Land*. Scripture and traditional poetry of the Judeo-Christian culture echo Isaiah at every turn, testifying to the richness of this poetic prophet.

## SOURCES

Comay, Joan, *Who's Who in the Bible*, vol. 1, New York: Bonanza Books, 1980; Hamilton, Edith, *Spokesmen for God*, New York: W. W. Norton and Company, Inc., 1949; Jeffrey, David L., ed., *A Dictionary of the Biblical Tradition in English Literature*, Grand Rapids, MI: William B. Eerdmans Publishing Company, 1992; Merrill, Eugene H., *An Historical Survey of the Old Testament*, Nutley, NJ: The Craig Press, 1972; Miller, Madeline S., and J. Lane Miller, *Harper's Bible Dictionary*, New York: Harper and Row, 1961; Sawyer, John F. A., "Isaiah," in *The Oxford Companion to the Bible*, edited by Bruce M. Metzger and Michael D. Coogan, New York: Oxford University Press, 1993.

## ISHMAEL

**Name and Etymology.** An angel told *Hagar that she would have a child and that she should "call his name Ishmael; because the Lord hath heard thy affliction" (Gen. 16:11). The name means "may God hear" or "God hears."

**Synopsis of Bible Story.** When *Sarai realized that she was growing old and was unable to bear an heir to *Abram, she suggested that he go to Hagar, her maidservant, as a surrogate wife. Once Hagar was pregnant and boastful about her superior fertility, Sarai grew angry with her, mistreated her, and caused Hagar to flee into the wilderness. It was there that an angel of the Lord appeared to the Egyptian bondswoman and told her that she should return to her mistress and submit to her, that she would bear a son who would be "a wild man; his hand will be against every man, and every man's hand against him; and he shall dwell in the presence of all his brethren" (Gen. 16:12). Hagar also was promised that her seed would be multiplied exceedingly. She did return and bear this son to Abram, and raise him in the midst of the tribe.

When he was thirteen, Ishmael was among those members of his household circumcised by Abram, in response to the commandment of the angel (Gen. 17:25). It was shortly after that time, when his half-brother *Isaac was born, that Ishmael became an outcast. At the weaning ceremony, Ishmael apparently "mocked" his baby brother (Gen. 21:9–14), infuriating Sarah once again. Ishmael and his mother were subsequently sent by Abraham into the desert with a few provisions. They were soon out of water and in dire peril. Hagar left Ishmael in the shade of a bush while she lamented his impending death. At this point, God provided a well and a promise that he would make of Ishmael "a great nation" (Gen. 21:18–19).

Ishmael and his mother lived in the wilderness of Paran, where he became an archer. When he was mature, his mother found him an Egyptian wife (Gen. 12:12–16), by whom he had twelve sons. Apparently, he continued some contact with his Hebrew family, since he did join Isaac in honoring his father at the Feast of First Fruits, and in burying Abraham shortly thereafter (Gen. 25:9). Later, his daughter married *Esau, one of the sons of Isaac (Gen. 28:9). Ishmael died shortly thereafter, at 137 years of age (Gen. 25:17).

**Historical Context.** Ishmael was the ancestor of the nomadic desert tribes in the Sinai region, the desert across Negev to southern Jordan. They came to be known as Ishmaelites, with individual tribes named after the sons of Ishmael. It is to this group of wanderers that *Joseph's jealous brothers would later sell the young man. They were known as the itinerant caravan traders, tent-dwellers, and cameleers (1 Chron. 27:30; Ps. 83:6). Because of their ancestry from an Egyptian bondswoman and her outcast son, they have traditionally been considered by the Jews to be of a lower rank than the sons of Isaac.

**Archaeological Evidence.** The Babylonian tradition of surrogate mothers, noted in the stories of Sarai and Hagar, created some difficulties for Ishmael. As the firstborn, he should have been the heir of Abraham. In the ritual sacrifice of the oldest son, he should have been the one offered to God on Mount Moriah. The cultures surrounding the Hebrews made ritual sacrifices of the oldest sons, often as fertility rites in times of famine.

**Character in Later Works.** Later legends told of various wives that Ishmael married, involving tests of their hospitality to visitors.

Later, when Mohammed traced the history of Islam back to Ishmael, the actions of the young man became more significant: in Islamic cultures, the young men are circumcised at thirteen; in each Muslim's life, he or she is expected to visit Ka'bah and the holy well of Zemzem, the traditional site of God's promise to Hagar. It is believed that Hagar came with Ishmael to the future site of their holy city, at that time a barren valley. Because her child was dying of thirst, she left him lying on the hot earth while she searched for water. The child, in a tantrum, kicked his heels into the ground, and the waters of Zemzem welled up into the depression and saved his life. This spot then became a place where pilgrims came in an exercise called the "Lesser Pilgrimage," which involved rapidly pacing back and forth seven times between two hills near the Ka'bah in imitation of Hagar's anguished search. Ishmael was thought to be the founder of the city, and veneration of his travails was gradually extended into the

"Greater Pilgrimage" which was performed during the holy month of Dhu'l-Hijja (Noss, 688). Muslim tradition makes Ishmael, rather than Isaac, the son whom Abraham was commanded to sacrifice (Coogan, 329).

In Western literature, Ishmael has traditionally been a lesser character of the story of Abraham, not a heroic figure as in Islamic culture. "Call me Ishmael . . . ," the opening words of Melville's novel *Moby Dick*, remind us that Ishmael, like *Cain, has become the archetypal wanderer, a great favorite among the Romantics, and the figure who haunts all of Melville's novels.

The close association and mutual distrust between the sons of Isaac and the children of Ishmael continues to this day, with the clashes between Israeli and Arabs. Their related religions, Judaism and Islam, still compete over the holy places in Israel. A visitor to the arid areas of the Near East can still see the tent dwellers with their flocks, living a nomadic life that bears strong resemblance to Biblical times.

## SOURCES

Coogan, Michael D., "Ishmael," in *The Oxford Companion to the Bible*, edited by Bruce M. Metzger and Michael D. Coogan, Oxford: Oxford University Press, 1993; Graves, Robert, and Raphael Patai, *Hebrew Myths: The Book of Genesis*, New York: McGraw-Hill Book Company, 1963; Noss, John B., *Man's Religions*, New York: The Macmillan Company, 1956; Westenbroek, Anthony, "Ishmael," in *A Dictionary of the Biblical Tradition in English Literature*, edited by David L. Jeffrey, Grand Rapids, MI: William B. Eerdmans Publishing Company, 1992.

# J

## JACOB (ISRAEL)

**Name and Etymology.** *Jacob* derives from the Hebrew word meaning "he grasped the heel," a reference to the story of the twin birth (Gen. 25:26), the first indication that Jacob would follow closely and finally supplant his brother Esau. He was renamed *Israel*, meaning "May El [or God] protect" or "man who saw God," after wresting with an angel (Gen. 32:28; 35:10).

**Synopsis of Bible Story.** Jacob was the ultimate trickster, who himself became the victim of others' tricks. A usurper of his brother's blessing and birthright when he was a young man, Jacob, as a middle-aged man, preferred a younger son, and finally, as an old man, extended his blessing to favorite grandsons whom he adopted. Although noted for his devious ways, he was beloved of God, the founder of the twelve tribes, and a key figure in Hebrew history. He dominates much of the book of Genesis, and the people who followed assumed his name, "Israel."

Jacob, the twin brother of *Esau, son of *Isaac and *Rebekah, who struggled with his brother in the womb, was born second, holding his brother's heel. Contrasted with the more brutal Esau from the beginning, Jacob was a "plain," "quiet" man who "dwelt in tents" (Gen. 25:27). Although Jacob was smoother and cleverer than Esau, Esau was their father's favorite, a rough-and-tumble hunter and outdoorsman. Using his brother's hunger as a tool against him, Jacob outwitted Esau by preparing and offering a pottage in return for his birthright (Gen. 25:29–34). Jacob, his mother's favorite, proved a willing party to her trick on the old, blind Isaac, disguising his voice, skin, and his clothing to win his father's blessing (Gen. 27). Realizing that he would be the object of Esau's anger because of this theft, Jacob then took his mother's shrewd advice and fled to Padan-Aram to seek a bride from the family's homeland.

Jacob's Ladder, c. 1490. The Art Archive/Musée du Petit Palais, Avignon/Dagli Orti.

It was on this journey to visit his uncle Laban, that Jacob had his famous dream, seeing angels going up and down on a ladder from heaven (Gen. 28). This occurred at Bethel, a place to which he would later return.

The scenes in Padan-Aram echo the earlier story of *Rebekah, with the meeting of the maiden at the well, the welcome to the home of relatives, and the eagerness to join the families in marriage. This time, though, it was *Rachel, the beautiful younger daughter, with whom Jacob fell in love. Laban, her father, tricked Jacob into first marrying his older daughter, Leah. He also demanded seven years of labor for each of the daughters. Jacob spent some twenty years in Laban's service before returning to Canaan. During those years, we see the birth of Jacob's many children to Leah and her maidservant, and to Rachel and her maidservant.

The story twists again: shortly before Jacob left, he made an agreement with Laban to divide their animals, taking the spotted and speckled ones for himself. He then bred them in such a way as to make his flock prosper at Laban's expense. Rather than departing with his host of wives, maidservants, children, and flocks openly and peacefully, Jacob stole away in secret. Rachel's theft of the household goods—which Jacob did not know about—brought her angry father in pursuit of them. She proved herself a perfect match for her shrewd husband and crafty father by hiding them under her dress (Gen. 31:1–21). Laban went peacefully home, leaving Jacob to return to face Esau.

Along the way, in a second dream, Jacob was again confronted with an angelic apparition. This time he wrestled the angel all through the night. By daybreak, the angel was defeated, Jacob was limping with a displaced hip, and he had a new name, "Israel" (Gen. 32:24–32).

The homecoming proved both sweet and sour for the colorful hero: he had a joyous meeting with his brother, who had forgiven him and required no bribe to make peace with Jacob and his vast family. Yet Jacob, ever suspicious, pretended he would follow Esau back home, only to stop instead at Succoth. He then purchased ground at Shechem, and finally journeyed to Bethel. His beloved Rachel bore him a second son, but died in childbirth. He buried her near Bethlehem, and then returned to Hebron, the family home, where he and Esau met once again at the death of their father, Isaac.

The later appearances of Jacob are part of the story of his favorite son, *Joseph, who was sold into slavery, became vizier of Egypt, tricked the family into coming to him, and finally brought Jacob to Egypt to live for the duration of the famine (Gen. 37–48). In a final scene, Jacob begged Joseph to bury him in his homeland, with his ancestors, in the Cave of Machpelah, near Hebron (Gen. 50:13). Joseph honored this final request.

**Historical Context.** Jacob was the eponymous father of the twelve sons from whom the tribes derived and is central to the understanding of Jewish history. The famine described in the story that took his family to Egypt in search of food was a common event at the time. The explanations of blessings and birthrights point to the increased importance of primogeniture—the primacy of the firstborn son. Every deviation from this rule required an explanation.

The marriage between cousins, which we see in the case of Jacob and both Leah and Rachel, parallels those of earlier members of the family, who also sought to avoid unions with pagan tribes in Canaan. It was also common in Egypt at the time.

Although Jacob was embalmed in the Egyptian mode, he was eventually buried in the tomb of his ancestors, according to the Hebrew custom. This was a reinforcement of his claim to the land and a reminder to his sons that they were not citizens of Egypt, where shepherds—such as they—were despised.

Even today, Jewish families use an echo of Jacob's blessing on the children: "God prosper you like Ephraim and Manasseh!" His deathbed blessing (Gen. 48:20) may have been the first use of the famous *Shema*, "Hear, O Israel!" (Graves, 276).

**Archaeological Evidence.** The places chronicled in the story have been clearly identified. Jacob's well near Sychar (or Shechem) is the spot where Jesus later asked the Samaritan woman for a drink of water (John 4:5–12). The well is still there today, still deep and full of cool, delicious water. Jabbok Wadi, a dramatic setting in ancient Gilead, now Jordan, provided an impressive locale for Jacob's wrestling with an angel and his reunion with his estranged brother. Tradition has placed Rachel's tomb, over which Jacob erected a pillar, along the road from Jerusalem to Bethlehem. It is marked by a small, Moorish domed structure erected by the Crusaders. In recent years, it has been the locale for much conflict between Israelis and Palestinians.

Artifacts discovered by scholars testify to the accuracy of other details of the story, for example, the piling of stones to mark significant locales, and the prevalence of "household gods"—small statues cherished by families.

**Character in Later Works.** Hebrew tradition elaborated on the conflict between Jacob and Esau, indicating that there was a heated battle after Isaac's death. Some believe that the angels on the ladder are signs of the four empires indicated in Daniel, providing a key to that prophecy (Kugel, 372–74). Jacob's name and history echo throughout the Old Testament. Over the centuries, scholars have labored to make Jacob a more worthy and less duplicitous ancestor.

Jacob was also referred to frequently by New Testament speakers and writers: Stephen recollected his journey to Egypt (Acts 7:8–16) and Paul cited his selection over Esau as a sign of the predestination of the elect (Rom. 9:10–13). The author of Hebrews saw him as an example of vital and pragmatic faith (Heb. 11:9, 11:20–22).

The various scenes in Jacob's life have proven rich sources of theological and literary discussion—the stone pillow, the angels descending and ascending the ladder to heaven, the pealed wand, the various tricks, including the stolen birthright—these have enriched sermons, poems, and stories. Dante used the image of the ladder in his vision of Paradise, and William Wordsworth used it as an expression of human aspiration. Francis Thompson is thought to have been inspired by Jacob's example in his own story of wrestling with God—"The Hound of Heaven."

Jacob's name appears frequently in literature, but not always in reference to the Biblical character. Hemingway apparently chose the name "Jake" for his hero quite deliberately in *The Sun Also Rises*, as an ironic image of modern man, wounded like Jacob, but, unlike him, a childless man, one who cannot find the comfort of God's guidance.

## SOURCES

Graves, Robert, and Raphael Patai, *Hebrew Myths: The Book of Genesis*, New York: McGraw-Hill Book Company, 1963; Jeffrey, David L., "Jacob," in *A Dictionary of the Biblical Tradition in English Literature*, Grand Rapids, MI: William B. Eerdmans Publishing Company, 1992; Kugel, James L., *Traditions of the Bible: A Guide to the Bible As It Was at the Start of the Common Era*, Cambridge, Mass: Harvard University Press, 1998; Miller, Madeline S., and J. Lane Miller, *Harper's Bible Dictionary*, New York: Harper and Row, 1961.

## JAMES

**Name and Etymology.** *James* is the English equivalent of the Greek word for *Jacob*, or "May El [God] protect."

**Synopsis of Bible Story.** In the New Testament, there are as many as six men named James, of whom two figured prominently: James "the Just" appears to have been one of four brothers (or half-brothers) of *Jesus (Matt. 13:55; Mark 6:3), one of those in his own family who was opposed to his ministry (Matt. 12: 46–50; Mark 3:31–35; Luke 8:19–21; John 7:3–5). James was won over to the faith by an appearance of the Resurrected Christ

(1 Cor. 15:7) and became an active member of the early Christian community, the head of the Church at Jerusalem, presiding over the council of the Church (Acts 15:13–34) and receiving *Paul's report of the third missionary journey (Acts 21:18).

Some believe him to have been the first bishop of the Church in Jerusalem (Brownrigg, 150). According to tradition, he was a strict Nazirite, and prayed so fervently his knees were as callused as a camel's. The Jewish historians Josephus and Hegesippus both record James's execution at the instigation of the high priest and the Sanhedrin shortly after the death of Festus, the procurator who dispatched Paul to Rome in A.D. 62. James was thrown into the Kidron ravine from the top of the Temple area wall and mercifully clubbed to death, putting him out of his misery, in the valley below.

Many scholars believe that James was the author of the epistle that bears his name and in which he referred to himself as "the servant of the Lord Jesus Christ." James, the son of Alphaeus (Acts 1:13), and James "the less" (Mark 16:1) may or may not have been this man.

A second James—"the Great," was the son of Zebedee, a fisherman who was called when mending his nets by the Sea of Galilee. He was the elder brother of *John, one of the "Boanerges" or "sons of Thunder," who apparently became his brother's partner in ministry. James was frequently mentioned as one of the inner group of the Disciples. He is thought to have been the son of Salome, who witnessed the Crucifixion. Like his brother and *Peter, he forsook his fishing business to follow Christ (Matt. 4:21f; Mark 1:19f; Luke 5:10). Because of his energetic activity along with Peter and John in Jerusalem, a ministry of teaching and healing, he was arrested and taken before the Sanhedrin. James was believed to have suffered martyrdom in the early days of the Church, a political victim of *Herod Agrippa I, executed shortly before Agrippa's own death (Acts 12:1–3).

**Historical Context.** The Epistle of James, one of the first "General" or "Catholic" epistles was addressed generally to Christians, not to specific churches. By the time James composed this letter, the "twelve tribes" (perhaps a reference to Jewish Christians) were scattered widely, and the Christians found themselves living in a pagan world, tempted to worldliness. The writer drew materials from "wisdom" literature, including two Apocryphal books—Ecclesiasticus and the Wisdom of Solomon. He emphasizes action rather than faith, the need to endure in the face of trial and temptation.

Among the apocryphal "Infancy Gospels" is the Infancy Gospel of James that was at one time thought to have been composed by "James the Lord's brother." It is now thought to have been written well after James's death in A.D. 62. Philip Jenkins refers to it as a "charming fiction which no scholar would dream of taking seriously as a historical source" (104). The early Church was interested primarily in the death of Christ and his final days on earth, while the writings about his earlier life, the circumstances of his birth, became popular in the second and later centuries.

**Archaeological Evidence.** The authorship of the Epistle of James has long been a subject of contention. The Hellenistic Greek language of the Epistle makes it less likely to have been the writing of the Aramaic-speaking brother of Jesus. Scholars also note that the authorship was not established prior to the third century, but by the fourth century the Epistle had a recognized place in the Canon. At the same time the Church was casting considerable doubt on the authenticity of the Infancy Gospel of James, which narrates the miraculous circumstances of Mary's birth, the unusual circumstances of her childhood, details of her coming-of-age and marriage, and additional stories surrounding the birth of Christ.

The place of martyrdom of James, the brother of Jesus, the Temple mount and the Kidron Valley below, still stands. The twelfth-century Armenian Cathedral of St. James, located on the western hill of the Old City of Jerusalem, contains the traditional shrine alleged to contain the head of James, considered the first apostle–martyr.

**Character in Later Works.** There was a seventh-century tradition that James "the Great" visited Spain before his martyrdom and established the Christian religion there. Upon his return to Judea, he was beheaded, but his body was subsequently taken back to Spain. Some believe that his body was transported to Santiago de Compostela in northwest Spain, where the shrine is still a center of pilgrimage. In the Middle Ages, Compostela became the center of the Christian national movement opposed to the Muslim occupation. James's body was said to have been taken during the Saracen invasion of the country, but recovered in A.D. 800 and returned to Compostela. Legends connected with "St. James the Great" have proliferated in Spain, where he was known as *Santiago*. He became one of the military patron saints of Spain.

In Spanish art he is usually represented on horseback, bearing a banner. Because of the great number of pilgrimages associated with him, the shell (a pilgrim symbol)—usually painted in the dress of the pilgrim, who also had a cockleshell in his hat—became his symbol. The gourd, often used to symbolize the Resurrection, was also used by pilgrims as a flask to carry water, and was associated with James. As one of the twelve apostles, he also bears a scroll in one hand, with selections from his text testifying to the Incarnation written on it.

The concept of "apostles" quickly became central to Christian teachings. Those who were "sent out" became the messengers of the faith. More precisely "the twelve" were particularly prominent in the considerations of the early Church, having considerable respect because of their close relationship with Jesus. In Acts, they were endowed with the power to work miracles in the name of Christ (Acts 2:43, 5:12) and even to forgive sins. Over time, the idea of succession of apostolic teaching increased the respect that followers felt for those connected with the original group of disciples (See Manganello, 48).

Although James, the brother of Jesus, and James, the son of Zebedee were both present at a number of important moments in the ministry of Jesus and in the life of the early Church, neither ever became a celebrated character in literature. The son of Zebedee was simply one more figure in paintings that portrayed the disciples together at occasions like the Last Supper. The dramatic death of Jesus' brother did have some attention: Mantegna, for example, did paint "The Martyrdom of St. James," in the late fifteenth or early sixteenth century. In portrayals of the virtues, "Hope" usually has James at her feet.

### SOURCES

Brownrigg, Ronald, *Who's Who in the Bible*, vol. 2, New York: Bonanza Books, 1980; Ferguson, George, *Signs and Symbols in Christian Art*, New York: Oxford University Press, 1966; Jenkins, Philip, *Hidden Gospels*, New York: Oxford University Press, 2001; Manganello, Dominic, "James," in *A Dictionary of the Biblical Tradition in English Literature*, edited by David L. Jeffrey, Grand Rapids, MI: William B. Eerdmans Publishing Company, 1992; Miller, Madeline S., and J. Lane Miller, *Harper's Bible Dictionary*, New York: Harper and Row, 1961; Miller, Robert (ed.), "The Infancy Gospel of James," in *The Complete Gospels*, San Francisco: HarperCollins, 1994.

# JEHU

**Name and Etymology.** *Jehu* means "Jehovah is He."

**Synopsis of Bible Story.** Jehu ben Nimshi, king of Israel for approximately twenty-eight years, was the warrior chosen by God to end the dynasty of Ahab. *Elisha, responding to God's command, sent a prophet to the battlefield at Ramoth-gilead to anoint him king of Israel (2 Kings 9:1–3). To this command, the young prophet added that Jehu was to destroy the house of Ahab and avenge the blood of the prophets and all the servants of the Lord shed by *Jezebel (9:7). Jehu, apparently a man of fast action and clear purpose, immediately informed his troops and undertook the mandated slaughter: first he killed Joram, then Jezebel, then the seventy sons, then the prophets of Baal.

The swift narratives picture him as a dashing chariot driver who shot his adversary with an arrow and threw his body into the disputed field of Naboth. He drove his chariot to the palace at Jerusalem and ordered the painted queen to be thrown down onto the stones. Curiously, he subsequently honored the dead *Jezebel as a "king's daughter" with a proper burial. He cleverly sent messages to the caretakers of the sons, demanding that they ship him baskets of the heads of the potential heirs and then rounded up the priests with a pretended invitation to a feast, surrounding and slaughtering them as well. In all this bloody activity, he saw himself as the fulfillment of *Elijah's prophecy, the sword of Jehovah. Apparently, he went too far in his activities, overstepping his mandate in his zeal for the Lord (2 Kings 10:14). He even converted the Baal temple into a "draught house" or latrine (2 Kings 10:27).

In his later days, he refused to destroy the golden images worshipped in the shrines at Dan and Bethel, and allowed pagan worship, thus limiting the dynasty that he established to five generations. After his death, Jehu was succeeded by his son Jehoahaz, who reigned from 814–798 B.C.

**Historical Context.** Jehu lived at a time when Damascus was already on the rise. It came to dominate Israel during his and Jehoaz's reigns, with Hazael of Syria seizing part of his land east of the Jordan. Later, Manasseh and Gad were forced to pay tribute to Shalmaneser II of Assyria. Although the author of 2 Kings approves of Jehu's bloody path to power, *Hosea deplored his brutal manner (Hos. 1:4).

**Archaeological Evidence.** The "Black Obelisk" of Shalmaneser II refers to a king of "Omri" who was named "Ia-u-a/Ia-a-u." This was probably Jehu, although he was not of the house of Omri, but rather the destroyer of that house. The annals of the Assyrian king would have little interest in the name of this insignificant subordinate, noting only that he was forced to pay tribute to Assyria.

**Character in Later Works.** Although Jehu has the barbaric quality of Greek epic heroes, he was not considered a great hero among the Jews. Later, St. Augustine saw him as an example of lying, and John Wesley thought him colorful in the openness of his opinions. Passing references appear in John Milton, John Dryden, O. Henry, and John Galsworthy, but Jehu never became a favorite figure for artists to depict.

## SOURCES

Baker, David W., "Jehu," in *A Dictionary of the Biblical Tradition in English Literature*, edited by David L. Jeffrey, Grand Rapids, MI: William B. Eerdmans Publishing Company, 1992; McKenzie, Steven L., "Jehu," in *The Oxford Companion to the Bible*, edited by Bruce M. Metger and Michael

D. Coogan, New York: Oxford University Press, 1993; Miller, Madeline S., and J. Lane Miller, *Harper's Bible Dictionary*, New York: Harper and Row, 1961.

## JEREMIAH

**Name and Etymology.** Jeremiah's name is linked to the roots for *God* and to the verb "to raise up against." Some scholars note that it comes from the Hebrew *Yirmiyahu*, "may God lift up" (Isaacs, 102).

**Synopsis of Bible Story.** Jeremiah was a remarkably self-revealing prophet. In the longest of the prophetic books, he tells us that he was the son of Hilkiah, of a priestly family, predestined to be a prophet; he did not marry, perhaps because of his strong sense of mission. He was lonely, forced by his calling to confront his countrymen with their sins. His ministry extended from c. 625 B.C. until after the destruction of the Temple and the overthrow of the Judean state in 586 B.C. He faced persecution and bondage, and was forcibly taken into Egypt by those who fled the wrath of Nebuchadnezzar. The narrative portion of the book, which alternates with the poetic sections, is a vivid portrayal of his adventures, including being thrown into a cistern, rescued, and then chained. Jeremiah lived a heroic life without a hero's glamour, setting himself against patriotic and romantic bravado, counseling safe surrender and wise action rather than defiance and death.

The more poetic interludes proclaim the sins of Judah in a series of vivid pictures, beginning with descriptions of Judah's prostitution to alien gods, burning incense and sacrificing children. This segment was probably a response to the Deuteronomic reformation and the message of *Hosea and his faithless wife. Jeremiah followed his attacks on syncretism (like *Zephaniah's) with a call for the "circumcision of the heart" (Jer. 4:4). Discovering that the reformation had led to defiant nationalism and external piety, he turned to an attack on the false worship of the era.

He used signs, or "enacted words," such as the linen waistcloth and the clay flask (chapters 13 and 19), in some of his prophetic utterances. He also used personification, splendid imagery from nature, vivid symbols, direct address and admonitions, threats, rhetorical questions, and an abundance of exclamations. His passionate utterances are detailed, addressed to specific events and names. Having searched through his landscape of perfidy and pain, he asks plaintively, "Is there no balm in Gilead?" (Jer. 8:22)

His book is a combination of prose and poetry, full of personal emotions, marked by his deep patriotism and intense anguish for the sufferings of his people. Known as the "suffering" or "weeping" prophet, Jeremiah mourned for his people and for the fall of Jerusalem. The final chapter of this anthology of poems and narratives tells of the last days of Judah, the destruction of the Temple, the murder of the king's sons, the blinding of the king, and his shackling and imprisonment in Babylon.

Jeremiah dictated his work to his faithful secretary, *Baruch, who wrote them down upon a scroll of leather, which the King of Judah slashed with a knife and burned. After this sacrilege, Jeremiah ordered his scribe to take another scroll and write the words again (Jer. 36:1–32).

His major ideas are God's authority, omnipresence, and power; the covenant obligations of God's people; the role of the non-Israelites; the importance of Jerusalem and the Temple; the meaning of the exile of the Israelites; and the hope for restoration.

**Historical Context.** Jeremiah witnessed the fall of Nineveh and the annihilation of the Assyrian Empire in 606 B.C. He also witnessed the death of King *Josiah in 605 B.C.

and lived through the two sieges of Jerusalem in 597 B.C. and 586 B.C. The book deals with the threat to Judah and to Jerusalem posed by the Babylonian campaigns at the close of the sixth century B.C. In 587 B.C., both Jerusalem and the Temple were destroyed and the people deported to "the rivers of Babylon" (Psalm 137:1). This effectively ended both the Davidic dynasty and the identity of Judah as a separate state.

Jeremiah also announced the judgment at Dan, but Jerusalem felt it was a long way from Dan and did not fear the loss of a remote area.

**Archaeological Evidence.** Because of Jeremiah's long involvement with the important events of his day, there is abundant archaeological evidence of Judah's history intersecting with that of Egypt and Babylon. Bernard Anderson specifically mentions the Lachish Letters (347), but many documents of Near-Eastern history testify to the monumental activities of the day.

For example, Babylonian clay receipts, which bear the date of Nebuchadnezzar's reign, mention specific people from the land of Judah who apparently belonged to the retinue of King Jehoiachim. Details of conquests on the one hand and diet on the other suggest the range of discoveries among these receipts. As Werner Keller says in his discussion of these cataclysmic times, "Jeremiah sketches with swift strokes of his brush scenes taken from the exciting and anxious events of the last days, which through discoveries in Palestine in our own day are confirmed as being startling in the accuracy and historically genuine" (305).

In addition, artifacts from the City of David have turned up in private collections. There are numerous clay bullae (small lumps of clay used to seal important documents) with seal impressions, mentioning the name of Baruch, the son of Neriah, and Jerahmeel, the son of King Jehoiakim. These provide important connections to the life of the prophet Jeremiah. Baruch, the scribe of Jeremiah, undoubtedly lived in Jerusalem, where he twice wrote down Jeremiah's prophecies beginning in about 605 B.C. It is likely that all these discoveries came from the City of David. Unfortunately, the precise locations of their discovery are unknown.

**Character in Later Works.** Jeremiah is thought to be the author of Lamentations, and perhaps even the Book of Kings. (Included in the prophet's book is a segment that duplicates a portion of Kings.) Some of the books of the Apocrypha carry on the ideas of Jeremiah, notably the Letter of Jeremiah, addressed to the captives in Babylon and *Baruch*, an expansion of his central story and ideas.

Tradition reports that Nebudchadnezzar, at the time of the destruction of Jerusalem, had instructed his general to treat Jeremiah with consideration and kindness, but the prophet insisted on sharing the hardships that were inflicted on his people. He continued his fiery speeches in Egypt, where he was finally killed. Apparently, Jeremiah's influence on his people was greater after his death than before. "Arrest and imprisonment were his lot when alive. After his death, the exiled Judeans in Babylon religiously meditated upon his lessons and were guided by them. Jeremiah's influence is clearly reflected in the visions of *Ezekiel, who became a prophet in Babylon and prepared his fellow exiles for King Nebuchadnezzar's destruction of Jerusalem" (Isaacs, 104–5).

Because Jesus also was thought by some to have followed a *via dolorosa*, he was considered to be another Jeremiah. The author of Hebrews identified Christ as the "new covenant" (Heb. 8:8–12, 10:16–17), fulfilling the prophecy of Jeremiah (Jer. 31:31–40).

Jeremiah does not figure significantly as a character in English literature, but we do find the concept of the "jeremiad," a type of declamatory lamentation that attributes a present calamity to past sins and promises better times in the future if the people reform their wicked ways. The great seventeenth-century religious poets John Donne and George Herbert refer to him, as do a number of the early Puritan preachers in America. (See Ronald Clements, 394–395 for specific references.) Most often, he is pictured as suffering or weeping for the children of Israel. Because of the confused chronology of his prophetic book, some have found the modern fictionalized account of his life by Franz Werfel, *Hearken Unto the Voice*, a useful retelling of his story in an orderly fashion.

## SOURCES

Anderson, Bernard W., *Understanding the Old Testament*, Englewood Cliffs, NJ: Prentice-Hall, Inc., 1966; Clements, Ronald, "Jeremiah," in *A Dictionary of the Biblical Tradition in English Literature*, edited by David L. Jeffrey, Grand Rapids, MI: William B. Eerdmans Publishing Company, 1992; Clifford, Richard J., "Letter of Jeremiah," in *The HarperCollins Study Bible*, edited by Wayne A. Meeks, San Francisco, CA: HarperCollins, 1993; Hamilton, Edith, *Spokesmen for God*, New York: W. W. Norton and Company, Inc., 1949; Isaacs, Ronald H., *Messengers of God: A Jewish Prophets Who's Who*, Jerusalem: Jason Aronson, Inc., 1998; Keller, Werner, *The Bible as History*, New York: Bantam Books, 1982.

## JESUS CHRIST

**Name and Etymology.** *Jesus* is a Greek form of the Hebrew word for "God is salvation." The Greek term *Christ* was added as a title, translating the Hebrew "Messiah" or "the Anointed One."

**Synopsis of Bible Story.** Jesus, son of *Mary, descendant of *David, was a Jewish rabbi, believed by his followers to be the Incarnate Son of God, the long-awaited Messiah. The four Gospels—*Matthew, *Mark, *Luke, and *John—tell the brief story of God's annunciation to the Virgin Mary, her pregnancy, the visit to Bethlehem for the child's birth, the star in the East followed by the *Magi, the visit of the shepherds, and the trip to Egypt to avoid the slaughter of the innocents commanded by *Herod the Great.

We learn also of Jesus's childhood, his early activities in Galilee, including his baptism by *John the Baptist; the selection of his disciples; his expanded ministry around the countryside; his battles with officials; his friendships; the many miracles of healing; his teaching and preaching; and his increasing popularity and fame, climaxing in the Triumphal Entry into Jerusalem.

This is quickly followed by the plots to destroy Jesus: the arrest, scourging, trial, and crucifixion on Golgotha between two thieves. *Joseph of Arimathea, a member of the Sanhedrin, provided a burial place for him. Three days later, the women who had followed Jesus came to his cave tomb to mourn him, only to discover that the rock had been rolled away, and the body was gone. An angel informed *Mary Magdalene that Jesus had risen from the dead. Subsequently, the risen Christ was seen by a number of the disciples and by others, walking with them, eating with them, talking with them, giving them comfort and advice.

His disciples and friends continued to gather in prayer after his death, finally blessed by the comfort of the Holy Spirit at the Pentecost, marking the beginning of the Church, which has continued to study and celebrate him over the centuries.

**Historical Context.** Born in the time of *Caesar Augustus, when Palestine was a thoroughly Hellenized portion of the Roman Empire, Jesus was thought by his followers to be the culmination of the Jewish messianic hope. His entire story is deeply rooted in Hebrew thought: the accounts of his ancestry, his life, and his death are all closely tied to Jewish prophecy—including his birth in Bethlehem, his youth in Nazareth, and his crucifixion. His words echo the imagery of the Old Testament, his beatitudes have the structure of Hebrew poetry; many of his sayings sound like Wisdom literature; his proclamations have the ring of the prophets.

His life was also intricately interwoven with the history of the period, including some of the era's most famous figures: *Herod the Great, king at the time of Jesus's birth, was a powerful and ruthless leader. The subsequent quarrels with others in the Herodian family explain the motivation for some of Jesus's travels, as he sought to avoid the fate that befell *John the Baptist at the hands of *Herod Antipas. Because some of his disciples were associated with John and some were probably Zealots, he was considered a threat to authorities at the Temple and on the throne. The complex governing structure of the era that segregated spiritual and political decisions is especially clear in the trial and crucifixion of Jesus: the arrest by Roman officers, the trial by the Sanhedrin, the imprisonment and scourging in the House of *Caiaphas, the political trial before *Pontius Pilate, and the final crucifixion by the Romans.

**Archaeological Evidence.** Evidence and tradition have settled on the actual places of much of Jesus' life, from the time of the Annunciation to the resurrection appearances. Long before the first church was built in Bethlehem, Christian pilgrims were coming to see the town. Accounts dating to the middle of the second A.D. century record that visitors saw the cave in which Jesus was born. Although the story of the cave is not in the Bible, caves would typically have been used for stables in the area. About A.D. 330, Constantine ordered a church to be built over the cave. Today a basilica rebuilt by Justinian is shared by a variety of Christian communities.

Modern pilgrims to the Holy Land continue to trace the travels of Jesus, as they have throughout the centuries. For example, the wilderness of Judea, where the "temptation" took place, is a specific area near Jericho. The "pinnacle" of the Temple appears to be the parapet where the trumpet was sounded. Recently, an inscribed stone was found at the foot of that area with the words: "To the place of trumpeting," marking the spot where the announcement of the holy days was made by the sound of the trumpet.

One of the few sites from Jesus's time that excavations have recently revealed is the Pool of Bethesda, adjacent to St. Anne's Church, the spot where Jesus healed the paralytic. The Synagogue at Capernaum, the Sea of Galilee, the Mount of Beatitudes, the rocky shore where Jesus cooked fish for his disciples—these are all actual places in Israel that modern pilgrims visit. The Mount of Olives, where Jesus expressed his sorrow for Jerusalem, lies on a path he knew from childhood from his family's many visits to Jerusalem. Later he also wept in the garden, prayed, was betrayed there, and it was there he was arrested. Tradition has identified the entire Via Dolorosa (the path Jesus took through Jerusalem to the place of his death), including the places he stopped—the Stations of the Cross—each of which is tied to special people and Scripture. Pilgrims regularly travel this route during Passion Week as an act of remembrance.

Scholars are currently trying to determine in greater detail the precise spots where Jesus was imprisoned, tried, scourged, and crucified. The triple-arched entry of the

The Crucifixion with the Virgin Mary and Saints John, Dominic, and Jerome, fresco 1437-45, dormitory, Convent of San Marco, Florence, Italy. The Art Archive/Dagli Orti.

Huldah Gate would appear to have been the entrance to Jerusalem that he most frequently used on his trips to the Temple Mount; and it is near the place he would have been tried. Evacuations of the House of Caiaphas have revealed a "pit" (now under the Church of Peter of the Cock Crow) where Jesus may have been beaten and held overnight. The bedrock of considerable height under the Church of the Holy Sepulcher is thought by many to be Golgotha. This is also believed by some to be the location of his tomb, though others identify a location outside the city walls as more likely. The burial in a cave with a rolling stone was unusual except among royalty, suggesting that Joseph of Arimathea must have been very wealthy.

The traditional location of the "Upper Room" (or Cenacle) is the so-called "Tomb of David," located in the Armenian Quarter of Jerusalem's Old City and is believed to be the place where Jesus appeared to his disciples after his Resurrection and where the Holy Spirit descended at Pentecost. This may indeed be the correct location. Epiphanius, a fourth-century bishop who lived in Palestine for at least 20 years, said that several first-century buildings had survived into the time of Hadrian (A.D. 135). Among these was a small Christian church. If the original Christian community continued to meet in the upper room, then it is likely that Epiphanius' small church was at that location. In addition, the mosaic floor in Madaba, Jordan (about A.D. 600) includes a depiction of the church in just this area of Jerusalem.

The centuries of building and destruction and rebuilding make the discovery of a specific time and place of a man without prestige or power exceedingly difficult. Ironically, it is far easier to find traces of Herod than of Jesus. Even Pontius Pilate has been reduced in historical memory to a couple of citations.

**Character in Later Works.** "The greatest story ever told," is the way numerous writers have described the life of Jesus and the whole history of God's relationship with his human creation. Without a doubt, for Christians, Jesus is the dominant man in Scripture. His words have been translated, quoted, interpreted, used, and abused by scholars, peasants, priests, and kings since they were first spoken. His actions have become the paradigm for his followers' lives, the source of images for painters and sculptors, the inspiration for music and literature.

It would be impossible to list the multitude of works that have flowed from the life and thought of Jesus: from his life, his parables, his healing touch, his sacrificial death. They continue to inspire artists even now, some two millennia after his death and resurrection.

In contrast to the Hebrews, who believed that their God strictly forbade the worship—or even the use in worship—of graven images, many Christians believed that the Incarnation liberated them from this prohibition. Since God had appeared in the flesh, he had blessed the image: since Christ could be seen by the human eye, artists were permitted to copy this image. From the early days of the Church, carved and painted images of Jesus appeared, sometimes picturing him as clean-shaven in the Roman style, sometimes bearded. Later the beard, the white toga, and the halo became iconographic elements in the repeated portrayal. Few signs in Western art are as universally understood as the cross. In time, the halo, a sign of charisma—the glow of God's glory—was added to pictures of Christ.

Jesus has often been portrayed as a healer, surrounded by children, preaching to the multitudes, or in a boat on the Sea of Galilee. Each of the moments leading up to the Crucifixion—the Triumphal Entry, the cleansing of the Temple, the Last Supper, the prayer in the Garden of Gethsemane, the betrayal by *Judas Iscariot, the scourging and the ironic coronation with a crown of thorns, the trial in front of Pontius Pilate, the Stations of the Cross on the Via Dolorosa, the Crucifixion, the descent from the cross, the "Pietà," the burial, the scenes of the resurrected Christ—these and many more form the core of Western art.

In literature as well, writers have used elements of his story—from the tropes to the mystery plays to modern television portrayals. Many authors have dwelled on his life—Dante, John Milton, T. S. Eliot—producing such works as *The Divine Comedy*, *Paradise Regained*, and *The Four Quartets*. Jesus appears as the model for a vast array of moderns—William Faulkner, John Steinbeck, William Styron, and many others have used his image in secular as well as religious writing. We also have parodies of Christ—messianic figures in popular art, especially science fiction and in the modern media, including the intergalactic messiah of *Star Trek*. The "Christ figure" has become the dominant archetype in Western literature and art.

Musicians as well have found in Christ's passion, his life and his words the inspiration for masterpieces of worship, the whole body of Christian music with all its variations. The hymns, chants, oratorios, and even modern popular music reflect the vast influence of this gentle man who was proclaimed the "Son of God."

## SOURCES

Chancey, Mark, and Eric M. Meyers, "How Jewish Was Sepphoris in Jesus Time?" *Biblical Archaeology Review*, 24(4) 18–33, 2000; Sayers, Dorothy L., "The Greatest Drama Ever Staged," in *The Whimsical Christian*, New York: Macmillan Publishing Co., Inc., 1969; Sayers, Dorothy L., *The Man Born to Be King*, Grand Rapids, MI: William B. Eerdmans Publishing Company, 1943.

## JEZEBEL

**Name and Etymology.** Jezebel's name probably derives from her worship of Baal, the god of the Phoenicians. "Where is the Prince?" is a cry of Baal's divine and human subjects when he is in the underworld.

**Synopsis of Bible Story.** Ahab, a late king of Israel, married the daughter of Ethbaal, the priest-king of Sidon and Tyre (1 Kings 16:31), who brought with her the worship of the Phoenician gods Baal and Asherah. A powerful woman who often led her weak husband into deeper sins, she outraged the people of Israel by supporting the worship of these pagan gods while on the throne of Israel. Claiming that her gods were equal to Yahweh, Jezebel killed the prophets of Jehovah, and brought a famine on the land (an ironic commentary on her "fertility" gods) (1 Kings 18:4). Her slaughter precipitated a challenge from *Elijah, who became her arch enemy. He demonstrated the mighty power of God on Mount Carmel by the massacre of her prophets (1 Kings 18:17–40).

This long-reigning queen was not only wife to Ahab, one of the longest-ruling kings in Israel, but also mother to Joram, the heir to the throne, and to Athaliah, who married Jehoram of Judah. Jezebel apparently chose to rule as an absolute monarch, not as one in a covenantal relationship with God and the people. Thus, when Ahab coveted Naboth's vineyard, but backed away from violent action, Jezebel imperviously ordered that it be seized and the owner murdered, showing in her high-handed action that she was more unscrupulous than Ahab and quite willing to usurp his authority. This power play led to the fulfillment of the prophecy of Ahab's destruction and to his violent death. Jezebel remained as queen mother, apparently a powerful role, for a number of years after her husband's death.

Her own brutal end was prophesied by her old enemy, Elijah, "The dogs shall eat Jezebel by the wall of Jezreel" (1 Kings 21:23). In an unforgettable scene, this prophecy came to pass with the attack by *Jehu in 842 B.C. The old queen, still in her ivory palace, hearing that Jehu was planning his attack, "painted her eyes, arranged her hair and looked out a window" at him—arrogant to the end. Her eunuchs threw her down from the window onto the courtyard, where she lay, splattered by blood, trampled by horses, and eaten by dogs (2 Kings 9:30–37).

Death of Jezebel, folio 150V of tenth-century Mozarabic bible. (Mozarabs were Spanish Christians living under Muslim rule, eighth to eleventh century.) The Art Archive/Real Collegiata, San Isidoro, Leon/Dagli Orti.

**Historical Context.** The marriage between Ahab and Jezebel was probably designed to ratify an alliance between the Phoenicians and the Israelites, offsetting the hostility of Damascus toward Israel (c. 880 B.C.) Jezebel, the powerful queen mother, who was devoted to the cult of Asherah, was not unusual for her culture (*New International Version*, notes 502–503). In that period it was the norm to worship both Yahweh and Asherah in the state temple in Jerusalem. (Note that Solomon had also built temples to pagan gods.) Her hosting of 450 of the prophets of Baal and 400 of the prophets of Asherah at her table, however, was a clear indication of fervent patronage, not simple tolerance. So was the slaughter of the prophets of Jehovah. *Joshua had sought to clear the land of these pagan influences, but Solomon and his foreign wives had brought them back. Now they were seen as a clear challenge to Jehovah.

**Archaeological Evidence.** King Ahab of Israel selected the site of Jezreel for his palace—a fertile area with fine vineyards, like Naboths's, close to the palace. The elegant "ivory" house, from whose window Jezebel looked down before being thrown to her bloody death and eaten by dogs, was assumed to be mythical until the recent discovery of shards of ivory, many of them with beautiful carving, in an old mound of ruins in Samaria.

**Character in Later Works.** "Jezebel" came to be synonymous with theological whoredom and sorceries. Her name is used in Revelation 2:20 for the seductive "prophetess" at Thyatira who encouraged immorality. The Church fathers equated her with all kinds of perfidy and wickedness, seeing her as the very image of pride. Although she does not appear to have been a central figure in literature or art, her name is so commonly used for a wicked woman that even the poor whites in William Faulkner's novel *Light in August* use "Jezebel" as a term of abuse.

Recently, revisionists have chosen to see the whole story from Jezebel's point of view. Janet Howe Gaines, for instance, considers that this woman was snatched from her own home and culture, taken to an alien land, pressed to worship a god she did not love, and criticized for loving her husband too much and helping him with excessive vigor. The term "harlot" is not justified by Jezebel's story in the Deuteronomic tradition, for there is no hint of sexual impropriety in her life. The term is uttered as an insult by her enemy, and yet became her enduring reputation. This is, of course, the feminist take on her story, picturing her as a victim of her era and her gender and quarreling with the obsessively masculine point of view of Scripture that favors Yahweh over Asherah.

### SOURCES

Ackerman, Susan, "The Queen Mother and the Cult in Ancient Israel," in *Women in the Hebrew Bible*, edited by Alice Bach, New York: Routledge, 1999; Gaines, Janet Howe, "How Bad Was Jezebel," in *Biblical Archaeological Review*, October 2000; Hackett, Jo Ann, "Jezebel," in *The Oxford Companion to the Bible*, edited by Bruce M. Metzger, New York: Oxford University Press, 1993; Keller, Werner, *The Bible as History*, New York: Bantam Books, 1982.

### JOB

**Name and Etymology.** There is no information on Job's name, which is unique in Scripture, nor is there any indication of his parentage, his tribe, or even his nationality—only the region in which he lived.

**Synopsis of Bible Story.** Job, a good man from the land of Uz, was prosperous and happy, a faithful servant of Jehovah. Suddenly, he found himself an unwitting pawn in a struggle between Satan and God. When Satan insisted that Job was good because he was blessed, God undertook to prove Job's genuine virtue. God permitted Satan to strip him of children, servants, and wealth. Steadfast, even in the face of one disaster after another, Job accepted this stoically: "Naked came I out of my mother's womb, and naked shall I return thither: the Lord gave and the Lord hath taken away; blessed be the name of the Lord" (Job 1:21–22).

In a second scene in heaven, Satan once again challenged God, insisting that Job would curse God if he were stricken in the flesh. This time, God allowed Satan to smite Job with boils, leaving him to sit among the ashes, scraping himself with potsherds. It was at this point that Job's wife recommended he curse God and die (Job 2:9). He resisted her advice, only to be visited by three friends, each of whom—after a time of silence—pointed out that his sufferings resulted from his own sins and rebuked him for his lament and his questioning. In a series of discourses and responses, Job and his "comforters" explored rich theological questions about the nature of God's justice and man's right to challenge God's will. Realizing that man is not prepared to confront God's justice, Job yet announced his enduring faith that his redeemer lived (Job 19:25).

This series of arguments and counter-arguments is followed by a new voice—a fourth friend—who was younger and had remained silent up to this point. Elihu castigated the others for their bad theology (chapters 34–37).

Finally, in the climactic scene, God appeared to Job out of a whirlwind, challenging him with a series of powerful rhetorical questions that end his quibbles (Job 38–40:2). This theophany, or appearance of the Lord, testifies to God's sovereignty, offering evidence of his creativity and power, asserting his authority while not answering detailed human inquiries. Job bowed meekly before his lord, agreeing to his own unworthiness. (Behold, I am vile . . .," he admitted; Job 40:4). In the end, his wealth and health were restored by God, and Job lived to a ripe old age, having seen his sons and his sons' sons, "even four generations" (Job 42:16).

**Historical Context.** The folk tale, probably originally in oral form, goes back to antiquity. The actual date of the composition of this book is clouded by its uniqueness—with words that appear nowhere else in Scripture. It is thought to date from some time after the seventh century B.C., and no later than 200 B.C.

The land of "Uz" from which the hero hails is a large territory east of the Jordan, which included Edom to the south. The land of Edom was often celebrated for Wisdom literature. The use of an Edomite hero strikes some critics as peculiar, indicating that the book was probably composed prior to 587 B.C.

Whoever the author, it is clear he was a man of vast learning and theological depth.

**Archaeological Evidence.** Other books from the Second Temple period suggest that the biblical text of Job was in circulation by the end of the second century B.C.

The fact that Job's wealth is measured in animals and the suggestion that he is related to caravan routes are clues that place him among ancients, perhaps as far back as the time of Abraham. As early as 1215 B.C., Moab is mentioned in the records of a punitive campaign organized by Ramses III. Scholars have found evidence that this was a rich and literate country by the sixth century B.C.

David was the first Israelite king to conquer Edom. In the sixth century, Edom was conquered by the Babylonians. After that, various nomadic tribes penetrated the country, pressing the Edomites westward into Judea, where they settled south of Hebron.

The court system portrayed in the story fits perfectly into Hebrew tradition, and the book is sometimes cited as a fine example of forensic literature. Terms such as "redeemer," for example, suggest understanding of legal procedures.

**Character in Later Works.** Job, whose book is categorized as Wisdom literature, quickly became the symbol of innocent suffering and faithful obedience to God. Extensions of the story, the Targum of Job and the Testament of Job, were elaborations of the original story, depicting his wife more favorably, emphasizing his fights against idolatry, adding to the speculations about Satan, and suggesting cosmological dualism, magic, and mysticism.

His patience is echoed in Scripture (as early as Ezekiel 14:14, 20), and is expanded to make him a symbol of endurance (or "perserverance" in more recent translations) in James (5:11). Medieval Christians, such as St. Gregory the Great, St. Jerome, St. Augustine, and St. Ambrose, saw him as a paragon of patience and an antetype of Christ. He became a popular symbolic figure among theologians through the ages, and among poets and playwrights. Many are familiar with his famous statement, "I know that my Redeemer liveth," because of its splendid presentation in Handel's *Messiah*. William Blake's beautiful illustrations of the Book of Job are particularly famous.

The modern adaptation by the American poet/playwright Archibald MacLeish, *J. B.*, precipitated a flurry of critical reassessments of the book. (See Hone, 255ff.) The preface in heaven, with the ironic conversation between God and Satan, is echoed in many literary masterpieces, including those by Dante, John Milton, Christopher Marlowe, and Goethe.

### SOURCES

Besserman, Lawrence, "Job," in *A Dictionary of the Biblical Tradition in English Literature*, edited by David L. Jeffrey, Grand Rapids, MI: William B. Eerdmans Publishing Company, 1992; Crenshaw, James L., "Job," in *HarperCollins Study Bible*, edited by Wayne A. Meeks, San Francisco, CA: HarperCollins, 1993; Hone, Ralph E., *The Voice Out of the Whirlwind: The Book of Job*, San Francisco, CA: Chandler Publishing Company, Inc., 1960; Miller, Madeline S., and J. Lane Miller, *Harper's Bible Dictionary*, New York: Harper and Row, 1961; Negev, Avraham, ed., *The Archaeological Encyclopedia of the Holy Land*, New York: Thomas Nelson Publishers, 1986.

### JOEL

**Name and Etymology.** *Joel* means "Yahweh is God."

**Synopsis of Bible Story.** The book of Joel reveals little about the author other than his family. He was the son of Petheul, also unidentified except for his name. Some critics speculate his concern for Judah indicates that Joel was a native of the region around Jerusalem.

The book of Joel consists of two sharply distinguished parts: the depiction of a locust plague and drought that descended on Judah and Jerusalem, and a series of apocalyptic visions of the "Day of the Lord." The plague is described with such detail—almost scientific accuracy, including the names of four different kinds of locusts—that most critics believe the prophet lived through this horror.

This is followed by a time of recovery and repentance, "Blow ye the trumpet in Zion, and sound an alarm in my holy mountain: let all the inhabitants of the land tremble: for the day of the Lord cometh, for it is nigh at hand" (Joel 2:1). Joel expresses his dream for a period "afterward," when they will be restored and "I will pour out my spirit upon all flesh; and your sons and your daughters shall prophesy, your old men shall dream dreams, and your young men shall see visions" (Joel 2:28). In his combined historical and apocalyptic vision, Jerusalem is delivered and the "remnant" called by the Lord. All nations will be gathered and brought down to the valley of Jehoshaphat. He graphically describes the dispersion of the Jews over all the earth that appears to precede a final judgment of the heathen in the "valley of decision" in the "day of the Lord." In beautiful language, he speaks of a time when "it shall come to pass in that day, that the mountains shall drop down new wine, and the hills shall flow with milk, and all the rivers of Judah shall flow with waters, and a fountain shall come forth of the house of the Lord. . . ." (Joel 3:18). The brief book ends with a promise that Judah shall dwell forever and Jerusalem will endure.

**Historical Context.** Apparently a contemporary of *Amos, Joel seems to have been a preexilic author of the Southern kingdom, much concerned with worship practices at the Temple. This prophet is not described as an individual. It is not, in fact, clear whether he is a "cult" or "nationalist" prophet, a prophet of "judgment" or of "salvation."

The book contains references to no datable historical events, leaving it unclear when it was written. Plagues of locusts, such as Joel describes in the opening chapter of his book, recurred over history. In addition, the intermingled bits of history which he included—with threats of the northern armies, battles, bloodshed, and enslavement—were also depressingly recurrent. The text points to a time when the political leadership of the Jews had, by default, devolved upon the high priesthood, but this does not help narrow the dating by much. The threat of the northern army (Joel 2:20) is typical of this country, which was especially vulnerable from the south (Egypt) and the north (Assyria and Babylonia), but not generally from the sea or across the desert (*New International Version*, 1334).

**Archaeological Evidence.** The reference to armies as locusts is also found in fifteenth century B.C. Ugaritic texts. Although this swarm of locusts was once seen as symbolic, it is now respected for the accuracy of its details: vast swarms of these insects emerge from desert breeding grounds in Africa, the Middle East, and parts of Asia. They may cover hundreds of square miles, laying waste to a whole countryside in a matter of hours. "The three stages of the insect's development, the great cloud darkening the sun and the stars, the noise of the whirring wings and chomping jaws, the fertile landscape turned into a bleached and burnt-up wasteland"—all of these are portrayed with a "startling realism" (Comay, 221).

The details of the Temple, including the blowing of the trumpet on high holy days, could date it either early or late. Some scholars believe that the prophecy includes details from as late as 400 B.C. The references to the destruction of Jerusalem and the Temple are thoroughly documented in history, occurring finally in A.D. 70. Others note that the fall of Judah that Joel predicts occurred in the sixth century B.C.

**Character in Later Works.** Joel seems to have been well known among other prophets of Israel, bearing striking parallels to *Amos, *Micah, Zephaniah, *Jeremiah, and *Ezekiel. As the *New International Version*'s introduction to the book notes, it all depends on the critic's view of the date of Joel: "If it was written early, the other prophets borrowed his phrases; if it was later, the reverse may have taken place. Some scholars maintain that all the prophets drew more or less from the religious literary traditions that they and their readers shared in common—liturgical and otherwise" (*New International Version*, 1330).

In addition, Joel's prophetic language is a source for many New Testament references—most notably those made by *Peter at Pentecost, when he quotes the prophet (Acts 2:16–21). The Qumran sect had seen their "teacher of righteousness" as a fulfillment of Joel 2:23 (*New International Version*, note 1334). It is also clear that the early Christians, in the book of Acts, thought that Joel's prophesy was fulfilled in the outpouring of the "spirit" after the "Crucifixion."

Joel has proven a great treasure trove for those seeking symbols: the image of beating swords into plowshares has been a common quote among people who dream of peace. His contrary images of destruction—fire and locusts—have also been standard in later apocalyptic visions. "The day of the locust," and the "Day of the Lord" have become common images of the Apocalypse. The archetypal wasteland imagery—desolation, sterility—mark the famous poem, *The Waste Land*, by T. S. Eliot, as does the contrary imagery of wine, fruition, and lush Edenic restoration. Authors from John Dryden to Thomas Wolfe have found imagery from Joel to be richly suggestive.

### SOURCES

Comay, Joan, *Who's Who in the Bible*, vol. 1, New York: Bonanza Books, 1980; Freedman, David Noel, and Bruce Willoughby, "Joel," in *A Dictionary of the Biblical Tradition in English Literature*, edited by David L. Jeffrey, Grand Rapids, MI: William B. Eerdmans Publishing Company, 1992; Miller, Madeline S., and J. Lane Miller, *Harper's Bible Dictionary*, New York: Harper and Row, 1961; Vawter, Bruce C. M., "Joel," in *Oxford Companion to the Bible*, edited by Bruce M. Metzger and Michael D. Coogan, New York: Oxford University Press, 1993.

## JOHN THE BAPTIST ("THE BAPTIZER")

**Name and Etymology.** *John* is derived from the Hebrew "the Lord is gracious."

**Synopsis of Bible Story.** John was a descendent of *Aaron on both sides, a member of a priestly family. Elizabeth and Zechariah, his parents, were childless when the angel Gabriel came to Zechariah and proclaimed that Elizabeth would bear a child who would be named John and would be great in the sight of the Lord and filled with the Holy Spirit (Luke 1:11–25). When Zecheriah challenged the angel over this announcement, he was struck dumb for the duration of the pregnancy, regaining his speech only when he wrote the name of the child for all to see.

A few months later, Elizabeth's cousin *Mary, also with child, came to their home in the hill country of Judea (traditionally identified as the village of Ein Karem), to see Elizabeth. When Mary entered the room, the child leapt in Elizabeth's womb, causing her to recognize that both Mary and her child were blessed (Luke 1:39–45). It was in response to this blessing that Mary uttered the splendid words of the Magnificat: "My soul doth magnify the Lord. . . ." (Luke 1:46–55).

At the time of John's birth and naming, *Zechariah prophesied that the child would become a prophet of the Highest, preparing the way for him to give his people the knowledge of salvation through the forgiveness of their sins because of the tender mercy of our God (Luke 1:70–79). We know little of John's youth, picking up his story only when he was an adult, a prophet following in the Old Testament tradition, living in the Judean desert, wearing camel's hair and leather garments, eating locusts and honey, baptizing and proclaiming the coming of the Messiah.

In his ministry near the Dead Sea and in the Jordan Valley, John gathered a group of disciples who heard and believed his message, a distinctive call to repentance, insisting on the need for individual rather than national salvation. Being a child of *Abraham would not save anyone (Luke 1:8). John realized that he had only "come to prepare the way" (Mark 1:3), and was not the "one to come." He acknowledged his own inferior position by announcing to those whom he baptized, "I indeed baptize you with water; but one mightier than I cometh, the latchet of whose shoes I am not worthy to unloose: he shall baptize you with the Holy Ghost and with fire (Luke 3:16).

It was to the region of the Jordan River, where John was baptizing, that his young cousin came, asking that he also be baptized. John, knowing that *Jesus was the Messiah, hesitated, noting that the roles should be reversed. When Jesus insisted on fulfilling "all righteousness," John agreed, only to witness the greatest theophany—experience of God—in Scripture: the three Persons of the Godhead appeared simultaneously, with God the Father speaking from heaven, God the Holy Spirit descending in the form of a dove, and God the Son welcoming the words, "This is my beloved Son, in whom I am well pleased" (Matt. 3:17).

Even after Jesus began his own ministry, John continued his preaching and teaching, admonishing and infuriating the Pharisees and the Sadducees (Matt. 3:7–15) and finally announcing God's judgment on *Herod the Tetrarch (Herod Antipas) for "all the evils he had done (Matt. 3:19). By this time, Herod had seduced and married his half-brother Philip's wife (Matt. 14:3–5) Herodias, who was also his own niece. Having spoken truth to power, John was thrown in prison, where he languished until Herodias—the wife/sister-in-law/niece in question—used the seductive dance of her daughter Salome to trick Herod into offering her whatever she wished. She asked for John's head on a platter—which Herod reluctantly delivered (Matt. 14:7–11). The news was reported to Jesus and his disciples, who mourned over the loss of their kinsman and friend. Some of them went and claimed the body and buried it (Mark 6:29).

**Historical Context.** In Judea, this was a period of anticipation, filled with talk of the coming Messiah. Palestine was now divided into regions ruled by the heirs of Herod the Great. Corruption among religious leaders encouraged the growth of ascetic communities like the Essenes and political activists like the Zealots. (If John was at one time a member of the Essene community at Qumran, he probably had left it prior to the period recounted in the Gospels.) Apparently, many saw him as an heir to the great Hebrew prophetic tradition, and he had a substantial following. In fact, it is thought that some of his disciples were later disciples of Jesus. The cousins did share some theology and some character traits—both emphasized the need for individual repentance and baptism, both confronted the powers of the Temple hierarchy.

John's battle with Herodias, ending with his own death, was a difficult confrontation for Herod Antipas. Those with understanding of the Hebrew traditions knew that it was a dangerous time to meddle with a holy man who had a popular following. The tetrarch Herod is thought to have feared John and would have preferred to protect him rather than kill him. The people of the region believed him to be *Elijah come back from the dead, a Nazirite, and a holy man, not a person that a smart ruler should risk turning into a martyr.

**Archaeological Evidence.** Josephus said that the Fortress of Machaerus on the eastern side of the Dead Sea was the scene of John's imprisonment and death. Most of the

The beheading of St. John the Baptist and presentation to Salome, lunette. The Art Archive/Collegio del Cambio, Perugia/Dagli Orti (A).

archaeological research regarding John has centered around the community of Essenes at Qumran and evidence in the Dead Sea Scrolls. Many scholars have thought that John was a member of this community, though orthodox scholars tend to disagree. The ideals of purity and holiness of the Qumran community do appear to be consistent with John's, and some believe that he was influenced, at least indirectly, by their ritual washings and cleansings, and by the company of disciples seeking to "fly from the retribution that is coming" (Brownrigg, 222).

John's activities appear to have been based at two principle sites on the Jordan River—one in the area of Salem, Ter er-Ricra, probably at the five wells of Aenon, located at Ed-Der; the other at Bethabara, the place of baptism. The Madaba mosaic shows the ferry above the place of baptism, with a house standing on piles, apparently designed to defend against floods of the river (Brownrigg, 221). Over the centuries, various churches and monastaries have been built in the region to memorialize the event. Pilgrims to the Holy Land often are baptized at this site.

**Character in Later Works.** Later in Scripture, we find that there were rumors that John was raised from the dead (Mark 6:14) and we also discover that followers have continued to baptize in John's name. Acts 18:25 tells of Apollos, who was continuing the practice 25 years later.

From the earliest documents, John was considered an important person in the Gospel narratives, appearing prominently in the synoptic Gospels. More recently, especially since the discovery of the Dead Sea Scrolls and the scholarly considerations of the community of Essenes, John has become an increasingly prominent subject for discussion, shedding light on debates within Judaism at the time Christ began his ministry.

Medieval art, which often portrayed the infant Jesus with the Madonna, also used the slightly older cousin, John, as a third figure in the pictures. Another popular image was the baptism of Christ, with the heavens opening up and the dove descending. Most appealing of all was the dramatic scene of the lascivious "Dance of the Seven Veils" and the presentation of John's severed head on a platter.

The mystery plays of the Middle Ages mention John frequently. He is often cited in other literature, notably by Herman Melville and Joseph Conrad. He even appears in the sardonic presentation of modern man, in T. S. Eliot's "The Love Song of J. Alfred Prufrock." Camille R. LaBossière and Charles H. H. Scobie list a host of novelists who refer to John the Baptist, including Margaret Laurence, John Updike, and Albert Camus (407–8).

## SOURCES

Brownrigg, Ronald, *Who's Who in the Bible*, vol. 2, New York: Bonanza Books, 1980; La Bossière, Camille R., and Charles H. H. Scobie, "John the Baptist," in *A Dictionary of the Biblical Tradition in English Literature*, edited by David L. Jeffrey, Grand Rapids, MI: William B. Eerdmans Publishing Company, 1992; Miller, Madeline S., and J. Lane Miller, *Harper's Bible Dictionary*, New York: Harper and Row, 1961.

## JOHN

**Name and Etymology.** *John* means "Jehovah hath been gracious."

**Synopsis of Bible Story.** The apostle John was one of the sons of Zebedee, a Galilean fisherman and brother of *James. Like the other fishermen/disciples from the region around the Sea of Galilee, John was one of the first called and one of the most regularly mentioned, suggesting that he was part of the inner circle of close friends of *Jesus (Matt. 10:2; Mark 3:17; Luke 6:14). He is usually thought to have been the disciple designated as the "one Jesus loved" in the Gospel that he is believed to have authored, though he is not mentioned by name in the Gospel of John. He is named at various times in the other Gospels: when Jesus called him (Mark 1:19–20; Matt. 4:21–22); when Jesus labeled him—along with his brother—as one of the "Sons of Thunder" or "Sons of Anger" (Mark 3:17); and when he and James (and their mother) approached Jesus, promising loyalty to the death, but at the same time seeking special honors for which they were rebuffed (Matt. 20:20–24; Mark 10:35–41). He was also present for special occasions: at the raising of Jairus daughter (Mark 5:37; Luke 8:51); at the Transfiguration (Matt. 17:1; Mark 9:2; Luke 9:28); and at Gethsemane (Matt. 26:37; Mark 14:33). If he was indeed the "beloved disciple" in the Gospel of John, he was additionally the one who leaned on Jesus' breast at the Last Supper (John 13:23); the one who was faithful all the way to the cross, at which time Jesus assigned him the special care of his mother (John 19:26f); the one who was the first to believe in Jesus's Resurrection at the tomb (John 20:10); and the one who was the first to recognize his risen Lord on the Sea of Galilee (John 21:1–7).

This extensive list would suggest that John was indeed the "beloved disciple" and the author of the Gospel of John. He appears somewhat less prominently in Acts: he was one of those who gathered in the upper room after the Ascension (Acts 1:13); he accompanied *Peter to the Temple to pray and stayed to heal the lame (Acts 3:1–4:22); and he also joined Peter on a journey to Samaria (Acts 8:14–17).

Traditions about his later years are legion: some believe that he and his brother were cousins of Jesus; St. Jerome records a tradition identifying John as the bridegroom at the marriage at Cana; St. Irenaeus reports that he lived to an old age, composing his Gospel in Ephesus (Jeffrey, 408); here he is thought to have established the nucleus of a church and written his epistles. After the death of John, some believe that his church at Ephesus published a final edited version of the Gospel, perhaps as late as A.D. 150 (Smalley, 375). As the author of the Revelation of St. John, he was also associated with the Isle of Patmos, where the Emperor Domitian or Trajan was thought to have banished him near the end of the first century A.D.

**Historical Context.** The author of the Gospel of John was extraordinarily well educated for a fisherman. The narrative is richly philosophical, beginning not with the genealogy or the nativity narrative, but with a poetic discourse on the Word or *Logos*, which echoes the opening of Genesis. He blends objective facts with religious interpretation, creating a dramatic narrative account infused with deeper meaning, and an artistic unity of considerable sophistication. Unlike the writers of the Synoptic Gospels, John ignores some of the events in the life of Jesus and includes other events and details, some of which appear to have been eyewitness accounts.

John is also thought to be the author of at least one, and perhaps all three of the Epistles of John. The first of these is more a homily or sermon than a letter. All three suggest a Hellenistic environment and a confrontation with gnosticism. The style and quality of thought have much in common with the Gospel.

The Revelation of St. John, which appears to be a somewhat later work, has sometimes been ascribed to John "the Elder." (John "the Elder" exists only in a quotation from Papias in Eusebius's history. Papias mentions two Johns and refers to the Scriptures as "the discourses of the elders." This reference is the basis of the speculation.) *The New International Version*, however, ascribes Revelation and all of the Johannine epistles to the apostle John, noting continuing patterns of language and style (See *New International Version* introductions to Epistles and to Revelation.)

**Archaeological Evidence.** Like the Virgin *Mary, John has been associated with both Jerusalem and Ephesus. On the other hand, Ignatius, who wrote (c. A.D. 116) to Ephesus, fails to mention John, who is thought to have died there. Other early writers—Papias and Polycarp—are also silent about John's residence in Ephesus (Miller, 340). Another unproven tradition, probably based on the *Chronicle* of Philip of Side (c. A.D. 430), asserts that James and John were killed by the Jews, presumably before A.D. 70. The mainstream view is that John lived in exile on Patmos, where he penned Revelation in the 90s A.D.

On the other hand, Ephesus, which has been extensively excavated, has a strong Johannine tradition. According to Josephus, there was a significant Jewish community there, and it was an early site for Christians as well. The Church of Saint John was purportedly constructed over the site of the apostle's grave (Oster, 189).

**Character in Later Works.** Tradition says that Mary, the mother of Jesus, lived with John until her death, and that he then traveled about Judea preaching the gospel with Peter. Some think he journeyed into Asia Minor and founded the seven churches mentioned in Revelation (2 and 3). He may have settled at Ephesus and endured persecution under Emperor Domitian. Legend has it that the emperor twice tried to take John's life, once ordering him to drink a cup of poisoned wine, which turned into a snake and departed. On another occasion, John was thrown into a cauldron of boiling oil, but emerged from it unhurt. He was then exiled to Patmos, where he had his revelation, going eventually to Ephesus as an old man, where he died a natural death (Ferguson, 126).

As a valued member of the inner circle of disciples, John figures prominently in stories of the life of Jesus and in many of the art works derived from that life. As the writer of one of the four Gospels, he was assigned the image of Ezekiel's eagle. Because he was consistently designated as "beloved," he is also portrayed as young and attractive, usually with a long beard (Jeffrey, 408–9). Since he was the one on whom Jesus leaned at the Last Supper, we see him in the many portrayals of that scene. And because he was also present at the Cross, we see him standing between Mary, the mother of Jesus, and Mary Magdalene in paintings of the Crucifixion. In contrast to the more impetuous Peter, John is often portrayed as the image of the contemplative life—an ironic image considering his designation as one of the "Sons of Thunder" (Mark 3:17). His friendship with Jesus is often compared with Jonathan's love of David. Even more powerful, of course, are his visions of the New Jerusalem in his Revelation—an inspiration for medieval church architecture and for numerous illuminated manuscripts.

## SOURCES

Ferguson, George, *Signs and Symbols in Christian Art*, New York: Oxford University Press, 1966; Jeffrey, David L., ed., *A Dictionary of the Biblical Tradition in English Literature*, Grand Rapids, MI: William B. Eerdmans Publishing Company, 1992; Miller, Madeline S., and J. Lane Miller, *Harper's Bible Dictionary*, New York: Harper and Row, 1961; Oster, Richard E., "Ephesus," and Stephen S. Smalley, "John, The Gospel According to," in *The Oxford Companion to the Bible*, edited by Bruce M. Metzger and Michael D. Coogan, New York: Oxford University Press, 1993.

## JONAH

**Name and Etymology.** *Jonah* means "dove."

**Synopsis of Bible Story.** Jonah, the son of Amittai, is best known for his career—not his prophetic message. He, apparently, like *Elijah and *Elisha, traveled in prophetic circles. We know only that part of his life and thought described in the brief book named for him.

Jonah's story begins with God's call to preach to the great city of Nineveh—a city usually perceived as an enemy to Israel and to Jehovah. Rejecting this mandate, Jonah instead raced to Joppa, taking a ship bound for Tarshish (assumed to be an early name for Cadiz, in Spain). Shortly after sailing, the ship ran into foul weather, and the sailors quickly discovered through the casting of lots that Jonah was the source of the trouble. He volunteered to help their cause by being cast into the sea, where a giant fish swallowed him, holding him for three days, and then hurling him onto dry land.

God again ordered his prophet to preach to the people of Nineveh (Jonah, 3); this time Jonah obeyed. His preaching proved a success, resulting in a decree by the king to repent and encouraging the people of the city to change their ways. God, in turn, relented and saved this Gentile people from destruction—much to Jonah's distress.

He prayed to die, only to be graced by a vine that grew over his shelter, providing shade for the petulant prophet. When God caused the vine to wither and die, Jonah again cried to God in distress, only to be told this time that he seemed more concerned about a vine than people and animals of the city of Nineveh. The abrupt and powerful ending contains the Lord's strong condemnation of this merciless and narrow-minded prophet. "Thou has had pity on the gourd for which thou has not laboured, neither madest it grow; which came up in a night, and perished in a night: And should not I spare Nineveh, that great city, wherein are more than sixscore thousand persons that cannot discern between their right hand and their left hand; and also much cattle?" (Jonah 4:10–11).

**Historical Context.** The Book of Jonah marks a turning point in Jewish history. It is set in the world of eighth century B.C., when Nineveh was the most powerful capital in the world. This was a century after the ten northern tribes had broken with Jerusalem and had begun their tradition of building pagan altars in high places and practicing pagan rituals. The Assyrians proved to be the avengers, working God's wrath on their apostasy and conquering the northern tribes in 722 B.C. The northern tribes were then assimilated into the Gentile nations, eventually disappearing from history. This is the cause of Jonah's great grief at the salvation of the people of Nineveh—they would survive to bring disaster on the people of Israel, Jonah's own people. (See Seiden's article.)

The book is unusual. It is a sea story, chronicling a voyage with Phoenician sailors. Because the Israelites were not seafaring people, stories of sea travel are rare in Scripture. Most of their references to boats are connected with the Sea of Galilee—as in the Gospels. Later, *Paul breaks this tradition with his tempestuous voyage over the Mediterranean. He may well have traveled by sea on several of his early journeys.

Jonah's story is also unusual as a tale of a miraculous animal–human experience. (The great fish in this story is apparently not the same as the Leviathan in Job.) References to threatening sea monsters are rare in Hebrew literature, as opposed to in Greek myth, which is full of sea adventures.

It is unusual, too, as an example of a successful prophetic outreach to Gentiles, peoples usually seen as enemies. This foreshadows the Book of Acts, suggesting that God's mercy is universal, not a national treasure belonging exclusively to the Jews.

The lots that were cast were a standard means of discovering the will of God, used later by the disciples to determine the replacement for Judas. From ancient times, this was considered a magical means of discovering divine wisdom.

**Archaeological Evidence.** Jaffa, or Joppa, was a city on the coast of the Mediterranean conquered by the Philistines and not included in Israelite territory. Solomon brought timber to Joppa from Lebanon for the building of his Temple, and later builders brought cedar wood there at the time of the restoration (Negev, 205). Mounds at Tel Aviv were first excavated in the 1950s, revealing remains of ancient Jaffa, the seaport from which Jonah sailed that dates back to the Bronze age.

Nineveh's remains have also been explored, uncovering the famous gates with the images of the great winged bulls of the palace of Ashurbanipal. It must, at one time, have had magnificent palaces. The walls were said to be "high like a mountain," with the whole city surrounded by gardens of scented plants irrigated by channels that drew water from neighboring rivers. Ashurbanipal also had a vast library. The 25,000 clay tablets found there document historical, literary, and religious matters. This was the last capital of the Assyrian empire. The city was probably founded early in the third millennium B.C., later serving as the sole capital under *Sennacherib. Today, the remains are hidden in two mounds on the banks of the Hzwsar River. Negev identifies the south bank's mount, Nebi Younis, as the site of Jonah's prophecy (283).

**Character in Later Works.** Jewish sources provide both serious and fanciful commentary on the book of Jonah, interpreting his flight from God as an echo of the fallen *Adam's efforts to hide from him, and Jonah's descent into the depths of the sea as a parallel to *Moses' ascent to the heights of Mount Sinai. One legend out of many dealing with the details of the whale's belly suggests that Jonah used the whale's eyes as windows into the depths (See Summerfield, Ryken, and Eldredge, 409).

*Jesus referred to the "sign of Jonah" in anticipation of his own death and resurrection, suggesting a comparison with Jonah's being swallowed by the great fish and vomited back onto the dry land. As a result, Jonah came to be considered a type of Christ, especially the resurrected Christ, figuring as an emblem of the Resurrection in many of the early Christian paintings in the catacombs.

In most of art history, he has been portrayed resting in the shadow of his gourd. When artists of the Italian Renaissance sought to picture his adventures at sea, being unfamiliar with the habits or appearance of whales, they often drew from their imaginations, portraying the fish as a dragon, a dolphin, or a great shaggy monster.

Jonah's influence on literature has been extensive, interesting different ages in different ways. His story is sometimes pictured as a model for the medieval miracle play (e.g., the Chester cycle of medieval plays). Frequent mention of his experiences appear throughout Western literature. Jonah is the subject of the sermon preached in Melville's *Moby Dick* by Father Mapple. Zora Neale Hurston used the image of Jonah in her comic tale of African-American life, *Jonah's Gourd Vine*. Robert Frost saw him as a contemporary Paul (who was also tossed into the sea) in *A Masque of Mercy*.

A "Jonah" became an image of bad luck among seamen, used famously in "The Rime of the Ancient Mariner" by Samuel Taylor Coleridge. In contemporary children's literature, the image is used in the tale of Pinocchio. Moderns consider this a richly comic tale, full of delightful psychological insights, but more fictional than historical.

The image of the rebellious poet arguing with God has appealed to Romantics and to moderns who relish the antihero with very human qualities. The beautiful psalm included in the text is a perennial favorite. The book is read on the Day of Atonement in the Jewish liturgical calendar, perhaps as a reminder of the mercy of God.

## SOURCES

Ferguson, George, *Signs and Symbols in Christian Art*, New York: Oxford University Press, 1966; Negev, Avraham, ed., *The Archaeological Encyclopedia of the Holy Land*, New York: Thomas Nelson Publishers, 1986; Seiden, Chaim, "Insight: Why Does Jonah Want to Die," in *Bible Review*, June 1999; Summerfield, Henry, Leland Ryken, and Laurence Eldredge, "Jonah," in *A Dictionary of the Biblical Tradition in English Literature*, edited by David L. Jeffrey, Grand Rapids, MI: William B. Eerdmans Publishing Company, 1992.

## JONATHAN

**Name and Etymology.** The name *Jehonathan* means "Jehovah hath given."

**Synopsis of Bible Story.** Jonathan, the oldest son of *Saul, appeared first in 1 Samuel 13:3 as the hero of a successful attack against the Philistines. In the following chapter, he won yet another victory over these traditional adversaries. A later story, in 1 Sam.

14:27–32, shows him the unwitting violator of his father's foolish rule against his soldiers eating. While in the woods, he discovered honey, tasted it, and found himself reinvigorated. His men followed suit, eagerly eating not only the honey, but meat as well, against Saul's express wishes and under his clear curse on those who disobeyed. In a subsequent confrontation with his father, Jonathan explained that the rule and the curse were both ill-considered, that men fight better when properly nourished. He was sentenced to die for his disobedience (1 Sam. 14:44), but forgiven at the last minute.

When *David entered the court, Jonathan established a covenant of friendship with the handsome young warrior/musician. He kept this covenant while seeking to remain faithful to his father and king, but he increasingly believed his father to be wrong. Caught between two powerful people, both of whom he loved, Jonathan made every effort to keep the peace. At one time, he convinced his father to desist in his repeated attempts to murder David, only to find that the old man was obsessed by jealousy. Saul even hurled a spear at this faithful son at one point. Jonathan's sad parting with David is chronicled in 1 Samuel 20:41–42.

A selfless hero, friend, and son, Jonathan willingly relinquished his own claim to the throne when *Samuel anointed David. He risked his own life to save David's, keeping his covenant at his own expense. He finally died, along with his father and brothers, on Mount Gilboa in a final battle (1 Sam. 31:11–13). David, in his famous lament for him (2 Sam. 1:25–27), paid tribute to this gentle, decent friend whom he loved more than a brother. David later brought his body back to the sepulcher of Saul's father, called Kish, where he buried his friend properly (2 Sam. 21:12–14). Later, as a final sign of his genuine love of this friend, David protected Jonathan's crippled son Mephibosheth (2 Sam. 9:1–13).

**Historical Context.** Jonathan bridges the end of Saul's dynasty and the beginning of David's. His battles against the Philistines are part of the continuing struggle to establish Israel as a unified force in this promised land. By the tenth century B.C., his friend David had established the centralized government needed to transform these tribes into a nation.

**Archaeological Evidence.** Jonathan's death along with his father and brothers on Mount Gilboa is one more sign of the numerous battles fought over the Jezreel Valley. A historian notes that there were at least 13 battles fought over this strategic location (Cline, "Why Meggido?" 20). Archaeologists continue to dig in this region and have uncovered relics of numerous civilizations.

**Character in Later Works.** Jonathan's gentle and faithful nature has appealed over the years to many Christians who have seen him as an ideal portrayal of charity. His friendship with David is usually understood as one of the greatest friendships of all time, paralleling those of Greek myth such as Achilles and Patroclus.

Jonathan is so central to David's story that he appears in almost every work that mentions King David. Edmund Spenser, for example, uses him as a symbol of friendship in *The Faerie Queene*. Jonathan figures large in D. H. Lawrence's *David* and in J. M. Barrie's play *The Boy David*.

He is also a secondary character in most stories of Saul, including Handel's oratorio *Saul*. Lord Byron, in *Hebrew Melodies*, has the old king bidding farewell to his men and expressing his affection for his son.

David's lament for his friend is considered one of the world's greatest dirges:

How are the mighty fallen in the midst of the battle!
O Jonathan, thou wast slain in thine high places.
I am distressed for thee, my brother Jonathan: very pleasant hast thou been unto me:
thy love to me was wonderful, passing the love of women.
How are the mighty fallen, and the weapons of war perished!

(2 Sam. 1:25–27)

## SOURCES

Cline, Eric H., *The Battles of Armageddon: Megiddo and the Jezreel Valley from the Bronze Age to the Nuclear Age*, Ann Arbor, MI: University of Michigan Press, 2000; Cline, Eric H., "Why Meggido?" in *Biblical Archaeological Review*, January 2001; Jeffrey, David L., ed., in *A Dictionary of the Biblical Tradition in English Literature*, Grand Rapids, MI: William B. Eerdmans Publishing Company, 1992.

## JOSEPH (SON OF JACOB)

**Name and Etymology.** *Joseph* means "may he [Jehovah] add" or "to take away" (Gen. 30:23–24); his Egyptian name was *Zaphnathpaaneah*, or "says the God: he will live."

**Synopsis of Bible Story.** Joseph, the eleventh son of *Jacob, was his father's favorite, the first child by his beloved wife *Rachel, who died at the birth of her second child, Joseph's brother Benjamin. Joseph was apparently a talented and attractive young dreamer who failed to notice the growing hostility of his siblings. Scripture notes (Gen. 37:2) that, when Joseph was 17, he notified his father of his brothers' unspecified bad behavior. After that, he unwisely shared with his increasingly jealous brothers the details of his dreams of superiority—their sheaves of wheat bowing to his, the sun and moon and stars bowing to him. Even his doting father was perplexed by this image of the sun and moon (suggesting his father and mother) bowing down before him. Yet, as a sign of his great love for this good and "comely" lad, Jacob (Israel), gave him a beautiful coat (Gen. 37:3).

This early hostility climaxed when Jacob sent Joseph out into the fields to check on his brothers, who were tending sheep. When his siblings spotted him, they plotted to kill him. His oldest brother, Reuben, saved his life by convincing the others to throw him into a pit instead of shedding his blood. Reuben had planned to rescue him later, but the brothers took the opportunity to sell Joseph to Ishmaelite traders from Gilead. After the merchants had carried him off to Egypt, the brothers took his coat of many colors, stained it with goat's blood, and pretended Joseph was dead (Gen. 37:23–32).

In Egypt, the resourceful Joseph quickly rose in the favor of his new master, Potiphar, one of the Pharaoh's officials, who made him a steward (Gen. 39). Potiphar's wife could not keep her eyes and thoughts off this handsome servant, whom she invited to her bed. When he refused her lascivious attentions, she turned on him and accused him of trying to ravish her. As a result, the innocent young slave was thrown into prison. There he again proved adaptable, winning the trust of the keeper of the prison, making friends with other prisoners—including the Pharaoh's cupbearer and his baker—interpreting dreams, and finally attracting the attention of the Pharaoh. Joseph interpreted Pharaoh's dreams to predict that the land was facing seven years of plenty followed by seven years of want (Gen. 41). When he advised that an administrator be placed in charge of storage of grain, he was rewarded for his good sense by being made viceroy.

It was in this role that he later found his own brothers seeking food in the midst of famine (Gen. 42). Testing their values in a series of complicated and prolonged trials, he found them to be honest and filled with genuine concern for his brother Benjamin and for their father. He broke into tears, told them his story, and brought the entire family to Egypt to avoid the famine in Canaan.

In the scenes of reconciliation with his half-brothers and his loving reunion with his younger brother and his father, we see the fulfillment of a lifetime of struggle and hope. By this time, he had married the daughter of the high priest of the temple at On and had two sons. He arranged for the family to settle in Goshen, close to the Asian border with its good grazing land (Alter, 346). After some years in this new home, the aged Jacob planned for his own death, calling Joseph to him and blessing Joseph's sons, making them his adopted children and heirs with his own boys. When Jacob died, Joseph had him embalmed and then carried the body back for burial with his family in Canaan.

When Joseph reached the ripe old age of 110, he also died. Like his father, he was embalmed, but his bones were not carried back to Canaan until they were taken there by Moses (Exod. 13:19).

**Historical Context.** Joseph's story, which spans the final chapters of Genesis, is the longest and most complex of the patriarchal narratives, explaining the sojourn in Egypt and establishing the basis for the tribes that were to return to the promised land under Moses' leadership.

Joseph's "coat of many colors" is now thought to have been a long-sleeved tunic. Some scholars note that this is the kind of garment worn by women or royalty and is apparently very costly (Kugel, 452). As a symbol of authority, it probably signified that Jacob, having already argued with Reuben, his eldest, was placing the eleventh son in the line of blessing.

The Hyksos Dynasty in Egypt, which ruled from c. 1720–1550 B.C., was noted for its friendliness to foreigners. Scholars believe that the Joseph saga began in the early years of this regime (Miller, 350). Egypt was—and still is—the breadbasket for the region, more fertile than the arid lands that make up much of Canaan.

The Ishmaelite traders from Gilead (Gen. 37:25) were descendants of *Ishmael. The products that they were carrying were common in trade with Egypt. Also referred to as Midianites, they were frequently seen in the desert along trade routes. Scholars note that the price they paid, twenty shekels of silver, was the current value of a male of Joseph's age.

**Archaeological Evidence.** The Jezreel Valley was the traditional path of trading caravans from east to Egypt. The Plain of Dothan, where today a modern hard-surfaced highway and an old caravan trail overlap, has a dry cistern or pit used for grain storage, probably the sort of place in which Joseph was held hostage.

The Egyptian elements in the story have the fullest archaeological documentation. Information on the Hyksos is particularly abundant, as are bas-reliefs showing starving Semitic peoples along with others seeking refuge in Egypt. The Egyptian relief from Horemheb is a vivid example of this. In carvings at the Temple of Rameses, we may also see miniatures of the granaries used in Joseph's day, as well as pictures of cattle, which had religious significance for the Egyptians.

The details of embalming are peculiar to the Egyptians. The Hebrews' burial customs, as we see in the stories of the other patriarchs, involved placing the bodies in caves or under piles of rocks. The preservation of the physical body was not necessary for immortality, as it was in Egyptian mythology.

**Character in Later Works.** In Jewish history, Joseph was seen as the ideal hero, a saintly figure. He is frequently cited in catalogues of the patriarchs and as the one who inherited the rights of the firstborn (1 Chron. 5:1–3). Joseph's descendants are divided into two tribes, Manasseh and Ephraim, the two sons adopted by Jacob. Parallels with *Daniel, another exemplary young man who became an interpreter of dreams, were frequently cited.

The Christians saw Joseph as a type of Christ figure, noting his unjust treatment by those close to him, and his sale for 20 pieces of silver, as well as the forgiving and loving resolution of the narrative. *Paul used him in Hebrews as an exemplar of faith (Heb. 11:22). Patristic writers Tertullian, Irenaeus, and Ambrose were moved by Joseph's moral uprightness.

Artists have painted various studies of Joseph, and used his image in stained glass windows—including a famous example at King's College, Cambridge.

Early literary references to Joseph focus on his coat of many colors and the betrayal by his brothers, but a very different type of Joseph appears in eighteenth-century English novels. Comic treatments, notably Henry Fielding's *Joseph Andrews*, turned Joseph's chastity into an ironic basis for the portrayal of his prissy hero. Here the innocent young man in the midst of a corrupt society, fending off lewd women who try to seduce him, seems absurd. The term "a real Joseph" became popular in the eighteenth century England as synonymous for prudish behavior.

Nineteenth- and twentieth-century novelists have returned to the Christ identification—as in Herman Melville's *Billy Budd*. Thomas Mann produced the fullest and most powerful rendering of the Joseph story in his four-volume series *Joseph and his Brothers*. The most recent treatment of the story, in the Webber and Rice rock cantata *Joseph and the Amazing Technicolor Dreamcoat*, lacks most of its moral or spiritual basis, becoming little more than an exciting story of a handsome young hero.

Joseph's narrative, a crucial one in Jewish history, is now appreciated as a remarkably artistic work, with the interweaving of dreams and fulfillment, the romantic tale of the bright young man off on a grand adventure, making rich use of suspense, intrigue, and clever devices for testing and recognition. It is seen as a masterpiece of storytelling. Sadly, the Joseph tradition has moved from the majesty of historical epic—people moving from their home into a land that will soon enslave them—into a mocking rock opera, full of flash and trickery.

## SOURCES

Alter, Robert, *Genesis: Translation and Commentary* (Anchor Bible Series), New York: W. W. Norton and Company, 1996; Graves, Robert, and Raphael Patai, *Hebrew Myths: The Book of Genesis*, New York: McGraw-Hill Book Company, 1963; Jacobs, Alan, "Joseph," in *A Dictionary of the Biblical Tradition in English Literature*, edited by David L. Jeffrey, Grand Rapids, MI: William B. Eerdmans Publishing Company, 1992; Kugel, James L., *Traditions of the Bible: A Guide to the Bible As It Was at the Start of the Common Era*, Cambridge, Mass: Harvard University Press, 1998; Miller, Madeline S., and J. Lane Miller, *Harper's Bible Dictionary*, New York: Harper and Row, 1961.

## JOSEPH OF ARIMATHEA

**Name and Etymology.** *Joseph* is one of the oldest names in Scripture, dating back to the son of Jacob, meaning "May God give increase." Arimathea was a town on the western slopes of the Judean hills, in the vicinity of Lod, thought to be near Ramlah or Ramataim-Zophim (Negev, 322).

**Synopsis of Bible Story.** Joseph of Arimathea, perhaps a secret disciple of Christ, was a member of the Jewish governing body, the Sanhedrin. He was apparently absent from the meeting at which *Jesus was condemned, or perhaps he simply abstained from voting (Luke 23:51). *Luke (23:50–53) mentions that he was "good and just" and that he explicitly dissented from the action taken by the council against Jesus. In *John 19:38–42, Joseph is paired with the Pharisee *Nicodemus; he hid his discipleship up to this point, probably for fear of the Jews.

After Jesus was crucified, this heretofore unmentioned man claimed the body, asking *Pilate's permission to take Jesus's body and entomb it. *Mark 15:43–46 notes that he was a respected council member awaiting the reign of God. He removed the body from the cross, wrapped it in a linen cloth, and buried it in a tomb he had prepared for his own burial; he then rolled a stone against the opening to seal it.

**Historical Context.** It is clear that Joseph was a law-abiding Jew, eager to follow the commandments concerning burial (Deut. 21:23; Tob. 1:17–18). According to Jewish law, the body of a person executed might not remain on the instrument of torture over night (Deut. 21:22f). According to Roman law, relatives could claim the body of the person who had been executed. Thus, it was appropriate for Joseph to petition Pilate for the body so that he could bury it before the Sabbath. When Pilate granted his request, Joseph arranged for the burial near Calvary, in a garden in which there was a newly hewn sepulcher intended by Joseph for his own use (Matt. 27:59). It was the practice of the Jews to bury their dead outside of the city walls, often in caves. Some believe that this cave may have been a temporary burial place. After the body decomposed, the custom was for the bones to be collected and placed somewhere else.

The place of the burial is thought to have been on the site now covered by the Church of the Holy Sepulcher. Pilgrims to Jerusalem are also shown a spot near the Garden of Gethsemane that may have served for Christ's burial.

**Archaeological Evidence.** Eusebius states that Arimathea was close to Lod, where Joseph lived. The biblical site of the ancient city has not been identified with certainty (Negev, 322–23).

Details of the stone and the burial cave have interested various scholars, who have studied the different stones used to cover cave entrances, noting that dozens of round "blocking stones" have been found from the Second Temple period (Kloner). Some believe that this was a square, rather than a round blocking stone, fairly small, as the tomb itself may have been.

**Character in Later Works.** Apocryphal writings variously present Joseph, rather than John, caring for *Mary after Christ's ascension (Levine, 383). The fourth-century apocryphal Acts of Pilate (or The Gospel of Nicodemus) gives information about Joseph's imprisonment, his miraculous rescue, and his testimony to Christ's ascension. The story of Christ's descent into hell, known as the "Harrowing of Hell," also was developed through Joseph (Walsh, 412).

In English tradition, he had developed into a local hero by the twelfth century. By c. 1250, monks at Glastonbury, England, had added a story to an earlier account that told of *Philip the apostle sending Joseph and companions to Britain, where they settled and built a church of wattles dedicated to Mary. From this tale was derived the tradition of the "Glastonbury Thorn," a species of Levantine hawthorn flowering twice a year (Brownrigg, 247).

A century later, John of Glastonbury developed the story of Arthur's descent from Joseph's nephew and made reference to the quest for the Holy Grail. (His reference was to two cruets "filled with the blood and sweat" of Jesus, for which Joseph cared.) Later legends developed Joseph's role as the Grail bearer, the ancestor of Galahad, and so on (Tuchman, 13–21). It was through this long tradition that Joseph became involved in the Grail legend, therefore appearing in the Arthurian legends. From Joseph was thought to have come the sacred sword—originally King David's—and the miraculous white shield. Eventually, he became associated with the Fisher King, the guardian of the Grail after Joseph died.

Later writers, including Spenser, Tennyson, Wordsworth, and Blake made reference to him because of this apocryphal tradition. In "Idylls of the King," Tennyson has a monk say:

> From our old books I know
> That Joseph came of old to Glastonbury
> And there the heathen prince, Aviragus,
> Gave him an isle of marsh whereon to build
> A little lonely church in days of yore.
> —Tennyson

This ancient tradition established for Britain its earliest link to Christianity, straight from Palestine, without any reference to Rome. Joseph was officially recognized as the founder of the Christian Church in Great Britain because of this legend.

## SOURCES

Brownrigg, Ronald, *Who's Who in the Bible*, vol. 2, New York: Bonanza Books, 1980; Kloner, Amos, "Did a Rolling Stone Close Jesus' Tomb?" in *Biblical Archaeology Review Archives*, September/October 1999; Levine, Amy-Jill, "Joseph of Arimathea," in *The Oxford Companion to the Bible*, edited by Bruce M. Metzger and Michael D. Coogan, New York: Oxford University Press, 1993; Miller, Madeline S., and J. Lane Miller, *Harper's Bible Dictionary*, New York: Harper and Row, 1961; Negev, Avraham, ed., *The Archaeological Encyclopedia of the Holy Land*, New York: Thomas Nelson, 1986; Tuchman, Barbara, *Bible and Sword*, New York: Ballantine Books, 1956; Walsh, Marie Michelle, "Joseph of Arimathea," in *A Dictionary of the Biblical Tradition in English Literature*, edited by David L. Jeffrey, Grand Rapids, MI: William B. Eerdmans Publishing Company, 1992.

## JOSEPH THE CARPENTER

**Name and Etymology.** *Joseph* is a Hebrew name meaning "may he [Jehovah] add." It is a traditional name taken from the Old Testament patriarch, the son of *Jacob.

**Synopsis of Bible Story.** Joseph, the earthly father of *Jesus, was betrothed to *Mary when the angel came to her with the astonishing announcement that she was to become the mother of the Messiah. A kind and just man who was reluctant to "make a publik example" of his pregnant spouse, Joseph "was minded to put her away privily" (Matt. 1:18). While he was making his decision, he was visited by an angel who encouraged him to continue his marriage plans, "for that which is conceived in her is of the Holy Ghost. And she shall bring forth a son, and thou shalt call his name Jesus: for he shall save his people from their sins" (Matt. 1:20–21). Joseph followed the directions of the angel, taking Mary as his wife, but he "knew her not till she had brought forth her firstborn son" (Matt. 1:25).

Since he was of the lineage of *David, Joseph was forced to leave his home in Nazareth to go to Judea, to be registered in the census required by *Caesar Augustus. Mary accompanied him on the difficult journey to Bethlehem, knowing that the time was near for the birth of the child. After *Jesus was born, Scripture notes that Joseph stood at her side when she was visited by the shepherds (Luke 2:16). He took the child to Jerusalem in solemn fulfillment of the law, where Jesus was circumcised and named—thus making him the legal child of Joseph (Luke 2:21). Scholars assume there was a space of time in which the news spread to the East, so the "wise men" made their journey to visit the child some months after the birth. When *Herod ordered the massacre of the Jewish infants, Joseph, the good father, being warned of the danger by an angel in a dream, fled with his family to Egypt (Matt. 2:13).

After the death of *Herod the Great, Joseph was again warned of dangers in Judea, but believed the way was clear to bring his family back to Galilee—Nazareth, (Matt. 2:22–23) where they apparently lived until his death. He must have had a role in the supervision of Jesus' younger days. Jesus' loving pictures of earthly fathers—as in the story of the "Prodigal Son"—suggest he knew something of a father's love and guidance. His references to God as "abba" or "father" are even more evidence of his admiration for the good-father figure.

Some traditions assert that Joseph continued to refrain from any sexual relationship with Mary, preserving her virginity. If this was the case, it would force us to assume that Joseph had children from an earlier marriage in order to explain references to brothers and sisters. This would explain the tradition that Joseph was much older than Mary. The Bible is not clear on this detail, but it does indicate that there were other children in the family—the most significant of them being *James.

We know that Joseph was pious, raising his sons in the traditions of his faith, including sacrifices and worship at the Temple. The last time he is mentioned as part of the story is when he took Jesus to the annual feast of the Passover in Jerusalem. The family must have traveled the long journey with others from Nazareth. When they started back, they found Jesus to be missing, forcing Mary and Joseph to return to Jerusalem, where they discovered their son in the Temple, "sitting in the midst of the doctors, both hearing them, and asking them questions" (Luke 2:46). Joseph must have been as astonished as the elders at this young man's understanding and at his answers, but it was Mary who admonished him for causing Joseph sorrow by his thoughtless behavior (Luke 2:48). It was then that the boy said, "How is it that ye sought me? wist ye not that I must be about my Father's business?" In this final reference to Joseph, when his role is subsumed in the greater role of God the Father, the Scripture notes that "they understood not the saying which he spake unto them" (Luke 2:49–50).

By the time his son entered his public ministry, Joseph is no longer mentioned, leading most scholars to believe that by then Joseph had died and Mary was a widow, relying on Jesus as her faithful son, who had not married, to serve as the "man of the house." This would explain the late start of Jesus' ministry and the close relationship with his mother, who accompanied him on some of his journeys. (Apparently, her other children also comforted her, even coming with her to plead with Jesus to return home.)

**Historical Context.** Both *Matthew, who tells the story of the Messiah from Joseph's perspective, and *Luke, who is inclined to tell it from Mary's point of view, consider the lineage of the earthly family significant. Both trace Jesus' heritage back through

*David. Matthew traces him to *Abraham and Luke traces him to *Adam, the son of God. They are both aware of the prophecy that the Messiah was to come from the House of David.

Joseph's nobility in desiring to protect his pregnant spouse and yet live in strict conformity to the law would have created a conflict in this decent man. It was forbidden to have sexual relations during the betrothal period; any violation of this law might be punished by divorce. In Hebrew Law, the betrothed woman is considered a "wife" (See notes in *New International Version*, 1436–1437). In addition, as an orthodox Jew who lived by the law of Moses, his community was clear on the punishment for a woman pregnant outside of marriage—she was to be stoned to death (Deut. 22: 23–24).

In documents of the era, we know of the events surrounding the Nativity narrative—the Roman requirements for census-taking in anticipation of taxation, the difficulties of travel, the bloodthirsty power grabs of *Herod the Great, the astrological studies of the wise men, and the habits of the shepherds. We know a great deal about the places Jesus lived, the larger world in which he worked, but we know little about this kind and thoughtful earthly father of Jesus. Joseph's work is usually assumed to be woodworking, but the term in Greek used for Joseph is "craftsman" (Matt. 13:55)—a word that could mean any number of things. The main form of construction in the Galilee was stonemasonry. Joseph may have worked in stone, but some historians think that he made plows and yokes, some that he was a cabinetmaker, and at least one thought he was a blacksmith (Manganiello, 413).

In some of the apocryphal books, such as The Infancy Gospel of Thomas and The Infancy Gospel of James, we see examples of a stern father, one who is disturbed by his son's enormous power and apparent abuse of it. In these apocryphal gospels, we also see a far more human and cruel Jesus killing children and raising the dead with great abandon and little spiritual benefit. (See examples in R. Miller, 371f, 387f.) Such a son would have required a stern father, but the accepted Scripture presents a far more loving relationship, suggesting that the earthly father would echo the words of the heavenly father—"this is my beloved son, in whom I am well pleased" (Matt. 3:17).

**Archaeological Evidence.** Joseph, a simple man from a small town, who had no known role in the major political or religious activities of the day, can be traced in archaeology only through the evidence of social patterns of common life. The homes, the tools, the clothing, and most of the accoutrements of daily life in Nazareth are lost to time. Little remains of the ancient synagogue where Jesus and his father may have worshipped. No church was built there until the time of the Emperor Constantine, and it was not mentioned prior to A.D. 570 (Negev, 279). The closest synagogue in the Galilee which has been discovered is at Capernaum, but it is unlikely that Joseph worshipped there. There are, of course, places in both Nazareth and Bethlehem that later traditions have designated holy sites related to Joseph, but no physical evidence of his life exists.

Nazareth is not found in the Old Testament, but it was a small settlement prior to the time of patriarchs. It was settled by 300 B.C., by newcomers who may have been a clan from the family of King David, forming the lineage of both Mary and Joseph. The Church of St. Joseph (also known as the Church of the Carpenter Shop) is north of the Basilica of the Annunciation, and is said to be built above the site of Joseph's carpentry shop. It is actually above some agricultural installations (a wine press and a silo). In Jesus' day, the village was tiny—with one spring and with not very fertile soil, it was a small agricultural settlement, where most families would have had modest plots for planting olive trees, grapevines, vegetables, and grain.

**Character in Later Works.** Joseph is an important part of all Nativity narratives and portrayals, the quiet presence behind the Virgin and the babe. Usually pictured in the traditional clothing of the time, bearded and older than his bride, he is invariably a secondary figure. Medieval mystery plays usually portray him as quite old, fearful that his spouse is an adulteress, and worried about having sexual relations with her.

Paintings of Joseph usually place him in his carpentry shop, on the trip to Bethlehem with the Christ Child, or on the journey to Egypt. He is almost invariably portrayed as a noble, dignified, sensible man, and an archetypal good father figure.

### SOURCES

Manganiello, Dominic, "Joseph the Carpenter," in *A Dictionary of the Biblical Tradition in English Literature*, edited by David L. Jeffrey, Grand Rapids, MI: William B. Eerdmans Publishing Company, 1992; Miller, Madeline S., and J. Lane Miller, *Harper's Bible Dictionary*, New York: Harper and Row, 1961; Miller, Robert J., ed., *The Complete Gospels*, San Francisco: HarperCollins, 1994; Negev, Avraham, ed., *The Archaeological Encyclopedia of the Holy Land*, New York: Thomas Nelson Publishers, 1986.

## JOSHUA

**Name and Etymology.** *Joshua* means "Jehovah is salvation"; this name in Greek is "Jesus."

**Synopsis of Bible Story.** Joshua, the son of Nun, from the Tribe of Ephraim (first mentioned in Exodus 17:9–13) was the natural successor to Moses, though not his son. In a series of incidents (Exod. 24:13, 32:17, 33:11), he proved his courage and his powerful faith. Because of his loyalty, he was sent to reconnoiter the land of Canaan, and then—unlike Moses and others—he was allowed to enter the promised land (Num. 14:6, 26:65, 32:12). When Moses "laid hands" upon him, Joshua was filled with the spirit of wisdom, so that the Israelites listened to him and did what the Lord commanded them to do (Deut. 34:9). As a military leader, he was able to conquer one city in Canaan after another, following carefully the directions given by God every step of the way. The book of Joshua is a chronicle of these heroic exploits, combined with the wisdom of a good leader and the orderliness of a farsighted administrator.

One of the most famous and frequently mentioned exploits of Joshua was the battle of Jericho. He marched his troops around the city for seven days; then his men blew their trumpets, and uttered a great shout, "For the Lord has given you the city!" (Josh. 6:15). Then the "walls fell down flat" (Josh. 6:20). The harlot Rahab (Josh. 2:1–21), who had helped the Israelites, was saved at the time of the siege, when Joshua's men destroyed every living thing in it—"men and women, young and old, cattle, sheep and donkeys" (Josh. 6:21). Later, Joshua also was once again helped by God in his conquests, in the battle over Gibeon, when the Lord made the sun and moon stand still (Josh. 10:12–13).

Not only a man of war, Joshua also set the stage for the peaceful settlement of the land, leading the people in a ceremony of covenant renewal (Josh. 24:1–25), reminding them of their promises and their laws. He arranged the allotments to the tribes, established the cities of refuge and the Levitical cities (Josh. 18–21). Never proud of his victories, he insisted that the Israelites' strength came from God: "One man of you shall chase a thousand: for the Lord your God, he it is that fighteth for you, as he hath promised you" (Josh. 23:10).

In his old age, Joshua gathered the elders around him at Shechem, reminding them of their long history, that they were a people set apart, partners with God in a covenant that forbade them to mingle with the Canaanite peoples, their gods, and their women. God, having given them a "land for which you did not labour, and cities which ye built not" (Josh. 24:13) expected their obedience to his law. At the end of the book of Joshua, we have his last words of advice, his planning of the great stone as a witness, and his burial at Timnathserah (24:26–33).

**Historical Context.** This epic hero—and "former prophet"—of the Hebrews, who led in the conquest and settlement of the promised land, deserved the prominence given him by being the subject of the first book in the Bible named for a man. ("*Former Prophets* are the historical books from Joshua through II Kings [except Ruth], which form a sequel to the Pentateuch and contain historical material on the period from the occupation of Canaan . . . to the fall of Jerusalem . . ." Miller, 583).

As *Moses grew old and learned that he required a successor, a man who could take the leadership in crossing the Jordan and claim the promised land for his people, he turned away from his own sons and chose a faithful follower and a strong warrior. The symbolic "laying on of hands" indicated a transfer of power and authority, still used in many churches today. Although moderns are concerned that Joshua was a man of war, he was also a man of faith, blending divine guidance and strict discipline with military strategy. He quickly settled the land, carefully apportioning the various sections to the tribes, allowing for special circumstances in an orderly and wise manner. He was the right man for the time—one who could be as ruthless as war required while attributing his victories to God's leadership, always seeing himself in the context of Hebrew history, as a servant rather than a hero.

The period of Joshua was the last era of harmony, when the Israelites were following faithfully the leadership of God's appointed leader. Joshua saw himself as "commander of the army of Yahweh." Victories were perceived as a result of the fusion of divine and human activity. The rituals involving the purification of the camp and the devotion of the spoils to God, the inclusion of the Ark in the battle, and even the battle cry have been cited as an effort to "sanctify" war.

Many of the cities he conquered and the lands he settled became important in later Israel history. For example, he met with his leaders at the Tabernacle at Shiloh, where the Ark of the Covenant was placed; this place then became the home of the Ark until the time of Samuel (1 Sam. 4:3).

Joshua's place in Jewish tradition among the "former prophets" makes him the final stage in a long history from the creation to the settling of the promised land. He is followed by the Judges and a tumultuous time of conflict with the peoples of Canaan. His story is history remembered through liturgy, a drama that unfolds through a series of repetitions, additions, and deletions, moving inexorably toward a climactic ending, which one critic calls a "cultic drama" (McEntire, 71–73). God is seen as the "divine warrior" who punishes idolaters and removes guilt through warfare.

**Archaeological Evidence.** Historians argue about the chronology of the book, believing that the gradual process of possessing the land was more peaceful than the text suggests and involved many years. Some track the various campaigns of the Israelites: the entry into Canaan, the central campaign, the southern campaign, and the northern campaign, noting the brilliance of the strategy. Starting with Jericho, they gained control over the strategic plains and roads, and used each location as a base of operations for future domination of the remainder of Palestine.

Archaeologists have explored the cities mentioned in Joshua with relish, excavating Hazor, Jericho, Gibeon, and so on. In various tells (mounds of debris), too numerous to mention, they have uncovered as many as twenty-one layers with significant Canaanite artifacts.

As for Jericho, a collapsed double wall found by archaeologist John Garstang may correspond to Joshua's conquest of the city (Hargis, 7). While some, such as Kathleen Kenyon, have asserted that Jericho was not inhabited at the time the Bible claims Joshua destroyed it, recent studies have shown that they may have disregarded evidence that would support the Biblical account. The city was inhabited by Israelites from the ninth century B.C. until the Babylonian exile.

Gibeon was inhabited from the third millennium B.C. onwards, but most of what is known about the site comes from the Biblical record. It was a Hivite city when the Israelites came into the land. During the battle, when the Israelites defended the Hivites against the Canaanite forces, the day was lengthened and large hailstones fell, killing many of the Canaanites. Denis Baly, a noted biblical and geographical scholar said that as late as May 23, 1957, "hail the size of small apples fell again in the same region" where Joshua chased the Canaanites.

Some scholars argue about the degree to which the Jews accepted the religion and culture of the Canaanites. Although God often commanded them to destroy the native population, these people were apparently not exterminated, but continued to live alongside the Israelites. Modern scholars continue to debate Joshua's era, many assuming that the pattern of the period was one of settlement rather than conquest of the land.

**Character in Later Works.** In later times, the Jews developed numerous legends about this heroic figure: that he was designated first of conquerors at the world's creation; that he was like the moon to Moses' sun; that he was, in fact, the man in the moon; that he married Rahab the (rehabilitated) harlot; and so on (Greenspoon, 416–47).

Christian writers were interested in Joshua as a type of Christ, largely because of their shared name (Joshua = Jesus in Greek). As a righteous warrior, he was occasionally mentioned in literature, but rarely as the central figure. The popular spiritual "Joshua 'Fit' the Battle of Jericho" is his most impressive appearance.

The bone of contention in modern circles is with Joshua's stilling of the sun and moon at the valley of Ajalon. This became an especial target by critics of Scriptural infallibility.

### SOURCES

Gaster, Theodor H., *Myth, Legend and Custom in the Old Testament*, vol. 2, New York: Harper and Row, Publishers, 1975; Greenspoon, Leonard, "Joshua," in *A Dictionary of the Biblical Tradition in English Literature*, edited by David L. Jeffrey, Grand Rapids, MI: William B. Eerdmans Publishing Company, 1992; Hargis, Merilyn, and Jeff Hargis, *The Hindsight Tour Guide*, USA: Hindsight, 1996; McEntire, Mark, *The Blood of Abel: The Violent Plot in the Hebrew Bible*, Macon, GA: Mercer University Press, 1999; Miller, Madeline S., and J. Lane Miller, *Harper's Bible Dictionary*, New York: Harper and Row, 1961; Negev, Avraham, ed. *The Archaeological Encyclopedia of the Holy Land*, New York: Thomas Nelson Publishers, 1986; Tucker, Gene M., "Joshua, The book of," in *The Oxford Companion to the Bible*, edited by Bruce M. Metzger and Michael D. Coogan,

New York: Oxford University Press, 1993; Whyte, Alexander, *Bible Characters from the Old and New Testaments*, Grand Rapids: Kregel Publications, 1960.

## JOSIAH

**Name and Etymology.** *Josiah* means "Jehovah heals."

**Synopsis of Bible Story.** In 2 Kings 22–23 and 2 Chronicles 34–35, we see Josiah, the final great king in the lineage of David. Son of a failed king who met death at the hands of murderers, grandson of a corrupt king who filled the land with blood and pagan rituals, Josiah inherited the throne when he was only eight years old. Noted for his piety and zeal, he reigned for thirty-one years, c. 640–609 B.C.

During his reign, he ordered an inventory and refurbishing of the Temple, during which process his scribes discovered a number of long-forgotten manuscripts. The priest Hilkiah was so impressed by the documents, he took them to the king. When he read the core of the materials—probably what we know today as Deuteronomy, the three addresses of Moses, plus groups of laws which proceeded from them—Josiah was awed by the words and shocked at the transgressions of his own people.

He undertook a cleansing of the countryside of vestiges of pagan worship, ". . . he put down the idolatrous priests . . . he brake down the houses of the sodomites that were by the house of the Lord . . . and he defiled Topeth, which is in the valley of the children of Hinnom, that no man might make his son or his daughter to pass through the fire to Molech. . . ." (2 Kings 23:5–10). When he had finished demolishing the images and cleansing the altars, Josiah even emptied the sepulchers, leaving only the ones he believed to be the resting places of pious men. He reinstituted the full ritual celebration of Passover, which had not been practiced in its full form since the days of the Judges (2 Kings 23:21–22). He put away the witchcraft that had infested the land. In short, he turned to the Lord "with all his heart, and with all his soul, and with all his might, according to the law of Moses" (2 Kings 23:25).

In spite of the exertions of this remarkable man, the Lord continued to frown upon the people of Judah, who had rejected him for so long and betrayed him so completely. Although Josiah was blessed by a long and prosperous reign, his kingdom nonetheless faced judgment. At the end, Josiah confronted Neco II, the king of Egypt, and was slain at the famous site of Megiddo. His body was brought back to Jerusalem, where he was buried in his own sepulcher (2 Kings 23:30). His heirs were soon set aside by the powerful forces attacking the tiny kingdom. Josiah was, in fact, the final king in the line of David to rule successfully over the people of Judah.

**Historical Context.** Josiah lived at an interval in history between the domination of Assyria and that of Babylon, which allowed him to focus on the internal concerns of Jerusalem. When he stepped out of this, in the more aggressive move against Neco II at Megiddo, he was mortally wounded. Ironically, his intervention appears to have helped the Babylonians and their allies to overcome the Assyrians and remove them from the world scene.

The Egyptians, however, took advantage of the situation to install themselves in Palestine while Babylon was stabilizing itself to the east of the Euphrates. Having slain Josiah, they took upon themselves the responsibility of appointing a king in his place, his own son Jehoahaz (2 Kings 23:30). Very shortly, though, this appointee was removed for insubordination and carried off to Syria and then to Egypt. Neco replaced him with Eliakim (609–597 B.C.), another of Josiah's sons, and changed his name to

Jehoiakim. Acting as a puppet of Egypt, he extracted the required taxes for Egypt and neglected the recent reforms of Josiah.

Historians continue to argue about the mystery of Josiah's motivations in confronting Neco II. But the outcome is clear: Judah lost its reformist leader and was forced to pay Egypt a heavy tribute. The gathering power of the Babylonian Empire would soon force Palestine and Syria to bow before it.

**Archaeological Evidence.** Evidence of the reeling Assyrian empire and of Egyptian power at the time has been found in numerous places. The destruction of Nineveh in 612 B.C. and the death of Ashurbanipal encouraged a revival of regional loyalties, leading to a fresh enthusiasm for native religions in subject countries and a cleansing of the gods of Nineveh. This nationalistic surge emboldened Judah and its neighbors. Hershel Shanks notes the discovery of a seventh-century seal that identifies its owner as "servant of the king," probably referring to one of his ministers, Asaiah, who was involved with the work on the scroll that was discovered in the Temple ("Fingerprint of Jeremiah's Scribe").

Evidence of the Egyptian efforts to bolster the Assyrian authority over Palestine was discovered in 1923 by Assyriologist C. I. Gadd: he found an inscription on a cuneiform text in the British museum that had been dug up in Mesopotamia many years previously. It read as follows: "In the month of Du'uz [June–July] the king of Assyria procured a large Egyptian army and marched against Harran to conquer it. . . . Till the month of Ulul [August–September] he fought against the city but accomplished nothing." Werner Keller (298) notes that the "large Egyptian army" was the forces of Pharaoh Neco. Fragments of temple reliefs and other relics testify to the prominence of Pharaoh Neco II of Egypt (610–595 B.C.). This was the army that Josiah foolishly confronted at Megiddo.

Using these and other accounts, archaeologists have reconstructed the story of Josiah's death: in the late spring or early summer of 609 B.C., Josiah marched his army into the Jezreel Valley and waited for the Egyptians to emerge from the narrow Musmus Pass. Josiah, dressed in disguise, was riding a chariot up and down his front line, encouraging his men. He sounded the attack, planning to annihilate the Egyptian invaders, but an Egyptian archer let fly an arrow that mortally wounded him. He was then transferred to a second chariot, spirited south to Jerusalem, "where he was buried, along with his dreams for a rejuvenated Judah" (Cline).

**Character in Later Works.** Josiah himself was not considered a significant personage in later works, although the events that led to his death are also described in the apocryphal First Book of Esdras (1:25–32) and in Josephus' *Antiquities of the Jews* (10:74). His interest in the manuscripts found in the temple did prove invaluable and led to much of the revival of faith in Judah. The Deuteronomic Code, discovered during his reign, restated the theology and religion of some of the great earlier prophets and influenced prophets of later times. Scholars continue to debate over the exact contents and nature of the manuscripts discovered and over the management of these documents. It is not clear, for example, why the prophetess Huldah was consulted and what her specific role was. The significance of the discovery and of Josiah's elevation of worship at the Temple in Jerusalem according to the Law of Moses, however, cannot be exaggerated: "Many leaders of post-Exilic Israel followed Josiah's ideals" (Miller, 353).

It is no wonder that Josiah is listed in Matthew's genealogy of Jesus (Matt. 1:10). As the last of the lineage of David who reigned over Jerusalem as an independent monarch, he became the very image of the good king and a presage of the Messiah who would return and restore Jerusalem to full glory. His death at Megiddo is considered the reason that the final battle of the Apocalypse is set in that spot—Armageddon.

## SOURCES

Baker, D. W., "Josiah," in *The Illustrated Bible Dictionary*, vol. 2, edited by J. D. Douglas, Sidney, Australia: Tyndale House Publishers, 1980; Cline, Eric H., "Why Megiddo? and "What Was Josiah Thinking," *Biblical Archaeology Review*, June 2000; Keller, Werner, *The Bible as History*, New York: Bantam Books, 1982; Merrill, Eugene H., *An Historical Survey of the Old Testament*, Nutley, NJ: The Craig Press, 1972; Miller, Madeline S., and J. Lane Miller, *Harper's Bible Dictionary*, New York: Harper and Row, 1961; Shanks, Hershel; "Fingerprint of Jeremiah's Scribe," in *Biblical Archaeology Review*, March/April 1996.

## JUDAS ISCARIOT

**Name and Etymology.** *Judas* is the Greek form of the Hebrew *Judah*; *Iscariot* may mean "a man of Kerioth."

**Synopsis of Bible Story.** Judas is listed as one of the twelve disciples in all four Gospels, usually appearing last in the listing. Only in *John is he called Simon's son (6:71), and only John calls him a "thief" who kept the "common purse" (John 12:6, 13:29). In all of the Gospels, he is also designated as the disciple who betrayed Christ. Some scholars believe that he is the only one of the twelve who was not a Galilean. His calling is not noted in Scripture, but we know he was interested in money.

Jesus knew that Judas would betray him (John 13:11), but Judas's motivation for the betrayal may well have been less mercenary than political. Some believe that he was a Zealot, expecting the coming of the earthly kingdom. If so, Jesus's words after the transfiguration must have been a bitter disappointment. It would not be surprising if his loyalty subsequently cooled. Judas may have been humiliated by Jesus's rebuke when he complained that *Mary was wasting precious oils on him (John 12:1–8).

His disappointment and isolation came at a crucial time, when Jesus had enraged the Temple hierarchy. Although Judas's offer to *Caiaphas and the chief priests (to betray his master) was probably unnecessary, it was nonetheless accepted. The scheming clerics offered to pay him "thirty pieces of silver"—the price of a slave—for this action. Shortly after this perfidy, we see him sitting near Jesus in the upper room at the Last Supper, leaving quickly when Jesus identified him as the one who would betray him (Mark 14:20–21; Luke 22:21). In the Garden of Gethsemane, when Jesus had spent the night in prayer, Judas came with the soldiers, approaching Christ and identifying him with a kiss of friendship (Mark 14:43–45). This traitorous kiss and Jesus's subsequent address to him as "friend" fixed forever the image of the arch-traitor on his character.

Some believe that he may have expected Jesus to perform a miraculous escape from his captors. His effort to return the money to the elders, to call off the plot and the trial, was rebuffed by the mocking priests and elders (Matt. 27:3–8). Throwing the blood money to the ground, he then went out to the field of Aceldama (which some believe that Judas had, in fact, bought with that money), and hanged himself. By contrast, the record in Acts indicated that he died as a result of a fall when "all his bowels gushed out" (1:18–19).

The Kiss of Judas. The Art Archive/Scrovegni Chapel, Padua/Dagli Orti (A).

**Historical Context.** Accounts of Judas are varied, inconsistent, and "influenced by theological opinions of the writers. . . ." This in turn makes it difficult to know the facts of his life and death (Freed, 395). If he was a political rebel, a member of a group of Zealots, this would explain much of his motivation, but this is never established in Scripture. He may have been seeking to force Jesus to proclaim his Messiahship or he may have been a jealous Southerner who wanted to repay the perceived favoritism afforded to the Galilean disciples.

There are references to a lost apocryphal Gospel of Judas, in which Judas was portrayed as the "enlightened secret agent of the redeemer" who foiled demonic powers that were trying to prevent the salvation of mankind (Besserman, 418). This would fit in with some of the Gnostic ideas that arose after the Crucifixion.

**Archaeological Evidence.** Kerioth was a village in southern Judea, tentatively identified with Khirbet el-Kariathein, north of Arad (Negev, 212). Aceldama, where Judas died, is now associated with the cemetery for foreigners in Jerusalem. The Field of Blood is south of the Western Hill, across the Valley of Hinnom.

**Character in Later Works.** The Church Fathers and many scholars over the years have puzzled over a number of issues connected with Judas: Why did Jesus choose him, knowing that he was selecting a traitor? What motivated Judas's treachery? Was he damned by betraying Christ, or by his subsequent suicide?

By the Middle Ages, literary men adopted the view of Judas as the villain, often portraying him in the English drama as an example of avarice, treason, and finally despair. Dante used him at the very center of hell, hanging out of Satan's mouth, as the image of the betrayer of a benevolent master. (Dante's other two villains in this circle betrayed Caesar.)

Dorothy L. Sayers, who discusses him at length in her notes on *The Man Born to Be King*, thought he was the most intelligent of the disciples, and eventually the most disillusioned. He thought he could use Jesus as his tool to usher in a political kingdom. Eventually, given his subtle intellect, he was the first to recognize the necessity of the Crucifixion. She believed that he had greater potential for good or evil than any of the others, that he was essentially an opportunitist, determined to be the chief business manager when the Kingdom came (Sayers, 52).

In much of art and literature, Judas came to be identified with all Jews, and his image became that of the stereotypical Jew—the unfortunate source, along with Caiaphas, of much of later anti-Semitism. He was usually dressed in dingy yellow (the color of dung), carrying a money bag. He was usually pictured as "a man with red hair and beard, ruddy skin, large hooked nose, big lips, and bleary eyes" (Besserman, 419). His image was the scorpion. In popular thought, Judas remains the basis for ascribing bad luck to the number thirteen—with Christ, he made the thirteenth person at the Last Supper.

In the nineteenth century, some scholars became increasingly interested in Judas's motivation and began work on sympathetic treatments of him. He continues to appear in stories, plays, and poems dealing with the last days of Christ, understood at times as a believer in political or social rather than personal redemption.

## SOURCES

Besserman, Lawrence, "Judas Iscariot," in *A Dictionary of the Biblical Tradition in English Literature*, edited by David L. Jeffrey, Grand Rapids, MI: William B. Eerdmans Publishing Company, 1992; Brownrigg, Ronald, *Who's Who in the Bible*, vol. 2, New York: Bonanza Books, 1980; Ferguson, George, *Signs and Symbols in Christian Art*, New York: Oxford University Press, 1966; Freed, Edwin D., "Judas Iscariot," in *The Oxford Companion to the Bible*, edited by Bruce M. Metzger and Michael Coogan, New York: Oxford University Press, 1993; Miller, Madeline S., and J. Lane Miller, *Harper's Bible Dictionary*, New York: Harper and Row, 1961; Negev, Avraham, ed., *The Archaeological Encyclopedia of the Holy Land*, New York: Thomas Nelson Publishers, 1986; Sayers, Dorothy L., *The Man Born to Be King*, Grand Rapids, MI: William B. Eerdmans Publishing Company, 1943.

## JUDAS MACCABEUS

**Name and Etymology.** The name *Maccabeus* appears to derive from "hammer," or "to mark, designate." It was first applied to Judas and then to the entire family as a tribute to the fortitude of this warrior clan. Thus, the hero is "Judas the Hammer," or "Hammerer" or perhaps "Judas, the one designated by Yahweh."

**Synopsis of Bible Story.** In the troubled times following the death of Alexander the Great and the brutal struggles by Seleucids and Ptolemaic powers over his vast empire, little Palestine became a pawn, captured by one tyrant after another. In 168 B.C. Antiochius IV, who was called Epiphanes, captured Jerusalem, looted the Temple, and violated the altar by sacrificing a pig on it. In response to such efforts to destroy Judaism, a band of guerrilla forces rose to protect their homeland and their faith. In the two books of Maccabees, the full story of the five brothers, sons of the priest Mattathias, includes a narrative describing the background of Hellenistic occupation of Palestine.

At first, outraged by the desecration of the Temple and the altar, Mattathias, the aged priest at Modein, refused to offer heathen sacrifices. He then killed an apostate Jew who was about to perform a ceremony honoring Greek deities, as well as the king's commissioner, who was compelling the men to sacrifice. Thus began the wars of the Maccabees. Mattathias and his sons fled into the countryside where they were joined by many Hasidim, who had previously been content with passive resistance. When Mattathias died, Judas took over the leadership of the band, defeated the Syrian detachments, and entered Jerusalem, where he purified the Temple and restored the worship of Yahweh.

More battles followed, with Judas demonstrating a combination of heroism and faithfulness. He succeeded against superior forces only when led by God. For a brief time, he married, settled down, and shared the common life (2 Macc. 14:25), but this contentment was soon interrupted by new villainies. His heroic exploits were driven by the martyrdom of Razis, "father of the Jews," who in his final torments threw his own entrails at the crowd. He was further enraged by the savage treatment of believers, and he felt the strong hunger for a national leader.

His calling was confirmed when Jeremiah awarded him a holy, golden sword, admonishing him to use it against enemies of the Lord (2 Macc. 15:15–16). While the enemy had great armor and instruments of battle, including elephants, Judas was God's warrior, supported by his angels in battle (2 Macc. 11:8–10). He fought against incredible odds, battle after battle, until he finally fell at the onslaught of the army of Bacchides (1 Macc. 9:18).

He was buried at the family tomb at Modein, which later became a memorial for the entire family. At his death, the people wept and cried, as they had at the death of *Saul: "How the mighty have fallen/the savior of Israel" (1 Macc. 9:21).

The leadership of the rebel forces was immediately assumed by one of his brothers, Jonathan, who was in turn succeeded by one after another of his brothers, until they had all been killed in service of their country and their faith. It all ended in 142 B.C. when Syria granted the Jews their political freedom (1 Macc. 15).

**Historical Context.** The forty years of Maccabean leadership (176–134 B.C.) are fully chronicled in the books named after them and in additional accounts of a more legendary nature, such as 3 Maccabees, and a sermon that is illustrated with stories of the Jewish martyrs in 4 Maccabees. Flavius Josephus, in his *Wars of the Jews*, also documents the history of this period, calling the Maccabees "Hasmoneans" because of Mattathias's father, Hashmon. The accounts are filled with copies of official documents, many of which are thought now to be fairly accurate copies of the originals. On the other hand, historians suspect that many of the numbers of the battle forces are exaggerated (Harrington, 1646–48).

The struggles over the vestiges of the once-great Hellenistic empire involved many pitched battles among various forces eager to attain power. At the end of the Maccabees' story, they were beginning to arrange truces with the Romans, the aspiring power to the west (1 Macc. 8ff).

The family of the Maccabees, the Hasmoneans, is credited with delivering Israel from her oppressors, and became the line of the Jewish high priesthood after this time.

**Archaeological Evidence.** For many modern archaeologists, the Greek cities and the events mentioned all through the books that chronicle the romantic history of Judas Maccabeus have become major centers of research. Sepphoris, for example, is a very productive site (*e.g.*, Chancy and Myers's article). These excavations demonstrate that the efforts to Hellenize the region were widespread, creating such impressive centers as Beth-shean.

Coins of the Maccabean period survive, demonstrating the autonomy of the Jewish state under high-priest rulers, and valuable Maccabean structures have been excavated at Beth-zur. The use of elephants in battle, cited in Roman battles with the Carthaginians, has been verified in earlier battles as well in recent times.

The community responsible for the Dead Sea Scrolls may have been early supporters of the Maccabean movement who fell away at the time the family took control of the high priesthood and temple worship.

**Character in Later Works.** From early times, Judas Maccabeus was seen as a kind of warrior for God, in the tradition of *Gideon and *David. His zeal for God's house was interpreted by early Christian writers as a prototype of Christ, who also cleansed the Temple and sacrificed his life for his people. Medieval writers thought of him as God's knight.

He thereby became one of the "nine worthies" often mentioned by the poets. By Milton's time, he is a contrary type of hero, one who seeks fame in the name of God. Later, he was celebrated in his former manner, appearing as a hero in Thomas Morell's libretto for Handel's *Judas Maccabeus* (1747) and Henry Wadsworth Longfellow's tragedy, also named *Judas Maccabeus.*

The books of the Maccabees are classified as deuterocanonical by Roman Catholics and Orthodox, but as apocryphal by Protestant Christians and Jews. The concepts of prayers for the dead, and the hope of the resurrection, including the concept of Purgatory, are based in part on the section in 2 Maccabees 12:41–45, in which Judas led the people in prayers for those who had fallen in battle wearing the symbols of idols, and therefore in need of atonement.

In the Jewish tradition, the Maccabean rebellion is very significant as a time of heroic defense of the faith. The cleansing of the Temple and restoration of worship are still celebrated by Hanukkah, or the Feast of Dedication, also known as the Feast of the Maccabees, a celebration mentioned in both 1 and 2 Maccabees. The symbol of the menorah and the eight days of gifts commemorate this revolt against a government that denied the Jews their religious freedom.

## SOURCES

Besserman, Lawrence, "Judas Maccabeus," in A *Dictionary of the Biblical Tradition in English Literature*, edited by David L. Jeffrey, Grand Rapids, MI: William B. Eerdmans Publishing Company, 1992; Comay, Joan, *Who's Who in the Bible*, vol. 1, New York: Bonanza Books, 1980; Chancy, Mark, and Eric M. Myers, "How Jewish Was Sepphoris in Jesus' Time?" in *Biblical Archaeological Review*, July/August 2000; Harrington, Daniel J., "Judas Maccabeus," in *HarperCollins Study Bible*, edited by Wayne A. Meeks, San Francisco, CA: HarperCollins, 1993; Keller, Werner, *The Bible as History*, New York: Bantam Books, 1982; Miller, Madeline S., and J. Lane Miller, *Harper's Bible Dictionary*, New York: Harper and Row, 1961.

## JUDE

**Name and Etymology.** *Jude*, in Hebrew, "Judah"; or, in Greek, "Judas," one of the oldest and most common of Hebrew names.

**Synopsis of Bible Story.** Jude calls himself the brother of *James, the brother of *Jesus, leading scholars to believe that he was the son of *Joseph and perhaps *Mary. Some believe that he was one of the apostles called "Judas" but not *Judas Iscariot. Others insist that Jude, the brother of Jesus, did not accept Jesus as the Christ until after his resurrection (Acts 1:13). He is mentioned as one of the family including "James and Joses and Juda and Simon" as well as sisters (Mark 6:3).

He is identified as the author of the general epistle or "catholic" epistle, who warned his fellow believers against the heretical teachings that were cropping up in the early Church. Jude's letter demonstrates the strength of the Old Testament Jewish traditions within the faith and life of the Church. Both Jude and his brother James were zealous observers of the law, demonstrating the continuing influence of Judaism in the early Church (Brownrigg, 251).

**Historical Context.** It is hardly surprising that members of Jesus's family should have been honored in the early Church and encouraged to hold high positions. Some believe that they may have even been treated almost like royalty. Jude may have become a missionary, but we know little of his character or life. Some traditions have Jude traveling through Syria to Asia Minor preaching the Gospel, only to end in Persia, where he was said to have been martyred. He was believed to have been transfixed with a lance or beheaded with a halberd, providing artists symbols for representing his sacrifice.

His deep concern regarding the Gnostic fallacy growing in the thinking of Christians led to writing the Epistle of Jude approximately A.D. 80. He was troubled that scoffers were misinterpreting the Gospel and that false teachers were leading Christians to become too free and undisciplined in their way of life. Both Jude and 2 Peter (which are close in idea and phrasing) seek to combat this rudimentary form of Gnosticism that plagued the early Church, reminding the members of the Old Testament law and message. The letter does not name the church to which it is addressed, but apparently local members—like disobedient angels who "have gone in the way of Cain" (Jude 11)—claimed some secret knowledge that perverted the grace of God and led others in the fellowship into licentiousness and heresy.

**Archaeological Evidence.** A number of recent discoveries of Gnostic texts have aided scholars in the determination of the problems that Jude was describing. His own interest in the Book of Enoch, which he quotes in verses 14–15, indicates that he had access to an apocryphal text that no longer exists. Jude refers to elements included in that text and to others available to the early Church—lost bits of prophecy, the story of Satan's fall, an account of the burial of Moses from the Testament of Moses, and so on. He also uses a denunciation which follows the form of commentary found in the Dead Sea Scrolls (Bauckham, "Jude," 396).

**Character in Later Works.** Scholars have noted that the New Testament does not tell us the names of Jesus's brothers nor the specific nature of their connection. The term "brother" need not refer to a full blood brother, as it was also used for half-brother, stepbrother, or even a cousin. Several positions on Jesus' relations have evolved over the years in different faiths: The Helvidian view, named for a fourth-century Roman, holds that the brothers and sisters of Jesus were children of *Joseph and *Mary, born after Jesus. The Eastern Orthodox churches hold to the traditional Epiphanian position, that these siblings were children of Joseph by an earlier marriage, and therefore older than Jesus. (This view was also held by some second-century Christian writers, found in such apocryphal writings as the Protoevangelium of James, The Infancy Gospel of Thomas, and The Gospel of Peter.) The traditional Western Catholic view is that the brothers and sisters were first cousins of Jesus—the Hieronymian view, named after Jerome (Bauckham, 2000).

There is almost no attention given to Jude in later art or literature, though his references to the fall of the disobedient angels, and their enchainment until the judgment of the great day, have encouraged a great body of discussion. Dante and Milton use this story of the Battle of Angels as background for their great works.

Except for the speculation on his ties to Jesus and the consequent nature of his relationship to Mary, Jude as a person was generally ignored. One of the few to fix on him was Thomas Hardy, who in *Jude the Obscure* (1895) chose the name for his hero, a man of sorrows who ended his days in despair. There is no reason to believe that Jude the apostle was such a man. He became the patron saint of craftsmen and of lost causes. In addition, the final words of his epistle have become the favorite doxology of "dissenting tradition churches" (Jeffrey, 422).

> To the only wise God our Saviour, be glory and majesty, dominion and power, both now and ever.
>
> Amen (Jude 25).

## SOURCES

Bauckham, Richard J., "All in the Family: Identifying Jesus' Relatives," in *Bible Review*, April 2000; Bauckham, Richard J., "Jude, The Letter of," in *The Oxford Companion to the Bible*, edited by Bruce M. Metzger and Michael D. Coogan, New York: Oxford University Press, 1993; Brownrigg, Ronald, *Who's Who in the Bible*, vol. 2, New York: Bonanza Books, 1980; Ferguson, George, *Signs and Symbols in Christian Art*, New York: Oxford University Press, 1966; Jeffrey, David L., ed., *A Dictionary of the Biblical Tradition in English Literature*, Grand Rapids, MI: William B. Eerdmans Publishing Company, 1992; Miller, Madeline S., and J. Lane Miller, *Harper's Bible Dictionary*, New York: Harper and Row, 1961; Miller, Robert J., ed., *The Complete Gospels*, San Francisco: HarperCollins, 1994.

## JUDITH

**Name and Etymology.** *Judith*, is Hebrew, meaning "from Judah"—the feminine form of "Judean."

**Synopsis of Bible Story.** Judith was a beautiful and wealthy widow still mourning for her husband, Manasseh, when her town of Bethulia was besieged by the army of *Nebuchadnezzar, led by Holofernes. Outnumbered and surrounded, running out of food and water, the town was on the brink of capitulation when Judith intervened. She broke her mourning, bathed, dressed herself, and went to the town's elders to share with them a plan. She assured them that God would protect them if they remained faithful, and then she arranged a hoax requiring immense courage and imagination on her own part.

She left Bethulia and went to the camp of Holofernes, where she offered to help him take her city, and won over his confidence and admiration. After three days, she pretended to fall prey to Holofernes' efforts to seduce her, joined him in a feast in his lavish tent, and watched as he grew increasingly drunk. When the others left for the night, she took her enemy's sword and hacked off his head; taking it in a food bag, she returned secretly to Bethulia. The townspeople were thrilled by her act of courage and listened eagerly as she outlined the rest of the plan.

The following morning, the men of her town raised a cry and attacked the enemy tents, where the army of Assyria fell into disarray upon the discovery of the headless trunk of their commander. Other fighters joined the jubilant warriors, driving the Assyrians out of the region, returning from the slaughter with abundant plunder.

Judith herself was rewarded with the contents of Holofernes' tent, which she donated as a votive offering. The town celebrated with dance and song and great merriment, and her name became famous throughout the whole country. She never remarried, though many men sought her hand in marriage. She died old and revered, and was buried in the cave of her husband Manasseh. The house of Israel mourned her death for seven days.

**Historical Context.** Although this apocryhal story seems related to events in the fifth century B.C., it is clear that the historical events in the story are from various eras, some dealing with Nebuchadnezzar, some with later rulers. Even the system of governance and the names of the cities do not match the historical setting of the Assyrian empire. The "conflated details" touch on periods from the time of Nineveh, Babylon, and the Second Temple (Craven, 1459). Some of the characters have Persian names (Holofernes and Bogoas; Judith 12:10–11) and appear to be part of campaigns in the fourth century B.C. One critic notes that it is probable that the story was composed in the time of the Hasmonean ruler and high priest John Hyrcanus I (c. 134–104 B.C.), when events may have inspired the revival of a patriotic narrative such as Judith's (Comay, 433–434).

**Archaeological Evidence.** Although the historical background and the text itself are both questionable, many of the details of Judith's story have been confirmed by archaeology. There are terracotta relics of women preparing bread just as Judith did, and the sites (such as the plain of Jamia and Jamia's harbor) mentioned in the text (Jth. 2:28), which are documented in this book and the books of the Maccabees (2 Macc. 12:8–9), are now being investigated by Tel Aviv University. Scholars have found evidence from the second century B.C. Maccabean revolt and are searching for evidence of Holofernes' role. Other cities mentioned in the text are also subjects of continuing exploration.

**Character in Later Works.** The Hebrew original of the story has disappeared, and the text was never accepted into the Hebrew canon. It is nonetheless a famous story that has impressed artists and writers down through the centuries.

Although the admirable character of the beautiful Judith was to appeal to many of the Church fathers—including St. Clement of Rome and St. Jerome—her devout life and faithful obedience to God's will and her concern for her people's welfare were the key ingredients, as they were for *Susanna and *Esther. They did not honor her as a figure from Scripture. Renaissance writers were interested in her as a image of resistance to idolatry and tyranny. Martin Luther, for example, wrote a preface to the book of Judith in 1534. (See longer listing of examples in Collette's article, 423–24.)

The dramatic action and pictorial quality of the story have encouraged artistic interpretation. There are numerous theatrical versions of her story and novel-length developments as well (*e.g.*, Arnold Bennett's *Judith*).

As a famous beauty, she also appealed to painters: Veronese (1528–88) and Caravaggio (1583–1610) both painted scenes from her story. One of the most famous paintings of "Judith and Holofernes" is by Artimisia Gentileschi, the daughter of the famous painter, Orazio Gentileschi. This painting is in the Capodimonti Museum in Naples. The image of the lovely woman holding the head of the once-powerful warrior is certainly visually compelling.

As an image of the moderns of the warrior-woman, Judith ranks with *Deborah and Jael, women who outwitted superior force in heroic acts of thoroughly unfeminine bravery.

## SOURCES

Collette, Carolyn, "Judith," in *A Dictionary of Biblical Tradition in English Literature*, edited by David L. Jeffrey, Grand Rapids, MI: William B. Eerdmans Publishing Company, 1992; Comay, Joan, *Who's Who in the Bible*, vol. 1, New York: Bonanza Books, 1980; Craven, Toni, "Judith," in *HarperCollins Study Bible*, edited by Wayne A. Meeks, San Francisco, CA: HarperCollins, 1993.

# L

## LAZARUS

**Name and Etymology.** *Lazarus* is a Greek word from the Hebrew, meaning "helped by God."

**Synopsis of Bible Story.** Although *Jesus used the name *Lazarus* for the beggar in the parable of the Rich Young Ruler (Luke 16:20), the main figure of this name was the brother of *Mary and Martha. Only John (11:1–44) tells the story of Lazarus's illness. His sisters sent a message to Jesus to come quickly to heal him, fearing that otherwise he would die. Jesus, strangely, lingered for two days beyond the Jordan, where his disciples asked him about his delay. His answer, that the illness was "not unto death" and would be the means by which the Son of Man might "be glorified," only puzzled them further. When they discovered that he did plan to return to Bethany, they warned him that he should not go back to the area around Jerusalem, where he had so many enemies. But Jesus responded that their friend Lazarus had "fallen asleep" and he must go to "awake him out of sleep." John also notes that this was a family Jesus loved.

When Jesus approached the house, he was told that Lazarus was already dead and had been in his grave for four days. Martha rushed out to greet him, admonishing him that Lazarus would not have died had Jesus come earlier, for "I know, that even now, whatsoever thou wilt ask of God, God will give it thee" (John 11:22).

Jesus promised that her brother would rise, and then, in response to her confusion about whether he meant in the "last day," he added, "I am the resurrection, and the life: he that believeth in me, though he were dead, yet shall he live: And whosoever liveth and believeth in me shall never die" (John 11:25–26).

Her response was a powerful affirmation of her faith. She then called her sister, who repeated Martha's complaint and fell down at his feet weeping. Jesus joined in the weeping. He then went to the cave where the sisters had laid the body of Lazarus, and commanded that the stone be rolled away. They objected, saying that the body would stink, but Jesus insisted.

When this was done, Jesus raised his voice, calling, "Lazarus, come forth." To the astonishment of all, Lazarus came out of the cave, with his graveclothes still hanging about him and his face. Some in the crowd immediately ran to tell the Pharisees of the miracle. Others believed in Jesus as the Messiah.

Jesus then escaped into the wilderness, avoiding any mingling with the Jews of Jerusalem, who were now clearly his enemies. When he returned to Bethany for Passover week, a crowd gathered to see him and Lazarus.

No other mention occurs in Scripture regarding Lazarus. No act or speech of his is recorded in any of the Gospel narratives.

**Historical Context.** In Jesus's life, this was a crucial moment—the time of his most dramatic miracle. The immediate response of the Pharisees was to murmur at the growing danger they faced from this miracle-worker. Among those who were already enemies of Jesus, the plan leading to the Crucifixion quickly gathered force.

This was also Christ's most important miracle symbolically. In this act of resurrecting Lazarus from the dead, Jesus foreshadowed his own resurrection; in the rolling away of the stone, he anticipated the actions of Easter morning.

Burials in New Testament times were immediate because of the warm weather and the lack of embalming. Almost always in Israel, even today, the person is buried on the day he or she dies (Bailey, 96). Bodies were wrapped in bands of cloth and placed in caves or rock-cut tombs, not in coffins. Caves frequently contained a number of bodies, sometimes serving as the burial site for entire families. They were sealed with a hinged door or—as in this case—with a heavy wheel-shaped stone.

Mourning involved songs, laments, and weeping, and often continued for seven days. The Middle Eastern convention of public displays of distress on the occasion of a death continue to be very dramatic.

**Archaeological Evidence.** The village of El-Azariah (the Arabic form of Lazarion, meaning "the House of Lazarus") is located on the site of Bethany, just below the Mount of Olives, facing east toward the wilderness and the Jordan Valley. Eusebius mentions the fourth-century church on the burial site that honored Lazarus, which was still extant in the twelfth century. Today, a new Franciscan church covers the remains of this older church, which St. Jerome also says was built over the tomb of Lazarus, originally within the cemetery of Bethany. S. J. Saller excavated Bethany from 1949 to 1953, discovering the remains of the four superimposed churches built to the east of Lazarus' tomb, all of which had mosaics. Associated with the churches are a large number of rock-cut tombs, some of which are within the precincts of the churches. Apart from these, the scholars discovered the remains of the ancient village of Bethany: houses, wine-presses, cisterns, silos, and other artifacts (Negev, 56).

**Character in Later Works.** Eastern tradition, speculating far beyond Biblical records, suggests that Lazarus and his sisters were put in a leaking boat on the Mediterranean, but managed to stay afloat long enough to reach the island of Cyprus, where Lazarus became bishop of Kitium, the place where he is thought to have died. In A.D. 890, his supposed relics were transferred to Constantinople, though some believe that they were taken to Vezelay, France, in the eleventh or twelfth century.

In Crusader times, pilgrims came to the house of Mary, Martha, and Lazarus at Bethany, and a legend became popular in the west that Lazarus was bishop of Marseilles and was martyred under the Emperor Domitian (Brownrigg, 257).

Augustine was among the first to see Lazarus not simply as a foreshadowing of Christ, but also as a type of awakening from sin (Siebald, 439). The portrayal of the raising of Lazarus was common in Corpus Christi plays, including the modern one by Dorothy L. Sayers, *The Man Born to Be King*. Sayers follows the pattern of Augustine, seeing in the raising from the dead symbolism of the joyous new life that the convert discovers in his redemption.

Poets have also found the story of Lazarus interesting for its symbolism and for an avenue to express their own skepticism. For example, Robert Browning, in "An Epistle Containing the Strange Medical Experience of Karshish, the Arab Physician" used the event to test the miracle by scientific evidence. Edwin Arlington Robinson in his "Lazarus" developed a psychological study of him after he had "lost the security of the tomb." Sylvia Plath related his experience to her own unsuccessful suicide attempt in "Lady Lazarus."

Novelists including Dickens, Melville, and James Joyce have made reference to him. One of the most impressive modern developments of Lazarus is in Eugene O'Neill's play *Lazarus Laughed*, in which the story is elaborated far beyond the scriptural source. (See Siebald, 440.)

The raising of Lazarus was also a common subject for art, with numerous paintings through the years, some among the earliest Christian artistic expressions. In some of them, comically, Lazarus is pictured holding his nose, apparently a reference to his "stench."

## SOURCES

Bailey, Kenneth E., "Lazarus," in *The Oxford Companion to the Bible*, edited by Bruce M. Metzger and Michael D. Coogan, New York: Oxford University Press, 1993; Brownrigg, Ronald, *Who's Who in the Bible*, vol. 2, New York: Bonanza Books, 1980; Ferguson, George, *Signs and Symbols in Christian Art*, New York: Oxford University Press, 1966; Negev, Avraham, ed., *The Archaeological Encyclopedia of the Holy Land*, New York: Thomas Nelson Publishers, 1986; Sayers, Dorothy L., *The Man Born to Be King*, Grand Rapids, MI: William B. Eerdmans Publishing Company, 1943; Siebald, Manfred, "Lazarus," in *A Dictionary of the Biblical Tradition in English Literature*, edited by David L. Jeffrey, Grand Rapids, MI: William B. Eerdmans Publishing Company, 1992.

## LEVI

**Name and Etymology.** Levi comes from the Hebrew word meaning "to join" (Gen. 29:34).

**Synopsis of Bible Story.** The third son of *Jacob and *Leah, Levi was born in Haran, in the Fertile Crescent. When his family moved back to Canaan, Levi joined his brothers in selling *Joseph into slavery. In the humiliating trip to Egypt to beg for food, Levi was obliged to beg Joseph's forgiveness. The only story told in Genesis about Levi as an individual apart from his brothers is the narrative of his sister Dinah's seduction by Shechem, a young man who subsequently asked for her hand in marriage. Jacob's sons, concealing their wrath at seeing a member of their family being treated like a prostitute, pretended to acquiesce. They agreed to the wedding, with the provision that the men of the town, including the seducer and his father, be circumcised. While the men of Shechem were recovering from this painful operation, Levi and his brother Simeon hacked them to death, thereby avenging their outrage against Dinah (Gen. 34:25–26).

On his deathbed, Levi's father, Jacob, recalled the barbaric act of vengeance and cursed it, scattering the family of Levi for their wrath and cruelty (Gen. 49:7). From this came the tradition of the Levites having no single territory, living in 48 towns and surrounding pasturelands. Levi himself died in Egypt at an advanced age (Exod. 6:16) and his sons, Gershon, Kohath, and Merari, carried on the "Levite" tradition. Ironically, this tradition became a blessed one.

Among Levi's descendants were *Miriam, *Aaron, and *Moses, through Kohath's line. Although Levi's descendants assumed the role of Temple servants, only the descendants of Aaron were considered the "exact center" of Israel's racial history, thus the perfect candidates for the chief high priesthood. Eventually, in the priestly code, only descendants of Aaron were to be the priests (Exod. 28:1; Num. 18:6–7).

**Historical Context.** Levi was part of the last generation of nomadic Hebrews. They were herdsmen and tent-dwellers as they had been since the time of Abraham. When drought struck and Levi and his brothers followed their brother Joseph to Egypt, they began a more settled lifestyle. In the early days, when Joseph was still in a position of prestige, Levi and his brothers were probably treated as honored guests by the Egyptians.

Later, after they were enslaved and abused and finally, when they sought to escape from Egypt, the tribe of Levi, called the Levites, assumed the position of leadership. Still later, when *Aaron and the worshippers of the golden calf rebelled against *Moses, it was the Levites who first rallied to him (Exod. 32:26–29).

After Moses had died and the Israelites had conquered the land of Caanan, the newly conquered land was divided among the tribes, but the Levites were not given their own region. Instead, each region had designated cities where the Levites were to reside, thereby continuing the practice of denying the children of Levi specific cities as their inheritance. Since they had become the priestly tribe, however, it was the obligation of the other tribes to provide for their support through tithes and offerings (Deut. 18:1–5; Num. 35:1–8).

In Deuteronomy, a priest was expected to be "levitical" (18:6–8); priests also served as judges (17:8–9), guardians of the Torah scroll (17:18), and were involved in covenant renewal (27:9). Moses stipulated that they were to be the "substitutes" for the first-born males of the Israelites (Num. 3:41). The Kohathites were to serve in the work of the tabernacle from the time they were thirty until they were fifty years old (Num. 4:34–35). Gradually, their role appears to have declined. Chronicles shows them cooperating with the Aaronoid priests, taking responsibility as Temple singers, gatekeepers, and teachers of the Torah (1 Chron. 6:31–48, 9–22–34; 2 Chron. 17:7–9).

Levites have also appeared as porters carrying the Ark and the Tabernacle (1 Kings 8:4; 1 Sam. 6:15). Although they might perform such sacred functions, most of the Levites as a group were apparently considered inferior to the descendants of Aaron, who supervised their work. *Ezekiel denounced the unfaithful and iniquitious Levites and confirmed their lesser status (44:4–14) while blessing those who "kept the charge of my sanctuary" (Ezek. 44:15–16). It was eventually Aaron's descendants who dominated the Jerusalem cult from the time of *Solomon (1 Kings 2:26–27) until the Seleucids overthrew Onias III in 174 B.C. Malachi, anticipating a time of cooperation with the descendants of Aaron, predicted a renewal of the Levites, perhaps because of the corruption of the priests in Jerusalem (2:1–9, 3:3–4), who required the "refiner's fire."

**Archaeological Evidence.** The evidence of the Levites' efforts may be traced through the preservation of the Ark of the Covenant over the years, until it finally disappeared in the sacking of the Temple by the Romans in A.D. 70. Although Titus gave specific orders to "Spare the sanctuary," the entire Temple was demolished and the contents removed. The triumphal arch of Titus (A.D. 81) pictures the looting of the Temple, the removal of the sacred objects and treasures.

**Character in Later Works.** The diminished view of the Levites is apparent in the New Testament, when Jesus cites a "Levite" as one of those who passes by the wounded man, refusing to help him, leaving him to the mercies of the Good Samaritan (Luke 10:32). When Jesus wept for the Holy City, he was weeping in part for the spiritual barrenness he saw there (Luke 19:41). Gradually, the physical Temple of Solomon and then of Herod were replaced with the Jewish eschatology of a Messianic Temple and an increasingly metaphorical use of the idea of the Temple. Finally, the "Lord God Almighty and the Lamb are the Temple" (Revelation 21:22), for there will be no need for a specific holy place. All the people are the keepers of the Lord's House; the priesthood will no longer be needed.

### SOURCES

Knoppers, Gary N., "Levi," in *The Oxford Companion to the Bible*, edited by Bruce M. Metzger and Michael D. Coogan, Oxford: Oxford University Press, 1993; Miller, Madeleine S., and J. Lane Miller, *Harper's Bible Dictionary*, New York: Harper and Row, 1961.

## LOT

**Name and Etymology.** *Lot* is Hebrew for "a covering."

**Synopsis of Bible Story.** Lot first is introduced (Gen. 11:27) as the son of Haran and the nephew of *Abram. He apparently became a ward of the older man when Haran died and the family undertook the migration from Ur of the Chaldees. He joined Abram's caravan in the journey to Egypt, but became increasingly prosperous and was not dependent on their return to Canaan. When Abram's and Lot's herdsmen began to quarrel, his generous uncle, recognizing that the sparse pasturege could not support the increasing number of animals, offered Lot his choice of land (Gen. 13:5–7). In response to his uncle's gracious offer, Lot revealed a greedy streak by selecting the fertile Jordan valley for his share. He also chose to settle near the corrupt city of Sodom.

When the five cities, including Sodom and Gomorrah, were invaded by Chedorlaomer and his confederates, Lot and his people were taken captive. Abram armed his own men and pursued the kings as far as Dan, battling with them at Hobah, west of Damascus, rescuing his nephew, and refusing to share in the booty (Gen. 14:1–24).

Lot, once again tempting disaster, then moved into Sodom (Gen. 14:12), where he apparently became a member of the ruling council, one who sat in the gateway (Gen. 19:1). On learning that the corrupt city was doomed, Abram tried to save Lot and his family by bargaining with God regarding the number of "righteous" inhabitants. When the angelic guests visited the notoriously inhospitable city of Sodom, only Lot offered them lodging and food. The townspeople gathered and threatened them while Lot sought to protect his visitors, offering his daughters in their place. The angry mob clamored for the male visitors instead. In response, the rioters were stricken blind though divine intervention. Finally told by God that he and his family must flee, Lot

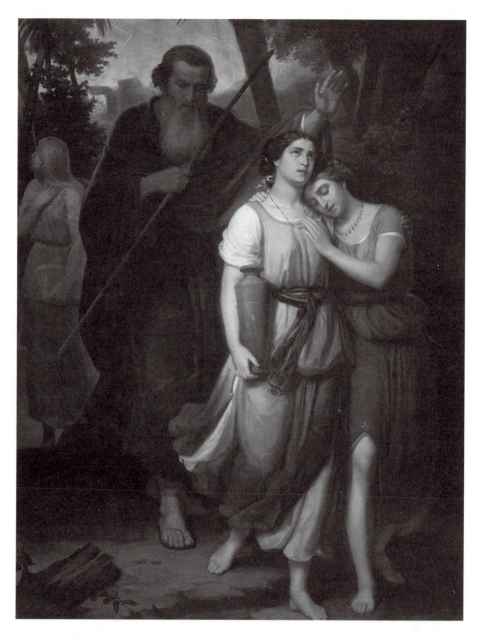

Lot and family leaving Sodom, 1853. The Art Archive/Queretaro Museum, Mexico/Dagli Orti.

could not convince his sons-in-law to accompany the family to safety. Once out of the city, his wife turned back, only to be transformed into a pillar of salt. Lot and his daughters escaped unharmed.

The final scenes in Lot's story suggest that he was a coward and a drunk. He feared Zoar, the place he was ordered to go, settling instead in a cave outside of the city, where he drank himself into a state of confusion. His daughters, believing perhaps that no other people survived the catastrophe of Sodom's destruction, went to him, seducing him. From these incestuous acts came two sons, Moab and Ben-ammi—the progenitors of the Moabites and the Ammonites (Gen. 19:36–38; Deut. 2:9, 19). Ironically, it is from this grotesque heritage that *Ruth descended, a Moabite widow who married Boaz and became the mother of Jesse, from whom *David and finally *Christ descended.

**Historical Context.** Like Abram, Lot was part of the eighteenth-century-B.C. culture, but unlike his uncle, he was inclined to city life, especially the seductive life in Sodom and Gomorrah. The incestuous activities that led to the birth of his two sons were used as evidence by the Hebrews of the debased heritage of their neighbors in Moab and Ammon as well as their shared ancestors.

**Archaeological Evidence.** Several of the sites in which Lot lived have been identified. Werner Keller, in *The Bible as History*, describes the verdant valley that Lot selected, as well as the geography of Lot's forced trip, after the kidnapping by the kings, up to Dan, where considerable archaeological work has been done. The battle between the two sets of kings apparently took place along the path called "The Kings' Way." The reference to sitting in the gate of Sodom has been verified by numerous scholars, who believe that this was a space where the city council of elders met, thus suggesting that Lot was a prominent member of Sodom's ruling body. When Lot and his wife fled Sodom, they paused at the edge of the Dead Sea, which to this day is the scene of astonishing salt deposits resembling statues.

Archaeology has proven that the Jordan valley was once a rich and fertile land, and that the five cities did indeed exist on the edges of the Dead Sea. In 1924, based on the scriptural references to the five cities of the plain, Dr. William Albright excavated the northernmost of the "Cities of the Plains." Later digging uncovered a 23-inch-thick wall around the cities along with numerous houses and a large temple. Most intriguing was evidence that a massive fire had destroyed the city, which lay buried under a coat of ash several feet thick.

**Character in Later Works.** Although the Bible suggests that Lot was not aware of his incestuous sins at the time he committed them, a Christian tradition held him guilty. A story developed over time that Lot later met Abraham and asked him how he might atone for this guilt. According to the legend, Abraham gave Lot three staffs that the visiting angels had left in his care, and told him to plant them near Jerusalem and to water them with water from the Jordan River. If the staffs were to blossom, he should take this as a sign that God had forgiven his transgression. In later centuries, the story was embellished to suggest that wood from the tree was used in Solomon's Temple and finally for the cross on which Christ was crucified. A monastery now stands on the spot where the miraculous tree was thought to have blossomed (Tzaferis, 37).

The Old Testament prophets frequently referred to the destruction of Sodom (Deut. 29:23; Isa. 13:19; Jer. 49:18). In later literature, Lot was considered a righteous man, saved from Sodom's punishment by his goodness (2 Pet. 2:7–8; Wisd. of Sol. 10:6). The dramatic destruction of the perverse cities, Sodom and Gomorrah, also plays a role in the teachings of Jesus and the Apostles (Jude 1:7; Matt. 10:15; 2 Pet. 2:6).

Although he had the reputation of a good man living amidst an evil people, Lot displayed few characteristics that would make him a hero. He was not generous, brave, wise, strong, sober, or pure. Though his wife appears occasionally as an example of second thoughts, Lot rarely appears in Scripture. He is cited, along with Noah, as a just man at the Last Judgment (Luke 17:28–33). Peter uses the destruction of Sodom as an image of the final destruction of the world.

Nor was Lot a major figure in later literature. He appeared in the Old English version of *Genesis*, and in Middle English plays—especially the Chester Cycle. In the seventeenth century, John Bunyan used him in *Pilgrim's Progress*; in the nineteenth century, Mark Twain made reference to him in *The Mysterious Stranger*; and in the twentieth century, he appeared in John Updike's novel, *Couples*, where he proved a useful image of modern man. His wife was central to D. H. Lawrence's poem "She Looks Back" (Horrall, 463–464). His weakness and lapses make him a natural for the image of the modern antihero, an example of the difficulties of living honorably amidst corruption.

## SOURCES

Horrall, Sarah, "Lot," in *A Dictionary of the Biblical Tradition in English Literature*, edited by David L. Jeffrey, Grand Rapids, MI: William B. Eerdmans Publishing Company, 1992; Keller, Werner, *The Bible as History*, New York: Bantam Books, 1982; Tzaferis, Vassilios, "The Monastery of the Cross: Where Heaven and Earth Meet," *Biblical Archaeology Review*, 27(5), 32–41, 2001.

## LUKE

**Name and Etymology.** *Luke* derives from the Greek *Loukas*, a shortened form of the Latin *Lucanus* or *Lucius*.

**Synopsis of Bible Story.** When he arrived at Troas, on his second missionary journey, *Paul was joined by Luke. At this point (Acts 16:11–12) the story in Acts changes from a third-person ("they") narrative to first-person plural ("we")—and then continues periodically in that mode. Two places in Scripture explicitly name Luke: in Colossians 4:14, Paul calls him "the beloved physician," and in 2 Timothy 4:11, Paul notes, "only Luke is with us." Nothing else about Luke is certain, but the speculation is extensive. Some believe that he was a Jew, some that he was a Gentile; Jerome said he was a Syrian of Antioch; some think he was the unnamed companion of Cleopas to whom Christ appeared on the road to Emmaus (Danker, 465); some believe he was the man of Macedonia who appeared to *Paul in a dream, urging the first evangelistic journey into Europe (Acts 16:9). We do know that he was the "beloved physician" to whom Paul refers in Colossians. We also know he was a faithful friend to the apostle and an enthusiastic evangelist.

If he was the author of Acts and of the Gospel bearing his name, we also know that he was a literary genius who knew and understood both Greek and Jewish culture and was able to interpret terminology for Gentile readers. Taking the forthright narrative of *Mark and the Hebrew-oriented narrative of *Matthew, Luke expanded the Christian worldview to a universal faith and to a Church that would serve to continue the traditions and fellowship of that faith. His narrative moves from Bethlehem to Jerusalem and then to Greek cities—Athens, Corinth, and so on—and finally looks forward to Rome.

In neither of the books attributed to him is he mentioned by name. In each he established his audience and his method in the prologue, addressing a Greek friend, Theophilus, and using the epistolary form, providing the account of the eyewitnesses and ministers of the Word, along with his own "perfect understanding of all from the very first," presenting the events in order (Luke 1:2). By providing both the story of *Jesus's earthly ministry and the beginnings of the Christian Church, Luke was able to present the miraculous story from the birth of *John the Baptist, expanding on the beautiful narratives of Christ's nativity; to move through the teaching years and the Crucifixion; to trace the Resurrection; and then to continue with the events in the Upper Room, the early preaching of the disciples, the stoning of *Stephen, the conversion of Paul, and the evangelizing of the Greco-Roman world. In his broad vision of the scope and meaning of Christianity, he was able to reach out to receptive Gentiles.

**Historical Context.** Most commentators assert that Luke was a Greek Jew or a convert to Judaism, a citizen of Antioch, who was writing after the fall of Jerusalem for an audience of Christians who no longer had firsthand knowledge of the events of Jesus' life, the major teachings of Christ, or the early history of the Church.

Some scholars have commented that Luke's practice of medicine is evidenced in his awareness of the diseases and of distresses of the people in the narrative. William K. Hobart, in the nineteenth century, searched out the "healing stories" in Luke's narratives; but his findings were soon refuted by Henry Cadbury, who found an equivalent frequency of such references in Josephus, Plutarch, and Lucian—all non-medical writers. (See Parsons.)

**Archaeological Evidence.** Generally scholars believe that Luke and Acts were originally a single narrative, perhaps divided when the canon was codified, moving the Gospel into the cluster of the four Gospels, and thereby separating it from its sequel. Some believe that the length of the text was limited by the scroll on which it was written: "Luke and Acts were simply too long to fit on one scroll" according to this theory, and were therefore divided prior to "publication" (Parsons, 2001). The Gospel title, which is unlike the others in its inclusion of "according to" appears at the end of the oldest extant manuscript of the Gospel of Luke—a papyrus in the Bodmer Library in Geneva. Parsons notes that this fragmentary manuscript dates from 125 years after the actual writing of the original scrolls.

**Character in Later Works.** One of the more interesting extrabiblical legends about Luke was that he was an artist who painted the image of the Virgin *Mary. As far back as the sixth century, such a painting was said to exist. As a result, in the Middle Ages, Luke became the patron saint of artists (and of doctors) and their guilds. In 1577, an academy in Rome devoted to the training of artists was named in his honor. Renaissance painters Rogier van der Weyden and Giorgio Vasari both painted pictures of him; van der Weyden even substituted his own face for the image of Luke to establish his identification with the saint.

A painting by Giovanni di Paolo, now in the Seattle Art Museum, shows him working on his Gospel and the winged ox in front of him. Like the other Gospel writers, Luke was assigned an image from Ezekiel and Revelation—in his case, the ox. Irenaeus was one of the first to identify Luke with this animal, noting that the ox "was like a calf, signifying sacrificial and sacerdotal order," and a link to the fatted calf which was sacrificed at the return of the Prodigal Son in the parable appearing only in Luke's Gospel (Parsons, 2001). This icon—with wings added as symbols of divine mission—was to appear frequently in illuminated manuscripts and in church architecture of the Middle Ages. In the MacDurnan Gospels, a ninth-century manuscript from Ireland, Luke has hooves, a ludicrous effort to identify him with his symbol of the ox.

The literary character of Luke's Gospel has made his work a favorite among the writers. Coleridge admired him, as did George Herbert and many others. The image of the good physician was to appear in Sholem Asch's novel *The Apostle* (1943) and in Maxim Gorki's play *The Lower Depths* (1902).

## SOURCES

Brownrigg, Ronald, *Who's Who in the Bible*, vol. 2, New York: Bonanza Books, 1980; Danker, F. W., "Luke," in *A Dictionary of the Biblical Tradition in English Literature*, edited by David L. Jeffrey, Grand Rapids, MI: William B. Eerdmans Publishing Company, 1992; Ferguson, George, *Signs and Symbols in Christian Art*, New York: Oxford University Press, 1966; Parsons, Mikeal; "Who Wrote the Gospel of Luke?" in *Bible Review Archives*, April 2001; Parsons, Mikeal, "Why the Ox?" in *Biblical Archaeology Review*, July/August, 1995.

## LYDIA

**Name and Etymology.** *Lydia* is the name of a region in western Asia Minor, where Croesus was the legendary king; it is also a popular name for girls.

**Synopsis of Bible Story.** When *Paul was in Troas, he had a vision one night in which he saw a man of Macedonia beckoning him to carry the gospel to Europe: "Come over into Macedonia, and help us" (Acts 16:9). With that encouragement, Paul, along with *Luke, *Timothy, and Silas, embarked on a missionary journey that led them to Philippi, "a Roman colony and the leading city of that district of Macedonia," where they stayed for several days (Acts 16:12). Finding no synagogue there, probably because there were so few Jews, Paul and his companions went outside the city gate to a spot along the river Ganga. There they discovered a prayer meeting being led by a wealthy woman named Lydia, from Thyatira, who was a worshipper of God. The tiny community of Jews, who gathered on the Sabbath for prayer by the river's edge, welcomed Paul and his companions, and listened to their message. Lydia insisted that Paul baptize her and her household. She then begged Paul, Silas, and Timothy to accept her hospitality (Acts 16:14–15).

On their way to Lydia's home, the group was harassed by a slave girl who could predict the future. She hounded Paul and his friends until Paul finally commanded the spirit to come out of her. This led in turn to a confrontation with the angry owner of the girl, who managed to have them stripped, beaten, and thrown into prison. After an exciting night involving an earthquake, threatened suicide by the jailer, baptism of the jailer and his family, and an offer of freedom from the frightened magistrates, Paul demanded a public liberation. As a Roman citizen, he had rights that had been violated. The magistrates begged them to leave town, but Paul and Silas chose the more deliberate and dignified path, going back to Lydia's home, meeting with the "brothers," and then leaving Philippi (Acts 16:38–40).

**Historical Context.** During this period, it was not unusual for a woman to develop a business on her own or through inheritance from her husband. In Lydia's case, we know only that she was a "seller of purple" (Acts 16:14) who employed a household of people. Lydia's household was the first in Europe known to have been converted and baptized (Brownrigg, 269). It was to this flourishing house-church that Paul wrote from time to time in his letters to the Philippians. Philippi was a Roman colony and city in Macedonia that was founded by Alexander the Great.

**Archaeological Evidence.** Purple dye was a murex secretion from mollusks used for coloring materials, much in demand in the Roman era and earlier. Near Easterners prized this rich red-blue color, using it for royal robes. It was used for the Tabernacle curtains, priests' ephods, and finally for the robe placed on Christ when he was ironically crowned "King of the Jews." The chief source for the famous Tyrian purple was the tiny mollusks found along the Phoenician coast and exported far and wide (Miller, 405, 594).

**Character in Later Works.** Although Lydia does not appear in much literature or art, she has become a favorite figure for analysis in recent years among feminists, who look to her as a businesswoman and a local leader, the central figure in founding the church at Philippi.

## SOURCES

Brownrigg, Ronald, *Who's Who in the Bible*, vol. 2, New York: Bonanza Books, 1980; Miller, Madeline S., and J. Lane Miller, *Harper's Bible Dictionary*, New York: Harper and Row, 1961.

# M

## MAGI

**Name and Etymology.** *Magi* is Greek for "wise men" or "sages." *The New English Bible* translates this as "astrologers." Others note that this is related to our term "magicians."

**Synopsis of Bible Story.** Matthew (2:1–12) recounts that wise men came from the East, having heard of the birth of the King of the Jews and having seen his star in the East. They told King *Herod that they had come to worship him—apparently assuming that they would find the newborn king in Herod's palace. When Herod inquired of his own wise men—his chief priests and scribes—where Christ should be born, they told him of the ancient prophecy that the Messiah would be born in Bethlehem, in the land of Judah. Returning to the Magi, Herod questioned them further about when they had seen the star and then sent them to Bethlehem to search for the child, adding, "and when ye have found him, bring me word again that I may come and worship him also" (Matt. 2:8).

They followed the star to the place where the young child lay, rejoicing "with exceeding great joy". (Matt. 2:10) "And when they were come into the house, they saw the young child with Mary his mother, and fell down, and worshipped him: and when they had opened their treasures, they presented unto him gifts; gold, and frankincense, and myrrh, and being warned of God in a dream that they should not return to Herod, they departed into their own country another way" (Matt. 2:10–12).

**Historical Context.** In Jewish history, the Persian concept of "wise men" as astrologers was reinforced by the long period during which the Hebrews were in Babylon. *Daniel, who lived in the court, also used the term (Dan. 1:20, 2:27, 5:15). By the period of the early Church, the term had broadened to refer to those who practiced the magic arts (Acts 8:9, 13:6, 13:8).

The prophecy that the Messiah was to be born in *David's city, Bethlehem, was quite ancient. Because Herod was not a Jew, this would not have been familiar to him; he saw the newborn babe as a threat to his sovereignty rather than as a fulfillment of

*Micah's prophecy (Mic. 5:2), quoted in *Matthew: "And thou Bethlehem, in the land of Judah, art not the least among the princes of Juda: for out of thee shall come a Governor, that shall rule my people Israel" (Matt. 2:6). Herod treated this information in the same bloodthirsty manner that he had handled any perceived threats in his own family—quickly and ferociously. (He had previously arranged to have his wife and some of his sons murdered; and to assure universal mourning at his death, he later ordered that thousands of men locked inside the hippodrome in Jericho be massacred when he died—an order which was mercifully ignored (Sheler, 200). If Josephus was correct regarding the resurgence of Messianic hopes during that period, Herod was shrewd in his brutal defense of his power.

The fact that the Magi—like Herod—were ignorant of this prophecy suggests that they were not Jews, but the first of the Gentiles who came to worship Christ. Some believe that they were members of a priestly caste of Media who worshiped fire and were versed in astrology and magic. These people believed that the appearance of new stars heralded the coming of great world leaders (Miller, 819). Such signs in the heavens were commonly accepted as prophetic by many ancient peoples. It is likely that they were astrologers from star-gazing communities, such as Persia or Mesopotamia, drawn to Bethlehem by a significant alignment of stars and planets indicating that a ruler had been born.

**Archaeological Evidence.** The gifts of the Magi, gold, frankincense, and myrrh, were treasured in Judah as in much of the ancient world and may have come from Arabia, where there had been Jews since the fall of Samaria and Jerusalem. Similar gifts are mentioned in stories of the *Queen of Sheba, whose country was apparently one source for the precious spices. Each of these gifts had symbolic meaning: the gold for a king, the frankincense for a priest, and the myrrh for a savior—one who died for his people.

Scientists have long puzzled over the nature of the star that they saw and followed. Some thought it might have been actually the conjunction of planets Saturn and Jupiter in the year 7 B.C. Astronomer Johannes Kepler recalled that rabbinic writers believed that the Messiah would appear when there was a conjunction of Saturn and Jupiter in the constellation of Pisces. In Jewish tradition, Saturn was supposed to protect Israel, an idea attested to by both Tacitus and by Babylonian documents (Keller, 361–365). Apparently, their prolonged sojourn in Babylonia influenced Jews with some of the mysticism of the Eastern stargazers. Flavius Josephus notes that the conjunction of the planets encouraged a number of rebels to unite in a strong Messianic movement, believing that God had decided to bring the rule of the Romans to an end with the coming of the Jewish Messiah. Such a savior would, of course, replace the Idumaen king, Herod the Great.

The phrase "in the east" (Matt. 2:2) apparently had special astronomical significance in ancient times, implying the early rising of the star or "the first rays of dawn," which would have corresponded exactly to the astronomical facts. By the nineteenth century, Halley's Comet (which appeared in 11 B.C.) was the preferred candidate for the star in the East. Astronomers now believe that the star of Bethlehem was either a comet or an exploding star—a nova. Excavations and ancient writings have come to light in recent years that provide astonishingly detailed information about the astronomical occurrences from Greek, Roman, Babylonian, Egyptian, and Chinese sources. On two occasions, the Romans noted in the heavens signals of earth-shattering historical events—one before the assassination of Caesar in 44 B.C. and yet another dazzling comet shortly before Nero committed suicide. Chinese astronomers note that they saw a comet between these two events. This comes from a very full account from ancient Chinese sources containing the first description of the famous Halley's comet, the great trailing star that always reappears close to the sun after an interval of seventy-six years.

**Character in Later Works.** This simple story of the wise men from the East, told only by Matthew, became the source of vast speculation. By the sixth century there were three of them, and they were considered kings—in fulfillment of the prophecy in Psalm 72:10. They were given the names Caspar, Melchior, and Balthasar. In the Middle Ages, they were venerated as saints: in the year 1162, their relics were said to have been taken by Frederick Barbarosa to Cologne Cathedral. Over time, they came to represent the different branches of the human race, taking on specific characteristics. A work attributed to Bede, for example, pictures Melchior as old, white-haired and bearded; Caspar as young, ruddy, and beardless; and Balthasar as black-skinned and thickly bearded (Goldberg, 472). They quickly took on the aspects of royalty as well, and were popularly portrayed by the nineteenth century as in the carol "We Three Kings."

The scene in which they appear is known as the visitation of the Magi, or Epiphany—the manifestation of Christ to the Gentiles. For many, this signifies the spread of Christianity to all lands, all peoples, in all ages (Ferguson, 78). In some faiths, Epiphany is considered the last of the days of the Christmas season—the "twelfth night."

With the flourishing of Nativity narratives in literature, especially in the medieval mystery dramas, the three wise men were a colorful and delightful addition, used in any pageant from early to modern days. Their confrontation with Herod also figured prominently in the mystery cycles. From earliest times to T. S. Eliot ("The Journey of the Magi") and Dorothy L. Sayers (*The Man Born to Be King*) the Magi have figured as symbolic characters, either for their gifts or their journey in faith. Sayers notes that she is following tradition, not the Bible, by representing them as kings, symbolizing the three races of mankind, the children of Shem, Ham, and Japhet (Asia, Africa, Europe) (Sayers, 25). She also makes them of three different ages and temperaments to suggest the stages and humors of human life.

## SOURCES

Brownrigg, Ronald, *Who's Who in the Bible*, vol. 2, New York: Bonanza Books, 1980; Ellis, E. E., "Magi," in *The Illustrated Bible Dictionary*, vol. 2, edited by J. D. Douglas, Sidney, Australia: Tyndale House Publishers, 1980; Goldberg, Michael, "Magi," in *A Dictionary of the Biblical Tradition in English Literature*, edited by David L. Jeffrey, Grand Rapids, MI: William B. Eerdmans Publishing Company, 1992; Ferguson, George, *Signs and Symbols in Christian Art*, New York: Oxford University Press, 1966; Keller, Werner, *The Bible as History*, New York: Bantam Books, 1982; Miller, Madeline S., and J. Lane Miller, *Harper's Bible Dictionary*, New York: Harper and Row, 1961; Sayers, Dorothy L., *The Man Born to Be King*, Grand Rapids, MI: William B. Eerdmans Publishing Company, 1971; Sheler, Jeffrey L., *Is the Bible True?* San Francisco, CA: Harpers, 1999.

## MARK

**Name and Etymology.** *Mark* is a Roman name, also *Marcus*, which appears frequently in Latin history. It is the Greek form from the Latin "large hammer." His Jewish name was *John*, thus he was also referred to as *John Mark* (Acts 12:12, 12:25, 15:37).

**Synopsis of Bible Story.** It is unclear which Mark was the author of the Gospel. There are at least three stories and ten references to "Mark" in the New Testament. Tradition has associated him with the John Mark of Acts, a Jerusalem Jew whose mother, Mary, was a prosperous property owner hospitable to Christians (Acts 12:12–17; Miller, 418). He is also noted as a kinsman to *Barnabas (Col. 4:10), who accompanied *Paul and Mark to Antioch (Acts 12:25, 13:1) and later went with them on their first missionary journey (13:5). For some reason, which is not specified in Scripture, Mark returned home, leaving his friends to continue without him. Paul apparently thought him undependable because of this action and was reluctant to include him on the second missionary journey, thereby causing some dissension between Paul and Barnabas. Some ten years later, Paul had apparently reconciled with the younger man and wanted him to come to Rome (2 Tim. 4:11).

Later references associate Mark with Simon *Peter, who calls him "my son" in a letter (1 Pet. 5:13). This reference may suggest that Peter had a role in converting Mark. He is thought to have remained in Rome after the martyrdom of the apostles, continuing the message of Peter, which is reflected in his narrative. The Gospel is marked as the work of a Jew who clearly knew Scriptures, Aramaic colloquial language, Jewish life and custom, and the political and geographical setting of his day. "He used such terms as Pharisees, Sadducees, Scribes, elders, priests, Temple, and synagogue with ease and accuracy" (Brownrigg, 274).

**Historical Context.** As the apostolic age drew to a close and the last of the firsthand memories of Jesus were fading, it is likely that Mark gathered together the oral traditions, many of which he had gleaned from his association with Peter, into the first and briefest of the Gospels. Peter and Paul were thought to have suffered martyrdom in Rome c. A.D. 64–65, thus suggesting that the Gospel of Mark was written after that time and perhaps before A.D. 70, the date for the destruction of Jerusalem—to which he refers in prophetic terms (Mark 13:13–33). The passage captures the tone of danger and suffering that one would associate with the terrors of the great fire (A.D. 64–5) and persecutions of Nero. The strong emphasis on the passion of Christ, told in clear, forceful language, made it a comfort to the early Christians and a model on which the other Synoptic Gospels, *Matthew and *Luke, appear to be based.

Traditions tie various cities to the Gospel writer. Alexandria names Mark the founder of the Church there, where he is believed to have been buried. The Egyptian Church attributes its principal liturgy to Mark, though Alexandrine Christian writers make no mention of his residence in Egypt.

One legend states that Mark was preaching along the shores of the Adriatic, when the vessel he was traveling on was caught in a great storm and driven to the place that was later to become Venice. An angel appeared to him saying, "On this site, a great city will arise in your honor." He then departed for Libya, where he preached for twelve years, then journeyed to Alexandria and founded the Christian Church in that city. He was martyred in Alexandria. Several centuries later, his body was carried to Venice by sailors. The city adopted his emblem, the lion—a symbol often found in Venetian art. (Ferguson, 132). He became the patron saint of Venice, where the Cathedral of San Marco became one of the masterpieces of church architecture

Modern scholars have debated a number of issues related to Mark's Gospel, including whether it is the true and solitary basis from which the other Synoptic Gospels derive or whether there was a prior document, now lost—the hypothetical "Quelle" or "Q."

The dating of the Gospel has focused on the prophecy—or perhaps recollection—of the destruction of Jerusalem. And, of course, the identity of Mark himself, his source of information and his creation of the form of a "gospel" have all busied scholars, who have subjected the Gospel to various types of analysis. (See Kee, Young, and Froehlich, 251ff.)

**Archaeological Evidence.** Papias, bishop of Hierapolis (60–130 A.D.), noted that Mark was an "interpreter" and "attendant" of Peter. Since Peter was originally thought to be a simple fisherman, this interpretation seemed vital to historians. In recent years, however, the discoveries in Capernaum, including a house that some identify as Peter's, suggest that Peter may indeed have been a prosperous man of business, not an illiterate fisherman as previously thought.

In 1958, a fragment of the "Secret Gospel of Mark" in a previously unknown letter by Clement of Alexandria (ca. A.D. 150–215) was discovered by Morton Smith, while he was cataloging manuscripts at the Mar Saba monastery near Jerusalem. These fragments tell stories of how *Jesus miraculously raised a young man who had died—a tale much like the raising of *Lazarus. The second fragment mentions Salome, indicating that Jesus refused to see her. Although these scraps of a larger document are not particularly valuable in and of themselves, they do point alternative Gospel that has not survived. (See the discussion and the fragments in R. Miller, 408–411.) (See also Jenkins, 101–102, 181, regarding the authenticity of this "find" about which scholars have "serious and enduring doubts.")

**Character in Later Works.** Later traditions link the upper room in the home in which Mark's mother lived on Mount Zion to where the early Christians congregated, and where Jesus gathered his disciples for the Last Supper. There is a Syrian Jacobite Church of John Mark in Jerusalem that marks that location, which is celebrated in Byzantine tradition.

An early portrayal of Mark preaching at Alexandria was painted by the Bellinis in the fifteenth century. The belief that his body was moved from Egypt to Venice in A.D. 832 by devout merchants inspired a series of mosaics in St. Mark's Cathedral in Venice, beneath the altar where his bones are thought to repose.

Over time, Christian iconography associated the four evangelists, or Gospel writers, with the four cherubim in Ezekiel and the four living creatures of Revelation 4:6. Mark came to be seen as the lion, and is thus portrayed frequently in medieval art and architecture—often, in fact, in illuminated manuscripts as a winged lion, marking his interest in the Resurrection. Because of his service as the secretary to Peter, he is also given a pen and, of course, the book of his Gospel.

## SOURCES

Brownrigg, Ronald, *Who's Who in the Bible*, vol. 2, New York: Bonanza Books, 1980; Ferguson, George, *Signs and Symbols in Christian Art*, New York: Oxford University Press, 1996; Jeffrey, David L., ed., *A Dictionary of the Biblical Tradition in English Literature*, Grand Rapids, MI: William B. Eerdmans Publishing Company, 1992; Jenkins, Philip, *The Hidden Gospels*, New York: Oxford University Press, 2001; Kee, Howard Clark, Franklin W. Young, and Karlfried Froehlich, *Understanding the New Testament*, Englewood Cliffs, NJ: Prentice-Hall, Inc., 1965; Miller, Madeline S., and J. Lane Miller, *Harper's Bible Dictionary*, New York: Harper and Row, 1961; Miller, Robert J., ed., *The Complete Gospels: Annotated Scholars Version*, San Francisco, CA: HarperCollins, 1994.

## MARY MAGDALENE

**Name and Etymology.** *Mary* is the Greek form of the Hebrew, *Miriam*. *Magdalene* refers to her home in Magdala.

**Synopsis of Bible Story.** One of the numerous women who were followers of *Jesus, Mary Magdalene has only a scattering of scriptural references in the various Gospels: Some believe she may have been the harlot who was rescued from her sinful life (Mark 16:9), who followed *Jesus out of gratitude. Some believe that *Luke's reference to the "certain woman which had been healed of evil spirits and infirmities, Mary called Magdalene, out of whom went seven devils" (Luke 8:1) may be an indication that Mary was an epileptic. She was clearly one of the devoted women who stood near the cross at the time of the Crucifixion (Matt. 27:56; Mark 15:40; *John 19:25). She also watched Jesus's burial in the cave provided by *Joseph of Arimathea (Matt. 27:61; *Mark 15:47). She came to mourn and to pay her respects at the sepulcher, only to discover the miracle of the Resurrection (Matt. 28:1; Mark 16:1; Luke 24:10; John 20:1). For her loyalty, she was rewarded by a vision of her risen Lord (Matt. 28:1, 28:9; John 20:11–18).

**Historical Context.** It would have been unusual—but not outrageous—at the time of Christ for a Jewish woman to be as independent as Mary Magdalene appears to be. Some traditions identify her as the woman at the well, or the woman filled with demons, either of which would imply she was a moral or social outcast. Her ability to follow along with the women as a disciple of the master suggests that she had no husband or family making claims on her, and that she may have had an income. She may have been a wealthy widow: she did have enough money to buy expensive oils to pour on Jesus's feet. In the early Christian world, women were influenced by the openness of the Greco-Roman culture. They were becoming more independent, moving freely in many spheres—the agora (marketplace), baths, businesses, and religious associations (Abrahamsen, 816).

**Archaeological Evidence.** Mary's hometown of Magdala in Galilee, now called "Mejdel," is located three miles from Capernaum on the northwest shore of the Sea of Galilee. Later, the town played an important role in the Jewish resistance and was besieged by the Romans. Excavations carried out from 1971 to 1973 and in 1975 revealed the remains of a Roman city, with a small synagogue of the Galilean type and a monastic complex (Negev, 226).

As the most prominent female figure in the Gospels outside of Jesus's family, Mary Magdalene has figured significantly in the continuing discussion of the role of women in the early Church. In the past century, certain forgotten and rejected documents of the Gnostics have thrust Mary back into prominence. In 1896, *Pistis Sophia* became available in English, revealing a tradition in which female disciples—including Mary Magdalene—played an important role in questioning Jesus about spiritual mysteries. Since that time, the rediscovery of other Gnostic texts, including the Gospel of Philip, the Sophia of Jesus Christ, the Dialogue of the Savior, and the Gospel of Thomas have also featured Mary Magdalene as a central figure among the disciples. The Gospel of Mary, however, is the document that has raised her role in a position of real contention. Although no complete copy of the apocryphal "Gospel of Mary" exists, three fragmentary manuscripts have survived into the modern period and have been published in the last half century. One is in Greek and the other two are in Coptic, a native Egyptian language written during the Roman period.

The brief gospel, which dates from the second century, is interesting for its Gnostic tendency and for its development of Mary as a disciple who was the first to see the resurrected Christ. In her gospel, Mary tells the other disciples of a vision that she has had that changes some of the earlier teachings, and which they reject (Miller, 357ff). They were suspicious of her claim to "see the Lord" in visions, a representation of the Gnostic claims to experience of his continuing presence (Pagels, 13). *Peter, who appeared to be jealous of Jesus's special love for her, was particularly negative about a woman assuming the role of teacher, but Levi defended her, insisting that Jesus "knew her completely and loved her devotedly ("The Gospel of Mary" 10:10, in Miller, 365). A historian notes that Mary was cowed by Peter, saying, "Peter makes me hesitate; I am afraid of him, because he hates the female race," and goes on to note that the male disciples agree that no woman be allowed to become a priest (Pagels, 65).

This is not a new discussion. Epiphanius, an early adversary of the Gnostics, noted that, "The Gnostic image of Mary Magdalen as Queen of the Apostles is purely a literary construction and contains not a shred of historical memory. . . ." (Quoted by Jenkins, 143). (See Jenkins's extensive discussion of this debate in his chapter on "The Daughters of Sophia," especially pp. 133–143.)

**Character in Later Works.** Although Scripture is limited in its references to Mary, popular legend abounds with tales and elaborations on her. Early disparagers of Christianity conflated her with the Virgin Mary to present Jesus's mother as an adulteress. The Latin fathers, Celsus and Origen, identified her with the sinner who washed Christ's feet with her tears and wiped them with her hair (Luke 7:37–50). Others identified her with *Mary of Bethany, making her sister to *Lazarus. Origen promoted the idea that she was a symbol of erotic asceticism, and St. Bernard of Clairvaux identified her with images of the Church as the bride of Christ.

One Byzantine tradition suggested that Mary went to Ephesus to preach with Lazarus and was buried there. Some thought her body was then taken to Constantinople (Brownrigg, 301). Later traditions asserted that she was a penitent in the desert in Egypt. One ninth-century tradition—which confuses her with *Mary of Bethany—ties her to a journey with Martha and *Lazarus by sea to the south of France, to Aix-en-Provence. This tradition describes her converting many people, eventually retiring to a desert near Marseilles, where she remained in solitude for thirty years, with nothing to eat or drink except what the angels supplied in the form of celestial food. In time, there was a cult of the Magdalene, with worshipful pilgrims going to her shrine at Saint Baume and writing hymns to her.

This tradition was terminated by the Reformation and by Calvin's clear separation of the three Marys, "devaluing Mary Magdalene as a symbol of the contemplative life" (Hannay, 487). Among Catholics, however, Mary remained a favorite saint during the Counter-Reformation and beyond. The Western Church, in the feast of Mary of Magdala on 22 July continues to make no distinction among the three women named Mary, while the Eastern Church regards each as a different person.

Mary has been a favorite of artists and writers throughout the ages, often as an erotic symbol or a penitential one. In paintings of the Crucifixion, she is often portrayed as a beautiful woman with long hair and uplifted eyes. She is usually dressed in violet, carrying a box of ointments, with a skull nearby (a symbol of the penitent saints). Donatello crafted a dramatic statue of her as a weeping penitent. She regularly appears in representations of the Crucifixion, the Pietà, and the Resurrection.

In medieval times, Mary became the subject of hymns and chivalric poetry, the image on calendars and the heroine of saints legends, carols, and ballads. As a balance to the purity of the Virgin Mary, she became central to medieval drama, appearing as one of the holy women in the brief dramatic portrayal of the Easter experience, the *Quem Quaeritis* trope, in continental plays, and in Townley, York, and Chester cycles—all scenes tied to the portrayal of the Crucifixion and the Resurrection.

Even after the Reformation, some Protestant poets continued to describe her in their religious poetry, and later Blake revived the image of her as a harlot (in "The Everlasting Gospel"). This follows the western tradition of a "magdalen" as a fallen woman. The twentieth century continues to demonstrate interest in her, portraying her in plays, poetry, and paintings. Nikos Kazantzakis cites her as Christ's final test in the novel *The Last Temptation of Christ*, where she becomes once again the image of erotic love. In the hit musical *Jesus Christ, Superstar*, Mary is presented as a love interest for Jesus, using the apocryphal Gnostic Gospel of Mary Magdalene as a source for this particular twist. Dorothy L. Sayers notes that Mary Magdalene and other women demonstrated Jesus's special attraction to women, whom he saw as fully human. This is why they were "last at the cross and first at the grave."

## SOURCES

Abrahamsen, Valerie, "Women," in *The Oxford Companion to the Bible*, edited by Bruce Metzger and Michael Coogan, New York: Oxford University Press, 1993; Brownrigg, Ronald, *Who's Who in the Bible*, vol. 2, New York: Bonanza Books, 1980; Ferguson, George, *Signs and Symbols in Christian Art*, New York: Oxford University Press, 1966; Hannay, Margaret, "Mary Magdalene," in *A Dictionary of the Biblical Tradition in English Literature*, edited by David L. Jeffrey, Grand Rapids, MI: William B. Eerdmans Publishing Company, 1992; Jenkins, Philip, *Hidden Gospels*, New York: Oxford University Press, 2001; Miller, Robert J., *The Complete Gospels: Annotated Scholars Version*, San Francisco: HarperCollins, 1994; Negev, Avraham, ed., *The Archaeological Encyclopedia of the Holy Land*, New York: Thomas Nelson Publishers, 1986; Pagels, Elaine, *The Gnostic Gospels*, New York: Random House, 1979; Sayers, Dorothy L., *Are Women Human?* Grand Rapids, MI: William B. Eerdmans Publishing Company, 1971.

## MARY (AND MARTHA) OF BETHANY

**Name and Etymology.** *Mary* is the Greek form of *Miriam*; *Martha* is an Aramaic word, not found in Hebrew, for "mistress," or "lady."

**Synopsis of Bible Story.** Mary and Martha, residents of Bethany, sisters of *Lazarus, and apparently good friends of *Jesus, provided hospitality for him and his disciples when they traveled to and from Jerusalem. Since the house is usually designated as theirs, not their brother's, historians suspect that one of them may have been a widow who inherited the property. Since Martha is often mentioned first and since her name means "mistress," she may have been the elder sister and the one who had the official possession of the residence.

Mary is often conflated with the other "Marys" of Scripture—*Mary the mother of Jesus and *Mary Magdalene. She and Martha are mentioned several times among the devoted women who followed Christ, in both *John (11:1–45) and *Luke (10:38–41). The visit to their home in Bethany is marked by Mary's decision to sit at Jesus's feet and listen to his teaching rather than to busy herself with the preparation of food, thereby choosing the "better part." In this case, Martha is portrayed as the complaining housewife who prepared the meal for her visitors, resenting her sister's avoidance of the work of the hostess.

When Lazarus died, however, it was Martha who ran eagerly out to meet Jesus on the road, proclaiming that her brother would not have died had Jesus come earlier. It was to her that Jesus made his great statement that he was the resurrection and the life (John 11:20–27).

It was Mary of Bethany who anointed Jesus's feet with precious oils (John 12:1–18), although another unnamed woman (perhaps Mary Magdalene) had anointed him at the house of Simon the leper at a much earlier time (Luke 7:36–50). Mary of Bethany's loving gesture occurred at their home, where they served as Jesus's hosts just before the feast of Passover.

**Historical Context.** The Jewish tradition for hospitality was quite elaborate and appears to have been a controlling concern for Martha. By contrast, women rarely assumed the role of disciple or student, sitting at the feet of the rabbi, as did Mary. Jesus, however, appears to have had numerous women among his regular retinue, who followed as informal disciples. They are mentioned several times in the Gospels, though not always by name. This would suggest a change from the strict Jewish tradition of clear demarcation of gender roles, with the women excluded from conversations. In the Old Testament, for example, we see *Sarai ministering to visitors while her husband enjoys the conversation—forcing her to eavesdrop from outside the tent. In the New Testament, we see women talking directly with Jesus, asking questions, debating his answers, as well as ministering to his needs.

The hospitality continued to follow the general pattern of the ancients. In New Testament history, we see that though inns were sometimes available, they were of low material and moral standards and generally unattractive to travelers. It became obligatory for the early Christians to show hospitality to their fellow believers. The pattern of hospitality is clear from several examples in the Gospels. Hosts greeted their guests with a kiss of welcome, offered them water to wash and refresh their feet, and oil for their heads.

The home of Martha and Mary is not described and may be simply metaphoric. Kenneth Bailey notes that the phrase "the house of" meant primarily a person's extended family, not necessarily the home itself (Bailey, 294).

**Archaeological Evidence.** Mary's anointing of the feet of Jesus in *John's account has led many to believe that she was actually *Mary Magdalene, but most scholars now believe this to be a different person from a different region. Also, because of the overlapping names and events, some scholars have thought that Martha may have been the wife or widow of *Simon the leper, but most believe that she was merely a capable neighbor who "went with her clay cookstove on her head, as women of Bethany still do, to lend a hand when company comes" (Miller, 423).

Bethany is a village near Jerusalem, on the eastern slope of the Mount of Olives. It was excavated by S. J. Saller in 1949, revealing four superimposed churches, all of which had mosaics. The remains of the ancient village of Bethany, with remnants of houses, winepresses, cisterns, silos, and pottery, were discovered on the site, dating back to Roman times (Negev, 56).

**Character in Later Works.** The two sisters are usually considered types of religious life: St. Augustine noted that "Martha was intent on how she might feed the Lord; Mary intent how she might be fed by the Lord" (Jeffrey, 485). These became images of the active and contemplative paths, often used in tandem with *Rachel and *Leah. The very term "Martha" was to become the description of the household drudge. This would explain that artists usually show Martha with a ladle or skimmer in her hand and a large bunch of keys attached to her girdle (or belt), as symbols of her housewifely qualities.

Yet there are nonscriptural legends that Martha, with Mary Magdalene (whom she is thought to have converted) and Lazarus set out, after the death of Christ, in an open boat which miraculously landed at Marseilles, France, where Martha converted the people of Aix-en-Provence and delivered them from a fearful dragon that was laying waste to the countryside. This would explain why artists also made the dragon the attribute of Martha (Ferguson, 16, 133).

The sisters appear in the Corpus Christi drama, the York "Raising of Lazarus," and in the modern version of the dramas by Dorothy L. Sayers, *The Man Born to Be King*. Sayers sees Martha as "house-proud" (Sayers, 171). Sayers also discusses the perverse readings of the story by modern preachers in *Are Women Human?* noting, "Mary's, of course, was the better part—the Lord said so, and we must not precisely contradict Him. But we will be careful not to despise Martha. . . . We could not get on without her. . . . For Martha was doing a really feminine job, whereas Mary was just behaving like any other disciple, male or female . . ." (46–47).

## SOURCES

Bailey, Kenneth E., "Houses, Furniture, Utensils," in *The Oxford Companion to the Bible*, edited by Bruce M. Metzger and Michael D. Coogan, New York: Oxford University Press, 1993; Ferguson, George, *Signs and Symbols in Christian Art*, New York: Oxford University Press, 1966; Jeffrey, David L., ed., *A Dictionary of the Biblical Tradition in English Literature*, Grand Rapids, MI: William B. Eerdmans Publishing Company, 1992; Miller, Madeline S., and J. Lane Miller, *Harper's Bible Dictionary*, New York: Harper and Row, 1961; Negev, Avraham, ed., *The Archaeological Encyclopedia of the Holy Land*, New York: Thomas Nelson Publishers, 1986; Sayers, Dorothy L., *Are Women Human?* Grand Rapids, MI: William B. Eerdmans Publishing Company, 1971; Sayers, Dorothy L., *The Man Born to Be King*, Grand Rapids, MI: William B. Eerdmans Publishing Company, 1943; Smalley, S. S., "Martha," in *The Illustrated Bible Dictionary*, vol. 2, edited by J. D. Douglas, Sidney, Australia: Tyndale House Publishers, 1980.

## MARY, MOTHER OF JESUS

**Name and Etymology.** *Mary* is the Greek form of the Hebrew name *Miriam*, meaning "bitterness."

**Synopsis of Bible Story.** This young woman, descended from the household of *David, was betrothed to *Joseph when she was visited by the angel Gabriel, who announced that she was to become the mother of the Messiah. Since she was still a virgin, her natural reaction was doubt that such a thing would happen. When assured that with God all things are possible, she accepted this troubling honor with modesty and obedience, saying, "Behold the handmaid of the Lord; be it unto me according to thy word" (Luke 1:38).

Burdened with the news of her condition, she visited her cousin Elizabeth, who was also pregnant with a promised child, *John the Baptist. As Mary saluted Elizabeth, the babe leapt in her cousin's womb, and Elizabeth proclaimed, "Blessed art thou among women, and blessed is the fruit of thy womb" (Luke 1:42). This verification of her angelic visitation led Mary to respond: "My soul doth magnify the Lord, And my spirit hath rejoiced in God my Savior. For he hath regarded the low estate of his handmaiden: for behold, from henceforth all generations shall call me blessed" (Luke 1:46–48).

Mary stayed with her cousin for three months before returning to her own house, probably in Nazareth. *Luke's story of the Annunciation is amplified by *Matthew's account of Joseph's gracious response to Mary's news. Knowing that he could quietly divorce her, he feared for her good name and even for her life. Joseph was visited by an angel who echoed Mary's explanation of the marvelous events that had led to the pregnancy and encouraged him to take her for his wife (Matt. 1:18–25).

When they were required to enroll for the Roman tax collection, she and Joseph journeyed to Bethlehem, their ancestral home (Luke 2:1–3). In primitive circumstances, in this small town that was no longer their home, Mary bore her child, wrapped him in swaddling clothes, and laid him in a manger. Remarkable events surrounded the birth—angels appeared to shepherds, a star stood over the place where the young child lay. Visitors came from afar bringing gifts, paying tribute to the long-awaited Messiah. The dark times that lay ahead were foreshadowed by *Herod's violent order to slaughter the Hebrew children, thus driving the small family out of their country and into Egypt.

Luke, who seems to know more about Mary than any of the other Gospel writers, tells us also about the trip to Jerusalem when the child was eight days old. There *Jesus was circumcised and named, becoming the legal son of Joseph, and Mary underwent the ritual purification rites and sacrificed a pair of turtledoves. There also, Simeon recognized the child and blessed God for sending the Messiah (Luke 2:25–34). The aged woman Anna echoed his blessings and gratitude for the redemption of Israel (Luke 2:36–38). Luke comments that Mary noticed such things, and kept them, pondering them in her heart (Luke 2:51).

When Jesus was an adolescent, Mary was astonished at this prodigy in her household. After the annual celebration of the Passover in Jerusalem, Mary discovered that Jesus was not with the crowd of "kinfolk and acquaintances," but had stayed behind to talk with the elders in the Temple. She was probably startled, saddened, and confused by his response to her admonition that he had caused his father sorrow by failing to tell them where he was: "How is it that ye sought me? wist ye not that I must be about my Father's business?" (Luke 2:49).

She had other children to raise along with Jesus. Four more sons, all of whom are named (Matt. 13:55) may have been Joseph's from an earlier marriage or may have been her own. She may have had daughters as well, but girls are rarely cited in Scripture. Joseph is often thought to have been somewhat older than she. He is not mentioned after the scene in the Temple, perhaps indicating he died soon thereafter.

We see her next with Jesus at the wedding at Cana (John 2:1–5). By this point, Mary accepted Jesus' supernatural powers, and at Cana she assumed that they might be used for her own purposes. She asked Jesus to change water to wine. Echoing his earlier admonition about his "Father's business," Jesus admonished her that his hour had not yet come. He nonetheless did as she requested.

Virgin Mary and Christ child, from Adoration of the Magi, tripytch, c.1495 (with donors Scheyven and Patron saints Peter Agnes and Joseph) (detail). The Art Archive/Museo del Prado, Madrid/Dagli Orti.

John indicates that this is the beginning of the miracles. Shortly thereafter, the family seems to have moved to Capernaum—where Jesus began his ministry and the gathering of his disciples. Mary played an active role in her son's ministry, traveling with him or following him on several occasions—as did other women, some of whom appear to have been her relatives.

*Mark records (3:31–5) the family's efforts to restrain miracles. Christ responded, "Who is my mother, or my brethren! . . . For whosoever shall do the will of God, the same is my brother, and my sister, and mother." Although this proclamation of separation from his earthly family seems powerful, the Scripture records other appearances of Mary, who followed him to the cross.

She was in Jesus' thoughts as he hung on the cross. Looking down at Mary and *John, Jesus assigned them to one another's care. She may have been one of the women who came to the tomb, and she was one of the mourners in the Upper Room who saw the miraculous coming of the Holy Spirit.

We do not know of her final years, though some traditions trace her to Ephesus, where it is thought she lived as a part of the young Church family. Roman Catholic tradition holds that she did not die, but was assumed into heaven.

**Historical Context.** Mary's story, which is largely a private history of a young Jewish woman in the days of *Caesar Augustus and *Herod the Great, provides interesting insights into the life of the average person in the first century A.D.: patterns of betrothal and marriage, worship and sacrifices, and festivals and weddings. She would have lived most of her life within a few miles of the place where she was born, amidst relatives who invited her to local weddings and religious festivals in Jerusalem. We know she was careful to follow the Jewish law of ritual purification and sacrifice. The choice of her offering of a turtle dove to sacrifice for the birth of her child signals her poverty.

Her presence at the foot of the cross and in the Upper Room suggest that she was part of a community that took care of her in her later years when she was no longer tied to Nazareth or to the family there. If she did move with John to Ephesus, she would have witnessed the impressive Roman culture there, along with the amazing growth of the new faith in her son, the Messiah.

The traditional Gospels mention Mary only a few times. Mark, the earliest Gospel, omits any mention of her by name. By contrast, the Gnostic "infancy gospels" (which Jenkins notes that "no scholar would dream of taking seriously as historical sources," 104) refer to her frequently. The Infancy Gospel of James (which appears in R. Miller, 383–396) is one of these "charming fictions" which extends the account of Mary's life back in time to include her birth and childhood, up to the birth of the Christ child.

The first five chapters of this text establish her nationality, homeland, ancestry, and parentage. Her early life is patterned on traditional stories of childless parents, with her mother, Anna, vowing to dedicate her child to God. Her infancy and childhood picture the purity of her life, not speaking or doing anything unclean or profane. At three, she was sent to the Temple, where she lived a life of absolute purity, "fed by the hand of an angel." When she was about to turn thirteen and become a woman, she posed a threat to the Temple's purity, so the priests invited suitors to whom "the Lord God shows a sign" (James 8:8 in R. Miller, 387). Joseph, a widower, immediately threw down his tools and rushed for the Temple. A dove flew out of his staff and perched on his head, a sign of God's selection of him as the protector, not the husband, of the maiden.

James presents the young wife/ward spinning when she had the angelic visitation. Various people come to her to proclaim her miraculous pregnancy. She faced questioning by Joseph, who assumed she had been seduced, and then by the priest, who was also suspicious of her behavior. She was forced to stand trial, undergoing a "drink test" in the wilderness, which she passed and was finally believed. (The Infancy Gospel of James, chapter 16, tells of Mary and Joseph each being subjected to the "Lord's drink test," involving drinking water and then being sent into the wilderness. This was to disclose their sin; but when each came back unharmed, the high priest marveled and said, "If the Lord God has not exposed your sin, then neither do I condemn you"; R. Miller, 391.)

A large segment of this Infancy Gospel is given over to Mary's virtuous deeds, demonstrating the four cardinal virtues: justice, self-control, wisdom, and courage. The stories that follow are detailed supplements to the records of Scripture. Ronald Hock notes, we are finally left "with an anonymous narrative written sometime after the Gospels of Matthew and Luke" (Hock, 2001).

The Council of Ephesus, in A.D. 432 affirmed the application of the term *Theotokos* (God bearer) to Mary in reaction to Nestorius' proposal of the word *Christotokos* (Christ bearer). He argued that Mary was mother of the human side of Christ only. The subsequent debate over the legitimacy of the Council and the nature of both Christ and his mother has continued down through the centuries. In this debate, the Infancy Gospel of James has exerted considerable influence over Christian piety and art.

**Archaeological Evidence.** At least two cities claim that Mary spent her last years in them: Jerusalem has the "tomb" of Mary and Ephesus has the house of the Virgin Mary. In Ephesus, where John is purported to have lived and become bishop and finally died, there is a convent over Panaya Kapulu, where Mary is thought to have died. On the other hand, the better documented site is the place where Jesus was betrayed, at the Basilica of St. Mary, which was supposed to have been her house (Mare, 251–52). The church apparently existed until the seventh century A.D. The present Church of the Tomb of Mary is thought to be on the same spot, near the Garden of Gethsemane.

Traditional sites of major events in Mary's life—the Annunciation, the birth, Pentecost, and so on—are marked by churches, frequently visited by pilgrims to the Holy Land.

**Character in Later Works.** Over the years, the veneration of the Virgin Mary has encouraged a series of celebrations of events in her life, some elaborated far beyond the literal scripture: the Virgin Birth, the Presentation, the Annunciation, Visitation, Purification, Assumption, and other ceremonial glorifications. Christians throughout the Roman Empire began to venerate Mary after the Council of Ephesus with festivals in her honor—her birth on September 8, her presentation in the Temple on November 21. During those festivals, portions of the Infancy Gospel of James were read (Hock).

In the Middle Ages, her role as "Mother of God" led to increasing veneration, with Latin hymns addressed to her, devotional poems, and miraculous appearances. Master artists drew and sculpted her image as Madonna and Pietà. Her iconography expanded so that she appeared not only in statuary and paintings in her traditional form, but also in such symbolism as the rose, the star of the sea, the moon, the lily of the valley, the temple of the Holy Spirit, and so on. Eventually, stained glass windows—most notably the great rose windows—and finally whole cathedrals were dedicated to "Our Lady" or "Notre Dame." Painters and mosaicists hired to decorate the churches and chapels honoring her often turned to the Infancy Gospel of James for appropriate subjects. By the fifteenth century, she was also assigned the titles "Redemptrix" and "Queen of Heaven." In 1854, Pope Pius IX proclaimed that from the moment of her conception, she was preserved free from all stain of original sin.

The medieval cult of Mary, which led to much of the concept of chivalry and courtly love is a long and curious story. Some of the more delightful of the miracle plays and tales deal with apparitions of the Virgin—as in "The Juggler of Notre Dame." The mystery cycles invariably portray her in the significant moments of Christ's life as a sympathetic figure.

Although Protestants, in the tradition of Calvin, rejected the veneration of the Virgin and she was banished during the Reformation from most of literature in the

Protestant countries, the romantics revived her and her symbols. Among the Victorians, with their Cult of Domesticity, Mary became the image of the perfect mother—the diametric opposite to the sin-filled *Eve.

In recent art and popular culture, a painting of the Virgin Mary in cow dung was displayed in the Brooklyn Museum amid storms of protest, and a painting of a defecating Virgin was recently removed from another museum's exhibit. More traditionally, however, moderns continue to use the image of Mary as the Madonna or as the Pietà—archetypes of woman's role in history. Apart from Christ, few biblical figures have had such a powerful influence on Western culture.

## SOURCES

Abrahamsen, Valerie, "Mary, Mother of Jesus," in *The Oxford Companion to the Bible*, edited by Bruce M. Metzger and Michael D. Coogan, New York: Oxford University Press, 1993; Hock, Ronald F., "The Favored One," in *Bible Review*, June 2001; Jeffrey, David L., ed., *A Dictionary of the Biblical Tradition in English Literature*, Grand Rapids, MI: William B. Eerdmans Publishing Company, 1992; Jenkins, Philip, *Hidden Gospels*, New York: Oxford University Press, 2001; Mare, W. Harold, *The Archaeology of the Jerusalem Area*, Grand Rapids, MI: Baker Book House, 1987; Miller, Madeline S., and J. Lane Miller, *Harper's Bible Dictionary*, New York: Harper and Row, 1961; Miller, Robert J., ed., *The Complete Gospels: Annotated Scholars Version*, San Francisco, CA: HarperCollins, 1994.

## MATTHEW

**Name and Etymology.** The name *Matthew* is a Greek form from the Hebrew, meaning "gift of God." In some of the Gospels, he is referred to as "Levi" instead.

**Synopsis of Bible Story.** Matthew was a tax collector or a "publican" (one who was employed by the state or public). He seems to have been in the employ of Rome, a collector of minor taxes: import, export, and transit fees. Jews who served a foreign government, as in this case, often extorted their own people and consequently were heartily despised by other Jews. Such men collected duty on goods carried to market (like salt), setting up toll gates on roads, bridges, and in harbors. Zacchaeus, who was also called a "tax collector" in Jericho, appears to have been of a higher status, a man who would have subcontracted much of his work to people like Matthew (Miller, 592).

*Mark indicates that Matthew's father's name was Alphaeus and that Capernaum was his home (Mark 2:14), suggesting that he may have been the brother of *James (Matt. 10:3; Mark 3:18). If he is the "Levi" referred to in both Mark and *Luke, he may have been a Levite, a descendent of Jacob's son *Levi. Perhaps he assumed the new name as a convert to *Christ.

The call of Matthew appears in three of the Gospels. Jesus himself spotted the tax collector by the roadside, perhaps at Capernaum, and said, "Follow me." And Matthew/Levi rose and "followed him" (Matt. 9:9). He is listed among the twelve without further elaboration, except in references to Jesus's dining at the "house of Levi," for which Jesus was reprimanded by the Scribes and Pharisees, who noted that he ate and drank with "publicans and sinners." To this Jesus replied that he had come to save those in need, not to call the righteous, but sinners (Matt. 9:12–13).

This disciple has generally been thought to be the author of the Gospel of Matthew, which draws on the earlier narrative of *Mark and adds the teachings of Jesus and the principles upon which life is to be lived under the rule of God. As a Jew, approaching the story from the perspective of Messianic prophecy and Hebrew law, Matthew included an account of Jesus's ministry as a fulfillment of Judaism, with emphasis on the new law and the new Israel. It is sometimes said that Matthew approaches the life and teachings of Jesus as a rabbi who admires and respects the rabbinical quality of Christ. The Gospel includes a combination of incidents in his life, the ethical teachings presented in an orderly manner, and instruction for those living in tension with Jews.

After an extensive genealogy, a birth narrative, and a rich portrayal of the ministry of *John the Baptist, Matthew portrays the temptation in the wilderness. He then presents the teachings of Christ, grouping them into five discourses—a "sort of Christian Pentateuch": (1) the Sermon on the Mount (chapters 5, 6, and 7), (2) the instructions to the Apostles (chapter 10:5–42), (3) a collection of parables (chapter 13:1–52), and (4) the discourse on the end of the world (chapters 24–25). The Gospel is crafted carefully to end with (5) the great commission: "Go ye therefore, and teach all nations, baptizing them in the name of the Father, and of the Son, and of the Holy Ghost: Teaching them to observe all things whatsoever I have commanded you: and, lo, I am with you alway even unto the end of the world" (Matt. 28:19–20).

This Gospel is generally thought to have been written sometime after A.D. 70 (the fall of Jerusalem). A noted historian says it was probably between 85 and 90 B.C., and attributes the Gospel to an "unknown Christian who was at home in a church located in Antioch of Syria" (Kingsbury, 502).

**Historical Context.** According to Papias (c. 60–130 B.C.), bishop of Hieropolis in Asia Minor, Matthew made a collections of the sayings of Jesus in Hebrew. Eusebius (c. 260–340 B.C.), bishop of Caesarea, noted that Matthew preached to the Hebrews, and some believe that he wrote his gospel in Judea, and then preached in Ethiopia, where he died. Various traditions record his martyrdom—in Ethiopia, in Persia, or in Pontus on the Black Sea.

The Book of Matthew, which was the most widely read and in some ways the most influential of the four Gospels, was apparently drafted by a Greek-speaking Christian of Jewish origin who used the Septuagint for translation of the Hebrew Scriptures. Some suggest it was a manual of discipline for the new Christians living in the midst of a Jewish culture, like the Dead Sea Scrolls in its focus on community instruction (Kee, Young, and Froehlich, 275).

Tax collectors were considered ceremonially unclean by their fellow Jews because of the necessity of their continual contact with Gentiles and their need to work on the Sabbath. Therefore, no orthodox Jew should eat with such a person. This would, in part, explain the outrage expressed by the Jews that Jesus shared with such a man—and at his house, perhaps in the company of other such men.

**Archaeological Evidence.** As a public servant in the region of the Galilee, Matthew is often mentioned in connection with discoveries in places such as Capernaum, where a synagogue of Jesus's day has been discovered. There is, of course, abundant evidence of the tax system used by the Romans to extract funds from their subjects. Records reveal that there were stock companies headed by wealthy Roman aristocrats, which had far-flung interests in the frontier provinces such as Judea. An overland customs route between Damascus and the Mediterranean would be an ideal place for collecting tolls.

Discussions regarding the dating and writing of Matthew's Gospel have focused largely on the possible order in which the Gospels were written, the use of Mark's

Gospel or some other source, and the clear appeal to the Jews. This last concern suggests that the Gospel was written early—when the church was largely Jewish, possibly as early as A.D. 50. It is one of the Synoptic Gospels, which scholars have examined extensively to determine the possible reliance on an oral tradition or a common source that has been lost, known as "Quelle" or "Q." Some believe that Matthew was the first of the Gospels, some that he wrote after Mark. (*The New International Version* has a useful summary of the debate on p. 1431.)

**Character in Later Works.** Like the other Gospel writers portrayed in illuminated manuscripts, statues, and paintings, Matthew is assigned the role of one of the four apocalyptic creatures of *Ezekiel and Revelation: in his case, the man—with wings. Because of his background as a tax collector, he also carries a money bag or purse. And because he is usually conceded to be the originator of the terms "holy catholic church" and "communion of the saints," Matthew is often portrayed with a scroll on which the Latin forms of these phrases are written. Like the other Gospel writers, he is usually painted with pen in hand. Sometimes an angel holds his inkhorn. Occasionally, an axe, thought to be the instrument of his martyrdom, is also displayed.

One of the most beautiful statues of him is an unfinished piece by Michelangelo. Numerous artists have painted some version of the company of disciples dining at the house of Levi—a happier portrayal than the one of the Last Supper. The National Gallery of Art has a painting of him by Simone Martini that includes most of his iconographic details mentioned above.

Like other of the disciples, Matthew appears in medieval mystery plays and even in the modern mystery play by Dorothy L. Sayers, *The Man Born to Be King*. She interprets him as a contemptible little turncoat, who was transformed by his love of Christ.

### SOURCES

Brownrigg, Ronald, *Who's Who in the Bible*, vol. 2, New York: Bonanza Books, 1980; Ferguson, George, *Signs and Symbols in Christian Art*, New York: Oxford University Press, 1966; France, R. T., "Matthew," in *A Dictionary of the Biblical Tradition in English Literature*, edited by David L. Jeffrey, Grand Rapids, MI: William B. Eerdmans Publishing Company, 1992; Harrop, J. H., "Tax Collectors," in *The Illustrated Bible Dictionary*, vol. 3, edited by J. D. Douglas, Sidney, Australia: Tyndale House Publishers, 1980; Kee, Howard Clark, Franklin W. Young, and Karlfried Froehlich, *Understanding the New Testament*, Englewood Cliffs, NJ: Prentice-Hall, Inc., 1965; Kingsbury, Jack Dean, "Matthew," in *The Oxford Companion to the Bible*, edited by Bruce M. Metzger and Michael D. Coogan, New York: Oxford University Press, 1993; Miller, Madeline S., and J. Lane Miller, *Harper's Bible Dictionary*, New York: Harper and Row, 1961; Tasker, R. V. G., "Matthew," in *The Illustrated Bible Dictionary*, vol. 2, edited by J. D. Douglas, Sidney, Australia: Tyndale House Publishers, 1980.

## MICAH

**Name and Etymology.** *Micah* means "Who is like Jah [Jehovah]?"

**Synopsis of Bible Story.** We know almost nothing of this eighth-century prophet, the apparent author of one of the twelve books of minor prophets. Internal evidence suggests that he was a younger contemporary of *Isaiah, a country man from the region of Moresheth-Gath (Micah 1:14), overlooking the coastal highway where the commercial caravans traveled through the ages. Like Isaiah, Micah also spoke of the troubled times that lay ahead for Judah, and of the later times when the Temple would become a place of international prominence. In this envisioned time of world peace, the true king would usher in a renewal of true worship in his spiritual kingdom. Some speculate that this forthright prophet may have been one of the "elders of the land" from the countryside, who was held in some esteem when he came to Jerusalem to prophecy (See Hans W. Wolff, quoted in Bulloch, 104–105.)

The book divides neatly into a series of segments, each starting with "Hear ye. . . ." and then presenting an oracle of doom and an oracle of hope. The central idea in each case is that the bloated self-confidence of leaders is damaging the faith of the rank and file, leading them away from true worship. Micah seems to be addressing the high and mighty quite directly. This is a parallel mode of speaking as an outsider, a man of the people, later used by *Jesus when he entered Jerusalem and also pointed to the iniquities of the religious leaders.

**Historical Context.** Micah's overarching concern is with the lineage of *David and the coming of a spiritual kingdom and a true king with genuine worship rather than with specific details of contemporary history. He may well have prophesied before the fall of Samaria and the Assyrian invasion. He is thought to have uttered his sayings during the reigns of Jotham (c. 742–735 B.C.), Ahaz (c. 735–715 B.C.), and Hezekiah of Judah (c. 715–687 B.C.) (Harrison, 996.) His exact dates, however, are difficult to determine. As with *Isaiah, the book of Micah has been the object of much textual and historical analysis, with quarrels over the possibility that certain of the later prophecies were added by later writers.

**Archaeological Evidence.** God's use of pagan nations to punish his own guilty people is fully evidenced in history. The path of the Assyrians and the Babylonians amply demonstrates the accuracy of Micah's prophecy. The area in which Micah lived was near Lachish, now being excavated as Tel el-Judeideh. Eusebius called his birthplace "Morasthei," and stated it was east of Beth-Gubrin. A later Christian tradition places Micah's tomb at a distance of ten stadia from that town, where a church was built.

**Character in Later Works.** Micah is frequently quoted as the one who articulated the Old Testament "golden rule," "What doth the Lord require of thee but to love mercy, do justice, and walk humbly with thy god" (Mic. 6:8).

Bearing a striking resemblance to other "prophets of devastation," he saw the sins of Samaria and Jerusalem bringing their doom. A generation later, *Jeremiah echoed his predictions regarding Jerusalem and the Temple (Jer. 26:18–19). He might have been put to death had not certain of the elders recalled that Micah of Moresheth had used similar words.

Like other prophets, Micah drew on the Exodus tradition, using the role of God in Hebrew history as evidence of God's faithfulness to the everlasting covenant. Like *Amos, *Hosea, and Isaiah, he too saw the Canaanite gods as sinister, with false and corrupting influences on the Israelites.

More plainspoken and specific than Isaiah, he foresaw the coming of the Messiah from a small town rather than Jerusalem, from Bethlehem Ephrathah (Mic. 5:2–3). It was this prophecy that *Herod's chief priests and scribes recalled (Matt. 2:5–6), leading this insecure and brutal king to conclude that the *Magi were in search of the prophesied true king of Israel. This in turn became Herod's justification for the Slaughter of the Innocents.

Micah's denunciation of the false prophets is echoed in the New Testament, where once again the elders of the Temple found themselves denounced publicly for their failure to be leaders who worshipped in goodness and in truth. Later, his law court imagery, with the trial, summons, witnesses, evidence, arguments, and judgment, became useful for *Paul, who also garnered legal arguments to defend his faith in the Roman courts.

His vision of a New Jerusalem, where swords would be beaten into ploughshares and spears into pruninghooks (Mic. 4:3) was—like Isaiah's—a strong influence on St. Augustine's *City of God*.

Micah's peasant-eye view of "civilized" history is a vivid contrast to the sophisticated and aristocratic view of Isaiah, who lived in the midst of the intrigue. This parallels that of such later authors as the eighteenth-century British writer, Thomas Gray, who saw the cities in vivid contrast to the pastoral landscape in "Elegy Written in a Country Churchyard."

The closing verses of the book of Micah are read each year by Jewish worshippers in the afternoon service on the Day of Atonement. He remembers God's mercy to his covenant people:

"He will turn again, he will have compassion upon us; he will subdue our iniquities; and thou wilt cast all their sins into the depths of the sea. Thou wilt perform the truth to Jacob, and the mercy to Abraham, which thou hast sworn unto our fathers from the days of old" (Mic. 7:19–20).

### SOURCES

Bullock, C. Hassell, *An Introduction to the Old Testament Prophetic Books*, Chicago: Moody Press, 1986; Harrison, R. K., "Micah," in *The Illustrated Bible Dictionary*, vol. 2, edited by J. D. Douglas, Sidney, Australia: Tyndale House Publishers, 1980; Miller, Madeline S., and J. Lane Miller, *Harper's Bible Dictionary*, New York: Harper and Row, 1961; Negev, Avraham, ed., *The Archaeological Encyclopedia of the Holy Land*, rev. ed., New York: Thomas Nelson Publishers, 1986.

### MIRIAM

**Name and Etymology.** *Miriam* derives from the Hebrew word for "bitterness" or perhaps "loved of Jehovah."

**Synopsis of Bible Story.** Miriam was the elder sister of both *Aaron and *Moses. Members of the tribe of Levi, the family lived in Egypt some years after *Joseph and his brothers had immigrated at a time of famine in Canaan. Over time, the Hebrews became unwelcome guests, enslaved, numerous, and believed to be a threat to Egyptians. The Pharaoh ordered that every newborn Jewish boy must be thrown into the Nile (Exod. 1:22). Miriam's mother hid the baby Moses from the Egyptians for three months. Then she prepared a papyrus basket for him and put it among the reeds along the "brink" of the Nile (Exod. 2: 3), thus fulfilling the literal obligations of the law.

Miriam, apparently resourceful and courageous, hid nearby, watching over to see what happened to the baby. When the Pharaoh's daughter, who had come down to the river to bathe, sent her servant to fetch the basket and recognized that the crying child was a Hebrew baby, Miriam came forward and offered to help: "Shall I go and call to thee a nurse of the Hebrew women, that she may nurse the child for thee?" she asked (Exod. 2:7). It was Miriam who arranged for Moses' own mother to serve as his nurse. As his older sister, she appears to have helped Moses bridge the Hebrew and Egyptian cultures. It is clear that by the time he was a "grown" man in the court of the Pharaoh (Exod. 2:11), he had developed a deep empathy with the Hebrew slaves: he risked his life in a fight with an abusive Egyptian overseer.

There is a gap in Miriam's story when Moses fled to Midian, settled there, married Zipporah, daughter of Jethro, and started a family. By this time, Miriam would have been middle-aged. If, as scholars believe, Moses remained in Midian for forty years, his sister would have been an elderly woman by the time God directed him to return to Egypt.

It was after her brothers, Moses and Aaron, joined forces, confronted the Pharaoh, and led the Hebrews out of Egypt that Miriam became prominent: She is quoted as singing the triumphant song as the procession emerged miraculously from the Red Sea (or the Sea of Reeds): "Sing ye to the Lord, for he hath triumphed gloriously; the horse and his rider hath he thrown into the sea" (Exod. 15:21). This song repeats (with slight variations) the first four lines of the victory hymn that Moses and the Israelites sang on the same occasion. Miriam took a tambourine in her hand and led the women in singing and dancing.

During the sojourn in the wilderness, she appears to have been a leader of the women. She was recognized as a prophetess who spoke to God on occasion. Over the years, she grew increasingly bold in her claim to authority, finally joining with Aaron (or possibly even inciting him) to challenge Moses's leadership. Why, she asked, did God not speak to her? (Exod. 12:2).

This escalating jealousy is foreshadowed in an earlier scene when she and Aaron taunted Moses about his Ethiopian wife. She may have been jealous of another woman's place in her brother's affections, or she may have been concerned that the marriage was interracial. The tribe of *Abraham had a long tradition of protecting its men from marriage to women of different cultural and religious backgrounds.

Curiously, her punishment for the insurrection was more severe than Aaron's. She was struck down with "leprosy," her skin turned white as snow. The affliction was relieved after only seven days. She returned to the community, and the remainder of her life is silence (Num. 12:15). Only her death is recorded, as is the mourning that followed her burial in Kadesh (Num. 20:1). Like her brothers, she died before crossing over into the promised land.

**Historical Context.** As a part of a persecuted slave culture, Miriam was the first of the Hebrew women who is pictured in a settled household and as a single woman. Women may have been expected to labor side-by-side with men in the fields or in the quarries. The Pharaoh's massacre of the male children may explain her status; if this was not the first such massacre, Hebrew husbands may have been scarce in Egypt. Although the Scripture makes no mention of Miriam's marriage, rabbinical tradition "makes her the wife of Caleb and mother of Hur." It would be unusual for a woman to remain unmarried in that period, but she might have been included in her brothers' households.

Later, in the Exodus and then in the wilderness, Miriam presents a lively portrait of the strong woman among the Hebrews. The reader can picture her singing and dancing while celebrating the bloody victory over the enemy. The singing of the triumphant song and the animated dance that followed were apparently traditional celebrations of victories in battle (See 1 Sam. 18:6; 2 Sam. 1:20). Although some claim her to be the first "poet" in Scripture, the song appears to belong to Moses as well as to Miriam.

Her identification as a "prophetess" reflects a role that women were to assume only occasionally in both the Old Testament and the New. "Your sons and your daughters shall prophecy . . ." (Acts 2:17; Joel 2:28). Other "prophetesses" identified in scripture were *Deborah (Judg. 4:4), *Isaiah's wife (Isa. 8:3), Anna (Luke 2:36), and *Philip's daughters (Acts 21:9).

Even though she was a leader among the women, she had no voice in the governance of her people (as Moses did) nor could she serve as priest (like Aaron). We assume that she would have lived her life in traditional ways: the care of the household and the children, the baking of bread, and the weaving of tapestries for the tabernacle in the wilderness.

Miriam's anger at Moses, possibly based on his marriage, begins with a reference to his "Cushite wife" (Num. 12:1–2 in the *New International Version*; "Ethiopian women" in the King James Version). For some reason, both Miriam and Aaron rejected her. Cush, the first son of Ham, was the father of a people who lived in the southern Nile valley. This "Cushite wife" may be Moses's wife Zipporah (see Exod. 2:15–22), or it may be a second marriage to a dark-skinned woman, or it may have been simply a pretext for a jealous outburst at God's favoritism for Moses.

Her punishment with the affliction of leprosy has puzzled many. Leprosy was often referred to in ancient literature, with detailed symptoms and treatment outlined in Leviticus. Priests were expected to identify the disease and separate the sufferer from the rest of the people because of its potentially contagious nature. In Numbers 5, the Lord commands Moses to tell his people "to send away from the camp anyone who has an infectious disease or a discharge of any kind or who is ceremonially unclean. . . . Send away male and female alike; send them outside the camp so they will not defile their camp, where I dwell among them."

The term *leprosy* apparently covered any number of skin diseases. It was often assumed to derive from sin, largely because many of the diseases covered by the term were sexual in origin. This particular case was unlikely to be what we now consider leprosy, perhaps being more like psoriasis, since it lasted only a brief time. The seven days of Miriam's separation may alternately be considered a punishment for her disgrace rather than a health precaution.

This isolation of the "unclean" takes on a symbolic meaning in Revelation 21:27, where it becomes clear that God expects his bride to be pure in order to enter into the Holy City of Jerusalem. This deeply entrenched tradition among the Hebrews explains Aaron's obligation to send Miriam out of the camp for seven days.

**Archaeological Evidence.** Egyptian tomb paintings do reveal the costumes of Hebrew women at the time and the relics of gold pieces indicate some of the jewelry they probably took with them.

**Character in Later Works.** Some believe that Miriam's song influenced the later Song of Deborah. St. Ambrose notes that the victory song anticipated *Mary and the "choirs of virgins" pictured in heaven, "singing to the Lord because they have passed through the sea of this world without suffering from its waves" (Jeffrey, 515). Miriam has traditionally been associated with the Virgin *Mary, partially because the name *Mary* is a variant of *Miriam*.

A few medieval writers referred to her in passing: Gower's *Mirour de l'omme*, and the fourteenth century *The Book of the Knight of La Tour* by Landry. References tend to be incidental until modern authors found her an early example of frustrated womanhood. D. H. Lawrence uses the name in *Sons and Lovers* for the sisterly lover of the hero, who hovers over him and prods him, demanding too much in exchange for her love. Other, more sentimental writers of popular religious fiction have seen her as a surrogate mother figure for Moses, focusing on her youthful heroism.

In recent years, she has been more widely celebrated as the first female poet in Scripture, and a leader who was born before her time.

## SOURCES

Douglas, J. D., *The Illustrated Bible Dictionary*, vol. 2, Sidney, Australia: Tyndale House Publishers, 1980; Jeffrey, David L., ed., *A Dictionary of Biblical Tradition in English Literature*, Grand Rapids, MI: William B. Eerdmans Publishing Company, 1992.

## MOSES

**Name and Etymology.** *Moses* may be a name of Egyptian origin, meaning "is born." Hebrew wordplay on the name means "drew him out," perhaps referring to his deliverance as a baby or perhaps the deliverance of his people from captivity.

**Synopsis of Bible Story.** This hero of the Hebrew people was a leader with an extraordinarily close relationship with God, a deliverer of his people from slavery, a lawgiver, a prophet, and a father to his erring children. (His story reaches from Exodus 2 to Deuteronomy 34.) Like many heroes, Moses had a miraculous birth and delivery, access to two cultures, and many wanderings and trials.

He was the youngest child of a Levite husband and wife, probably Amram and Jochebed, born at a time when the Egyptians were throwing Hebrew male children into the Nile to control the population. His mother hid him for three months and then put him in a papyrus basket among the reeds in the river. *Miriam, Moses's sister, watched over him, coming forward when the Pharaoh's daughter and her attendants discovered him with an offer to arrange for a Hebrew nurse. This informal adoption by Egyptian royalty gave Moses access to education, enriching his early training, expanding his contacts with life and people in the Egyptian aristocracy so as to make him sophisticated enough to confront another Pharaoh at a later time in life, and preparing him for the leadership role he would assume.

His Hebrew family's nurturing kept him in touch with the faith and culture of his people, developing in him a sensitivity to the indignities the slaves were suffering. This awareness burst forth when he was incensed by the sight of an Egyptian beating a Hebrew. In this clash of his two cultures, he instinctively chose the Hebrew side, killing the Egyptian. Shortly afterwards, the Pharaoh heard the rumors and sought to kill him.

Moses escaped to Midian and lived there as a shepherd, a husband, and a father. His father-in-law, the priest Jethro, proved a wise guide and counselor for him during this exile. This wilderness period lasted forty years, coming to a close when the Pharaoh (possibly Thutmose III) died and God called Moses to return to his enslaved people. On the "mountain of God" in the desert, God spoke to Moses from the burning bush (Exod. 3), identifying himself and commanding Moses to "bring forth my people the children of Israel out of Egypt" (Exod. 3:10). Displaying either modesty or recalcitrance, Moses questioned God and argued against his mission. God responded to each question and objection, providing details, methods, miracles, and assistance.

With his older brother *Aaron at his side, serving as his spokesman, Moses returned to confront the Israelites (Exod. 6:9) and the Pharaoh (Exod. 7:10). This godly leader experienced challenges and disbelief at every step, forcing him to call on God again and again for a series of signs and finally for a series of plagues (Exod. 7–11). Only with the shock of the final plague—the deaths of the first-born sons of the Egyptians (a grim

Moses in the Sinai desert (wth the tablets of the law). The Art Archive/Musée des Beaux Arts, Troyes/Dagli Orti.

echo of the earlier slaughter of the Israelite babies)—did the Pharaoh relent and allow the Hebrew slaves to leave.

The escape, detailed in Exodus 13–14, involved another reversal: the Pharaoh changed his mind, sent his armies in hot pursuit, and triggered yet another calamity for the Egyptians—the drowning of the charioteers in the Red (Reed) Sea. God's providential concern for his people was evident in the escape, the opening and closing of the waters, the leading of the tribes as a cloud by day and a pillar of fire by night.

In the wilderness, Moses called on the wisdom of his long years in Midian, leading his people like a flock of sheep, attending to their health and safety. He relied on God for food (manna) and water (striking the rock with his rod). In a climactic scene, Moses brought them back to the mountain, where he once again knew God face-to-face. On Mount Sinai, he used the education of the court to transcribe the law revealed to him by God. This complex and rich system of laws was to serve the Israelites for the remainder of their long history. The commandments and elaborations of God's wise regulations were to keep this people faithful, healthy, and orderly through the centuries. He is also credited with having written the first five books of the Bible—the Pentateuch.

As a leader during his forty years in the wilderness, Moses was often stern, angry at the disobedience of his people when they built a golden calf to worship, then rebelled against his leadership and moaned for a return to the fleshpots of Egypt. In his final years, he directed the division of the land they were promised, the census of the tribes, and he determined the succession of the leadership. Though he lived to a ripe old age, Moses was never allowed to cross over into the promised land. Just before his death, he did stand on the top of Mount Nebo to view the land God promised his people (Deut. 34). He died in the land of Moab—after 120 years—still clearsighted and powerful to the very end. As the Scripture tells us:

> And there arose not a prophet since in Israel like unto Moses, whom the Lord knew face to face, In all the signs and wonders, which the Lord sent him to do in the land of Egypt to Pharaoh, and to all his servants, and to all his land. And in all that mighty hand, and in all the great terror which Moses shewed in the sight of all Israel.
> (Deut. 34:10–12).

**Historical Context.** From the time of Ramses II and the building of the great pyramids in Egypt, we know a great deal about ancient history, of which the Hebrews were only a modest part. The Egyptians had vast numbers of slaves whom they used in their great building projects. Those monuments to human pride, with their carvings and their paintings, still testify to the varied enslaved peoples who groaned under the burden of these engineering marvels.

Moses was the transitional figure, who led his people out of slavery, through the wilderness, to the verge of the promised land. In the forty years of wandering, he solidified the legal, moral, and religious culture of the young nation, providing a basis for the warfaring people who would then cross the Jordan and take the land under *Joshua. (Werner Keller dedicates several chapters to this epic of nation-building.) As the author of the Pentateuch, Moses is usually credited with bringing writing to the Hebrews, giving them the law, providing the rituals and worship practices, developing in this band of ex-slaves a sense of national identity, and leading them to the promised land. Modern textual critics have quarreled with the tradition of Moses' sole authorship of the Pentateuch (especially the account of his own death), but generally he has retained his status as the great Hebrew hero.

**Archaeological Evidence.** Historians have argued over which pharaohs were part of Moses' life, the actual time of the events, and the specific places to which the text refers. Ernest Wright identifies Seti I as the Pharaoh of the initial oppression. Both he and Bernard Anderson place the Exodus in the reign of Ramses II, as do many others, about 1290 B.C., in the XIX Dynasty. He believes that the pharaoh, who immortalized himself with colossal statues throughout Egypt and who used the Apiru (Habiru) in his public projects, would have been the likely antagonist. Ramses had shifted his political center to the Delta so as to control Egypt's dwindling Asiatic empire. Having signed a treaty with the Hittites, the Egyptians knew a long period of tranquility and immense construction projects at Karnak and Luxor, where the Hebrews apparently labored. Paintings discovered in the tombs reveal Asiatic laborers, some of them in the process of making bricks and building monuments. Pithom and Ramses have been excavated by archaeologists.

The stations of the travel route that they took, avoiding the King's Highway and wandering through the wilderness, are specifically listed in Numbers 33. Kadesh-Bernea undoubtedly was a stopping place, since it had a spring large enough to supply a great multitude. The construction of the monastery of St. Catherine at Mount Sinai is based on faith that this is the actual location of the events surrounding the bringing of the Law to the Jews, though other scholars have argued that the mountain was in Midian.

**Character in Later Works.** All through the Old Testament, Moses is revered as the great leader and prophet. Psalm 90 is, in fact designated "A prayer of Moses the man of God." This same veneration continues in the New Testament, leading the Pharisees to confront Christ with his apparent challenge to the law of Moses. *Jesus stated clearly that he had not come to overturn the law, but to fulfill it (Matt. 5:17). His respect for Moses and the law continued into the early Christian Church, with *Paul listing Moses among the faithful Hebrews (Heb. 11:23–24). In Matthew 17:2, Christ's transfiguration includes a vision of Moses and *Elijah—representatives of the old covenant and the promise of salvation. *Peter suggested the building of three shelters to signify these three great leaders, only to find his idea canceled by God's proclamation: "This is my beloved Son. . . ." (Matt. 17:5). Here we see clearly that Moses, for all of his greatness, is no equal to Christ, the only begotten son of God.

Paul continued this reevaluation of the prophet of the Jews by indicating that the wondrous experience on the mountaintop had now been transformed into the new covenant, mediated by Jesus: Mount Sinai replaced by Mount Zion, the dream of the promised land replaced by the hope for the new Jerusalem (Heb. 12:18–24). In Romans, Paul explained the true meaning of the law (Rom 2:17–29).

The Christian tradition has tended to reduce the authority of Moses and the law: medieval Catholics thought of him as an ascetic, contemplative, monastic type. He became a standard figure in medieval and Renaissance art, sometimes pictured erroneously with horns because of an error in translation of Scripture. After the Reformation, he was often portrayed as a stern giver of the law, superseded by the Christian emphasis on faith and love.

In English literature, he appeared in late medieval plays based on Scripture—both the York and N-Town "mystery" cycles. He was also referred to by Chaucer and the author of *Piers Plowman*. John Bunyan presented him as a stern fellow along the path that Pilgrim trod in *The Pilgrim's Progress*, and William Blake pictured him as a symbol of the bondage of the law in *Africa* and *Ahania*.

American tradition has found a different image in Moses: the African-American community particularly came to venerate him as the prophet who led an enslaved people out of slavery. Not only in their spiritual "Go Down, Moses," (a title Faulkner uses for a story of African Americans in Mississippi), but also in stories and sermons, Moses became a hero. Faulkner chose to recount an entire sermon Dilsey hears in a black church in *The Sound and the Fury*; the story is one of Moses and his people escaping to freedom.

Others have returned to the identification of Moses with the law—Thornton Wilder (who used him as a judge in *The Skin of Our Teeth*) saw Moses as the image of uncompromising legalism. For Jewish writers, such as Saul Bellow, Moses is simply a standard name for Jewish boys, as in "Moses Herzog."

## SOURCES

Anderson, Bernard W., *Understanding the Old Testament*, Englewood Cliffs, NJ: Prentice-Hall, Inc., 1966; Jeffrey, David L., and John V. Fleming, "Moses," in *A Dictionary of the Biblical Tradition in English Literature*, edited by David L. Jeffrey, Grand Rapids, MI: William B. Eerdmans Publishing Company, 1992; Keller, Werner, *The Bible as History*, New York: Bantam Books, 1982; Marcus, Amy Dockser, *The View from Nebo*, New York: Little, Brown, 2000; Wright, G. Ernest, *Biblical Archaeology*, Philadelphia, PA: The Westminster Press, 1962.

# N

## NAHUM

**Name and Etymology.** *Nahum* means "comforts" or "God is comforted"; he is also known as "Nachum."

**Synopsis of Bible Story.** Nahum, a minor prophet identified only as "the Elkoshite," spoke boldly of the doom of Nineveh. Unlike other prophets of the seventh century B.C., this man focused his attention on the invaders and conquerors, not the people of Judah—although his audience must have been Judah. The brief book begins with an incomplete acrostic poem (only a portion of an alphabetical psalm) and a declaration of judgment (Nahum 1:1–15). The remainder consists largely of judgment oracles, written in poetic language, with vivid word pictures, many metaphors and similes, and much repetition.

Nahum painted a graphic picture of the fall of Nineveh: "The sight of warriors dressed in red, flashing steel, madly racing chariots, frantic Assyrian soldiers hurrying to the wall, galloping horses, piles of corpses, combined with the sounds of women moaning like doves, leaves the audience with the feeling of having tuned in on the devastation" (Bullock, 215). The staccato phrases and powerful rhetorical questions accumulate in a rush of condemnations that culminate in a devastating overall proclamation of God's powerful vengeance. When the day of wrath did come to Nineveh, the city was destroyed and never rebuilt. With obvious relish, this writer described the specific details of the Assyrian iniquities and the means of the final obliteration.

**Historical Context.** Because Nahum spoke of the fall of Thebes or No-ammon in Egypt (663 B.C.) and the coming fall of Nineveh (612 B.C.; Nahum 3:7–9), most scholars date the composition between the two events. This would place Nahum himself in the reign of *Josiah, and make him a contemporary of *Zephaniah and the young *Jeremiah.

By the time Nahum prophesied, Assyria had already destroyed Samaria, conquered Israel, and carried away the captives. By the seventh century B.C., the Assyrians were threatening tiny Judah, having already demanded tribute and attacked most of her neighbors. The brutality of Assyria "is amply attested both in literature and art. Assyria was essentially a nation of warriors whose chief delight was to plunder, ravish, and destroy" (Paterson, 116). As John Paterson notes, "With his own hand the king would gouge out the eye of noble captives or flay them alive and pin them to the ground to perish. Impalement of prisoners was a common practice. The Assyrian sculptures show us how the king could sit down to dine with the bleeding hands of captives hung around to give zest to his appetite" (Paterson, 116–17).

**Archaeological Evidence.** Quotations from Nahum (Nahum 3:6–9) along with commentary referring to the "Seeker-after-smooth-things" appear in the Dead Sea Scroll from Qumran Cave 4. These fragments helped to establish the dates of the scrolls and to identify some of the obscure references.

When the Assyrians defeated the Egyptians at Thebes in 663 B.C., they had real cause to celebrate their victory. According to Homer, this city had 100 gates and was regarded as impregnable. Ashurbanipal bragged that his troops had plundered the metropolis whose temples contained boundless wealth: "I conquered the whole city . . . silver, gold, precious stones, the whole contents of its palace, coloured vestments, linen, magnificent horses, slaves, both men and women, great obelisks of shining bronze weighing 2,500 talents; I took the temple gates from their place and brought them to Assyria" (Keller, 293–94).

*Sennacherib made Nineveh capital of the Assyrian empire about 700 B.C., thereby providing a symbol of the brutal and aggressive nation he commanded. Archaeologists have discovered among the ruins of this city evidence of the city *Jonah had visited earlier and Ashurbanipal governed, with its great palaces and temples to the goddess Ishtar. The famous lion gates, celebrating the lion-hunter Ashurbanipal, are reflected in the imagery of Nahum.

Mounts called Kuyunjik and Nebi Yunus ("Prophet Jonah") on the banks of the Tigris river opposite Mosul in northern Iraq have been excavated. Discoveries in Assyria have included the uncovering of a city wall with a moat 150 feet wide and 8 miles long with 15 gates, heavily fortified against battering rams and arrows. As is prophesied in Nahum (2:6), the Assyrians had dams that could be released to wash away the palace walls. The city was full of plunder from its victims, as is testified to by the Babylonian Chronicles (See Nahum 2:10). Among the most famous of the discoveries at Nineveh are the enormous lion statues.

One particularly gory reference in Nahum 3:3 to "piles of dead" (*The New International Version* translation) may refer to the bloody practice of Shalmaneser III, who boasted of erecting a pyramid of chopped-off heads in front of the enemy's city. *The New International Version of the Bible* notes that other Assyrian kings stacked corpses "like cordwood by the gates of defeated cities" (footnote, p. 1377). The reference in Nahum 3:10 to binding great men in chains is also a literal description of the practice of humiliating the defeated kings by putting dog chains on them and displaying them in dog kennels at the eastern gate of Nineveh.

**Character in Later Works.** The images of bloody warfare pictured in this vivid book echo throughout history. As recently as Picasso's *Guernica*, artists have portrayed the horror of man's brutality to man.

Although Nahum is seldom mentioned in later Scripture or in secular art works, his symbol of the evil city of Nineveh with its foundation of wickedness and tyranny became fundamental to the image of the great cities ruled by satanic forces—what James Thompson called "The City of Dreadful Night." This is the City of Man, which St. Augustine so beautifully separated from the "City of God"—the heavenly Jerusalem. Shelley wrote of the great symbols of human pride covered by the desert sands in "Ozymandias"—a portrayal of the bloody victories of men whose greatness was soon forgotten. The city of Nineveh was so completely destroyed by its enemies that it was covered with windblown sand and never rebuilt.

## SOURCES

Anderson, Bernard W., *Understanding the Old Testament*, Englewood Cliffs, NJ: Prentice-Hall, Inc., 1966; Bullock, C. Hassell, *An Introduction to the Old Testament Prophetic Books*, Chicago: Moody Press, 1986; Isaacs, Ronald H., *Messengers of God: A Jewish Prophets Who's Who*, Jerusalem: Jason Aronson, Inc., 1988; Keller, Werner, *The Bible as History*, New York: Bantam Books, 1982; Paterson, John, *The Goodly Fellowship of the Prophets*, New York: Charles Scribner's Sons, 1948; Young, E. J., "Nahum," in *The Illustrated Bible Dictionary*, vol. 2, edited by J. D. Douglas, Sidney, Australia: Tyndale House Publishers, 1980.

## NATHAN

**Name and Etymology.** *Nathan* comes from the Hebrew for "he gave."

**Synopsis of Bible Story.** Nathan was a prophet in the court of King *David. It was he who rebuked David at the time of his affair with *Bathsheba and the murder of Uriah. "There were two men in one city; the one rich, and the other poor. The rich man had exceeding many flocks and herds: But the poor man had nothing save one little ewe lamb, which he had brought and nourished up: and it grew up together with him, and with his children; it did eat of his own meat, and drank of his own cup, and lay in his bosom, and was unto him as a daughter." So begins the touching story, which continues, "And there came a traveler unto the rich man, and he spared to take of his own flock and of his own herd, to dress for the wayfaring man that was come unto him; but took the poor man's lamb, and dressed it for the man that was come to him."

David, angered at this tale insisted, "As the Lord liveth, the man that hath done this thing shall surely die: And he shall restore the lamb fourfold, because he did this thing, and because he had no pity" (2 Sam. 12:4–7).

It is at this moment that Nathan pounced: "Thou art the man. Thus saith the Lord God of Israel, . . ." (2 Sam. 12:4–7). In telling the story of the pet lamb and the greedy rich man with many sheep, Nathan forced David to acknowledge his own sins and repent them. Nathan pronounced God's judgment and, seeing the genuine remorse of the ruler, also prophesied future blessings. Later he reported God's love for *Solomon, David and Bathsheba's second son (2 Sam. 12:24–25), thereby setting the stage for helping Solomon succeed to the throne rather than Adonijah (1 Kings 1:11–48). Apparently, through his role in confronting the guilty lovers with their sin and later comforting them at the death of their child, Nathan won the trust and affection of both David and Bathsheba, thus becoming a confidant and source of support for Bathsheba during David's final days. He participated in the anointing of Solomon at the Spring Gibon outside Jerusalem (1 Kings 1:38–40).

Earlier, Nathan's had been the prophetic voice that informed the enthusiastic King David that he would not be allowed to build the Temple. After first endorsing the plan to erect a suitable "house" for Yahweh (2 Sam. 7:2–7), Nathan had a vision in which he carried to David, announcing that the building of the Temple was to be done in Solomon's day (2 Sam. 7:12–13). At the same time, the Lord assured David of his love for him and his dynasty. God communicated, via Nathan, his covenant that David's descendants would rule after him forever. His was also the voice of doom, pronouncing the consequences of David's sin—that the sword would not depart from his house (2 Sam. 12:10).

After David's death, Nathan's two sons were given high office by Solomon: Azariah was put in charge of the officials responsible for tax districts and Zabud became Solomon's confidential advisor.

**Historical Context.** As a God-inspired prophet, Nathan is often used as the illustration of the close connection between the prophetic mission, moral and political reforms, and the true religious revival which took place when the scattered tribes were consolidated under King David and King Solomon. He broke new ground spiritually, gave guidance and encouragement to David, provided a link between his reign and Solomon's, and lifted the moral tone of Hebrew life during the early monarchy.

**Archaeological Evidence.** A minor figure in the midst of major monarchs, this prophet is supported only by the frequent references to him in Rabbinic sources, which make Nathan a nephew of David, reared by Jesse, Nathan's grandfather and David's father.

The story that Nathan tells David, as if it were a current court case, is based in tribal law: It was permissible to slaughter an animal from a neighbor's livestock if someone found it absolutely necessary to conform to the rules of hospitality. However, this privilege was forbidden to anyone whose own property included available livestock, and it was strictly forbidden when the neighbor's animal was a personal pet—as is the case in this parable.

Nathan, a tenth-century Hebrew prophet, is credited with recording the events of the reigns of David and Solomon in the "Book of Nathan" (1 Chron. 29:29 and 2 Chron. 9:29, 29:25). Though some consider this merely a pious tradition, some scholars believe it to be a reasonable claim. Recent scholars have noted that "The Acts [or Chronicles] of Nathan" may be among the "Lost Books of the Bible," a long list of oral and written texts to which we find scattered references through much of the Bible.

**Character in Later Works.** Nathan set the pattern for the ideal court prophet, one who speaks Truth to Power. He appears in commentary rarely, except as a foil to David.

The famous image of "one little ewe lamb" became the symbol for one's most cherished possession. It occurs regularly in nineteenth-century literature, particularly in novels of Thomas Hardy and the Brontës.

The concluding lines of this passage, "Thou art the man!" also became a famous echo of the confrontation with David. It appears frequently in Western literature and was a favorite line for revivalists such as George Whitefield and John Wesley.

SOURCES

Christensen, Diane, "The Lost Books of the Bible," in *Bible Review Archives*, October 1998; Comay, Joan, *Who's Who in the Bible*, vol. 1, New York: Bonanza Books, 1980; Metzger, Bruce M. and Michael D. Coogan, eds. *The Oxford Companion to the Bible*, New York: Oxford University Press, 1993; Miller, Madeline S., and J. Lane Miller, *Harper's Bible Dictionary*, New York: Harper and Row, 1961; Willis, Timothy M., "Nathan," in *A Dictionary of the Biblical Tradition in English Literature*, edited by David L. Jeffrey, Grand Rapids, MI: William B. Eerdmans Publishing Company, 1992.

# NEBUCHADNEZZAR (NEBUCHADRESSAR)

**Name and Etymology.** *Nebuchadnezzar*, a Babylonian name, means "O (God) Nabu, protect my son!" or "the [god] Nabu has protected the succession."

**Synopsis of Bible Story.** Nebuchadnezzar II, "the Great," son of Nabololassar, became king of Babylon at a significant time in Judah's history. He was the most effective leader in Babylon since Hammurabi. Even before his father's death in 605 B.C., he had acted as commander-in-chief at the battle of Carchemish, where he defeated the Egyptians and drove them back inside their own borders. He was responsible for three deportations of the citizens of Judah: in 598 B.C. after Jehoiakim's uprising, in 587 B.C. after the rebellion of Zedekiah, and in c. 582 B.C. after the murder of Gedaliah (Miller, 481).

Among these captives were the prophet *Ezekiel and the young man *Daniel (Dan. 1:1) from Judah. The prophet *Jeremiah stayed in Jerusalem during much of this period, tolerated by Nebuchadnezzar because he counseled his people to submit to the invader, whom he portrayed as a tool of God, a scourge for their wickedness. Finally, Nebuchadnezzar sacked Jerusalem, carrying away the treasures of the Temple, bringing an end to the Southern Kingdom. He so reduced Jerusalem and the surrounding countryside that for more than a century it remained what *Isaiah called a wilderness of thorns and briars.

The Babylonian captivity that followed saw the prophecy of *Daniel, including the interpretation of the king's dream of madness and death. Nebuchadnezzar survived many years after this, in control of a far-flung empire. Little is known of the final thirty years of his rule. He is known for the massive building programs in Babylon, its walls, palaces, temples, and defenses. He died in 562 B.C., and was succeeded by his son Amel-Marduk (Evil-Merodach of 2 Kings 25:27).

**Historical Context.** As the son of the founder of the Chaldean dynasty, Nebuchadnezzar was a central figure in Hebrew history, the ruthless foreigner who brought the little kingdom of Judah to its knees. Jehoiakim paid tribute to him for years, stripping the Temple of the vast treasures *Solomon had brought for its adornment. *Jeremiah saw Nebuchadnezzar as God's servant, wreaking God's violent judgment on Judah, carrying out God's purpose in punishing Israel. (See Orlinsky, 50.)

Nebuchadnezzar's vast kingdom and power had catastrophic impact on the rebellious people of Judah: the rebellion of Jehoiachin led to the siege and sack of Jerusalem in 587 B.C. and the subsequent rebellion and cruel punishment of the rebel king Zedekiah (Jer. 39:5–6 and chapter 52) in 588 B.C., and marked the end of Judah as a separate kingdom.

**Archaeological Evidence.** A large library of cuneiform tablets was discovered and carried to Berlin in 1899 by Robert Koldewey, who had led a large expedition in search of ancient "Babil" (Keller, 302–3). An addition to these discoveries was made in 1955 through the examination of tablets found in the British Museum, deciphered by D. J. Wiseman. These Babylonian texts describe the invasion of Judah, identifying Jehoiachin as "Yaukin, king of Judah." They also describe the life of Jehoiachin and his family and retinue in the palace of Nebuchadnezzar in Babylon.

The famous Ishtar gateway is thought to have been built during Nebuchadnezzar's long reign, as a portion of his extensive building program. The inscriptions found there laud his rebuilding of Babylon, and his exercise of law, order, and justice, as well as his religious devotion—not his military exploits.

**Character in Later Works.** The Babylonian captivity was a watershed event in Hebrew history, calling forth the lovely Psalm,

> By the rivers of Babylon, there we sat down, yea, we wept, when we remembered Zion.
> We hanged our harps upon the willows in the midst thereof.
> For there they that carried us away captive required of us a song; and they that wasted
>     us required of us mirth, saying, Sing us one of the songs of Zion.
> How shall we sing the Lord's song in a strange land?
> If I forget thee, O Jerusalem, let my right hand forget its cunning. . . . (Psalm 137).

This famous Psalm in turn inspired Verdi's "Chorus of the Hebrew Slaves" in the opera *Nabucco*.

Later Biblical texts tend to portray Nebuchadnezzar—and his city—as the very epitome of evil. In Revelation, for example, *John speaks of Babylon as the great whore. It appears to have represented the very image of secular power—parallel to Rome among the early Christians.

Herodotus spoke of the hanging gardens of Babylon, which many attributed to Nebuchadnezzar, as one of the Seven Wonders of the World. His tremendous building program astonished much of the ancient world, especially the Jews who prospered in this pagan culture.

Literature has picked up on imagery from Daniel related to Nebuchadnezzar's dreams, particularly the images of the man and of the tree, using them in extensive references. Dante, for example, sees the man as the symbol of the various ages of mankind from the Golden Age to the present debased era.

Daniel's portrayal of Nebuchadnezzar as a madman, down on all fours, eating grass (Dan. 4:23–33), is vividly portrayed in William Blake's engravings.

## SOURCES

Keller, Werner, *The Bible as History*, New York: Bantam Books, 1982; Merrill, Eugene H., *An Historical Survey of the Old Testament*, Nutley, NJ: The Craig Press, 1972; Miller, Madeline S., and J. Lane Miller, *Harper's Bible Dictionary*, New York: Harper and Row, 1961; Orlinsky, Harry M., "The Situational Ethic of Violence in the Biblical Period," in *Violence and Defense in the Jewish Experience*, edited by Solo W. Baron and George S. Wise, Philadelphia, PA: The Jewish Publication Society of America, 1977; Wiseman, Donald J., "Nebuchadrezzar," in *The Oxford Companion to the Bible*, edited by Bruce M. Metzger and Michael D. Coogan, New York: Oxford University Press, 1993.

## NEHEMIAH

**Name and Etymology.** *Nehemiah* means "God has consoled." His Babylonian name, according to talmudic sources, was Zerubbabel (Jeffrey, 546).

**Synopsis of Bible Story.** Nehemiah was a child of the Babylonian captivity, a prominent member of the Persian king's court, a cupbearer. When he heard of the sad circumstances of Jerusalem, even decades after Cyrus had issued a decree allowing Jews to return to their homeland, he was deeply distressed. He explained his anguish to the king, telling him of the trouble and shame of the once-great city—the wall broken down and the gates destroyed by fire (Neh. 1:3). In 445 B.C., with King Artaxerxes' permission, Nehemiah left Susa and began the long journey to Jerusalem, determined to rebuild the city walls. Endowed with the king's authority to serve as governor of Judah, and fully equipped with permissions and protection, he surveyed the situation and determined on a plan of action that involved most of the inhabitants of the old city.

As the citizens began their work, they discovered that they were surrounded by enemies who sought to discourage them, shouting taunts and laying traps. Nehemiah proved to be a wise and strong leader, as well as an efficient administrator. He evaded his enemies, organized workers—both men and women—and quickly rebuilt the crumbling wall. Toward the end of this perilous endeavor, he insisted that the workers divide their time between protecting their fellows and engaging in the actual building (Neh. 4:18).

After serving twelve years as governor, Nehemiah returned to Susa for a time, then came back to Jerusalem (c. 430 B.C.) to revisit his work. Disappointed to discover that the Temple was being misused and the priests not paid, he instituted strong laws, cleansed the Temple, and insisted on proper payment to the Levites. He also demanded that Jews remain faithful to their vow to marry within the faith, a vow they had taken at the insistence of *Ezra. He also forced the merchants out of the city for the Sabbath. Citizens were relocated to homes within the city walls to ensure that this would be a representative city of the Jews. For this activity, he is sometimes described as the "First of the Pharisees."

In addition to a number of social and economic reforms, he is thought to have reinstituted the observance of the Feast of Booths, a popular Jewish festival first commemorating the Exodus and later the return from Babylonian exile (Neh. 8:13–18). Like *Ezra, he encouraged instruction in the Torah and warned against practices that could lead to abuse of the faith and become offensive to fellow believers.

His story ends abruptly with this reinstatement of order, leaving the reader unsure of the rest of his life's story. This may be a result of the focus on Nehemiah's relationship with the Jews in their work in Jerusalem, thus limiting the narrative to his leave of absence from the court to seek to make Jerusalem a safe, happy, and holy city.

**Historical Context.** The book that bears his name, and which tells his story, was originally yoked with *Ezra in a single narrative that completed the history of 2 Chronicles. The actual chronology of the two stories of the priest and the administrator who rebuilt Jerusalem is cloudy, but Ezra does seem to have gone to Jerusalem earlier than Nehemiah, who apparently heard news from Jerusalem while he was still in Susa, c. 444 B.C. Ezra must have been a witness to the work done by Nehemiah and his men, and he was present at the time that the rebuilt wall was completed and celebrated. The process of return and rebuilding was divided between these two men, one a priest of the line of *Aaron, the other an administrator and perhaps a eunuch. Their efforts, ending with the reconstruction and resettling of Jerusalem, marks the completion of the story of the Babylonian captivity.

**Archaeological Evidence.** Details of Nehemiah's life in Susa and in Jerusalem have been verified by archaeological studies, providing a host of footnotes in study Bibles on every page.

Especially interesting are the excavations in Jerusalem which have revealed vestiges of the stones involved in Nehemiah's reconstruction efforts. Archaeologist Kathleen Kenyon followed the details of the accounts of the devastation and reconstruction, especially around the gates in the southeastern wall, and has identified a few of the points: the King's Pool (the Pool of Siloam), the Fountain Gate, and the Dung Gate, among others. Archaeologists argue about the current names of some of the other gates, such as the Valley Gate and the Broad Wall, which were probably not used in the postexilic period. "Kenyon and Shiloh agree that Nehemiah's western wall ran north and south along the eastern side of the western scarp of the summit . . ." (Mare, 121–128). Some believe that approximately 10,000 people lived in Jerusalem at that time.

**Character in Later Works.** Told in part as an autobiographical memoir, Nehemiah, like Ezra, is the tale of one man caught up in important historical events. As a builder of the walls, a strong image of restoration, he became a symbol for the post-Reformation Protestant leaders, especially in America. Jeffrey lists a number of examples of American Puritans who saw the image of Nehemiah, the builder, as an American image of faith and endeavor. T. S. Eliot, who used Nehemiah as a central figure in his choruses from *The Rock* (4–5), described him as one who builds with "the trowel in the hand, the gun rather loose in the holster" (Jeffrey, 546). This imagery sounds like the pioneers of the American West.

For others, he is the symbol of good works and good organization. Moderns have used him as a forerunner for *James' admonition that "faith without works is dead," and a model of the diaconate of which *Stephen was a famous example. He has been the inspiration for many Christian magazines over the years named "Sword and Trowel." And a modern preacher recently spoke of the need to rebuild a devastated city as a call for a "Nehemiah generation."

## SOURCES

Comay, Joan, *Who's Who in the Bible*, vol. 1, New York: Bonanza Books, 1980; Jeffrey, David L., ed., *A Dictionary of the Biblical Tradition in English Literature*, Grand Rapids, MI: William B. Eerdmans Publishing Company, 1992; Mare, W. Harold, *The Archaeology of the Jerusalem Area*, Grand Rapids, MI: Baker Book House, 1987; Merrill, Eugene H., *An Historical Survey of the Old Testament*, Nutley, NJ: The Craig Press, 1972; Miller, Madeline S., and J. Lane Miller, *Harper's Bible Dictionary*, New York: Harper and Row, 1961; Whyte, Alexander, *Bible Characters from the Old and New Testaments*, Grand Rapids, MI: Kregel Publications, 1990.

## NICODEMUS

**Name and Etymology.** *Nicodemus* is Greek for "victor over the people."

**Synopsis of Bible Story.** Nicodemus, who appears by name only in the Gospel of *John, was a Pharisee, a ruler of the Jews, and a member of the Sanhedrin or Great Council. He came first to visit *Jesus by night—either from fear that he would arouse talk or because he wanted to have an extended visit, which would have been difficult in the daytime, when Jesus was usually surrounded by crowds. The questions he asked (in John 3:1–4) were basic to an understanding of Jesus's ministry and purpose, eliciting some of the most memorable responses in all of Scripture.

Later, in John 7:50–51, he was the lonely voice of dissent when the Sanhedrin attacked Jesus. When Jesus proclaimed himself to be the source of "living water," it was Nicodemus who insisted that the council follow the proper procedures under the law.

And finally, he joined *Joseph of Arimathea in burying the body of Jesus after the Crucifixion (John 19:39). This final act of kindness would seem to indicate that he had become a follower of Christ by this time.

Jesus instructing Nicodemus. The Art Archive/Musée de Tournai/Dagli Orti.

**Historical Context.** Legends passed on from early times indicate that Nicodemus was baptized by Peter and John, and banished from Jerusalem during the Jewish uprising against Stephen (Miller, 490). These stories, however, have no Scriptural basis.

Nicodemus is interesting as a representative of the most highly placed and prestigious of the Jewish religious establishment. The Pharisees, primarily a school of zealous students and teachers, were specialists in the law, enjoying the subtle details of their constant debate and analysis. In their conversation, Nicodemus designates his respect for Jesus as a teacher by calling him "Rabbi."

It was the Pharisees who confronted Jesus on several occasions with challenging questions. Jesus often responded to these leading questions, designed to cause problems for him, with reciprocal questions aimed at the Pharisees. By contrast, the questions that Nicodemus asked were sincere, and apparently led to his being convinced—at least intellectually—Jesus was the "Son of Man" born to give his life that others might have eternal life. As a Pharisee, Nicodemus used his standing and his knowledge of the law during the trial of Christ, to quarrel with his fellows on the Sanhedrin for failing to follow proper procedure in challenging the judgment of a man without first giving him a hearing (John 7:46–51).

Jewish burial practice involved immediate arrangements for disposal of the body. To this ceremony, Nicodemus brought a hundred pounds of myrrh and aloes to embalm the body before he and Joseph wrapped it in linen and laid it in the cave tomb.

**Archaeological Evidence.** The Pharisees grew out of the period of the Maccabean revolt (166–159 B.C.). This renewed zeal for the law also spawned the Essenes, a group much studied of late because of the discoveries at Qumran. Central to the Pharisees' teaching is the belief in the twofold law: the written and the oral Torah. As an historian noted, this led to an elaborate tradition of interpretation of the law in the debates and sayings of the elders; these complex arguments were, in turn, finally written down in the Mishnah and documented in the Talmud (Riches, 589).

**Character in Later Works.** St. Augustine found Nicodemus a provocative figure, a strong defender of the Torah, and a thoughtful questioner of Christ, who apparently came to a saving faith through his spirit of inquiry.

In English literary tradition, a late work called the "Gospel of Nicodemus" became widely popular by the fourteenth century for its description of the Harrowing of Hell. Many of the medieval cycles included scenes of this aprocryphal portion of Jesus's narrative—e.g., the Townley play "The Deliverance of Souls." Nicodemus was less popular in the period following the Reformation, largely because his "Gospel" was by this time rejected as apocryphal. In addition, Calvin cast an unsympathetic interpretation over Nicodemus's interview with Jesus—calling him a "proud man" who wasted Christ's time, considering Jesus's words as a "fable." Later Protestant critics, such as Matthew Henry, have proven more sympathetic (Jeffrey, 549).

Writers have used Nicodemus's character and questions in a variety of ways: Dickens bases a character in *Our Mutual Friend* on him, Edwin Arlington Robinson used him in the poetry collection *Nicodemus*, and Sholem Asch used him as a major character in his novel *The Nazarene*.

Rembrandt was one of many who sought to capture the clandestine conversation between Jesus and Nicodemus on canvas or paper (Brownrigg, 318). He, of course, appears in scenes of Jesus's trial, his crucifixion, and his burial.

SOURCES

Brownrigg, Ronald, *Who's Who in the Bible*, vol. 2, New York: Bonanza Books, 1980; Jeffrey, David L., ed., *A Dictionary of the Biblical Tradition in English Literature*, Grand Rapids, MI: William B. Eerdmans Publishing Company, 1992; Miller, Madeline S., and J. Lane Miller, *Harper's Bible Dictionary*, New York: Harper and Row, 1961; Riches, John, "Pharisees," in *The Oxford Companion to the Bible*, edited by Bruce M. Metzger and Michael D. Coogan, New York: Oxford University Press, 1993.

## NOAH

**Name and Etymology.** The meaning of Noah's name is not clear, but may be derived from the Hebrew word for "rest" or "comfort." Genesis 5:29 says his father, Lamech, called his name "Noah," saying, "This same shall comfort us concerning our work and toil of our hands, because of the ground which the Lord hath cursed."

**Synopsis of Bible Story.** Scripture tells two stories of Noah, picturing very different views of the man and his relationship with his sons. In the first (Gen. 6:5–9:17) God selected Noah, a man who had found grace in his eyes, out of wicked mankind to save from destruction. He provided detailed instructions for the building of an ark and the selection of those people and animals that were to be taken on board in preparation for the approaching flood. Noah built the ark and assembled his own family and "two of every sort" of animals before the rains came for forty days and forty nights. At the end of that time, only Noah remained alive—"and they that were with him in the ark" (Gen. 7:23).

At the end of a hundred and fifty days, when the rain stopped and the water abated, the ark rested upon the "mountains of Ararat." Noah opened the windows and sent forth a raven, then a dove, and finally a second dove, which returned with an olive leaf. He waited another seven days, and then God told him to "Go forth of the ark. . . ." and bring forth the creatures which had survived (Gen. 8:16).

Noah then built an altar and offered burnt offerings. God, pleased with his action, promised that he would not again curse the ground for man's sake. "While the earth remaineth, seed-time and harvest, and cold and heat, and summer and winter, and day and night shall not cease." Establishing a covenant with Noah and his seed after him, the Lord set the rainbow as a token for perpetual generations to signify that "my covenant, which is between me and you and every living creature of all flesh; and the waters shall no more become a flood to destroy all flesh" (Gen. 8:22).

In the second Noah story (Gen. 9:18–27), the man is pictured after the great flood, now a "husbandman" who planted a vineyard, drank of the wine that he produced, was drunken, and "uncovered" within his tent. One of his sons, Ham, the father of Canaan, saw his nakedness and told his brothers. They refused to look at him, but approached him backwards and covered his nakedness. When Noah woke, he knew what Ham had done, and cursed his progeny to be servants while the other sons would be enlarged and "dwell in the tents of Shem."

Concluding both stories, Genesis 9:28–29 tells us that Noah lived after the flood three hundred and fifty years, a total of nine hundred and fifty years, "and he died."

**Historical Context.** Dr. Aaron Smith, an expert on the flood, has discovered 80,000 works in 72 languages about this catastrophic event, of which 70,000 mention the wreckage of the ark (Keller, 38). This cataclysmic prehistoric event survives largely in ancient myth, two examples of which—one Greek, one Akkadian—parallel the Genesis story of the deluge. The Akkadian story, found in the *Gilgamesh Epic* was also current among Sumerians, Hurians, and Hittites. It echoes the punishment of mankind for bad behavior, the building of the ark, the extended deluge (but only six days), the sending out of birds to test for dry land, and the subsequent worship in gratitude for bringing the survivors through the ordeal. In the Greek myth, Zeus let loose the flood to wipe out the whole race of men, but Prometheus warned Deucalion, who built an ark, and survived along with his wife Pyrrha. Again, a dove was the signal of the end of the flood, but this time, the people repopulated the land by throwing rocks over their shoulders (Graves and Patai, 116).

The story of Noah's drunkenness has a very different tradition, involving ambiguous meanings for "uncovered," some concern that either castration or sodomy was involved, and a possible tie to later history. The Hebrews enslaved Canaanites (or Phoenicians), and this is thought to have been an explanation of the master/slave roles.

**Archaeological Evidence.** From very early times, there have been continuing references to a great flood with specific locations: the historian Josephus mentions remains of the ark on Ararat. Evidence of the reality of a flood has been discovered in numerous sites, including Ur and Kish. (See the map of excavations in Keller, 28.) According to Woolley, an archaeologist who spent years studying the region, a cloudburst flooded the Tigris and Euphrates about 3200 B.C., covering all but the highest mountains in the region.

Different expeditions have sought to discover the remains of the ark. The past century has seen a series of sightings and discoveries, but as yet nothing that is verifiable, and scientific. The term "Ararat" may refer to a region—modern Armenia—rather than a specific mountain.

In a recent article in the *New York Times*, scholars cited fresh evidence supporting the actuality of the catastrophic flood that struck the Black Sea region more than seven thousand years ago, turning the sea saline, submerging surrounding plains, and possibly inspiring the flood legends of Mesopotamia and the Bible. In this case, the use of sonar allowed the archaeologists on the expedition to discover stone blocks underwater off Sinop, a city on the northern coast of Turkey. The core samples yielded chemical evidence that the site was once occupied by people, confirming an important element of the flood theory, according to Dr. Bruce Hitchner, of the University of Dayton, Ohio, and editor of *The American Journal of Archaeology*. An entire book recently published, *Noah's Flood: The New Scientific Discoveries About the Event That Changed History*, by William Ryan and Walter Pitman, focuses on the new discoveries.

**Character in Later Works.** Early rabbinical commentators tried to explain the sin of Ham as sexual abuse or castration. His role in the humiliation of Noah has frequently appeared in history, alleged by some to justify the enslavement of African peoples. The Hamites were located in southwestern Asia and northeast Africa, Cush, Put, and Egypt (Gen. 10:6).

Noah's wife was a leading character in the Gnostic Book of Noria, now lost. The portrait of her as a shrew who attempted to keep her husband from building the ark became a staple for medieval mystery plays at Chester, York, and Townley.

Early Christian commentators focused more on Noah himself and his role as a new Adam, a righteous man (Luke 3:36), a preacher of righteousness (2 Pet. 2:5), and an example of faith (Heb. 11:7). The covenant (Gen. 9:9, 11–13) was considered a major covenant in the Old Testament, the sign of the rainbow perpetually attesting to God's promise to sustain life on earth.

Poets have made passing reference to Noah as a key Old Testament figure, but the novelists have found him more interesting: Melville's *Confidence Man*, Mark Twain's *The Mysterious Stranger*, Dickens' *Bleak House*, and D. H. Lawrence's *The Rainbow* have all used the character and his symbolism. Lawrence was especially interested in the promise of the rainbow, the design of the arch, and its relationship to architecture, especially the rounded Norman arch. He thought this represented the ideal balance needed for human relationships. Recent science fiction writers and authors concerned with the end of the world have revived Noah as the image of the second Adam, starting all over after a new cataclysm. One of the more fanciful examples of this is the modern American play by Thornton Wilder, *The Skin of Our Teeth*.

The story of Noah and the ark has resurfaced among moderns arguing the truth of creationism and the nature of myth. The understanding of this story, including whether it is literally true, has intrigued both scholars and laymen, proving essential in ongoing debates over creationism and evolution.

## SOURCES

Goetsch, Paul, "Noah," in *A Dictionary of the Biblical Tradition in English Literature*, edited by David L. Jeffrey, Grand Rapids, MI: William B. Eerdmans Publishing Company, 1992; Graves, Robert, and Raphael Patai, *Hebrew Myths: The Book of Genesis*, New York: McGraw Hill Book Company, 1963; Keller, Werner, *The Bible as History*, New York: Bantam Books, 1982; Ryan, William, and Walter Pitman, *Noah's Flood: The New Scientific Discoveries About the Event That Changed History*, New York: Simon and Schuster, 1998; "Scholars Find Further Signs of Big Flood Evoking Noah," *New York Times*, 1 October 2001.

## PAUL

**Name and Etymology.** *Saul* was his Hebrew name, but he is usually referred to by his Roman name, *Paul*, which he used more frequently after his conversion experience. *Paul* means "little," leading some critics to assume he was small in stature.

**Synopsis of Bible Story.** Paul, born in Tarsus, a crossroads of commercial traffic in Cilicia (Acts 9:11), was a Roman by birth, perhaps from a family of "freemen" who had been enslaved by the Romans and freed to return to Judea. He was a Hebrew of the Hebrews, from the tribe of Benjamin (Phil. 3:5), named for King *Saul, the first hero of his tribe. Well tutored in the law, Paul was a Pharisee (Acts 23:6) educated under the noted scribe Gamaliel. A fanatical persecutor of the Jews, Paul was witness to the stoning of *Stephen (Acts 8:1). He was on the road to Damascus, planning further persecutions, when he was struck blind by God and began his long and painful process of conversion and education as a Christian (Acts 9:1–19, 22:1–21, 26:1–23).

The Christian community in Damascus welcomed him, saved him from a plot to murder him, and helped him begin his preparation for the ministry, a period of about thirteen years, some of which were spent in the Arabian Desert. He also went to Jerusalem, met with *Peter and *James, the brother of *Jesus (Gal. 1:18). From these various followers of Jesus, Paul learned about the earthly ministry of Christ. Settling for a time in Antioch, where the early believers were first called Christians, he agreed to join *Barnabas in his first missionary journey.

In the years that followed, Paul became the Apostle to the Gentiles, carrying the Gospel message to regions around the Asia Minor coast, up into Macedonia, and over into the cities of Greece. His usual pattern was to find the local synagogue, gather a group of believers, and then preach to the larger congregation. In some places, where there were few Jews—as in Athens (Acts 17:16–33)—he made ingenious use of his wide reading in Greek and Roman literature and philosophy to draw listeners into the Christian faith.

Along the way, although plagued by a physical disability he referred to as a "thorn in the flesh," and often living a hand-to-mouth existence, stopping for a time to work as a tentmaker with his friends *Priscilla and Aquila, he was able to establish a number of small congregations of believers. His written words of encouragement formed a series of cherished letters that became the core of Christian theology. In those rich epistles to the Galatians, Corinthians, Thessalonians, and so on, Paul explored a series of theological challenges to the new faith and provided the structure and interpretation for believers. At the same time, he told more of his own story, of his companions, of his hardships, and of his love for individuals in their communities—Silas, *Timothy, *Lydia, and many others. It is from these letters and from the narrative in the book of Acts, written by one of his first companions, the "beloved physician *Luke, that we discover much of the history of the early Church.

When, in his final days, Paul was charged with crimes, he pleaded his Roman citizenship and was imprisoned, tried, and sent to Rome. The narrative of Acts breaks off at this point, leaving Paul on his way to Rome, encountering storms at sea, with the expectation of further imprisonment, trials, and eventual beheading by a sword, the Roman punishment for its convicted citizens. The record of his earthly end is not complete, leaving some to hope that he was acquitted and continued his ministry on to Spain before he returned to visit Crete, Macedonia, and Greece, only to be rearrested and returned to Rome for further imprisonment and, finally, execution (Miller, 533). Luke undoubtedly knew the details of Paul's death, but preferred to leave the story incomplete.

**Historical Context.** From the narrative in Acts and the many personal details in the various epistles attributed to Paul, we learn much of the first-century A.D. Roman world. Greek culture was still dominant, though the Roman imperial system was firmly in place. Paul spoke in amphitheaters, such as the one in Ephesus, where the pagan rituals were celebrated. He confronted the numerous gods, and was himself thought to be Mercury by the people of Lystra. Using this understanding and a background in philosophy and theology, he approached the Athenians at their famous Aeropagus (Mars Hill) by using their own openness to an "unknown god." His visits to Corinth and his words of encouragement to the Corinthians provide a lively picture of this vigorous city with its colorful mix of sailors and prostitutes—along with good, faithful believers.

Paul was proud of his Roman citizenship, which he had apparently inherited, and used his knowledge of Roman legal practices to avoid punishment by local magistrates, appealing to Rome when he was in difficulty. His speeches to Felix and King Agrippa (Acts 24, 25, 26) when he was imprisoned at Caesarea are models of classical rhetorical strategy.

The many stories of his final days also echo the history of the era. Tertullian of Carthage (c. A.D. 198–200) declared that Paul was beheaded in Rome. Galus of Rome, a third-century churchman, said that he suffered martyrdom on the Ostian Way. Origen later wrote that he died in Rome under Nero. Based on early records, Church leaders in Constantine's time built a church on the spot where Paul was thought to have died, and later believers replaced it with the magnificent basilica of St. Paul-Without-the-Walls in Rome, near the Ostian Way to commemorate his martyrdom (Miller, 533).

In recent years, fragments of apocryphal Acts of Paul have emerged, as well as spurious Letters of Paul and Seneca to supplement the legendary Visio Sancti Pauli—a legendary fantasy purported to have been found under the foundation of Paul's house in Tarsus, which was popular and influential in the Middle Ages (Jeffrey, 588–89).

**Archaeological Evidence.** The Mediterranean world is filled with sites and bits of buildings Paul may have visited: for example, the expansive ruins of Caesarea, King Herod's property, which was probably the most populous city in Israel at the time of the early Church, still has the evidence of the harbor, the prison, the amphitheater, and many other of the buildings he would have seen. *Philip the Evangelist was the first Christian to preach the gospel to the people at Caesarea (Acts 8:40), *Cornelius was stationed there as a centurion in the Italian Regiment (Acts 10:2). Paul came as a visitor to stay with Philip, who had settled in Caesarea. Later he returned to Caesarea as a prisoner awaiting trial, appeared before Felix and then Portius Festus (A.D. 57–59), and preached to *Herod Agrippa II.

In Asia Minor, visitors can see the amphitheater at Ephesus and the relics of the silver trade, where the worship of Diana was profitable and where the local silversmiths chased Paul from their midst. In Phillipi, visitors can still see the prison where he was beaten. In Athens, the hill on which Mars and the other Greek gods were worshiped, still attracts visitors who, when visiting the Parthenon on the Acropolis, may pause at the spot where Paul was thought to have preached to the Athenians.

**Character in Later Works.** "No single figure, except that of Christ himself, has more influenced the subsequent interpretation of Scripture and the formulation of biblical tradition: the writings of St. Paul not only interpreted the kerygma for Mediterranean communities of Gentile Christians but laid down . . . principles for typological interpretation of the Hebrew Scriptures which became foundational for Christian religion and culture" (Jeffrey and LaBossière, 588).

Paul's Damascus Road conversion experience, his trade as a tentmaker, and his decapitation became part of the Christian tradition. Paintings and statues usually portray him as short, bald, bearded, and dressed as a Roman. He is also often chained. He is usually pictured with the symbolic sword by such painters as Durer, van Dyck, and Rembrandt. Michelangelo chose to portray the blinding light of his conversion experience.

During the Reformation, his authority grew in its influence on theologians. In recent years, however, this influence has been debated—it is often seen as pernicious. Slaveowners used arguments from the epistle to Philemon, leading to attacks on both slavery and on Paul by emancipators. Paul's recommendations to both the Corinthians and to Timothy regarding the role of women in the Church and in the family have drawn the ire of feminists. Nietzsche also argued that Paul perverted the message of Christ.

Nonetheless, for all of his detractors, no writer or interpreter of Scripture has had a more pervasive and profound influence on Western Christendom.

## SOURCES

Brownrigg, Ronald, *Who's Who in the Bible*, vol. 2, New York: Bonanza Books, 1980; *Eusebius' Ecclesiastical History*, trans. by C. F. Cruse, Peabody, MA: Hendrickson Publishers, Inc., 1998; Ferguson, George, *Signs and Symbols in Christian Art*, New York: Oxford University Press, 1966; Jeffrey, David L., and Camille R. LaBossière, "Paul," in *A Dictionary of the Biblical Tradition in English Literature*, edited by David L. Jeffrey, Grand Rapids, MI: William B. Eerdmans Publishing Company, 1992; Miller, Madeline S., and J. Lane Miller, *Harper's Bible Dictionary*, New York: Harper and Row, 1961.

## PETER

**Name and Etymology.** Peter was also known as "Simon," "Cephas," and "Simeon." Both *Simon* and *Peter* are Greek, while *Cephas* is the Aramaic equivalent to the Greek *petros* or rock, symbolic of the man's solid character (Miller, 541).

**Synopsis of Bible Story.** Peter, the son of Jonah, was a prosperous fisherman on the Sea of Galilee, living in Bethsaida, on the edge of Capernaum, when *Jesus called him to be his disciple (John 1:44). He was apparently in business with his brother Andrew, who introduced him to Jesus and who also became one of the core group of disciples, along with the sons of Zebedee, *James and *John. We know from scripture that Peter was married and may have lived in a large household with his mother-in-law (1 Cor. 9:5). Most Bible scholars assume that their household was the favorite gathering place for the disciples when they were in the area. Like his brother Andrew, Peter seems at one time to have been a disciple of *John the Baptist before being called by Jesus.

Almost immediately after being called, Peter became a leader among the Apostles: he was the first of them to declare Christ was the Messiah (Matt. 16:13–16; Mark 8:27–29; Luke 9:18–20); he was outspoken in his loyalty and was on occasion the chief spokesman for the disciples; at the Last Supper, he declared his faithfulness; in the Garden of Gethsemane, it was Peter who defended Jesus against the soldiers, cutting off the ear of one of the arresting officers; on hearing the news of the Resurrection, Peter was the first to run to investigate the women's story of the open tomb (John 20:2–6), although a younger disciple, *John, who outran him, arrived first. Peter shared a meal with the resurrected Christ on the shores of Galilee, and it was Peter who became the leader of the early Christian Church, preaching the first sermon at Pentecost, encouraging the believers in Jerusalem, and opening up the doors of the faith to Gentiles (Acts 10). Like the other apostles, he worked miracles: he healed Aeneas, the paralytic; he raised Dorcas to life; and he converted and baptized Cornelius and his household. His last appearance in Scripture was in his role at the Council of Jerusalem (Acts 15:7–11). *Paul mentioned Peter's visit to Antioch (Gal. 2:11–21); Peter seems also to have visited Corinth (1 Cor. 1:12) and to have engaged in evangelism in Rome before Paul's arrival (Rom. 15:20–22).

Simon Peter was a complicated man with great energy, enormous talents, and many weaknesses. He is remembered for his tendency to blurt out his feelings, to act out his anger, and to display his cowardice. It was typical of Peter that he was the one who stepped out of his boat to join the Master in walking on the water, but also to have doubts and to begin to sink, only to be rescued and lectured for the failure of his faith. Although he was a hothead and a backslider, he is also remembered for his humility and repentance after his threefold denial of his master (Matt. 26:75; Luke 22:34). His great love and earnest desire to serve were rewarded by experience of the resurrected Christ and by a vision that taught him to "feed my sheep" without judging what was "clean" and "unclean" (Acts 10:15). Even after this admonition, Peter still needed a rebuke from Paul to keep him on the right path (Gal. 2:11).

**Historical Context.** The prominence of Peter and the narrative of his travels and labors, which ends with Acts 15, is continued in the New Testament apocryphal writings and in the traditions that point to his enormous influence in Christian circles everywhere—especially around Antioch—and his final martyrdom in Rome. The Epistle of Clement to the Corinthians and Eusebius's *History* both tell of Peter's and Paul's joint labors in building the church at Rome and their martyrdom there. The apocryphal Acts of St. Peter and St. Paul adds details about Peter's death: like Paul, Peter was believed to have suffered martyrdom in Rome under Nero (A.D. 64–65). At his own request—in response to a vision—he was crucified "downward; not otherwise" (R. Miller, 542) because he did not consider himself worthy to die in the same manner as Christ. He was buried in a cemetery near Nero's Circus, where Constantine's Basilica of St. Peter was built in the fourth century A.D.

According to Irenaeus, as early as A.D. 85, Peter was considered the "mind behind" the Gospel of *Mark. Clement of Alexandria, Irenaeus, and other Church fathers declare that the Second Gospel was either dictated by Peter or represented the recollections of Peter as compiled by Mark. A fragmentary Gospel of Peter was discovered by French archaeologists in Upper Egypt in 1886. Scholars have dated it from the eighth or ninth century A.D. This fragment seems to have come from Syria, and is associated with the church at Rhossus. The pastoral letters, both included in the New Testament, are also attributed to Peter, but some scholars argue that they are the works of later Church leaders who used Peter's name to give them reverence.

**Archaeological Evidence.** Different sites in Israel are pointed out to visitors as related to the life and ministry of Peter. On the Sea of Galilee, at Capernaum, is an excavation of "the house of Peter," revealing the outlines of several rooms in what was apparently the home of a prominent fisherman's family. Apparently Peter and his brother were partners with James and John, had employees, and were free to come and go as they chose. Historians speculate that they were men of substance who controlled their own lives, as suggested by the quality of their house at Capernaum (Strange and Shanks). (This excavation is the site of the modern basilica in the Franciscan area near the synagogue ruins.)

In addition, scholars have studied the fishing industry on the Sea of Galilee, discovering much about this ancient activity. It was clearly prosperous work, serving the people who enjoyed fish as a central element of their diet, using it fresh, dried, and salted. Bethsaida was one of 13 ancient harbors on the coast of the Sea of Galilee (Murphy-O'Connor).

In Jerusalem, one prominent tourist attraction is the Church of St. Peter in Gallicantu (the Cockcrow), the traditional site of the House of Caiaphas, the place of Peter's dramatic failure during the long night of Christ's imprisonment and flagellation.

In Rome, there are other sites: recent excavations beneath the present Basilica of St. Peter have revealed many tombs, both pagan and Christian, indicating that this was a vast cemetery of ancient Rome and a likely burial place for Peter. A number of places in this city are tied to the ministry of Peter and Paul.

**Character in Later Works.** Peter's proclamation of Jesus' divinity was followed by Christ's assertion that Peter (or his confession) was "the rock" on which he would build his Church (Matt. 16:16–19). This, along with Peter's early leadership in the apostolic Church in Jerusalem and in Rome has led Roman Catholics to consider him the first pope, with apostolic leadership deriving from his power as the keeper of the "keys of the kingdom of heaven" (Jeffrey, 504–606). Peter is therefore a central figure in much of Roman Catholic literature, challenged by Protestants after the Reformation, who interpreted papal claims and the Petrine tradition differently.

The epistles attributed to Peter reinforce his role as a leader: the first appears to have been written from Rome—or "Babylon"—and was addressed to the Christians in the Roman provinces of Asia Minor, who needed encouragement. The second epistle, another pastoral letter, was addressed to Christians everywhere, and contained warnings against false teachings. They reveal a man with considerable wisdom in spite of his limited theological training.

In art, the oldest extant representation of Peter is a bronze medallion from the late second or early third century A.D., in which he is depicted with a roundish head, prominent jaw, receding forehead, and thick curly hair and beard. Later iconographic representations show him holding the keys and sometimes a fish. Occasionally, he is portrayed as a ploughman; sometimes he is shown in chains. Rocks are also his symbols, from Christ's indication that he was "the rock" on which he would build his Church. He, of course, is also often accompanied by a cock, signaling the night of rejection.

As the first among the disciples, he was a standard figure in the Corpus Christi dramas of the medieval world and recently was a prominent part of Dorothy L. Sayers *The Man Born to Be King*. Thornton Wilder, Henry Sienkewicz, Morris West, and Peter Marshall have all used the big fisherman in their stories and plays (Jeffrey, 607). He has remained, over the years, a compelling figure, flawed yet heroic.

## SOURCES

Brownrigg, Ronald, *Who's Who in the Bible*, vol. 2, New York: Bonanza Books, 1980; Ferguson, George, *Signs and Symbols in Christian Art*, New York: Oxford University Press, 1966; Jeffrey, David L., ed., *A Dictionary of the Biblical Tradition in English Literature*, Grand Rapids, MI: William B. Eerdmans Publishing Company, 1992; Miller, Madeline S., and J. Lane Miller, *Harper's Bible Dictionary*, New York: Harper and Row, 1961; Miller, Robert J., ed., *The Complete Gospels: Annotated Scholars Version*, San Francisco: HarperCollins, 1994; Murphy-O'Connor, Jerome, "Fishers of Fish, Fishers of Men," in *Bible Review*, June 1999; Strange, James F., and Hershel Shanks, "Has the House Where Jesus Stayed in Capernaum Been Found?" in *Biblical Archaeology Review*, November/December, 1982.

## PHILIP

**Name and Etymology.** *Philip* is from the Greek, "lover of horses." There is no Hebrew equivalent name.

**Synopsis of Bible Story.** In Matthew 10:3 and Mark 3:18 we first meet Philip, a resident of Bethsaida. He was probably a disciple of *John the Baptist during John's ministry beyond the Jordan River (Luke 6:14). It was from among the crowds on the banks of the river that *Jesus called him to be a disciple (John 1:43). A friend of *Peter and Andrew, who also lived in the Galilee region, he was probably also a fisherman. Although he was of a retiring disposition, he did introduce his friend Nathaniel to Jesus. Nathaniel was thereby convinced that he was the Messiah, "the Son of God," "the King of Israel" (John 1:45).

Some scholars believe that Philip was the disciple who was reluctant to leave before he buried his father (Luke 9:57–60). It also appears from the story of the feeding of the five thousand, that Philip managed the provisioning of the disciples, for he was staggered at the idea of feeding such a crowd. He was probably a practical, sincere, open, and generous person, not so much a leader as an approachable man who asked forthright questions.

During Jesus' final visit to Jerusalem prior to the Crucifixion, Philip invited some inquiring Greeks to "Come and see" the Master. At the Last Supper, he was the disciple who asked, "Lord, show us the Father, and we shall be satisfied." Jesus rebuked him, saying that he who has seen Jesus has seen the Father. After the Crucifixion, Philip continued in fellowship with the other followers of Christ, praying in the Upper Room in Jerusalem and being a witness to the Pentecost (Acts 1:12–14).

Philip the evangelist, probably a different man who was an early member of the church in Jerusalem, was the man selected as one of the seven to administer the business affairs of the twelve and the growing Church, and to distribute relief to the poor, including widows and orphans of the Christian community (Acts 6:1–6). He also preached and healed at Samaria after the martyrdom of *Stephen (Acts 8:4–8), where he freed people of unclean spirits. He led Simon the sorcerer to become an active believer in Christ. An evangelist of considerable effectiveness, he helped convert the Ethiopian eunuch to the Gospel message (Acts 8:26–39), and thereby was responsible for helping to spread Christianity throughout northeast Africa. Later he took up residence at Casarea, where *Paul and *Luke visited him and his four prophetess daughters (Acts 21:8–15).

**Historical Context.** Philip the apostle was a significant part of the ministry of Christ during his lifetime, helping with the management of the disciples' practical affairs, to the time after the Crucifixion, when he continued to preach the gospel message. Philip the evangelist had an equally significant role in the young Church, as a person who could reach out to Jews and Gentiles, and as a deacon, responsible for the social and healing ministry of the community.

**Archaeological Evidence.** From the elaborate scholarship following the discoveries of Qumran, we know a great deal of the background of John the Baptist and his followers, including those who moved into the ministry of Christ. We also know, from recent scholarship, a great deal about the region around the Sea of Galilee, the fishing industry there, and its relationship to the disciples. (See Murphy-O'Connor.)

The fountain of St. Philip near Beth-zur is traditionally identified as the place where Philip the evangelist baptized the Ethiopian eunuch (Brownrigg, 364).

Philip the apostle's home town, Bethsaida, a small fisherman's village on the northeastern shore of the Sea of Galilee, was known under the name of Beth-Ramtha. Herod Agrippa conferred on it the rights of a *polis* and renamed it *Livias*, in honor of his wife. Archaeologists identify it with et-Tell, east of the Jordan River (Negev, 58–59).

The discoveries at Nag Mammadi included the Gospel of Philip, a heterodox document that ridicules belief in the Resurrection, provides Gnostic positions on the feminine nature of the Holy Spirit, and purports to document the relationship between Jesus and *Mary Magdalene. It is attributed to Philip the apostle, but appears to have a late third-century provenance. Philip Jenkins notes, ". . . there is no hint that this work contains any kind of independent historical tradition" (117).

**Character in Later Works.** Some believe that Philip the apostle carried the Gospel to Scythia, and remained there for many years. According to one tradition, in the city of Hierapolis he found that the people were worshipping a great serpent. Philip used a cross to make the serpent disappear; unfortunately, it left behind such a horrible stench that many people died, including the son of the king. Philip, however, was able to bring the youth back to life. Having enraged the priests who led the serpent-worship, Philip found himself threatened with death. He is thought to have died on a Latin-style cross, which became his symbol—often with a serpent at the foot. A beautiful Byzantine church, a hundred miles inland from Ephesus is thought to mark the spot of this martyrdom.

In medieval art, when not portrayed with the serpent and the Tau cross, Philip the apostle is pictured with five loaves because of his role in the feeding of the five thousand.

Philip the evangelist is usually credited in Ethiopian ecclesiastical history as being the first head of their church. There was previously a Jewish tradition in Ethiopia, dating from the time of the Queen of Sheba, to which the eunuch converted by Philip belonged. The scene of the conversion is celebrated in medieval art. This Philip is also thought to have become a bishop in Lydia, the northern district of Asia Minor. His effectiveness in driving out the evil spirits is portrayed by Filippino Lippi (1457–1501) in the painting "St. Philip Exorcising the Devil."

Dorothy L. Sayers uses him in her cycle of plays on the life of Christ, *The Man Born to Be King*, as a simple, engaging, "puppylike" young man who, for all of his simplicity asks the right questions and performs miracles (Sayers, 99, 126).

### SOURCES

Brownrigg, Ronald, *Who's Who in the Bible*, vol. 2, New York: Bonanza Books, 1980; Ferguson, George, *Signs and Symbols in Christian Art*, New York: Oxford University Press, 1966; Jenkins, Philip, *Hidden Gospels*, New York: Oxford University Press, 2001; Miller, Madeline S., and J. Lane Miller, *Harper's Bible Dictionary*, New York: Harper and Row, 1961; Murphy-O'Connor, Jerome, "Fishers of Fish, Fishers of Men," in *Bible Review*, June 1999; Negev, Avraham, ed., *The Archaeological Encyclopedia of the Holy Land*, New York: Thomas Nelson Publishers, 1986; Pagels, Elaine, *The Gnostic Gospels*, New York: Random House, 1979; Sayers, Dorothy L., *The Man Born to Be King*, Grand Rapids, MI: William B. Eerdmans Publishing Company, 1943.

## PONTIUS PILATE

**Name and Etymology.** "Pontius" may derive from fighting in the Pontus (the Black Sea region) for Rome; "Pilate" may stem from *pilatus*, "javelin" or from pileus, the felt cap worn by freedmen and their descendants (Miller, 558). D. H. Wheaton suggests that his cognomen, *Pilatus*, may have been handed down by his military forbears (1229).

**Synopsis of Bible Story.** Each of the Gospel accounts tells—in somewhat different form—of *Jesus's appearance before Pontius Pilate, the Roman governor of Judea. The Sanhedrin—the Jewish authority—had no power to put a prisoner to death, and was therefore forced to lead Christ to their Roman procurator, where they accused him of "perverting the nation, and forbidding to give tribute to *Caesar, saying that he himself is Christ a King" (Luke 23:2).

Not convinced after examining the defenseless man before him, Pilate tried several ways to escape making this final judgment: he noted that since Jesus was a Galilean, he should be tried before *Herod, under whose jurisdiction Galilee was administered, but Herod returned the prisoner to him, indicating that Jesus had broken no law in his jurisdiction (Luke 23:11). Pilate then suggested that he might release him in celebration of the Passover Feast, but the crowd called for the release of *Barabbas instead.

Ecce Homo, c.1522. Christ shown to people by Pontius Pilate from Sta Cruz Coimbre, Portugal. The Art Archive/Album/Joseph Martin.

When his wife warned Pilate that she had had an ominous dream about this man, he continued to evade the decision, asking of Jesus, "What is truth?" He then washed his hands, and handed this innocent man over to his soldiers to flog, before delivering him to be crucified (Mark 15:15).

**Historical Context.** The Romans had settled on a structure and a process for governing their provinces by Pilate's time. Pontius Pilate was the fifth Roman procurator, or governor, of Judea, Samaria and Idumaea (A.D. 26–36 or 37). We know from very early historical records that he was a faithful but overzealous administrator prone to making clumsy errors. Both Tacitus and Josephus verify that he was the Roman authority at the time of Jesus' death. Philo describes Pilate as "inflexible, merciless, and obstinate" (Brownrigg, 368). Josephus relates that Pilate's first action upon arriving in Judea was to place Roman standards (or banners) in Jerusalem, violating the Jewish prohibition against both graven images and "other gods," and thereby inciting a riot. After six days of uproar, he was forced to back down and remove the images. He then tried to dedicate a set of golden shields bearing no image, but with an inscription with the names of the procurator and the emperor in his own residence in Jerusalem; again he was forced to back down and remove them, this time at the order of Tiberius, who did not want to incite further wrath among the Jews.

As a final act of outrage, Pilate used money from the Temple to construct an aqueduct that would carry water from a spring to the city. This time tens of thousands of Jews demonstrated against the project, forcing him to send in troops, and resulting in many deaths. This is thought to be the Galilean riot referred to in Luke 13:1–2, when the blood of the slain was mingled with their sacrifices (Wheaton, 1229).

Given this background, it is not surprising that Pilate was nervous about the large crowd gathering in Jerusalem for the Passover, and particularly about the following that Jesus was attracting. His clumsiness, his bad relationship with the Jews, and his clear failure to understand their faith would have made him an easy administrator to intimidate.

Later, he was blamed for the slaughter of a number of Samaritans assembled at Mount Gerizim, leading to a delegation of Samaritans protesting to Vitellius, then governor of Syria, who ordered Pilate to stand trial on charges before the emperor. It was while he was returning to Rome that Tiberius died. Although we know nothing of the outcome of the trial, Eusebius reports that Pilate was forced to commit suicide during the reign of Gaius (A.D. 37–41). Other authorities suggest that Pilate was tried at Rome, detained in prison, and may have committed suicide to escape execution by Caligula. He may also have been beheaded by Nero.

His wife, Claudia Procula, was the granddaughter of the Emperor Augustus and the illegitimate daughter of Claudia, the third wife of the Emperor Tiberius; she was a royal princess, sophisticated, cultured, and sensitive. She may well have been the source of her husband's influence, explaining her presence at the time of Jesus's trial. It was unusual for wives to accompany their husbands to foreign assignments. Because of her prescience and the later tradition that she became a follower of Jesus, she was canonized by the Greek Orthodox Church (Miller, 559).

**Archaeological Evidence.** Apparently the most impressive structure in Jerusalem at the time of Pontius Pilate was the four-towered Antonia. The praetorium in which Pilate tried Jesus has been proven to have been part of the Tower of Antonia in the ancient Temple area. In fact, some of the original pavement where he displayed Jesus to the people has been discovered under the Church of the Dames de Zion.

Pilate spent most of his time in Herod's beautiful new city on the Mediterranean coast. Current excavation is focused on Caesarea Maritima, one of ancient Israel's most majestic sites, covering a vast area of 235 acres. It was occupied from the third or fourth century B.C. through the Crusades, first becoming an important city when Herod had the harbor cleared and built a temple, a palace and numerous other buildings. During the excavation of the theater at Caesarea, archaeologists discovered a stone being reused as a step in one of the aisles, inscribed: "Pontius Pilate, the Prefect of Judea, has dedicated to the people of Caesarea a temple in honor of Tiberius." (Tiberius was the emperor to whom he owed his appointment.) The site has yielded a vast assortment of statuary, inscriptions, coins, mosaics, ceramics, and many other finds. One significant discovery is a coin that bears the name of Pontius Pilate as the Roman governor.

**Character in Later Works.** The earliest traditions fastened on Pilate's evasiveness, placing greater blame on "the Jews"—particularly Annas, *Caiaphas, and the Sanhedrin. His role, however, was fixed for all time by the Apostles' Creed: ". . . and suffered under Pontius Pilate." The medieval mystery cycles invariably presented Pilate as a braggart, whose pompous rhetoric created comic effects. Peter Groth (622) notes that Pilate appears in at least twenty-six European Passion plays, including all the English cycles. Milton uses him as a representative of the state, largely because of Christ's remark to him, "My kingdom is not of this world" (John 18:36). Others have used him in curious ways—as in the cases of Joseph Conrad, Toni Morrison, and James Joyce. Recent novelists have become interested in understanding him better in the context of his times. Paul Luther Maier and Ann Wroe have both written extended fictional accounts of him.

Because he is so much a part of Western thought, his image is a standard part of Christian art, appearing in portrayals by the great artists such as Rembrandt and Tintoretto. He is usually presented as a judge, puzzled and troubled, sometimes washing his hands in a vain effort to wash away his guilt.

## SOURCES

Brownrigg, Ronald, *Who's Who in the Bible*, vol. 2, New York: Bonanza Books, 1980; *Eusebius' Ecclesiastical History*, trans. by C. F. Cruse, Peabody, MA: Henrickson Publishers, 1988; Groth, Peter, "Pontius Pilate," in A *Dictionary of the Biblical Tradition in English Literature*, edited by David L. Jeffrey, Grand Rapids, MI: William B. Eerdmans Publishing Company, 1992; Miller, Madeline S., and J. Lane Miller; *Harper's Bible Dictionary*, New York: Harper and Row, 1961; Wheaton, D. H., "Pontius Pilate," in *The Illustrated Bible Dictionary*, vol. 3, edited by J. D. Douglas, Sidney, Australia: Tyndale House Publishers, 1980.

## PRISCILLA AND AQUILA

**Name and Etymology.** *Priscilla* or *Prisca* was the Greek name from the Latin "ancient." *Aquila* was the Latin from the Greek word for "eagle." Of the six times that this pair are mentioned in Scripture, Priscilla's name is put first four times—twice by Luke and twice by Paul (Brownrigg, 32, 374).

**Synopsis of Bible Story.** On his missionary journeys, *Paul frequently stayed with members of the local church or synagogue, often sending messages back to them after he had left. Of all the people he met on these far-flung travels, Priscilla and Aquila appear to have been among his favorites. Perhaps because they shared the trade of tentmaking with him, or perhaps because they were eager to be his hosts for extended periods, he found their love and support invaluable.

This married couple were originally Jews from Pontus in Asia Minor. They had migrated to Rome and then had been exiled by the edict of Claudius in A.D. 49, when all Jews were expelled from the imperial city. They subsequently went to Corinth, where they set up their trade, working either in canvas or leather, and met Paul, who came to live with them (Acts 18:1–3). They also became his partners in evangelism, sailing with Paul from Cenchrae, the Aegean port of Corinth, and then apparently settled for a time at Ephesus, where they again set up their business. It was there that they confronted Apollos, who was a strong but confused advocate for *Christ as the Messiah. At some point during their stay in this great city, they "risked their necks" for Paul's life—perhaps at the time of the silversmiths' uprising.

After Claudius died, they were free to return to Rome, which they did, retaining their thriving business in Ephesus, and traveling back and forth between the two cities.

**Historical Context.** This pair of weavers and leatherworkers shed some light on the economic life in which the early Church flourished. They apparently lived in the "weavers' sections" of several towns, including Corinth and Ephesus, and there provided a gathering place for Christians (Miller, 580). Many of the early churches were apparently house churches, and the leaders had "tentmaking ministries," that is, they supplied their own upkeep by plying a trade.

In Aquila, as a Jew of Pontus (a region of northern Asia Minor bordering the Black Sea), a citizen of Rome, and a victim of Claudius' dispersion of the Jews, we see the Jewish survivor, taking his trade with him to establish a new base of operations when old avenues have been closed.

Priscilla is noted as an early example of Paul's willingness to include women in the outreach activities of the Church, as evidenced by his naming of her along with her husband to his evangelistic team. She is also mentioned with her husband in the instruction of Apollos (Acts 18:24–28), and is given particular notice in Paul's letters (1 Cor. 16:19; Rom. 16:3–5).

This openness to the work of women, unlike the Jewish tradition, is reinforced by Paul's statement in Galatians 3:28: "There is neither Jew nor Greek, there is neither bond nor free, there is neither male nor female: for ye are all one in Christ Jesus."

**Archaeological Evidence.** Numerous relics of the cities where Priscilla and Aquila lived have survived—in Rome, in Corinth, and in Ephesus. Historians have discovered that the tents were often made of goat's hair cloth, or *cilicium*—a name derived from Paul's region—Cilicia. Handling goats' hair was considered pollution by Jewish law: "and purify all your raiment and all that is made of skins and all work of goats' hair . . ." (Num. 31:20; Miller, 741).

Some have speculated that the precedence given to Priscilla suggests that she was a Roman lady of higher rank than her husband or that she was more prominent in the Church, but this is not clear from the text (Walls, 82).

**Character in Later Works.** This committed pair of Christians have not become the subject matter of much art or literature. In recent years, with the advent of the feminist movement, Priscilla's role in the early Church has assumed particular importance.

SOURCES

Brownrigg, Ronald, Who's Who in the Bible, vol. 2, New York: Bonanza Books, 1980; Miller, Madeline S., and J. Lane Miller, Harper's Bible Dictionary, New York: Harper and Row, 1961; Walls, A. F., "Aquila and Priscilla," in The Illustrated Bible Dictionary, vol. 1, edited by J. D. Douglas. Sidney, Australia: Tyndale House Publishers, 1980.

# R

## RACHEL

**Name and Etymology.** *Rachel* is derived from the Hebrew word for "ewe"—probably indicating she was a shepherdess at the time she met Jacob.

**Synopsis of Bible Story.** When *Jacob fled his brother's wrath, using the opportunity to seek a wife in his family's homeland, Padan-Aram, he met a shepherdess "beautiful and well favoured" (Gen. 29:16–18). After proving both his strength and good manners by lifting the great stone cover from the well so that she could water her flock, he introduced himself as a kinsman and stole a kiss. Rachel, like her relative *Rebekah, welcomed the stranger and invited him to her father's home. After a month's visit, when Jacob asked Laban, her father and his uncle, for Rachel's hand in marriage, the shrewd old man demanded seven years' service for this treasure. Scripture tells us that these years of service seemed to Jacob "but a few days, for the love he had to her" (Gen. 29:20). Then, on the wedding night, Laban substituted Leah, Rachel's older sister, as the bride. Instead of apologizing for the ruse, he required yet another seven years of labor for Jacob to win Rachel.

Both Leah and Rachel offered their maidservants to Jacob as concubines in their protracted competition for his love. Unlike her fecund sister, Rachel proved barren for some years, in spite of the apparently happy married life she and Jacob shared in Padan-Aram and later at Succoth, Shechem, and Bethel. Finally, in response to prayer and promise, God blessed her with *Joseph (Gen. 30:24). At Ephrath, after the birth of her second son, Benjamin, Rachel died, leaving a mourning husband to build her memorial "pillar" and lament their brief time together (Gen. 35:16–20).

Rachel broke from the traditional mold of the ideal wife and mother when the family was fleeing from the crafty Laban. Rachel, unknown to Jacob, took the teraphim, or god images, causing her father to chase after them and accuse Jacob of theft. When he declared his innocence and invited Laban to search the family, Rachel cleverly hid the images under her saddle, pretending that she was menstruating and was unable to move. Laban accepted her word, judged the family innocent, and agreed to a vow of peace between the two sides of the family (Gen. 31:20–35). Scripture provides no explanation of her rationale for this atypical act.

**Historical Context.** Rachel was the last of the matriarchs, and the last of the wives from the "homeland" of the Hebrews. From her story we can glean some of the marriage customs of the Middle East. Most young men from prosperous families would have brought a bride-price to the family of Laban. Because Jacob left *Isaac in great haste, he apparently came emptyhanded and was therefore forced to provide labor in compensation for the bride. This may, in fact, have been Isaac's intended punishment for his trickster son. The rule of the elder sister's marrying first, which is a neat parallel to Jacob's own reversal of birth order, was validated by the Book of Jubilees and recommended for all of Israel (Graves and Patai, 213).

The wedding arrangements of the era would have involved a sealed covenant, including the dowry that the bride brought—in this case, servants. The lavish wedding festivities often continued for a week or more. Even today in some Middle Eastern cultures, the bride may wear an opaque veil that can easily disguise her identity. Men were allowed to have more than one wife, a tradition we see in royal households as late as *Solomon's day and remains legal among certain groups in much of the Middle East. Although marriage to sisters was tolerated as late as the sixth century B.C., later regulations forbade this custom (Lev. 18:18).

The view of women's status, later clarified in Hebrew law, is anticipated in Laban's refusal to touch his daughter. Apparently she knew that her announcement that she was menstruating would repel him, as did any contact with blood. According to the old Jewish rabbinical tradition, this indicated her father considered her "unclean."

This story is particularly valuable for the insights into practices among women to encourage fertility. For example, the use of mandrakes as a cure for barrenness, largely because of their human appearance, was mentioned as late as Shakespeare's day. The narrative also reveals the perils of childbirth: death in childbirth was not unusual for women until recent times.

Because Rachel was Jacob's favorite wife, her children were his favorites, preferred over all ten of his other sons. This favoritism is reinforced by Jacob's protection of her when he returned for his confrontation with *Esau, placing *Joseph behind Leah, her children, and his maidservants and their offspring. Later, he would cherish both Joseph and Benjamin for her sake, and give special blessing to Joseph's children.

**Archaeological Evidence.** Rachel's tomb is still marked by a site at the edge of Bethlehem of Judea, where Jacob is said to have erected a pillar over her grave (Gen. 35:20), though some scholars believe that "Ephrath" is the northern Bethlehem near the border of Zebulun and Asher, southeast of the Mount Carmel ridge.

The graven images that Rachel stole were the kind explicitly forbidden by the second commandment. These teraphim were probably small figurines of metal, wood, or terracotta, not necessarily cultic or obscene, used as good-luck charms for expectant mothers. In some cases, as this one, they were family gods, perhaps an indication of ancestor worship. For many folk, the possession of such gods apparently was not considered a conflict to the worship of Jehovah. These images reappear in Micah, Samuel, and long after. Hosea did not see them as a rival to

Yahweh, but Zechariah finally denounced the superstitious use of teraphim to secure rain and officially outlawed them—though they continued to remain popular until after the exile.

Keller notes that, according to the Nuzi tablets (clay tablets discovered in the old Hurrian city of Nuzi), teraphim were used to establish the rights of inheritance (Keller, 52). If this was the case among the people of Padan-Aram, it would explain Laban's eagerness to recover them. It might also explain Rachel's motive in taking them, hoping to claim the family property for her husband or sons. Recent scholars doubt this theory, but they think that such images may have indicated family headship. A more likely motivation for Rachel, whose brothers, still at home, were the probable inheritors of their father's property, was that the teraphim, often associated with divination practices, may have seemed a kind of protection for the travelers on a dangerous journey to Palestine

**Character in Later Works.** In the Book of Ruth, the elders and the witnesses prayed that the Lord will "make the woman that is come into thine house like Rachel and like Leah, which two did build the house of Israel" (Ruth 4:11). They were apparently using a traditional blessing for the marriage of Ruth and Boaz. Jeremiah had a more symbolic reference to Rachel: "A voice was heard in Ramah, lamention and bitter weeping: Rachel weeping for her children refused to be comforted for her children, because they were not" (Jer. 31:15).

Rachel has sometimes been contrasted with Leah in much the same way *Mary of Bethany is contrasted with Martha: she is the image of faith, not works. While Leah bore multiple children, Rachel was loved for herself, even though barren for some years. St. Augustine pictured her as one of the elect, and St. Thomas Aquinas pictured her as an image of the contemplative life as opposed to the active life we see in Leah.

In literature, Rachel was used as the image of the mother mourning for her unborn children. In the nineteenth century, novelists began to use her as the image of the beloved wife who dies young. This particularly appealed to Charles Dickens, who named one character "Rachael" in *Hard Times*. William Makepeace Thackeray utilized Jacob's long courtship and labors for the woman he loved in both *Henry Esmond* and *The Virginians*. More recently, Margaret Laurence, in *A Jest of God*, portrayed an ironic version of the woman hungry for children, only to find her "pregnancy" was really a tumor. In a recent novel by Anita Diamant, *The Red Tent*, Rachel, her servants, and her sisters are described from the point-of-view of the only surviving daughter of the clan—Dinah.

Rachel continues to serve as a type of woman who is loved by romantics and despised by feminists. The beauty that led Jacob to fall in love with her at first sight, her patience that allowed her to wait for years for marriage, and her dedication to her husband and her children all mark her as an old-fashioned woman. The only element of her story that feminists would applaud is her theft of the teraphim and deceit that pays back her greedy father.

## SOURCES

Beamer, Linda, "Rachel," in *A Dictionary of the Biblical Tradition in English Literature*, edited by David L. Jeffrey, Grand Rapids, MI: William B. Eerdmans Publishing Company, 1992; Comay, Joan, *Who's Who in the Bible*, vol. 1, New York: Bonanza Books, 1980; Douglas, J. D., ed., *The Illustrated Bible Dictionary*, vol. 3, Sidney, Australia: Tyndale House Publishers, 1980; Graves, Robert, and Raphael Patai, *Hebrew Myths: The Book of Genesis*, New York: McGraw-Hill

Book Company, 1963; Keller, Werner, *The Bible as History*, New York: Bantam Books, 1982; Miller, Madeline S., and J. Lane Miller, *Harper's Bible Dictionary*, New York: Harper and Row, 1961.

## REBEKAH

**Name and Etymology.** *Rebekah* is derived from the Hebrew word from "a looped cord for tying young animals," parallel to the Greek word for "to tie fast."

**Synopsis of Bible Story.** Rebekah, the wife of *Isaac, was the daughter of Bethuel of Padan-Aram and the sister of Laban. She figured prominently in three scenes: when she was chosen as Isaac's wife, when she pretended to be his sister, and when she tricked him into giving his blessing to *Jacob.

In the first instance, she was the gracious woman at the well, whom the servant immediately recognized as the God-ordained bride for Isaac and the ideal progenitor of the seed of *Abraham. She welcomed the stranger, gave him and his camels water, accepted his generous gifts, and invited the caravan to her home (Gen. 24). When the servant, Eliezer, speaking for his master, offered a marriage contract, Rebekah's brother turned to her and asked her preference. Displaying a lively interest in adventure, the maiden readily accepted the offer, agreeing to leave her childhood home, accompany a stranger, marry a man she had never met, and live in a country she had never visited. On arrival, properly chaperoned, she acted modestly, veiling herself, and going with Isaac to his mother's tent, where she became his wife—"and he loved her: and Isaac was comforted after his mother's death" (Gen. 24:67).

Isaac's enthusiastic response to her is evident in his fidelity to her as his only wife in spite of her apparent barrenness (Gen. 25:21). Her beauty, which is mentioned at least twice, is implied by Isaac's subterfuge: When he took his family to Gerar in an effort to escape the famine, he realized—as Abraham had done earlier—that the husband of a beautiful and desirable woman was in peril of his life. He therefore asked Rebekah to pretend she was his sister. When Abimelech saw them embracing ("sporting" in the *King James Version*—Gen. 26:8), he confronted Isaac, charging that he had endangered the woman and any man who might have been guilty of adultery (Gen. 26:10). Her protection against such violation is a tribute to God's providence.

Eventually, she was blessed with the birth of fraternal twin boys. Even in her womb, they were at war for precedence. Heeding God's specific designation of the younger, *Jacob, to be the son of the blessing, she showed a marked preference for him. Scripture mentions of her favoring of the younger, smoother Jacob over her husband's favorite, the hairy *Esau, a hunter (Gen. 25:28). Later, when Isaac was near death, realizing that her husband planned to ignore God's prophecy and grant his blessing to Esau, his firstborn, Rebekah plotted with Jacob to steal the blessing. Using the time-honored strategies of the powerless, Rebekah listened to a conversation between her husband and his favored son, and then used this secret knowledge to thwart his will. She designed a scheme, cooked the food, found the skin, and instructed Jacob on the means to pretend that he was Esau.

Ever the dominating mother, fearful that Jacob would follow Esau's lead and marry Hittite wives, she arranged for her chosen son to visit her brother Laban, hoping that he would find a bride from among his own people. Thus she helped make his exile the source of his new, prosperous adventures. By her shrewd plotting, she won a bittersweet reward—a prize for Jacob, and his exile, which left her with a feeble, disillusioned husband, an angry son, and foreign daughters-in-law (Gen. 27:42–46).

When she died, she was buried in the cave of Macpelah with her husband and his family (Gen. 49:31).

**Historical Context.** In patriarchal times, a woman was cherished for her virginity before marriage, her fidelity and fecundity during marriage. In the tribe of Abraham, it was also important that a wife have the cultural and religious traditions of this family—not the habits of the Canaanites. A marriage with a cousin or an even closer relative, like Abraham's marriage to his half-sister, was preferable to taking a "foreign" wife among the tribes who surrounded this clan, though this level of familial intermarriage was later forbidden in Israel's marriage laws.

Marriages usually involved contracts negotiated by third parties, who established the amount of the bridal gift and the other details. (Much of this tradition continues among some Bedouins and Orthodox Jews even today.) Usually, the husband would have come to the bride's home, but in this case the bride accompanied the servant to the husband, where she assumed the standard veil. A bride was not supposed to be seen by a groom prior to the wedding. The reference to Isaac's mother's tent may refer to the place of the ceremony, such as the canopy still used in Jewish wedding ceremonies, or perhaps the place for the consummation of the wedding. Esther Fuch notes that the betrothal was merely a transfer of the woman from her father's to her husband's custody, as when Laban says, "Take her and go" (Gen. 24:51). The woman was clearly a prized object, exacting a price. There was no parallel reference to the groom's appearance or his virginity.

**Archaeological Evidence.** The items of jewelry mentioned were common in wealthy families, especially nose-rings and bracelets. The meeting at the well and the drawing of water was a standard activity, with pitchers and buckets surviving from ancient ruins. The mention of camels at the well has caused some questions, since camels were thought to have been adopted as beasts of burden several centuries after the patriarchal period. Given the precision of the other details of the betrothal and marriage, some critics note that they may have been an "inadvertent anachronism" introduced in the story because they were so commonly associated with desert travel in later years (Alter, 114).

**Character in Later Works.** Earlier cultures honored Rebekah, largely because she was a key figure in the patriarchal narrative. *Paul (Rom. 9:10) saw her as one through whom God chose to fulfill his promise. She appeared to be a prefiguring of the woman at the well (John 4:6–15), a type of *Mary, serving as an instrument of God. St. Clement and St. Ambrose saw her as the bride of Christ, the figure of the holy Church.

Medieval writers (*e.g.*, the Townley Cycle) saw her as a wise counselor to Isaac. She then disappeared as a reference in English literature, only to be revived in nineteenth and twentieth century novels, where she took on a more unscrupulous characterization. She appears as the Jewish heroine in Sir Walter Scott's *Ivanhoe*. William Makepeace Thackery, who made her famous as the model for Becky Sharp in *Vanity Fair*, also used her in *Rebecca and Rowena*, and she became the model for Daphne du Maurier's romantic portrayal of the image in *Rebecca*.

In the numerous modern works on women in Scripture, Rebekah has become an interesting example of the woman who seeks power through men. She easily convinces the servant that she is the ideal wife for Isaac and quickly wins Isaac's love. A clever and devious woman, she is willing to lie to Abimelech to protect her husband and to trick her old husband into giving his blessing to her favorite son. While feminists tend to admire her, the more traditional critics, like Alexander Whyte, view her as a woman who fails to respect or reverence her husband (Whyte, 106–110).

## SOURCES

Alter, Robert, *Genesis: Translation and Commentary*, New York: W.W. Norton & Company, 1996; Fuch, Esther, "Structure and Patriarchal Functions in the Biblical Betrothal Type-Scene," in *Women in the Hebrew Bible: A Reader*, edited by Alice Bach, New York: Routledge, 1999; Norman, J. G., "Rebekah," in *The Illustrated Bible Dictionary*, vol. 3, edited by J. D. Douglas, Sidney, Australia: Tyndale House Publishers, 1980; Peck, Russell A., "Rebekah," in *A Dictionary of the Biblical Tradition in English Literature*, edited by David L. Jeffrey, Grand Rapids, MI: William B. Eerdmans Publishing Company, 1992; Whyte, Alexander, *Bible Characters From the Old and New Testaments*, Grand Rapids, MI: Kregel Publications, 1990.

## RUTH

**Name and Etymology.** The name *Ruth* may derive for the Syriac word for "woman companion"; it also has some parallels to a seventeenth century B.C. Babylonian term used in administrative texts for a woman involved in agricultural administration.

**Synopsis of Bible Story.** The Book of Ruth is one of only two books in the Bible named for women. It tells of the family of Elimelech, who were driven by famine to journey from Bethlehem to Moab; they settled there for some years, and the two sons married Moabite women. Later, the father and both of the sons died, leaving the three women without masculine protection or support. Naomi, the wife/mother, having determined to return to her home in Bethlehem, encouraged both of her daughters-in-law, Orpah and Ruth, to go back to their families. Although Orpah agreed, Ruth refused, insisting on staying with Naomi. Her famous response was: "Intreat me not to leave thee, or to return from following thee: for whiter thou goest, I will go; and where thou lodgest, I will lodge: thy people shall be my people, and thy God my God. . . ." (Ruth 1:16).

When the two widows arrived in Bethlehem, Ruth sought out a means for survival, deciding to become a gleaner in the fields of Boaz, a kinsman of her dead husband. Impressed by her loyalty to her mother-in-law, Boaz provided Ruth protection from the other workers and special favors (Ruth, 2). When the harvest was complete, Naomi suggested that Ruth approach Boaz after the threshing and lie at his feet in a risky strategy designed to elicit his continuing protection. The plan worked: Boaz, touched at her interest in him, rewarded her, and designed his own plan for proper legal action. He confronted the closer kinsman of Ruth's husband and father-in-law, providing him the opportunity for the Leverite marriage, and clearing the way for their wedding (Ruth, 3–4).

Their union was blessed with a son, who was put on Naomi's bosom, bringing her joy at last (Ruth 4:16). This child, Obed, was to be the father of Jesse, the father of *David, and the ancestor of *Jesus.

**Historical Context.** The story took place at the time of Judges (Ruth 1:1). The customs in the story, including the use of the sandal to seal a covenant (Ruth 4:7–8), were apparently already obsolete by the time the story was written. Generally, Israelites were discouraged from marriage to foreign women, especially those of Moab, largely because of the pagan worship practices, including child sacrifice. Their worship of Chemosh and Ashtora-chemosh, fertility gods, was especially horrifying to the Israelites. Apparently, Moab's relationship with Israel was nonetheless sometimes relatively cordial, possibly because of ancient kinship ties. These people were thought to be descendants of *Lot through incest with his daughter.

The Leverite marriage (marriage of a man and his relative's widow) and the act of land redemption are echoed in other portions of Scripture, notably in the story of Tamar (in Gen. 38) and the regulations in Jewish law (Deut. 25:5–10) appear to apply to Boaz's relationship to Ruth and her in-laws. The life of a dead man was to be supported and protected by his surviving family, and the family property traditionally remained within the family.

**Archaeological Evidence.** Life of the period was largely agricultural, not lending itself to archaeological evidence. Nelson Glueck's explorations in Moab, which identified hundreds of town sites, testify to a lively and highly cultivated land, with irrigated fields from early times.

The scene of adjudication of property rights—and Ruth's hand in marriage—was at the city gates. Excavations of the gates of the city of Gezer reveal the kind of spot, including the location of a ceremonial judgment seat, where Boaz and his kinsman would have negotiated this covenant. Excavations have also uncovered threshing floors, often large enough for many people of the town to thresh and winnow at the same time, exposed to the prevailing west wind, and probably near the city gates, where the harvest could be protected. The American excavations at Gezer in 1971 also uncovered a granary in the acropolis region dating back to the twelfth century B.C.

Fragments of four manuscripts of the book of Ruth were discovered at Qumran.

**Character in Later Works.** The Book of Ruth is the festal reading for Shavu'ot in Jewish tradition. Ruth herself is an image of reverence for both Jews and Christians, as the ancestress of both David and Jesus. She is also a dramatic image of the proselyte. Augustine saw her as an ideal portrait of the widow who was blessed in her second marriage.

The book is a favorite, especially among women, who have responded to it as a romantic love story as well as a tale of God's providential care. Artists have enjoyed it for its exquisite structure and the scenes it conjures. Both poets and painters have touched us with their images of Ruth and Naomi returning home and of Ruth gleaning in Boaz's fields. Among the most famous are Blake's portrayal of her in *Jerusalem* and Keats' reference to Ruth standing "in tears amid the alien corn" in "Ode to a Nightingale." Goethe called the book of Ruth the most beautiful "little whole" in the Old Testament.

Moderns have fixed on Ruth as an indication of the plight of women in ancient times and the possibility of a lesbian reltionship between Ruth and Naomi. Exum studies a famous painting of Ruth and Naomi by Calderon, a film about their adventures, and various other artifacts through the ages to demonstrate how different periods have found different messages in this ancient text (Exum, 129ff). Most women find it a rich study of the different roles of woman in Hebrew culture.

## SOURCES

Campbell, Edward F., Jr., "Ruth," in *Anchor Bible*, vol. 7, edited by Robert G. Boling, Garden City, NY: Doubleday and Co., 1975; Exum, J. Cheryl, *Plotted, Shot, and Painted: Cultural Representations of Biblical Women*, Sheffield, England: Sheffield Academic Press, 1996; Metzger, Bruce M., and Michael D. Coogan, eds., *The Oxford Companion to the Bible*, New York: Oxford University Press, 1993; Miller, Madeline S., and J. Lane Miller, *Harper's Bible Dictionary*, New York: Harper and Row, 1961; Ryken, Leland, "Ruth," in *A Dictionary of the Biblical Tradition in English Literature*, edited by David L. Jeffrey, Grand Rapids, MI: William B. Eerdmans Publishing Company, 1992.

## SAMSON

**Name and Etymology.** *Samson* comes from the Hebrew for "son" or "sun."

**Synopsis of Bible Story.** This hero from the Tribe of Dan was a combination of invincible warrior, naïve lover, and worthy judge (Judg. 13–17). Like other heroes of Scripture, his miraculous birth was signaled by an angel. His mother was told that her son was to be raised a Nazirite, never to cut his hair, nor to touch wine (Judg. 13:2–24). His supernatural strength—the ability to slay thousands at a time—was constantly attributed to the power of God coming upon him, and seemed to be related to the austere life he lived as a Nazirite. Because of his relationship with God, he was purportedly able to tear a lion apart, slay 30 men single-handed, kill 1,000 Philistines with the jawbone of an ass, and pull down the pillars of a temple.

The story describes his early attraction to a Philistine woman, whom he married in spite of his parents' admonitions. On his way to "take" his bride, he discovered the carcass of a lion, in which he found a beehive. Later, he used this curious event for a riddle: "Out of the eater came forth meat, and out of the strong came forth sweetness" (Judg. 14:8–14). The wedding feast, which was attended by 30 of the bride's people, was marred by his challenging of them to solve his riddle or forfeit clothing. Unable to solve his riddle, they pressured his new wife to wheedle the answer out of her husband. Over three nights, she queried him repeatedly until he finally capitulated to her nagging and told her about his discovery of the lion carcass filled with honey. She then relayed this information to her people, enabling them to win the wager. Samson sought revenge by slaying 30 of their fellow countrymen, whose clothing he handed over to their horrified relatives at the feast, and then left the wedding, returning to his own home.

The following year, when he went back to see his wife, he found that she had been married to another member of the wedding party. Rather than settling for her sister, whom the distressed father-in-law offered in her stead, Samson again went on a

Samson and the lion, folio 148 of 1526-29 manuscript Latin Bible from Abbey of St Amand, France. The Art Archive/Bibliothèque Municipale, Valenciennes/Dagli Orti.

rampage, this time slaughtering so many Philistines that they, in turn, murdered the young wife and her family.

This set of violent events is followed by Samson's twenty years of faithful service as a judge. (Like the minor judges, Samson is not remembered for his "ordinary" service but for his extraordinary brutality.)

The placid interval ended when another pair of events occurred, mirroring the earlier stories. Samson spotted a prostitute whom he desired (Judg. 16:1); then he set his heart on *Delilah of Sorek, a tool of the Philistine lords. They used her in a set of three tests to try to discover the source of Samson's strength, and found the real answer in the final test. When Delilah cut his hair, thus breaking his Nazirite vow, his strength failed. The Philistines were then free to blind and enslave him, making him the butt of their torments (Judg. 16:30).

In a grand finale, the Philistines and their blind slave gathered at Gaza, at the temple of their god Dagon, where the newly reinvigorated hero, his hair again grown long, used his enormous strength to bring down the pagan temple on the Philistine crowd, killing more in his death than he ever killed in his life (Judg. 16:30).

**Historical Context.** Historians have long debated the origins and history of the Philistines or the "Sea Peoples." This aggressive group of tall, feather-helmeted people appear to have come from the Aegean region, probably from Crete. *Moses had made an especial effort to avoid them in the Exodus, choosing instead to go inland rather than face the perilous pathway along the Philistine shoreline. Yohanan Aharoni notes that they did not settle down until the second half of the twelfth century B.C. The various peoples of Transjordan settled simultaneously with the Israelites and clashed with them mainly in the border regions. By the mid-eleventh century, there was a change. The Philistines challenged many of the open villages, moving the Israelites toward strongly fortified fortresses and royal cities of the monarchy (Aharoni, 67–70). By the time of Samson, they had gradually assumed power over the region to the west of Judah, exercising authority over the Israelites.

Scripture notes that God used Samson to stir the people of Israel into combat with this pagan force, which had superior weapons and a more sophisticated fighting force. The gods of Philistia—Dagon and Ashteroth in particular—were a lure to the Israelites, who were beginning to intermarry with these pagan folk. After Samson, the hostility between the peoples increased, notably during the time of *David.

As a member of the Nazirites, Samson was an anomaly. Generally, men took vows for a set period of time, including those that Samson's mother took on his behalf. Delilah's cutting of his hair was parallel to the revocation of the vow, but unusual because it was done for Samson—as was the original acceptance of the ascetic lifestyle—reducing him to a curiously passive actor in the drama of his own life.

**Archaeological Evidence.** Although historians had long doubted that the Jews were really a separate and identifiable group in the days of the Judges, recent archaeological discoveries demonstrate that there are clear differences between remnants of the two cultures of the Hebrews and the Philistines. Some remains, identified as ancient Israelite, have different architecture and different agricultural techniques, with terraced cliffs. Neither the Israelites' pottery nor their weapons were as advanced as those of their enemies.

Archaeological remains, particularly from Egypt, which also had antagonistic relationships with the "Sea Peoples," clearly reveal the Aegean heritage and the extraordinary appearance of these "giant" folk. Their early use of bronze and iron weapons made them superior to the more primitive Israelites. Remains of pottery with the spiral designs of the Aegean culture, and clay coffins have been discovered, reinforcing the earlier theories of a massive exodus from their Aegean homelands approximately 1200 B.C.

These people were to give their name to the land—"Philistia"—and provide the basis for the modern term "Palestine."

**Character in Later Works.** Although listed in *Paul's famous catalogue of the saints (Heb. 11:32), Samson is not usually seen as a saint or a great judge. He rather appeared as a vengeful and foolish hero, more Greek than Hebrew in his life and death. Josephus expanded his characterization and motivation in an effort to make him more noble, and later commentators treated him as a saint, a prefiguration of *Christ, and as a classical hero (Hill, 678). The tale of Delilah was frequently used for evidence of feminine deceit.

Chaucer and Boccaccio both make him an example of the noble man brought low by a wicked woman. Milton saw in him potential for a tragic drama, basing his *Samson Agonistes* on the final scene of Samson's colorful life. In more recent literature, D. H. Lawrence used him in a short story, "Samson and Delilah," that is largely autobiographical.

Musical composers have also found him an inspiration: both Saint-Saëns and Handel wrote major works on the theme of Samson and Delilah. A number of artists have painted scenes from his life, including Montegna and Doré.

Recent scholars have become interested in Samson's possible identification with the sun and his archetypal aspects as the "hero." His mysterious birth narrative, tied to the locale of Beth-shemesh ("house of the sun"); his name ("sun"); his destruction of the harvest; and his death in the temple in the West (suggesting sunset) all contribute to the idea that he was a sort of sun-king figure.

### SOURCES

Aharoni, Yohanan, "Violence and Tranquility in Ancient Israel: An Archaeological View," in *Violence and Defense in the Jewish Experience*, edited by Salo W. Baron and George S. Wise, Philadelphia, PA: The Jewish Publication Society of America, 1977; Hill, John Spencer, "Samuel," in *A Dictionary of Biblical Tradition in English Literature*, edited by David L. Jeffrey, Grand Rapids, MI: Eerdmans Publishing Company, 1992; Leith, Mary, and Joan Winn, "Samson," in *The Oxford Companion to the Bible*, edited by Bruce M. Metzger and Michael D. Coogan, New York: Oxford University Press, 1993.

## SAMUEL

**Name and Etymology.** The name *Samuel* suggests the Hebrew word for "heard of God" (1 Sam. 1:20)—"Because I have asked him of the Lord," as Hannah says, perhaps basing her name for him on puns on the verb meaning both "request" and "dedicate."

**Synopsis of Bible Story.** Samuel, whose name encompasses two books of the Old Testament, is the main character in only 1 Samuel. Immensely important, he was a bridge between the judges and the kings, serving as the final judge and anointing the first two kings of Israel. He was also a priest and a prophet.

Samuel's birth and infancy signaled his dedication to God. His mother, Hannah, was apparently barren. Like other blessed women of her tradition, she prayed for a child, promising that she would dedicate her baby to the service of the Lord. When her prayer was answered, she responded with a majestic song of praise (1 Sam. 2:1–10) that foreshadowed *Mary's "Magnificat" (Luke 1:46–55). In keeping with her promise, Samuel's mother returned to the priest Eli when her child was weaned—approximately three years later—and gave him to the Lord. Each year, she would return with a new garment for her son, who grew in his faith and his service under the tutelage of the wise old priest. While still a boy, Samuel heard the voice of the Lord calling him, and telling him of Eli's own sons, who had proven to be unfaithful in their priestly duties. They eventually were killed in battle, to the shock of Eli, who died immediately afterwards. With this series of catastrophes, and the Philistines' capture of the Ark of the Covenant, the "glory" departed from Israel and God's hand was heavy upon his people (1 Sam. 4:21).

For twenty years, the ark remained with the Philistines, and we hear nothing of Samuel, who apparently served as a judge in this period. Then Samuel called an assembly at Mizpah (1 Sam. 7:5) to demand that the people of Israel put aside the Philistine gods and serve the Lord only. Because of their willingness to put away their "Baals and Ashtoreths," Samuel agreed to serve as their leader and intercessor with the Lord, leading them in a confession of their sins. His worship was interrupted with an attack by the Philistines, who were routed by a combination of God's thunder and the Israelites' savage defense. During the rest of Samuel's lifetime, "the hand of the Lord was against the Philistines," allowing the restoration of cities previously attacked by these old enemies (1 Sam. 7:13). In this, we see Samuel as a warrior-judge, leading Israel in the great tradition of the charismatic judges of this period.

Like Eli, he had hoped to name his own sons as his successors, but like Eli's sons, these young men did "walk not in his ways" (1 Sam. 8:3), forcing Samuel to acquiesce to the increasing demand for a king for Israel. Although he recognized the perils of kingship and spoke eloquently against the proposition, he finally took the popular demand to the Lord, who agreed to give his people a king.

Responding reluctantly to this order, Samuel anointed *Saul (1 Sam. 10:1), but soon found him to be disobedient to God's orders. Having twice disobeyed God's commands, *Saul met with stern rebukes from Samuel. "Thou hast done foolishly," the old prophet told the brash young king. "Thou hast not kept the commandment of the Lord thy God, which he commanded thee: for now would the Lord have established thy kingdom upon Israel forever. But now thy kingdom shall not continue: the Lord hath sought him a man after his own heart, and the Lord hath commanded him to be captain over his people, because thou hast not kept that which the Lord hath commanded thee" (1 Sam. 13:13–14). On the second occasion, Samuel was forced to tell Saul once again that the Lord was grieved with his behavior, to admonish him, and then to kill the king of the Amalekites as the Lord had commanded. From this day until he died, Samuel did not go to see Saul again—"though Samuel mourned for him" (1 Sam. 15:34). Thus Samuel turned away from Saul, lamenting that he had anointed him king in the first place, and responded to God's leading by searching out *David, a "man after God's own heart," whom he anointed king.

Samuel's death is briefly noted: "And Samuel died; and all Israelites were gathered together and lamented him, and buried him in his house at Ramah" (1 Sam. 25:11). In a curious codicil to this story, Samuel came back briefly from the dead, summoned by Saul and the witch of Endor. Even in death, his anger at Saul continued, and he told the tormented king that the Lord had turned away from him (1 Sam. 28:16).

**Historical Context.** Samuel is considered the greatest spiritual leader of Israel since the time of *Moses, his career marking the transition from judges, the old type of charismatic leadership, to kings and prophets, the new divided leadership, with the separation of the political and the religious authority. From this time on, the prophets confronted the kings in contention over Israel's life. The beginning of Samuel's time as judge, when he led Israel in a religious renewal, marked a time of protection from the powerful Philistines. His wisdom in foreseeing the path of the monarchy was proven out by history. As a priest and prophet, Samuel led his people back from their compromise with Canaanite naturalism, the worship of the fertility gods so common in the farmers' world.

Historians note that the first chapters of Samuel's narrative deal with the events at Shiloh, the central sanctuary of the Congregation of Israel, to which it was customary for Israelites to make a pilgrimage each year in order to make a sacrifice (Josh. 18:1). It was their worship of Yahweh that held them together as a people, ruled by a priesthood who represented God to them. But with the loss of the Ark of the Covenant and the defeat by the Philistines, Shiloh was no longer seen as the Israelite sanctuary. Eventually, the transfer of authority would move to Jerusalem instead, probably because Shiloh was destroyed by the Philistines at the battle of Ebenezer.

**Archaeological Evidence.** Mizpah, where Samuel judged, was frequently mentioned during the period of the judges, which archaeologists call the Iron Age I (1200–1000 B.C.) In a recent article, Jeffrey Zorn notes that Tell en-Nasbeh is now considered the best candidate for biblical Mizpah. The old city gate of the city still stands. This site is about eight miles northwest of Jerusalem, on the southern outskirts of modern Ramalah. Although the Bible says Samuel was buried in Ramah, there is a mosque on top of Nebi Samwil marking the traditional tomb of Samuel. Below the mosque are the foundations of the Crusader church, suggesting a tradition dating from the early Christian era. In this traditional tomb have also been found terracotta figures of Ashtoreth.

Remains of the places mentioned in Samuel's chronicle, including Shiloh, where the tabernacle once stood, and the Philistine fortress at Ashdod have all been excavated. Some of the richest sources of information have been discovered at Beth-Shean, which apparently had temples of Dagon and Ashtoreth as late as 1000 B.C. The debate over the identification of the Biblical references and these excavations continues to flourish in archaeology journals.

**Character in Later Works.** In the New Testament, because of his role as prophet (Acts 3:24), judge (Acts 13:20), and priest, Samuel is seen as a forerunner of *Christ. Augustine thought his supplanting of the house of Eli a symbol of the supplanting of the old law by the new.

Although cited as one of the great heroes of the faith, Samuel has rarely appeared as a major figure in literature or art. The old prophet is the main character in Laurence Housman's *Samuel the Kingmaker*, appearing as a scheming politician, and as narrator of Robert Penn Warren's long monologue "Saul of Gilboa."

## SOURCES

Anderson, Bernard W., *Understanding the Old Testament*, Englewood Cliffs, NJ: Prentice-Hall, Inc., 1966; Comay, Joan, *Who's Who in the Bible*, vol. 1, New York: Bonanza Books, 1980; Kinsley, William, "Samuel," in *A Dictionary of the Biblical Tradition in English Literature*, edited by David L. Jeffrey, Grand Rapids, MI: William B. Eerdmans Publishing Company, 1992; Negev, Avraham, ed., *The Archaeological Encyclopedia of the Holy Land*, rev. ed., New York: Thomas Nelson Publishers, 1986; Zorn, Jeffrey R., "Mizpah: Newly Discovered Stratum Reveals Judas's Other Capital," in *Biblical Archaeology Review*, September/October, 1997.

## SARAH (SARAI)

**Name and Etymology.** *Sarai* was later changed to *Sarah*, both names apparently meaning "princess."

**Synopsis of Bible Story.** Sarai, the wife, and perhaps the half-sister of *Abraham/Abram, was the first biblical matriarch. (Her story appears in Genesis 11:29–23:2.) Abram claimed that they were born of the same father, but of different mothers (Gen. 20:12), yet in Genesis 11:31, Sarai is cited as the daughter-in-law, not the daughter of Terah.

When Sarai first appeared on the scene, at the time Abram and his tribe were moving from Ur of the Chaldees, she was already an old woman by the standards of the day, yet she must have been incredibly beautiful, attracting the attention of the most powerful men in both Egypt and Canaan. Knowing that such a treasure was a potential threat to his own life, Abram asked her to say she was his sister and hide their husband-wife relationship. Later, this drama was repeated with yet another king in yet another country.

In spite of her long relationship with a loving husband, Sarai was childless. After their sojourn in Egypt, where the Lord (rather than her husband) protected her from the Pharaoh, she and Abram faced the consequences of her apparently barren state. If she did not provide a son for her husband, their property would be inherited by another member of the family.

Thus, she offered her Egyptian maidservant, *Hagar, to Abram as a proxy-wife. When Hagar did become pregnant, she must have flaunted her superior fecundity, raising Sarai's ire. In response, Sarai demanded that Abram decide between them; her docile husband then drove the pregnant bondswoman into the wilderness. When, in acquiesence to the Lord's command, a submissive Hagar returned, Sarai seems to have allowed her back into the family, suggesting that Sarai was quick to anger and quick to forgiveness. Her later rejection of Hagar, however, confirms that the bad blood between them continued.

As part of the extensive caravan, this volatile old beauty was not simply a pampered woman. Although Sarai did have servants, she herself was responsible for providing the food and wine for guests. While she followed the conventions of the time by remaining outside of the tent when Abram entertained visitors, she satisfied her curiosity about their conversation by eavesdropping. When she overheard an angel tell Abraham that she would now be called "Sarah" and that she was to be blessed with a son and would become the mother of nations, she laughed out loud—either in scorn or in joy. Sarai, now named *Sarah*, cursed by a lifetime of barrenness, doubted that a woman well past childbearing age could indeed become a mother. The angel's response was powerful: "Is any thing too hard for the Lord?" (Gen. 18:6–14)

When *Isaac was born, Sarah and Abraham gave him a name signifying their laughter, and his old mother delighted in her ability to "give him suck." At the time of Isaac's weaning, she was once again infuriated by Hagar, this time because *Ishmael, Hagar's son, mocked her child. She again demanded that Abraham cast out this bondswoman as well as her son. It is clear that this is not simply a response to the mockery, for she added, that he "shall not be heir with my son. . . ." (Gen. 21:10)

After her defense of Isaac, Sarah ceased to be noted in Scripture until the time of her death at 127 years of age. She died in Hebron, in the land of Canaan, where Abraham mourned her, wept for her, and bought the land for her burial (Gen. 23:1–2).

**Historical Context.** Apparently in the eighteenth century B.C., it was not unusual for attractive women to be taken by powerful kings and pharaohs. Unwilling husbands were often killed, willing ones were rewarded. This would suggest that Abram was justified in his apparently crowded by subterfuges.

The stories of barren women are repeated in Scripture—e.g., *Rebekah, *Rachel, Hannah, and Elizabeth. God was seen as the key to fertility, and a woman's worth was closely tied to her fecundity. Nor was it unusual for a woman to use her maidservant to provide children by her husband—as in the case of *Jacob's wives. The Code of Hammurabi contains a close parallel to the strange relationship among Abram, Sarai, and Hagar, allowing for a man to substitute a bondswoman for his wife in order to produce a legal heir (Graves and Patai, 159).

Nursing apparently lasted for one or two years in ancient times, with the celebratory feast coming at the end of that time. There is a parallel story of prolonged nursing in the birth narrative of *Samuel.

From the structure of the story, it is evident that Sarah's long-delayed fruitfulness is key to the entire narrative. It begins with her apparent barrenness, a threat to the genealogy of Abraham, and ends with the birth and weaning of her son, followed by a lean obituary. The emphasis on the purity of the race (God's protection of Sarai in times of danger, the need for her—not an Egyptian maidservant—to be the mother of Isaac) continues into the New Testament, with the focus on Mary's virginity and genealogy.

Feminists (such as Phyllis Trible) see Genesis 22 as "The Sacrifice of Sarah," not of Isaac. Although the focus is on Abraham, the Scripture clearly indicates that Sarah's central role was her jealous protection of her son and his rights. It is ironic that her response to the aborted sacrifice of her beloved son is not noted. Some stories suggest that Sarah died of joy when she discovered that Isaac was not sacrificed (Graves and Patai, 175).

**Archaeological Evidence.** Numerous circumstances and customs in the story are easily verified by archaeological evidence, including the caravan route, the location of the cities, the treatment of slaves, the Hurrian habit of adopting a wife as sister, the importance of hospitality rituals, and the burial customs. Sarah's burial cave, which was eventually shared with Abraham and others, is in the Cave of Machpelah, which still survives, surrounded by the beautiful walls constructed in the days of Herod, lying deep beneath the Mosque of Abraham. The nearby Tel er-Rumeideh is believed to contain remains of Bronze and Iron Age Hebron (*New International Version*, 40).

**Character in Later Works.** The relationship between these two strong women, Sarah and Hagar, each of whom became the mother of a dynasty, has fascinated scholars over the years. Jewish scholars elaborated on the Hebrew legend of Abram and Sarai, adding adventures in Egypt and Gerar, explaining how Sarai was kept pure in the face of powerful temptation. Amplified stories of Hagar appear in both the Talmud and Islamic writings (Miller, 645).

Scripture has numerous echoes of various facets of this story: the barren wife, the threats to purity, the captivity, the plagues, and the escape with God's help. The question-and-answer dialogue with God parallel earlier Genesis scenes (in Eden, and in the Cain and Abel story). The powerful old beauty, still able to make demands of her husband David, is repeated in *Bathsheba's story when she too was able to pressure David to honor her son. *Paul later saw the mothers as allegories of two different covenants, the old and the new, one for slaves, one for freemen (Gal. 4:21–31). In 1 Peter 3:6, we see Sarah as a symbol of faith and obedience, a type of *Mary because of the miraculous nature of her child's conception and her calling Abraham "master."

Over time, Sarah, as the first matriarch, became a standard part of Abraham's story, usually portrayed as an example of the good wife. Medieval plays in England presented her as opposing the sacrifice of Isaac, arguing with Abraham. Charles Dickens characterized her as a beautiful woman, strong and merciless with her servants (Twomey, 681).

Sarah continues to have an important role in Jewish homes, in the parental blessings of girls on Sabbaths and holidays. She is also an important figure in Christian thought, a stunning portrayal of the wife as partner, willing to join her husband on his pilgrim path. Her enduring influence is suggested by the large number of infant girls who have been named for her over the centuries.

## SOURCES

Bach, Alice, ed., *Women in the Hebrew Bible: A Reader*, New York: Routledge, 1999; Graves, Robert, and Raphael Patai, *Hebrew Myths: The Book of Genesis*, New York: McGraw-Hill Book Company, 1963; Keller, Werner, *The Bible as History*, New York: Bantam Books, 1982; Miller, Madeline S., and J. Lane Miller, *Harper's Bible Dictionary*, New York: Harper and Row, 1961; Negev, Avraham, ed., *The Archaeological Encyclopedia of the Holy Land*, rev. ed., New York: Thomas Nelson Publishers, 1986; Trible, Phyllis, *Texts of Terror: Literary-Feminist Readings of Biblical Narrative*, Philadelphia, PA: Fortress Press, 1984; Twomey, M. W., "Sarah," in *A Dictionary of the Biblical Tradition in English Literature*, edited by David L. Jeffrey, Grand Rapids, MI: William B. Eerdman's Publishing Company, 1992.

## SAUL

**Name and Etymology.** *Saul* comes from the Hebrew "loaned."

**Synopsis of Bible Story.** Saul's tragic story is found in 1 Samuel. When the Israelites found their loose confederation of tribes ineffectual against their many enemies, they demanded a king. *Samuel, following guidance from God, anointed Saul the first king of Israel. Saul had all the makings of a hero: he was a large and powerful man from a prominent family, the son of Kish, a man of substance in the tribe of Benjamin. The family home was at Gibeah, three miles north of Jerusalem. Saul was described as a "choice young man, and a goodly" (1 Sam. 9:2). In one telling of his story, Samuel was sent to Saul by God, who had also warned against substituting a human king for the divine guidance. Samuel anointed the younger man secretly and admitted him into his prophetic school (1 Sam. 10:11–13). (There is an alternate telling in 10:21–24.) This was followed by the siege of Jabesh Gilead. When the people begged Saul for help against the insulting king of the Ammonites (1 Sam. 11:1–7), he responded by raising an army and defeating the enemy, causing the grateful people to respond by acclaiming him king (1 Sam. 11:15). This was followed by a public ceremony of anointing.

Other victories followed at Geba and, with the help of his son *Jonathan, at Michmash (1 Sam. 13:3–16, 14:1–16). The Philistines, however, proved too powerful for Saul and his band of warriors, who lacked the sophisticated metal armaments of their neighbors. Although they won a series of small victories, they could never fully vanquish this enemy.

An impatient man, Saul took sacrifices into his own hands rather than waiting for the priest, thereby raising the ire of God and Samuel. Later, Saul again disobeyed the

Samuel chooses Saul as King of Israelites fresco 13th century AD. The Art Archive/Anagni Cathedral, Italy/Dagli Orti (A).

clear instructions of God by refusing to kill his enemy, choosing instead to pardon him. At this point, Samuel announced that the glory of God had departed from this disobedient king, and God would choose another to be his anointed (1 Sam. 15:35).

Although he reigned over Israel for twenty years, Saul appears to have declined rapidly. He wavered between deep depression and great exaltation. In one of these bouts of depression, he invited the shepherd boy *David into his court to comfort him with music, not knowing that the lad was the Lord's anointed, his successor to the throne. Although he loved the boy, who was a good friend to his son Jonathan and finally the husband of his daughter Mical, he grew increasingly jealous of him, overhearing the people compare their exploits and shower their love on the younger man: "Saul has killed his thousands, and David his ten thousands," they shouted (1 Sam. 18:7). Saul then plotted to murder his young rival. Over a period of time, he tried repeatedly to kill David, who avoided being hurt or harming the old king. Saul finally drove David out of the kingdom.

By this time, Samuel was dead and the kingdom was in disarray. In a curious episode near the end of his tortured life, Saul sought out the witch of Endor, begging her to call the spirit of Samuel from the dead. The old seer, prophet, priest, and judge responded with wrath, showing no more mercy to this fallen hero in death than he had in life.

The Philistines, taking advantage of the weakness and dissension within the ranks of the Israelites, attacked through the Valley of Jezreel, and killed Jonathan, Abinadab, and Malki-Shua, Saul's sons (1 Sam. 31:2). The old king died by his own hand on Mount Gilboa. The victorious Philistines cut off his head and carried it through their villages, displaying his armor in the temple of Ashtaroth, and fastening his body to the walls of Beth-Shean. The men of Jabesh Gilead rescued the bodies of Saul and his three sons from the city and buried their bones under an oak (1 Sam. 31:8–13).

**Historical Context.** Saul was a transitional figure, an example of the kind of powerful military leader needed by the beleaguered Israelites, and the hero of a cautionary tale admonishing the kings of Israel to be humble and obedient servants of Jehovah. Sometime around 1050 B.C., Israel was threatened with the loss of all the fruits of its labors for the previous two hundred years: the Philistines were victorious, Shiloh stood in ruins, and the Philistines were at the point of enslaving the people of the region. Saul was able to bring the tribes together through his strength of character, and he prepared the way for his more able and charismatic successor, David. One critic notes that the Bible narrative does not give Saul adequate credit for his work. The two decades of his reign fully justified the first Hebrew experiment in kingship: he gave the weak and poorly organized Israelite tribes the military and political cohesion needed to hold their enemies at bay; and he paved the way for the expansion of the kingdom under David (Comay, 341). His successor, David, was so beloved; Samuel, his predecessor, became so antagonistic and his own character was so flawed that Saul survives in memory more as a tragic figure than as a great hero.

There is plenty of evidence that the Philistines were superior to the Israelites in metallurgy. These "Sea Peoples" had chariots, armor, daggers, and other implements that were unavailable to the more primitive, nomadic Israelites.

**Archaeological Evidence.** Numerous students of the Bible have discovered evidence from different parts of Saul's career: Professor W. F. Albright uncovered Saul's citadel, the first royal castle in Israel, at Tell el-Ful. Major Vivian Gilbert, a British army officer in Allenby's army in Palestine during World War I, believing the stories of Saul's victories were based in fact, used the geographical markers to plan his own successful attack on the Turks at Michmash (Keller, 187–88).

The valley of Jezreel, the scene of Saul's defeat and death, was the classic battleground in the Old Testament, associated with *Deborah, *Gideon, and in the New Testament, with Armageddon. At Beth-Shean, temples to Dagon and Ashtaroth, in which the Philistines put Saul's armor as trophies, have been uncovered. (After Saul died on nearby Mount Gilboa, the headless bodies of Saul and his three sons, Jonathan, Abinadab, and Malki-Shua, were taken by the Philistines and hung on the walls of Beth-Shean. His armor was then placed in the temple of Ashtaroth in Beth Shean. The Israelites of Jabesh Gilead, however, came by night and took down their bodies, giving them a decent burial.)

The view of the high tell of Beth-Shean evokes memories of David's moving lament over the ignominious deaths of Saul and his three sons: "The beauty of Israel is slain upon thy high places: how are the mighty fallen!" (2 Sam. 1:19).

**Character in Later Works.** The importance of this leader is evident in the perpetuation of his name. *Paul's name was originally *Saul* from Tarsus. In Jewish history, Israel's first king sometimes had a number of defenders, but Christians have usually criticized him for his failure to follow God's lead and for his lack of spiritual discipline, leading to his suicide. St. John Chrystostom, St. Augustine, Luther, and Calvin all condemned him.

The emotional heights and depths of his nature inspired Rembrandt's portrait and Handel's oratorio. As a tragic figure, he was an ideal subject for artists: Milton referred to him frequently in his work, condemning him as a bad and treacherous king. Byron used him in *Hebrew Melodies* (1816), and Browning gave an entire poem over to him in *Saul* (1845–47). D. H. Lawrence wrote a play, *David*, using Saul as a major character (1926). Most creative treatments of the hero David would invariably begin with Saul as mentor and then as antagonist. Saul's descent from greatness into madness is the stuff of heroic tragedy.

## SOURCES

Comay, Joan, *Who's Who in the Bible*, vol. 1, New York: Bonanza Books, 1980; Keller, Werner, *The Bible as History*, New York: Bantam Books, 1982; Lipizin, Sol, and Joseph McClatchey, "Saul," in *A Dictionary of the Biblical Tradition in English Literature*, edited by David L. Jeffrey, Grand Rapids, MI: William B. Eerdmans Publishing Company, 1992; Miller, Madeline S., and Lane Miller, *Harper's Bible Dictionary*, New York: Harper and Row, 1961.

## SENNACHERIB

**Name and Etymology.** *Sennacherib* means "Sin [moon god] has increased the brothers."

**Synopsis of Bible Story.** This proud Assyrian king came to the throne in 705 B.C. after the assassination of his father, Sargon II, and lost it when his sons assassinated him in 681 B.C. He was a bold strategist, a ruthless warrior, and a boastful victor who conquered and plundered much of the Middle East. He entered Judah's history when he turned his attention east to the rebellious provinces along the Mediterranean coast. These events are recorded in 2 Kings 18:13–19:37, and Isaiah 37. Among the leaders of the rebels was Hezekiah, in the fourteenth year of his reign (701 B.C.). After attacking and capturing forty-six Judean walled cities, he turned toward Jerusalem (2 Kings 18). Frightened when Lachish was overcome, Hezekiah offered tribute, stripping the gold and silver from the Temple, which he later sent to Assyria. On one military excursion, Sennacherib attempted to breach the walls of Jerusalem, but was mysteriously stopped on the night before the attack was to take place. After he suffered heavy losses due to the plague, Sennacherib returned to Nineveh, where he received the promised tribute from Hezekiah.

**Historical Context.** Sennacherib was a powerful leader at a crucial time in history. The violence against his father that brought Sennacherib to the throne also led him to fear divine disfavor and to distance himself from his father's traditions. He abandoned the capitol that Sargon had just built and chose the old city of Nineveh for his capital, "installing wide boulevards, bringing in mountain water by aqueduct, planting trees, and laying out parks." Recognizing the threat of Babylon, he destroyed it, "diverting a watercourse through the ruins so that the site would be permanently obliterated" (Brinkman, 686). Given this ruthless drive for power, Sennacherib may have intended the destruction of the Palestinian cities as instrumental in the larger goal of establishing Assyrian authority.

At times, *Isaiah saw Sennacherib as a force for God's justice, at others as the enemy of Jerusalem. It was on his advice that Hezekiah resisted the temptation to capitulate and hand over Jerusalem to this fearsome foe (Isa. 37:33–37). The miracle of the Angel of Death descending on the camp was explained in part by Herodotus, who recorded the scourge of mice, which probably brought with them the bubonic plague.

**Archaeological Evidence.** The famous tunnel of Siloam was built by Hezekiah in anticipation of the siege of the Assyrians. Archaeology supplements our knowledge about the extent of his preparations. He strengthened his defensive network of forts in the low rolling hills west of Jerusalem, built huge towers to guard the gateways of key cities in his fortification network, and established four supply depots and had storage jars made with special inscriptions on the handle ("for the king") for gathering supplies into the depots. More famously, Hezekiah blocked up the outer entrance to the Gihon Spring; he then had workers tunnel through the hill on which the City of David was built in order to bring the water into the walled area of the city. He also built additional reservoirs for water. He condemned private houses in order to build a massive wall to defend the newer areas of the city. The "broad wall" is still visible in the Jewish Quarter of Jerusalem. After the Six-Day War in 1967, extensive excavations left "windows" to reveal remains as far back as 586 B.C., the time of *Jeremiah.

The annals of Sennacherib, written in cuneiform on a clay prism, record his mighty deeds, including his massive building projects and his many victories. He did record the victory over Lachish and the walling up of "Hezekiah the Jew" "like a caged bird" (Keller, 280) in his self-aggrandizing records, (but not the mysterious events of the night when the plague struck his army, preventing his attack on Jerusalem). The columns of the annals and many reliefs on the walls of the royal palace excavated in Nineveh testify to his deeds. One in particular shows the Assyrians storming Lachish, using ramps and showing the bloody battle in great detail. One of the portrayals of Sennacherib reviewing the booty of Lachish describes him as "Sennacherib, king of the universe, king of Assyria. . . ."

**Character in Later Works.** Rabbinical tradition portrays Sennacherib as wicked and proud. The most famous literary use of the career of this powerful man was by George Gordon, Lord Byron, in his famous poem "The Destruction of Sennacherib," which pictures the "Angel of Death" descending on the doomed troops. For most of history, his vicious invasion of the land was portrayed as nothing more than one in a catalogue of foreign powers which swept like so many plagues over Israel.

## SOURCES

Baker, David W., "Sennacherib," in *A Dictionary of the Biblical Tradition in English Literature*, edited by David L. Jeffrey, Grand Rapids, MI: William B. Eerdmans Publishing Company, 1992; Brinkman, James A., "Sennacherib," in *The Oxford Companion to the Bible*, edited by Bruce M. Metzger and Michael D. Coogan, New York: Oxford University Press, 1993; Comay, Joan, *Who's Who in the Bible*, vol. 1, New York: Bonanza Books, 1980; Hargis, Merilyn, and Jeff Hargis, *The Hindsight Tour Guide*, USA: Hindsight, 1996; Keller, Werner, *The Bible as History*, New York: Bantam Books, 1882; Miller, Madeline S., and J. Lane Miller, *Harper's Bible Dictionary*, New York: Harper and Row, 1961.

## SHEBA, QUEEN OF

**Name and Etymology.** Only her title, not her name, is given; we know that this woman was the queen of "Sheba," a country also known as "Saba," located in southern Arabia, near the Gulf of Aden. She is later referred to as the queen of the "south." (See Matt. 12: 42 and Luke 11:31.)

**Synopsis of Bible Story.** The dramatic meeting of the Queen of Sheba and *King Solomon is chronicled in two locations—1 Kings 10:1–13 and 2 Chronicles 9:1–12. Having heard of Solomon's great fame, the queen came to Jerusalem to meet him and to test his wisdom, bringing with her great treasures of spices, gold, and precious stones. Impressed by what she saw on her visit and with the evidence of his wisdom, she proclaimed his people happy indeed to have such a king. She lavished gifts on him and then left to return to her own land.

**Historical Context.** One of many visitors to the court at Jerusalem in the tenth century B.C., the Queen of Sheba represents the vast international contacts and the great prestige of Solomon's era. During a time when the great kingdoms that always surrounded and threatened Israel were quiet or weak, Solomon was able to reach out in a manner that impressed the people. The land of Saba (now identified as eastern Yemen) apparently had queens in position of power from time to time, but Josephus, the Jewish historian, doubted Sheba's authenticity. The land was noted for its wealth, largely due to its protected position and its abundance of valuable spices, though the enormous quantity of gold cited in 1 Kings seems an exaggeration to the historians.

Because of the close relationship between Saba and Ethiopia, and the conflation of the story of Candace, the queen of Ethiopia with the queen of Sheba, the Ethiopians trace their ancestry to this historic meeting. The text hints at a possible affair between Solomon and the queen (he gave "to the queen of Sheba all her desire, whatsoever she asked"; 2 Chron. 9:12). This has traditionally been cited as the background of Menelik I and the "Throne of *David," to which all Ethiopian emperors down to Haile Selassie traced their lineage.

**Archaeological Evidence.** At Hajar Bin Humeid, forty miles from Marib, archaeologists have found deposits from the period of Sheba. It is clear that there was a culture flourishing in this region even before the time of Solomon, with caravan trade in spices, gold and precious stones. This apparently made a journey over some 1,400 miles of desert for the queen herself and her retinue possible; this trade route and the strength of her economic system protected her retinue. (See Gus W. van Beek, 40 ff.)

One debate among historians has centered on the tradition that Menelik, the son of the Queen of Sheba and King Solomon, brought the Ark of the Covenant to the Elephantine Temple, a Jewish temple that Menelik had constructed on the Nile in the style of Solomon's famous Temple in Jerusalem. One scholar rejects this Ethiopian legend, suggesting instead that the temple was constructed and used during King Manasseh's reign (c. 687–642 B.C.).

**Character in Later Works.** The romantic meeting of these two characters has resulted in a grand array of folk elaborations and artistic presentations. In Jewish tradition, the Queen of Sheba came to be identified as Lilith, queen of demons, who strangled infants in their cradles, summoned by magic charms, and coupled with men in their sleep. In Christian tradition, she came to be identified with the *Magi, who also brought gifts of gold, frankincense, and myrrh from the East. For them she became an early image of a pagan admiring Israel and Israel's god. In Eastern tradition, she came to be seen as the mother of *Nebuchadnezzar, a curious woman who had hairy feet and magical powers. This imagery was further elaborated by later oriental tales which identified her as the goose-footed queen.

The celebrated meeting between the two monarchs decorates a large number of medieval cathedrals, becoming the subject of carvings, paintings, and windows—Ghiberti's "Gates of Paradise" at the Baptistry in Florence is a lovely late example. Sheba also appears in music—Handel's oratorio *Samuel*—and was the topic of literature, especially in the modern era. Flaubert used the Lilith version of the Queen of Sheba in his story of the temptation of St. Anthony; Arthur Symons used her liaison with Solomon in *The Lover of the Queen of Sheba*; and William Butler Yeats wrote about the pair several times, including his poem "Solomon to Sheba." Moderns, especially in the African-American arts community, have revived the tale, using it as a symbol of black history and ancient magnificence. Romare Bearden's *She-ba* is a good example of this blend of feminism and black history.

## SOURCES

Isaac, Ephraim, "Is the Ark of the Covenant in Ethiopia," in *Biblical Archaeology Review*, July/August 1993; Jeffrey, David L., *A Dictionary of the Biblical Tradition in English Literature*, Grand Rapids, MI: William B. Eerdmans Publishing Company, 1992; Porten, Bezalel, "Did the Ark Stop at Elephantine?" in *Biblical Archaeology Review*, www.biblicalarchaeology.org, May/June 1995; Pritchard, James B., ed. *Solomon and Sheba*, London: Phaidon Press Ltd., 1974.

## SOLOMON

**Name and Etymology.** *Solomon* probably means "peaceful." *Nathan the prophet (2 Sam. 12:25) also called him *Jedidiah*, "beloved of the Lord."

**Synopsis of Bible Story.** Solomon's majestic and tragic story appears in 2 Sam. 12:24–25; 1 Chron. 22:5–23:1; 1 Kings 1:28–40. He was the third king of Israel (965 to 926 B.C.) and the second son of *David and *Bathsheba, the designated heir to the throne from the beginning.

His brothers Absalom and Adonijah plotted to deny him this role, but *Bathsheba, always her son's strongest supporter, knew of this threat to the authority of Solomon (1 Kings 1:11–21). On Nathan's wise advice, Bathsheba reminded David of his promise that Solomon would sit on the throne. The old king responded in a final act of authority, setting forth the arrangements for the anointing of Solomon. The ceremony at Gihon, to which Solomon rode on David's mule, included a horn of oil taken out of the tabernacle, the blowing of the trumpet, and the proclamation: "God save king Solomon" (1 Kings 1:39). Solomon, in an act of grace, forgave his brothers' and Joab's perfidy and allowed them to live—at least until after David's death.

The ambitious Adonijah, exploiting Solomon's weakness for his mother, went to Bathsheba and begged for the Shunammite Abishag (David's handmaid during his final days), whom he sought to marry. Recognizing the continuing threat of Adonijah, who was his elder brother and believed himself to be the true heir, Solomon ordered his death and his co-conspirator's as well. After this display of power, Solomon had no serious threats to his throne and was able to preside over a united and prosperous kingdom for many years.

Early in his reign, while at Gibeon, he had a dream in which the Lord asked him what he most desired. Solomon responded with his famous request: "Give . . . thy servant an understanding heart to judge thy people, that I may discern between good and bad: for who is able to judge this thy so great a people?" (1 Kings 3:9) The Lord, pleased by Solomon's humble and thoughtful request, granted him wisdom and understanding. In doing so, God established a clear condition for his long and powerful reign over the children of Israel: "And if thou wilt walk in my ways, to keep my statutes and my commandments, as thy father David did walk, then I will lengthen thy days" (1 Kings 3:13).

The fruit of this exchange was soon obvious to the people through a series of judgments that displayed Solomon's wise heart. Among the most famous was his decision in the case of two harlots quarreling over a baby. The king's threat to cut the child in two and divide the infant equitably between the would-be mothers revealed the motherly instincts of the true mother, allowing Solomon to make the proper judgment (1 Kings 3:16–28). Over time, this wisdom mellowed, making him famous. Collections of aphorisms, Israel's famous "wisdom literature," that are recorded in the books of Proverbs and Ecclesiastes as well as nonbiblical texts such as the "Wisdom of Solomon" (Meeks, 1499–1529) are commonly attributed to him. His court was undoubtedly the center of enormous cultural and literary activity, a place where visitors could share the wisdom literature of their peoples, and perhaps a place where these proverbs were collected by scribes.

He apparently developed an orderly system of governance and provided safety for "every man under his vine and under his fig tree" (1 Kings 4:25). With heavy taxes and conscripted labor, he was able to begin the building ordained by God during the time of David—the Temple at Jerusalem. During the years of his grandiose building program, the people delighted in the new affluence and magnificence that Solomon's rule brought to Israel. Unfortunately, when the Temple was complete, he did not relax the taxation nor reduce his zeal for construction.

While raising massive armies, Solomon also arranged a series of strategic partnerships with kingdoms that were potential threats to Israel, thereby securing a peaceful reign. Through many marriages, beginning with the Pharaoh's daughter and extending to many counties with whom he had treaties, he was able to secure his borders and encourage extensive trade. From the outset these marriages to foreign women posed a threat to his faith. Scripture asserts that "he had seven hundred wives, princesses, and three hundred concubines: and his wives turned away his heart" (1 Kings 11:3). Although Solomon "loved the Lord," he built temples for his wives' worship of alien deities in "high places," and also sacrificed and burned incense there himself (1 Kings 11:7–8).

The most famous of these foreign alliances was with the *Queen of Sheba. Some believe that she was the inspiration for that lovely paean to the flesh, "The Song of Solomon." (Others believe it was the earlier Shunammite maiden, who nursed David in his final days and was coveted by Adonijah.)

The later years of Solomon's life, after the completion of the Temple, were increasingly painful. His many women, both wives and concubines, with their many children and quarrels and various worship practices, led him into moral and intellectual confusion. Refusing to respond to the grumbling of the priests and other true believers among the Jews, he continued to tolerate diverse worship practices. His latter days were marred by cynicism and boredom, the sense of "vanity" so strong in Ecclesiastes, another portion of Scripture often attributed to him.

The people of Israel began to complain of his imperial tone, growing disrespectful and lawless, and even robbing the tax collectors. His designated heir, Rehoboam, displayed signs of haughtiness and dissolution—traits that he himself had nurtured and failed to correct. *Nathan warned Solomon of potential threats, and finally, in a solemn vision, the Lord told him of looming troubles. In a great gesture intended to

Solomon meeting the Queen of Sheba, 19th-century Ethiopian. The Art Archive/Private Collection/Dagli Orti.

reinforce these messages of disruption and decline, the prophet Ahijah tore a cloak into 12 pieces, handing him only two of them, giving the others to his faithful helper Jereboam, signaling that the kingdom would be divided at his death (1 Kings 11:28–33) and his heirs would reign over a far smaller portion of Israel.

**Historical Context.** Solomon's long and glorious reign (965–926 B.C.) was the high point of splendor for the Kingdom of Israel. His building of the Temple, using the foreign architect Hiram and bringing materials from far and wide gave a sense of national identity to the Jews that reinforced the pride they had known under David. Under Solomon, Israel enjoyed the final days of a united kingdom. For a brief and shining moment, Israel was famous as a center of culture, industry, building, and religion.

The lingering tradition of King Solomon's mines was thought to refer to copper mines, but archaeologists have gradually come to believe that the ones that have been discovered may well date from a later period. Solomon was thought to have been a thoroughly progressive ruler with a flair for exploiting foreign brains and foreign skill, thus moving beyond the simple peasant regime of his father, David, into a far more sophisticated and eclectic kingdom.

His marriages to foreign women, much frowned on by his people, brought many allies in the surrounding regions. These alliances also ensured a peaceful reign. The worship "in high places," which Solomon encouraged, was apparently the worship of the goddess Ashtar or Astarte, the mother goddess figure often tolerated by the Hebrews. Myth holds that Solomon actually married the Queen of *Sheba, who bore him a son, Menelik I, the traditional founder of the royal house of Ethiopia.

Some believe that the idyllic kingdom described in the "royal" psalm, which mentions Sheba (Psalm 72:10), refers to the grand court over which Solomon presided. It is also thought that he collected the great minds of his time to his palace, where he encouraged a flowering of literature, perhaps producing the collections of "Proverbs," "Ecclesiastes," the "Wisdom of Solomon," and the "Song of Solomon." Scholars are not sure the extent to which any of these may be his own individual creations.

**Archaeological Evidence.** The greatest of Solomon's structures, the Temple, which was destroyed in 586 B.C. and later served as the base for Herod's grand reconstruction, is lost forever. For political and religious reasons, it is impossible to dig on the Temple Mount, where this building and his palace would have been constructed. Nonetheless, archaeologists have uncovered numerous examples of Solomon's grandiose building projects elsewhere, including those at Megido, Hazor, and Gezer. His defense strategy for his empire consisted of a ring of cities strategically located around the borders of Israel, manned by companies of soldiers, including charioteers. Among the requirements of his vast militia were stalls for 4,000 horses mentioned in 1 Kings 10:26.

The records of the extensive trade in which Solomon engaged suggest an interest in countries far flung from earlier days, and he apparently lived in oriental splendor in the midst of silver and gold. His fleet, manned by Phoenicians, sailed to Ophir carrying smelted copper and brought back gold, silver, hardwood, jewels, ivory, and varieties of apes and peacocks. Archaeologists have long debated the actual identity of this city, considering possibilities in modern Zimbabwe.

**Character in Later Works.** No character in the folk literature of Israel achieved such international fame as Solomon, who assumed the mythical quality of a magician as well as a wise and rich king. Postbiblical tales about Solomon appeared not only among the Jews of the Diaspora, but also among Ethiopians and Arabs. He, like King Midas, became the image of wealth and splendor. He continues to symbolize the triumphal kingdom—a time of peace and prosperity—that is portrayed in the royal or Messianic psalms, when the kingdom of God will prevail (Psalm 72).

Perversely, he is also the symbol of perfidy, of syncretism that ultimately destroyed the kingdom. His lust after foreign women led to his lust after foreign gods; his "tolerance," which grew from his intellectual arrogance, soon turned into assimilation of goddess worship, and his heirs proved to be even more arrogant and less faithful and religious than he. In him, we see the seeds of the destruction of the line of David, even at its zenith.

Many works are attributed to him—the "Wisdom of Solomon," "Psalms of Solomon," "Odes of Solomon," and "Testament of Solomon." Jewish tradition also has him authoring works on medicine, mineralogy, and magic. In the New Testament, Jesus used him as an image of "glory" that derives from human wealth and of wisdom, comparing him unfavorably to the "lilies of the field" (Matt. 6:28).

In European literature, Solomon often serves as an example of wealth or magic or syncretism. Chaucer and Dante both refer to him, though more as a wise ruler than as a magician. Rarely does he appear as the model for a character or the subject of a story.

On the other hand, those Biblical passages attributed to him have had enormous influence in both English and American literature. The tone of Ecclesiastes with its references to vanity found its most picturesque and influential form in "Vanity Fair," an unforgettable scene in John Bunyan's *Pilgrim's Progress*. A derivative appearance is in William Makepeace Thackeray's *Vanity Fair*. This structure of "Wisdom" facing "Folly" sets the underlying tone for Melville's *Typee* and *Moby Dick*, for Hardy's somber novel, *Far from the Madding Crowd*, and for the comic novel by Mark Twain, *The Adventures of Huckleberry Finn*. The most famous use of his hidden wealth is *King Solomon's Mines*, a popular romance by H. Rider Haggard.

More recently, Toni Morrison picks up on "The Song of Solomon." In her novel by that name, she uses it as a key to the plot and the family line. The lush celebration of physical love has also appealed to a number of writers from the Renaissance on, inspiring a number of marriage songs or "epithaliamia" from the time of Edmund Spenser to the moderns.

## SOURCES

Hubbard, D. A., "Solomon," in *The Illustrated Bible Dictionary*, vol. 3, Sidney, Australia: Tyndale House Publishers, 1980; Keller, Werner, *The Bible as History*, New York: Bantam Books, 1982; LaBossière, Camille R., and Jerry A. Gladson, "Solomon," in *A Dictionary of the Biblical Tradition in English Literature*, edited by David L. Jeffrey, Grand Rapids, MI: William B. Eerdmans Publishing Company, 1992; Mare, W. Harold, *The Archaeology of the Jerusalem Area*, Grand Rapids, MI: Baker Book House, 1987; Meeks, Wayne A., ed., *HarperCollins Study Bible*, London: HarperCollins Publishers, 1993; Patai, Raphael, *The Hebrew Goddess*, Detroit, MI: Wayne State University Press, 1990.

## STEPHEN

**Name and Etymology.** *Stephen* is Greek for "crown."

**Synopsis of Bible Story.** Stephen, whose story appears in Acts 6 and 7, was the first Christian martyr. Apparently a Hellenistic Jew living in Jerusalem, he was selected by the apostles to be one of the first deacons, to relieve these busy men of the care of widows and orphans, the distribution of food and other necessities. As his powers and his faith increased, Stephen began to teach, preach, and heal in the synagogues. The Hellenistic group within the Synagogue of the Libertines or Freedmen, however, grew jealous of him and trumped up charges against him, parallel to those used against *Jesus. They accused him of blasphemy against *Moses, thus stirring up the Jewish elders and scribes, who brought him before the Sanhedrin, elaborating the charges to include the proposed destruction of the holy place of Jerusalem.

Rather than proclaiming his own innocence, Stephen took the opportunity to review the history of the Jews as a stiff-necked people, "uncircumcised in heart and ears" who repeatedly disobeyed the clear directions of God. Like *Jesus and *Isaiah, he insisted: ". . . the most High dwelleth not in temples made with hands; as saith the prophet, Heaven is my throne, and earth is my footstool . . ." (Acts 7:48–49). He then spoke of his vision of Jesus in glory, at the right hand of God.

Convinced of his blasphemy, the mob stopped their ears and seized him. As he prayed for God to receive his soul and forgive his murderers, they stoned him to death (Acts 7:59–60). Those engaged in the brutal stoning deposited their garments at the feet of *Saul (later Paul), a tormentor of the early Christians, who "was consenting unto his death" (Acts 8:1). Stephen was buried with great lamentation by devout men.

**Historical Context.** The Hellenized Jews came from various parts of the Greek and Roman empire; they were Jews who had been dispersed and then returned to Jerusalem. The Synagogue of the Freedmen was composed, in part, of those who had been carried away as slaves and had earned or been granted their freedom. At this time—shortly after the death of Christ—the Christians still considered themselves a part of Judaism, and therefore met in synagogues. Stephen's message, with its critique of Judaism and the Jews, became a pattern of disagreement that would eventually separate the Christians from their Jewish heritage, making them no longer a Jewish sect, but a separate religion.

The manner of his death—stoning—was in accordance with Jewish law (Lev. 24:15–16), which required that those who were witnesses against the defendant throw the first stones (Deut. 17:7). If Jesus had been executed by the Jews instead of the Romans, this would have been the manner of his death as well.

Stephen's martyrdom touched off a persecution that scattered Christians to Samaria (Acts 8:1) and probably as far as Damascus, thus laying the foundations for the extension of Christianity to the Gentile world. His speech is thought to have been the beginning of a theological revolution in the early Church, as the principles of the universal mission were clearly stated for the first time—apparently the rationale for *Luke's extended record of Stephen's speech (Nixon, 1486).

A medieval legend states that 400 years after Stephen's death, a priest named Lucian had a vision of the place where his body was buried. His remains were subsequently removed and reburied in Rome beside the relics of St. Laurence. The legend notes that, when the tomb was opened, St. Laurence moved to one side and gave his hand to St. Stephen, leading someone to give St. Laurence the title "the courteous Spaniard" (Ferguson, 143). Stephen became one of the most popular of all saints during the Middle Ages, especially in the West, where his feast followed Christmas Day (Brownrigg, 426).

**Archaeological Evidence.** The present Stephen's Gate, in the east wall of Jerusalem is considered by many to be the site of his martyrdom. A Dominican complex, the St. Étienne Church, was built by the Damascus Gate in 1882, thought to be the place of the stoning of St. Stephen in 35 A.D. In the fifth century A.D., the Byzantine empress Eudoxia built a large church there to commemorate his sacrifice; a Crusader church was later build nearby (Barkay, 2000). Other candidates for the place of his stoning, which would have been outside the city, in an area where there was no city wall or city gate in his day, include the Kidron Valley, where there is a Greek Orthodox Church, and Geth Gemal, where a body was found in a tomb and brought to Jerusalem and buried in the Zion Church on the western hill.

**Character in Later Works.** Stephen's references to the tabernacle and the whole invisible Christian culture is developed in the Epistle to the Hebrews.

Stephen's saintly manner and angelic face have made him the very model for the Christian martyr. In most catalogues of the martyrs, including Foxe's *Book of Martyrs*, the listing begins with Stephen (David Jeffrey, 735). John Bunyan picks up on Stephen's idea that pilgrims of the faith live as "resident aliens" in the land, using him as a model repeatedly in *Pilgrim's Progress*. (This is a concept still discussed by Christian writers such as Peter Augustine Lawler, who recently wrote *Aliens in America*. Walker Percy also used it in an echo of St. Augustine's statement that we humans are pilgrims or "aliens" in this world.) T. S. Eliot uses the occasion of St. Stephen's Day and a sermon on him by St. Thomas à Becket in *Murder in the Cathedral*. His name is so famous that it is used as the symbolic image of the Christian artist in Stephen Daedalus, the hero of Joyce's *Portrait of the Artist as a Young Man.*

Painters have represented Stephen in the costume of a deacon, bearing the palm of martyrdom. Nearby are the stones used to kill him. Because of a legend that ties his burial with St. Laurence, the two are often portrayed together (Ferguson, 143).

## SOURCES

Barkay, Gabriel, "What's an Egyptian Temple Doing in Jerusalem," in *Biblical Archaeology Review*, May/June 2000; Brownrigg, Ronald, *Who's Who in the Bible*, vol. 2, New York: Bonanza Books, 1980; Ferguson, George, *Signs and Symbols in Christian Art*, New York: Oxford University Press, 1966; Jeffrey, David L., ed., *A Dictionary of the Biblical Tradition in English Literature*, Grand Rapids, MI: William B. Eerdmans Publishing Company, 1992; Madeline S., and J. Lane Miller, *Harper's Bible Dictionary*, New York: Harper and Row, 1961; Nixon, R. E., "Stephen," in *The Illustrated Bible Dictionary*, vol. 3, edited by J. D. Douglas, Sidney, Australia: Tyndale House Publishers, 1980.

## SUSANNA

**Name and Etymology.** *Susanna* is Hebrew for "lily."

**Synopsis of Bible Story.** In the apocryphal book Susanna, we learn of a "very beautiful woman and one who feared the Lord" (Susanna 1:2). She lived with her wealthy and honored husband, Joakim, in Babylon. Her father, Hilkiah, and her unnamed mother were righteous people who "trained their daughter according to the law of Moses" (Susanna 3). Her blissful world grew dark when two elders, filled with lust, began to frequent the house of her wealthy husband, and fixate on his beautiful wife. Susanna, modest and proper, waited each day for visitors to leave before walking in her husband's garden, but the elders spied on her and forgot their duties as judges as their passion for her intensified. They finally recognized their shared obsession and hatched a plot to find her alone (Susanna 13).

Their opportunity came when Susanna was bathing in the garden and sent her maids away to bring olive oil and ointments for her use. The elders accosted her, demanding sexual favors in exchange for their silence about a lie they had concocted. Shocked, Susanna cried out for help. When the people rushed in, the elders told their trumped-up story of discovering her with a young lover. It was only at the trial that followed that she was forced to tell her tale of their efforts at extortion, crying out for the Lord's help (Susanna 28–42).

In response to her prayer, God sent *Daniel to her defense. He tested the lustful elders by separating them and asking them details of their story. When they contradicted one another, the people proclaimed Susanna innocent, and Daniel ordered that the elders be put to death. Susanna returned to her family and to her position of an honored member of the community (Susanna 44–63).

**Historical Context.** The Babylonian setting for this story suggests that there was a community of prosperous Jews in Babylon in Daniel's time. Daniel's own elevation to high status in the court of *Nebuchadnezzar also testifies to this prosperity of selected Jews in captivity. It is thought that this story may actually reflect social conditions of some Jews of a later century.

The portrayal of the trial reveals some interesting details of judicial practice, including the veiled appearance of Susanna, the "scoundrels" stripping her, and the laying on of hands (Susanna 32–34). The final judgment in the case suggests that the punishment for bearing false witness was like that for adultery—death.

**Archaeological Evidence.** The text itself appears to be a portion of the book of Daniel, following either Chapter 12 or perhaps serving as an introduction to the entire book, before Chapter 1 (Wills, 1637). Another historian notes that the book seems to be of Palestinian origin: "The date could be as early as the Persian period and certainly no later than c. 100 B.C.E., when the Septuagint translation was completed" (Dentan, 721).

**Character in Later Works.** The beautiful central character of an ancient detective story, a Hebrew courtroom drama, and a nefarious plot by two old hypocrites, Susanna is a delightful heroine. Her chastity, modesty, and steadfastness in the law all make her a character beloved by medieval writers. There are 67 plays based directly on her story, 28 in German alone (Walker, 741–2). She also appears frequently in poetry from ancient to modern times, including a reference by Wallace Stevens in his poem "Peter Quince at the Clavier."

Painters have also loved the image of the beautiful woman bathing in the garden as nasty old men in all their long robes lurk in the shadows lusting after her. Tintoretto's "Susanna and the Elders" is a good example of an artist's portrayal of this melodramatic scene, which has the additional benefit of justifying of painting a female nude.

## SOURCES

Comay, Joan, *Who's Who in the Bible*, vol. 1, New York: Bonanza Books, 1980; Dentan, Robert C., "Susanna," in *The Oxford Companion to the Bible*, edited by Bruce Metzger and Michael D. Coogan, New York: Oxford University Press, 1993; Walker, Steven C., "Susanna," in *A Dictionary of the Biblical Tradition in English Literature*, edited by David L. Jeffrey, Grand Rapids, MI: William B. Eerdmans Publishing Company, 1992; Wills, Lawrence, "Susanna," in *HarperCollins Study Bible*, edited by Wayne A. Meeks, San Francisco, CA: HarperCollins, 1993.

# T

## THOMAS

**Name and Etymology.** He is named only "Thomas" in Matthew 10:3; Mark 3:18; Luke 6:15, but in John 11:16, he is further identified as *Didymus*, or the Greek word from the Aramaic, for "twin," though it is never clear whose twin he is. (The Gnostics apparently thought him to be a twin of *Jesus.) He is also known by the full name, "Didymus Judas Thomas."

**Synopsis of Bible Story.** Thomas is listed with the disciples of Jesus in all the Gospels and appears in the roll of those who chose a replacement for *Judas after the ascension of Jesus, but no incident is recorded in the Synoptic Gospels or in Acts regarding him individually. Only *John notes Thomas's role in the closing days of Jesus's life: Jesus was hounded out of Jerusalem but proposed to return to Judaea in spite of Jewish hostility. Though he was frightened, Thomas displayed courage and loyalty, offering to die with him if that proved necessary (John 11:16). Thomas revealed his spiritual limitations in his conversation with Jesus after the Last Supper. When Jesus said he was going to prepare a place for them, Thomas interrupted, saying, "Lord, we do not know whither thou goest; and how can we know the way" (John 14:5). On another occasion, Thomas was with the disciples once again in the Upper Room. A man of practical faith, he refused to accept the testimony of the others regarding their risen Lord, proclaiming, "Except I shall see in his hands the print of the nails, and put my finger into the print of the nails, and thrust my hand into his side, I will not believe" (John 20:25). This led to a confrontation with Christ, when he again appeared, offering to allow Thomas to feel his wounds in order to satisfy his doubts. In response, Thomas made a powerful confession of faith, "My Lord and my God!" (John 20:26–29). The final scriptural reference to Thomas is to an additional post-Resurrection appearance of Jesus to a group in the Galilee, which included Thomas (John 21:2).

**Historical Context.** In "The Acts of St. Thomas," a second- or third-century history about this disciple, the later history of Thomas is expanded: the apostles in Jerusalem were believed to have sent him as a missionary to India. When he resisted the mission, he was sold as a slave to the messenger of the Indian king and arrived at his destination in that condition. In India, he performed miracles and converted many people. The folklore includes many Gnostic elements, including a Gnostic "Hymn of the Pearl," probably of Syriac origin. (In this text, he is presented as the twin of Christ, who sometimes appeared in Thomas's likeness [Jeffrey, 766; Jenkins, 104–105].)

Eusebius also says that Thomas was a missionary to India and later to Parthia (between the Tigris and Indus rivers). Thomas is thought to have met his death by martyrdom, pierced by four spears.

Among other works ascribed to him are: The Apocalypse of St. Thomas, The Gospel of Thomas, a Book of Thomas the Contender [Athlete], and coauthorship of the apocryphal Epistle of the Apostles (all included in The Complete Gospels).

**Archaeological Evidence.** The Mar Thoma Church in Travancore and Cochin, now called Kerala, is reputed to be the one Thomas founded during his missionary work in India.

In 1945, a number of Gnostic manuscripts were discovered in a jar unearthed near Chenoboskion in upper Egypt. The library consisted of 13 leather-bound volumes, containing 49 works written in various Coptic dialects during the fourth and fifth centuries. This collection of ancient religious texts were known as the Nag Hammadi Library, so called after the Egyptian city near which they were found (R. Miller, 301). One of these was the Gospel of Thomas, a collection of the "sayings of Jesus," which were supposedly recorded by Thomas from his days with Jesus. Some members of the Jesus Seminar (a modern, influential, academic group who edited The Complete Gospels) are inclined to believe that such records could be authentic, because students of famous philosophers often collected wise, witty, and insightful sayings of their masters, as is evidenced in scriptural tradition by the Wisdom literature we find in Proverbs and Ecclesiastes. On the other hand, the great majority of scholars who worked with the establishment of the canon thought these documents dubious.

The opening line of The Gospel of Thomas reads, "These are the secret sayings that the living Jesus spoke and Didymus Judas Thomas recorded." "Didymus Judas Thomas seems to have been a popular legendary figure from apostolic times, especially in Syria. In fact, it is only in eastern Syria that we find precisely this form of the name, where it occurs in the Acts of Thomas. In early Christianity the names of particular apostles often acquired special significance within specific geographical areas. . . ." Thomas was apparently the patron apostle for Syria (Miller, 302). Scholars believe this collection of sayings may have dated from the first century A.D., a time when the Christian communities were still appealing to the authority of individual apostles, not "the twelve" as a whole. By the end of the first century, such sayings collections appear to have fallen into disuse, being replaced by the narrative Gospels.

**Character in Later Works.** There is a story about the construction of a magnificent palace, which Thomas was hired to build for Gondophorus, King of the Indies; he used the money instead to feed the poor, and was imprisoned. When the king's brother died and went to heaven, he found the palace was built there instead; he appeared to Gondophorus in a dream to tell him about the rewards for charity in this world, and effected the freeing of Thomas. Because of this legend, Thomas is often portrayed with a builder's rule or square, matching the older tradition that he, like Jesus, was a carpenter (or craftsman). As a result, he later became the patron saint of architects, masons, and stonecutters.

Known for his deliberate testing of facts, Thomas has endured in popular legend as "Doubting Thomas." One colorful tale regarding Thomas, which probably dates from the Middle Ages, tells that he was absent when the *Virgin Mary's body and soul were reunited and transported to heaven. He therefore refused to believe in her bodily assumption, demanding that her grave be opened so that he could examine the body. In order to convince him of her assumption, Mary flung down her belt (girdle) as evidence. For this reason, the Virgin's belt is often present in portrayals of him (Ferguson, 75).

Thomas has rarely assumed a major role in the stories of Christ's life, appearing primarily in the one scene of the Resurrection for which he is best known, when he tested Jesus's wounds (John 20:28–29). There are paintings and carvings of the scene in which Thomas is thought to have reached out to touch the wounds of Jesus (though Scripture does not indicate that he did so), and there are also portrayals of his martyrdom, such as the one in William Caxton's *Golden Legend* (1483).

Dorothy L. Sayers, in *The Man Born to Be King*, characterized him as an eternal pessimist, but fiercely loyal and courageous. In her view, it is breathtaking that from such a practical man came "the one absolutely unequivocal statement, in the whole Gospel, of the divinity of Jesus. . . ." This is the only place, she notes, where the word "God" is used of Jesus without qualification of any kind (127, 315).

### SOURCES

Brownrigg, Ronald, *Who's Who in the Bible*, vol. 2, New York: Bonanza Books, 1980; Ferguson, George, *Signs and Symbols in Christian Art*, New York: Oxford University Press, 1966; Jeffrey, David L., ed., *A Dictionary of the Biblical Tradition in English Literature*, Grand Rapids, MI: William B. Eerdmans Publishing Company, 1992; Jenkins, Philip, *Hidden Gospels*, New York: Oxford University Press, 2001; Miller, Robert J., ed., *The Complete Gospels: Annotated Scholars Version*, San Francisco: HarperCollins, 1994; Pagels, Elaine, *The Gnostic Gospels*, New York: Random House, 1979; Sayers, Dorothy L., *The Man Born to Be King*, Grand Rapids, MI: William B. Eerdmans Publishing Company, 1943.

## TIMOTHY

**Name and Etymology.** *Timothy* or "Timotheus," means "honorer of God."

**Synopsis of Bible Story.** From scattered references in the "Acts of the Apostles," the pastoral letters addressed to Timothy, and from others among *Paul's epistles, we learn many things about Paul's good friend and helper. Timothy was the son of a Greek father and a Jewish mother (Acts 16:1). Paul first met him in either Derbe or Lystra and converted him to Christianity in approximately A.D. 48. (Miller, 762). A young man, willing to undergo circumcision in order to make himself more acceptable to the Jews, Timothy soon became Paul's secretary and helper. He accompanied Paul on his second missionary journey. When Paul fled from Berea, Timothy and Silas remained there until they had a summons from Paul to join him in at Athens. Finally overtaking him at Corinth (Acts 18), they remained for a while, later spending time at Ephesus as well, and eventually going on a mission into Macedonia and Corinth. Finding the problems in Corinth too difficult, Timothy was replaced by Titus. Later he helped to organize the offering for the Church at Jerusalem and accompanied Paul as far as Troas (Acts 20:4–6).

Some believe Timothy may have eventually gone to Paul when he was imprisoned in Rome, but he is not mentioned in the documents related to this period. After Paul was released from prison in Rome in A.D. 62–63, he apparently wrote the first letter to Timothy. Under Nero, Paul was again imprisoned, and it was during this time that he wrote 2 Timothy (*New International Version*, 1844). Languishing in a cold dungeon, Paul was chained like a common criminal. His friends had a hard time finding where he was being kept. In his loneliness, he came to believe he was deserted and thus begged Timothy to join him: "Do thy diligence to come shortly unto me. . . . When thou comes and bring with thee the cloak that I left at Troas . . . and the books, but especially the parchments" (2 Tim. 3:9–13).

According to Hebrews 13:23, Timothy himself was imprisoned and released, but we do not know whether this was in Rome or another city. We do not, in fact, know whether he responded to Paul's anguished urging.

Timothy was not an apostle; apparently not an "overseer," but only an "apostolic representative," a delegate who carried out special work (Titus 1:5) (See *New International Version*, 1834–35). He was the child and grandchild of believers whom Paul loved deeply. He was a modest man, who had to be urged to boldness—not the typical hero of literary adventure.

**Historical Context.** Some believe that Timothy continued as a leader in the early Church, becoming the first bishop of Ephesus. This would be a reasonable assumption based on his long service to the Christians of that city.

Scholars have long battled over the differences between the beloved Timothy of the "general" epistles and the Timothy in the "pastoral" letters bearing his name. Although some doubt that these epistles were written by Paul, both early tradition and the salutations in the letters themselves name Paul as the author of these letters (*New International Version*, 1834).

**Archaeological Evidence.** Ephesus, the city most closely associated with Timothy, was the site of the great battle between Paul and the followers of the goddess Diana. Silversmiths in the region apparently made a fortune by making and selling images of the multibreasted fertility goddess. The temple of Diana (or Artemis), considered one of the Seven Wonders of the World, was decorated with great statues by famous artists. The statue of the goddess was ornamented with gold and brilliant marble, dazzling to the worshipper. Today, only a huge ditch remains where the great temple stood, near the Isa Bey Mosque. Guidebooks note that it was burned by a madman named Herostratos in A.D. 356.

**Character in Later Works.** Timothy is usually seen as a young companion, a helper, never the main character in stories. Although Paul gave him considerable advice on the choice of leaders, he never indicated that Timothy was himself an impressive leader. He was instead encouraged to persevere in spite of his youth. He was clearly a devoted and loving "son" to the older man. Thus, his name is used primarily as a term for a companion for a stronger character.

## SOURCES

Brownrigg, Ronald, *Who's Who in the Bible*, vol. 2, New York: Bonanza Books, 1980; *Eusebius' Ecclesiastical History*, trans. by C. F. Cruse, Peabody, MA: Henrickson Publishers, 1998; Miller, Madeline S., and J. Lane Miller, *Harper's Bible Dictionary*, New York: Harper and Row, 1961.

## TOBIT

**Name and Etymology.** *Tobit* is the Greek form of the Hebrew *Tobi*, "my good," which may be an abbreviation for *Tobiah*, "Yahweh is my good" (Nichelsburg, 1439).

**Synopsis of Bible Story.** Tobit (whose story appears in the apocryphal Book of Tobit) was a faithful and righteous worshipper of God, who was among the exiles of the Northern Kingdom carried off to Nineveh. While in captivity, he struggled to keep the Jewish law while also working to succeed within the new culture. He was such a success that he amassed a small fortune, which he left with a friend in Media.

Blind Tobit in bed tended by lay sister preparing medicine by fire from Bible Historiale by Guyart des Moulins 1470, Bruges. The Art Archive/British Library.

After the advent of *Sennacherib to the throne, the highways were closed, cutting Tobit off from his prosperous trading activities. He nevertheless continued to do good works among his fellow Jews. He was especially concerned with the proper burial of the dead, and defied the king's explicit orders by burying those whom the king had executed. Eventually, Sennacherib confiscated Tobit's property and drove him into hiding with his wife and son.

When Esat-haddon, Sennacherib's son, came into power, Tobit's life continued to spiral downward. He lost his sight, and his wife was forced to work for their subsistence. Under such conditions, and even while asking that his life be brought to an end, Tobit continued to praise God.

Meanwhile, his kinsman Raguel's daughter, Sarah, was tormented by demons who killed each of her seven husbands on their wedding night, leaving her a widow and a maiden. Like Tobit, this distressed woman was brought to the point of begging God to deliver her from the burden of her life.

God answered both of their prayers by blessing them: Tobit recalled the money he had left with his friend Gabael in Media and sent his son, Tobias, to recover the money and to seek a bride from his kinsmen. God sent his angel Raphael to go along as a companion and helper. On the journey to Rages, accompanied by a dog, the men camped at the Tigris river and fished for their supper. A large fish leaped up, and the young men caught it. Raphael explained that the fish would serve for more than supper: its gall, heart, and liver would help rid people of demons and cure blindness.

The story then unfolds neatly using these solutions: Tobias discovered the demon-ridden Sarah and proposed to her, using the smoke from the fish's heart and liver to cleanse the room of evil spirits. He went to Rages to recover the lost fortune, returned to his father, and used the fish's gall to cure Tobit's blindness. Tobit's death is portrayed in a series of generous gestures and blessings, with thanksgiving to God for his manifold blessings.

**Historical Context.** The story of Tobit grows out of the deportation of the people of the Northern Kingdom to Assyria under Sargon II in 722 B.C. Its roots are thought to be in folklore rather than in literal history, involving such motifs of ancient tales as "the dangerous bride" and "the grateful dead." The occasional use of Wisdom literature is also a mark of its folkloric origins, yet the details of family life, marriage, burial, social customs, religious rituals, and other elements mark it as a real-life narrative embellished with retelling.

In some ways, this is a modified version of the much richer story of *Job, with a dog and a fish introducing a kind of divinely inspired magic into the tale. It picks up on the material prosperity that *Ezekiel encouraged, pointing to the period when the Jews would find that they could survive as a special people within an alien culture. While working toward material prosperity, they found strength in maintaining their rituals and laws.

**Archaeological Evidence.** The many historical inaccuracies in the story make it a confusing artifact to study. Composed in Aramaic, textual fragments of the document were found among the Dead Sea Scrolls, along with a Hebrew translation. The book was bound into English Bibles until 1640, and became optional thereafter.

**Character in Later Works.** Although considered apocryphal by Protestants, the book is used by the Anglican Church in the marriage service, with the words of Tobias's wedding prayer included in the *Book of Common Prayer* as an alternative wedding rite.

The humor of the work makes Tobit a kind of comic version of Job. Authors have seen it as an early example of the short story, full of complications and neat solutions. The magical elements of the animals give it something of the flavor of a fable as well.

Artists have been interested in the story partially because of its colorful aspects—particularly the dog and the fish. Diane McColley lists hosts of artists, including Perugino, Verrochio, and Rembrandt, who painted Tobit and Tobias (769). Theologians have explored the work as symbolic, and artists have seized on events in Tobit and Tobias's lives as variants of themes seen elsewhere. Thus, Tobias's travels appear to be a type of the "road to Emmaus" experience; his marriage is seen as a foreshadowing of the Virgin Mary's betrothal; and Tobit's extended and prophetic death scene is interpreted as a type of the death of the Virgin.

Although Tobit appears in some medieval and renaissance literature, the designation of the book as apocryphal diminished its authority and influence among Protestant writers. Milton mentions Tobit in *Paradise Lost*, as do Lord Byron in *The Deformed Transformed* and Robert Browning in *The Ring and the Book*. James Joyce also uses Tobit's blindness as the basis for a pun in *Finnegan's Wake*. It is rare, however, to find Tobit or Tobias references in modern literature or art.

## SOURCES

McColley, Diane, "Tobit and Tobias," in *A Dictionary of the Biblical Tradition in English Literature*, edited by David L. Jeffrey, Grand Rapids, MI: William B. Eerdmans Publishing Company, 1992; Nickelsburg, George W. E., "Tobit," in *HarperCollins Study Bible*, edited by Wayne A. Meeks, San Francisco, CA: HarperCollins, 1993.

## ZECHARIAH

**Name and Etymology.** *Zechariah* means "Jehovah hath remembered."

**Synopsis of Bible Story.** The name *Zechariah* is used for 29 persons in the Bible, but the most significant of those known by this name is the minor prophet of postexilic Jerusalem, who prophesied at the same time as *Haggai. He is introduced only as the son of Berechiah and grandson of Iddo, and the head of a priestly family that returned from the Babylonian exile (Zech. 1:1–7; Neh. 12:4). Some scholars believe that the name *Berechiah* has been inserted in error, and that Zechariah was actually the son of Iddo (Paterson, 227). Most believe that he was a priest who came back with the returning exiles from Babylon, serving first as a priest in the restored community when he was only in his twenties, and then succeeding as high priest when his father died at an early age.

The book named for him opens with a series of visions: horses, horns, carpenters, olive trees, candlesticks, a flying roll (or scroll), a flying ephah (or measuring bushel), and flying chariots. In each vision, Zechariah notes, "I lifted up mine eyes," and each time he sees something—a man with a measuring line (a plumb line) or an enormous flying scroll—and each time he inquires of the meaning. Each of these questions is met by a response from an angel, who instructs him and orders him to "cry" or run and speak to his people.

In his first vision, Zechariah saw a placid world in which Darius had apparently succeeded in quelling rebellious vassal states, and the convulsions of the empire had ceased. He comforted his people with the assurance that the nations that oppressed Israel would be destroyed, clearing the way for a New Jerusalem—a city without walls—ruled by a Messiah who would build the Temple of Jehovah, and "he shall bear the glory, and shall sit and rule upon his throne" (Zech. 6:13). The later parts of the book deal with problems of fasting, the restoration of Jerusalem and its purification, and the future of the king.

Zechariah was an idealist, concerned about the religious and political life of the people of Judah—not only their sins and their failure to rebuild the Temple, but also their need for a Messiah, and their need to return to the rituals of their faith. Underneath his social sympathies lay a much deeper concern for the spiritual life of Judah. His visions for his people were apocalyptic and powerful.

**Historical Context.** The prophecies of Zechariah began the same year that *Haggai prophesied (520 B.C.) and extended almost to the time when the Temple was restored, 516 B.C. The Book of Zechariah tells of the same problems as the Book of *Haggai. Under the reign of Darius the Persian, the people of Judah had returned to their homeland, but they had halted the work on the Temple. Various of their neighbors—probably the Samaritans and their Arabian and Ammonite allies—had managed to frustrate the work, it was resumed under Haggai and Zechariah. A neighboring governor sent a letter to Darius informing him of the Jews' activity, asking that he search for a legal basis for this revived activity. When Darius did arrange the search, he found the original decree from Cyrus, which not only gave permission, but also offered help. As a result, Darius ordered Tatnai, the neighbor who had asked the questions, to supply the Jews with those materials they might lack. The Temple was completed within six years, though the city itself remained a pile of rubble and the walls remained shattered until *Nehemiah's time, c. 445–430 B.C.

Carrying his ministry on some two years beyond that of Haggai, Zechariah supported the coronation of Zerubbabel, but the plot was thwarted and the proposed leader disappeared, perhaps through the machinations of the Persian secret police. A Babylonian was subsequently appointed civil administrator of Judea, thereby thwarting the Jewish dream of a sovereign, independent state.

**Archaeological Evidence.** There is no archaeological evidence of Zerubbabel's rebuilt Temple in Jerusalem other than the literary evidence that it was 90 feet high and 90 feet wide (Ezra 6:3). The Ark of the Covenant is not mentioned, suggesting that it may have been lost when Jerusalem was destroyed. Jeremiah (41:5) implied that there was a shell of the burned Temple still existing, where persons came to the "house of the Lord," bringing grain offerings and sacrifices. It is assumed that Zerubbabel used what was left of *Solomon's Temple walls and platform. The east wall of the Temple platform has masonry at the so-called straight joint, probably from Zerubbabel's time. "This masonry is characterized by large stones with heavy irregular bosses . . ." (Mare, 119–120).

Zechariah is thought to have been buried among the Herodian rock-cut tombs in the Kidron Valley in the tomb that is traditionally associated with him.

**Character in Later Works.** A number of Zechariah's prophecies came to pass, including those that appear to anticipate the conquests of Alexander the Great (Zech. 10:10), and the annual pilgrimages of the Jews of the Diaspora to Jerusalem during that period (14:16). He also foretold the siege of Jerusalem (12:1–3), the initial victory of Judah's enemies (14:2), the Lord's defense of Jerusalem (14:3–4), the judgment on the nations (12:9; 14:3), and the topographical changes in Judah (14:4–5) (*New International Version*, 1399). His vision of the candlestick and the seven lamps along with the two olive trees is traditionally recited as the prophetic portion on the Sabbath of Hanukkah. Zechariah beheld a "candlestick all of gold . . . and his seven lamps thereon," which he learned to mean "not by might, nor by power, but by my spirit, saith the Lord of hosts" (Zech. 4:2–6) then he saw two olive trees, which "are the two anointed ones, that stand by the Lord of the whole earth" (Zech. 12:14).

A number of his ideas of the final judgment have parallels in Muslim thought and some sound like Christian ideas of the millennium. The echoes of this prophet in Revelation are numerous—the scroll, the horns, the golden lampstand, and the New Jerusalem.

Regarding Messianic emphasis, Zechariah foretold Christ's coming—in lowliness (6:12), his humanity (13:7), his rejection and betrayal (11:12–13), his crucifixion (13:8), his priesthood (6:12–13), his reign (9:10, 14:9), and his establishment of enduring peace and prosperity (3:10, 9:9–10). A number of his visionary sayings became significant in Christian writing, including the Triumphal Entry into Jerusalem (9:9), the betrayal for 30 pieces of silver (11:12), the pierced hands (12:10, 13:6), the smitten shepherd (13:7), and the universal reign (14:10).

Because of Zechariah's accurate prophecies of the coming Messiah, he is frequently pictured among the prophets in cathedrals and paintings of the Church. One of the finest examples is in Michelangelo's fresco in the Sistine Chapel in Rome.

## SOURCES

Bullock, C. Hassell, *An Introduction to the Old Testament Prophetic Books*, Chicago: Moody Press, 1986; Comay, Joan, *Who's Who in the Bible*, vol. 1, New York: Bonanza Books, 1980; Isaacs, Ronald H., *Messengers of God: A Jewish Prophets Who's Who*, Jerusalem: Jason Aronson, Inc., 1998; Mare, W. Harold, *The Archaeology of the Jerusalem Area*, Grand Rapids, MI: Baker Book House, 1987; Merrill, Eugene H., *An Historical Survey of the Old Testament*, Nutley, NJ: The Craig Press, 1972; Miller, Madeline S., and J. Lane Miller, *Harper's Bible Dictionary*, New York: Harper and Row, 1961; Paterson, John, *The Goodly Fellowship of the Prophets*, New York: Charles Scribner's Sons, 1948.

## ZEPHANIAH

**Name and Etymology.** *Zephaniah* means "the Lord hides" or "the Lord protects." The name probably refers to God's protection of Zephaniah during the infamous reigns of Manasseh and Amon.

**Synopsis of Bible Story.** Of the man Zephaniah himself, we know only that he was the son of Cushi, the son of Gedaliah, the son of Amariah, the son of Hezekiah, and that he lived during the reign of Josiah of Judah (Zeph. 1:1). Critics debate whether the Hezekiah mentioned as an ancestor might have been the King Hezekiah, but there is no firm consensus on this identification. Scholars do agree that the prophet began to prophesy when he was in his early twenties, that he was a member of the ruling class, perhaps of noble blood, and that he was like *Isaiah in his ability to move regularly in court circles.

His prophecy divides into two major sections: Zephaniah 1:2–3:8 is about universal judgment, including oracles against Philistia, Moab, Ammon, Ethiopia, Assyria, and Judah. This thunderous proclamation of doom is followed by promises of salvation (3:9–20), including a general salvation of the nations, and of Judah. The powerful tone of judgment and the importance of the Day of the Lord, in which God will judge both Judah and the nations, is mingled with a strong sense of God's covenantal commitment of grace. In spite of Judah's sins, the people of the "Lord of Hosts" remain the cherished children of God.

**Historical Context.** Scholars debate the exact timing of Zephaniah's prophecy. His main ministry apparently took place before 621 B.C. and may have been instrumental in encouraging King *Josiah to undertake the reforms of Temple worship (2 Chron. 34:1–7). The kinds of worship that Zephaniah condemns are parallel to those that Josiah rooted out—the worship of Molech, of Baal, and of the planetary deities. Several of the prophets also note that the functionaries on whom the Judean society depended to convert the wandering people from popular religions to an orthodox faith were themselves corrupt: "Her princes are roaring lions; her judges are evening wolves; . . . her prophets are light and treacherous persons; her priests have polluted the sanctuary, they have done violence to the law" (Zeph. 3:3–4) (Bullock, 167). Apparently, Zephaniah was describing his land in the wake of Mannasseh's pro-Assyrian administration, a time of particular horror and degradation. Second Kings characterizes this Manasseh, who reigned for 55 years, as doing that which was "evil in the sight of the Lord, after the abominations of the heathen, whom the Lord cast out before the children of Israel" (2 Kings 21:1–2). This is the reign that *Hosea and *Isaiah described in terms of "harlotry."

Zephaniah was writing early in the years that followed, during the benevolent reign of *Josiah, at a time when Josiah was still a young king, and before the destruction of Nineveh. He was an older contemporary of *Jeremiah, one of the first persons to break the long silence of more than fifty years that followed the death of the prophet Isaiah. His condemnation of the pro-Assyrian court ministers who served as regents during Josiah's minority suggest that he was of the upper class, as does his understanding of the wicked nations—including Judah—that have forgotten Jehovah.

Some believe that this brief, three-chapter book was occasioned by the Scythian invasion of western Asia, which marked the beginning of the end of the Assyrian empire. Although it is not clear who is the foe that will be the agent to punish God's people, the Scythians may well have been the ones he describes. Other candidates might be the Assyrians or the Chaldeans. In 612 B.C. Nineveh was destroyed by an alliance of Medes and neo-Babylonians—as Zephaniah had prophesied (Zep. 2:13).

**Archaeological Evidence.** The "abominations of the heathen," which provide the context for Zephaniah, are mentioned by Philo of Byblos, who describes the worship practices that so outraged the prophets. Gruesome, ferocious, obscene, and bloody practices are documented in abundance as evidence of the widespread zeal for the fertility gods who were a constant threat to the children of Israel and their rulers (Keller, chapter 26).

The identification as the Scythians, a "wild horde" who burst out of the Caucasus Mountains, is based on a suspect passage in Herodotus, who describes the Asiatic horsemen as ferocious plunderers who swept through the countryside and then turned and disappeared as "an evil apparition." Scholars argue about the events and the identification of the armies. Keller pictures the scene Zephaniah foresees this way: "Through the maritime plain by the Mediterranean stormed this unruly mob of Scythian horsemen. Fearful and frightening rumours heralded their approach. The inhabitants of Judah must have seen them as they looked down from the mountains" (Keller, 296). If so, surely Zephaniah's words must have come to mind: "For Gaza shall be forsaken, and Ashkelon a desolation: they shall drive out Ashdod at the noon day and Ekron shall be rooted up . . . in the houses of Ashkelon shall they lie down in the evening. . . ." (Zeph. 2:4, 2:7).

Zephaniah's prophecy of the utter destruction of Nineveh did indeed come to pass in 612 B.C., and as he stated, the site was "utterly desolate" (Zeph. 2:13). One commentary notes, "Even the site of Nineveh was later forgotten—until discovered through modern excavations" (*New International Version*, 1390).

**Character in Later Works.** The "puritan" of the prophets, Zephaniah proclaimed the coming of the "Day of Wrath." Having seen God in his full glory in his holy city, the prophet is convinced that righteous God was coming in judgment. His wrathful tone, which may have influenced Josiah's program in 621 B.C., perhaps prepared the way for the reception of the law. In this sense, "he may be considered one of the earliest founders of Judaism" (Paterson, 108). He was also important in *Haggai and *Zechariah's vision of the rebuilding of the Temple, and Malachi's view of the opportunities and responsibilities of God's people in the postexilic era.

He was a forerunner of the other apocalyptic prophets, including St. *John of Revelation, who shared the strong sense of the coming of the "Day of the Lord" and the judgment on all the nations. For Christians, this vision of the "Day of the Judgment" was to blend with the promise of the Second Coming, when Christ would return to earth—as portrayed by such painters as Michaelangelo in the magnificent Sistine Chapel fresco.

## SOURCES

Bullock, C. Hassell, *An Introduction to the Old Testament Prophetic Books*, Chicago: Moody Press, 1986; Isaacs, Ronald H., *Messengers of God: A Jewish Prophets Who's Who*, Jerusalem: Jason Aronson, Inc., 1998; Keller, Werner, *The Bible as History*, New York: Bantam Books, 1982; Paterson, John, *The Goodly Fellowship of the Prophets*, New York: Charles Scribner's Sons, 1948; Watts, John D. W., "Zephaniah, The Book of," in *The Oxford Companion to the Bible*, edited by Bruce M. Metzger and Michael Coogan. New York: Oxford University Press, 1993.

# BIBLIOGRAPHY

*Note:* For the most part, the text relies on the traditional Authorized, or King James Version of the Bible for direct quotations. For most of the basic research, however, I have used the *New International Version*, which I rarely cite because its presence is so pervasive in the text. For many of the articles on archaeology, I have referred to the website for *Bible Review* and *Biblical Archaeology Review*— www.biblicalarchaelogy.org

I have avoided extensive duplication of information on history and archaeology, hoping that those using this book will check the cross-references.

## Bibles, Extracanonical Texts, and Translations

Alter, Robert. *Genesis: Translation and Commentary*. Anchor Bible Series. New York: W. W. Norton & Company, 1996.

Barker, Kenneth. *The New International Version Study Bible*. Grand Rapids, MI: Zondervan Publishing House, 1995.

Boling, Robert G. *Judges*. Anchor Bible Series. Garden City, New York: Doubleday and Co., Inc., 1969.

Campbell, Edward F., Jr. *Ruth*. Anchor Bible Series. Garden City, New York: Doubleday and Co., Inc., 1975.

*The Holy Bible* (King James Version). Philadelphia: A. J. Holman Company, 1960.

*The Lost Books of the Bible and The Forgotten Books of Eden.* New York: New American Library, 1974.

Meeks, Wayne A., ed. *The HarperCollins Study Bible* (New Revised Standard Version with the Apocryphal/Deuterocanonical Books). San Francisco, CA: HarperCollins, 1993.

Miller, Robert J., ed. *The Complete Gospels: Annotated Scholars Version*. San Francisco, CA: HarperCollins, 1994.

Propp, William Henry. *Exodus I–XVIII*. Anchor Bible Series. New York: Doubleday and Co., Inc, 1999.

Speiser, E. A. *Genesis*. Anchor Bible Series. Garden City, New York: Doubleday and Co., Inc., 1979.

### Dictionaries and Encyclopedias

Brownrigg, Ronald. *Who's Who in the Bible*, vol. 1. New York: Bonanza Books, 1980.

Comay, Joan. *Who's Who in the Bible*, vol. 2. New York: Bonanza Books, 1980.

Douglas, J. D., ed. *The Illustrated Bible Dictionary*, vols. 1–3. Sidney, Australia: Tyndale House Publishers, 1980.

Fairbairn, Patrick, ed. *Imperial Standard Biblical Encyclopedia* (20 vols.). Grand Rapids, MI: Zondervan, 1956.

Ferguson, George. *Signs and Symbols in Christian Art*. New York: Oxford University Press, 1966.

Gaster, Theodor H. *Myth, Legend, and Custom in the Old Testament*, vol. 2. New York: Harper and Row, 1975.

Jeffrey, David L., ed. *A Dictionary of the Biblical Tradition in English Literature*. Grand Rapids, MI: William B. Eerdmans Publishing Company, 1992.

Metzger, Bruce M., and Michael D. Coogan, eds. *The Oxford Companion to the Bible*. New York: Oxford University Press, 1993.

Miller, Madeline S., and J. Lane Miller. *Harper's Bible Dictionary*. New York: Harper and Row, 1961.

Negev, Avraham, ed. *The Archaeological Encyclopedia of the Holy Land*, rev. ed. New York: Thomas Nelson Publishers, 1986.

Whyte, Alexander. *Bible Characters from the Old and New Testaments*. Grand Rapids, MI: Kregel Publications, 1990.

### General Scholarship

Anderson, Bernard W. *Understanding the Old Testament*. Englewood Cliffs, NJ: Prentice-Hall, Inc., 1966.

Bach, Alice, ed. *Women in the Hebrew Bible: A Reader*. New York: Routledge, 1999.

Baron, Salo W., and George S. Wise, eds. *Violence and Defense in the Jewish Experience*. Philadelphia, PA: The Jewish Publication Society of America, 1977.

"The Book of Confessions." In *The Constitution of the United Presbyterian Church in the United States of America*, part 1. New York: Office of the General Assembly, 1970.

Bullock, C. Hassell. *An Introduction to the Old Testament Prophetic Books*. Chicago: Moody Press, 1986.

Cline, Eric H. *The Battles of Armageddon: Megiddo and the Jezreel Valley from the Bronze Age to the Nuclear Age*. Ann Arbor: University of Michigan Press, 2000.

*Eusebius' Ecclesiastical History*. Translated by C. F. Cruse. Peabody, MA: Henrickson Publishers, Inc., 1998.

Exum, J. Cheryl. *Plotted, Shot, and Painted: Cultural Representations of Biblical Women*. Sheffield, England: Sheffield Academic Press, 1996.

Freeman-Grenville, G. S. P. *The Holy Land: A Pilgrim's Guide to Israel, Jordan and the Sinai*. New York: Continuum, 1998.

Graves, Robert. *The Greek Myths*. Baltimore: Penguin Books, 1955.

Graves, Robert, and Raphael Patai. *Hebrew Myths: The Book of Genesis*. New York: McGraw-Hill Book Company, 1963.

Hamilton, Edith. *Spokesmen for God*. New York: W. W. Norton and Co., Inc. 1949.

Hargis, Merilyn, and Jeff Hargis. *The Hindsight Tour Guide*. USA: Hindsight, 1996.

Hone, Ralph E. *The Voice Out of the Whirlwind: The Book of Job*. San Francisco, CA: Chandler Publishing Company, Inc., 1960.

Isaacs, Ronald H. *Messengers of God: A Jewish Prophets Who's Who*. Jerusalem: Jason Aronson, Inc., 1998.

Jenkins, Philip. *Hidden Gospels: How the Search for Jesus Lost Its Way*. New York: Oxford University Press, 2001.

Josephus, Flavius. *The Works of Josephus*. Translated by William Whiston. Peabody, MA: Hendrickson Publishers, Inc., 1987.

Keddie, Gordon J. *Even in Darkness*. Darlington, England: Evangelical Press, 1985.

Kee, Howard Clark, Franklin W. Young, and Karlfried Froehlich. *Understanding the New Testament*. Englewood Cliffs, NJ: Prentice-Hall, Inc., 1965.

Keller, Werner. *The Bible as History*. New York: Bantam Books, 1982.

Kollek, Teddy, and Moshe Pearlman. *Jerusalem, Sacred City of Mankind: A History of Forty Centuries*. Jerusalem: Steimatzky's Agency, Ltd., 1968.

———. *Pilgrims to the Holy Land: The Story of Pilgrimage through the Ages*. New York: Harper and Row, 1970.

Kugel, James L. *Traditions of the Bible: A Guide to the Bible As It Was at the Start of the Common Era*. Cambridge, MA: Harvard University Press, 1998.

Marcus, Amy Dockser. *The View from Nebo*. Boston: Little, Brown, 2000.

Mare, W. Harold. *The Archaeology of the Jerusalem Area*. Grand Rapids, MI: Baker Book House, 1987.

Mazar, Amihai. *Archaeology of the Land of the Bible: 10,000–586 B.C.E.* New York: Doubleday and Co., Inc., 1992.

McEntire, Mark. *The Blood of Abel: The Violent Plot in the Hebrew Bible*. Macon, GA: Mercer University Press, 1999.

McKenzie, Steven L. *King David: A Biography*. New York: Oxford University Press, 2000.

Merrill, Eugene H. *An Historical Survey of the Old Testament*. Nutley, New Jersey: The Craig Press, 1972.

Miller, Patrick D. *The Divine Warrior in Early Israel*. Cambridge, MA: Harvard University Press, 1973.

Noss, John B. *Man's Religions*. New York: The Macmillan Company, 1956.

Ohlsen, Woodrow, ed. *Perspectives in Old Testament Literature*. San Diego, CA: Harcourt Brace Jovanovich, 1978.

Pagels, Elaine. *The Gnostic Gospels*. New York: Random House, 1979.

———. *The Origin of Satan*. New York: Random House, 1995.

Patai, Raphael. *The Hebrew Goddess*. Detroit, MI: Wayne State University Press, 1990.

Paterson, John. *The Goodly Fellowship of the Prophets*. New York: Charles Scribner's Sons, 1948.

Pritchard, James B., ed. *Solomon and Sheba*. London: Phaidon Press Ltd., 1974.

Ryan, William, and Walter Pitman. *Noah's Flood: The New Scientific Discoveries About the Event That Changed History*. New York: Simon and Schuster, 1998.

Ryken, Leland, and Tremper Longman III. *A Complete Literary Guide to the Bible*. Grand Rapids, MI: Zondervan Publishing House, 1993.

Sayers, Dorothy L. *Are Women Human?* Grand Rapids, MI: William B. Eerdmans Publishing Company, 1971.

———. *The Man Born to Be King*. Grand Rapids, MI: William B. Eerdmans Publishing Company, 1943.

———. *The Mind of the Maker*. Westport, CT: Greenwood Press, 1941.

———. *The Whimsical Christian*. New York: Macmillan Publishing Co., Inc., 1969.

Sheler, Jeffery L. *Is the Bible True?* San Francisco, CA: Harpers, 1999.

Trawick, Buchner B. *The Bible as Literature*. New York: Barnes and Noble, 1970.

Trible, Phyllis. *Texts of Terror: Literary-Feminist Readings of Biblical Narrative*. Philadelphia: Fortress Press, 1984.

Tuchman, Barbara. *Bible and Sword*. New York: Ballantine Books, 1956.

Wooley, C. L. *Ur of the Chaldees*. New York: W. W. Norton, 1965.

Wright, Ernest. *Biblical Archaeology*. Philadelphia: The Westminster Press, 1962.

Young, Edward J. *Daniel*. Carlisle, PA: William B. Eerdmans Publishing Co., 1949.

Young, Karl. *The Drama of the Medieval Church*, vol. 2. Oxford: Clarendon Press, 1967.

# INDEX

## ABOUT THE AUTHOR

**Nancy M. Tischler** is Professor Emerita of English and the Humanities at Penn State University.